Property, Predation, and Protection

What threatens the property rights of business owners, and what makes these rights secure? This book transcends the conventional diagnosis of the issue in modern developing countries by moving beyond petty bureaucratic corruption or expropriation by the state ruler. It theorizes "agent predation" as a novel threat type, showing it to be particularly widespread and detrimental. The book also questions the orthodox prescription: institutionalized state commitment cannot secure property rights against agent predation. Instead, this volume argues that business actors can hold the predatory state agents accountable through firm-level alliances with foreign actors, labor, and local communities. Beyond securing ownership, such alliances promote rule of law in a rent-seeking society. Taking Russia and Ukraine between 2000 and 2012 as its empirical focus, the book advances these arguments by drawing on more than 150 qualitative interviews with business owners, policy makers, and bureaucrats, as well as an original large-N survey of firms.

Stanislav Markus is an assistant professor of political science at the University of Chicago. His research has been published in *World Politics*, *Socio-Economic Review*, and *Polity*. He is the winner of the 2014 Gregory Luebbert Article Award for the best article in comparative politics awarded by the American Political Science Association. Professor Markus received the Academy Scholar award from the Harvard Academy for International and Area Studies, 2008–2009 and 2011–2012. He holds a PhD in government from Harvard University.

In memory of my grandmother, Lina Andreevna Gvozdeva

Property, Predation, and Protection
Piranha Capitalism in Russia and Ukraine

STANISLAV MARKUS
University of Chicago

CAMBRIDGE
UNIVERSITY PRESS

32 Avenue of the Americas, New York, NY 10013-2473, USA

Cambridge University Press is part of the University of Cambridge.

It furthers the University's mission by disseminating knowledge in the pursuit of education, learning, and research at the highest international levels of excellence.

www.cambridge.org
Information on this title: www.cambridge.org/9781107088344

© Stanislav Markus 2015

This publication is in copyright. Subject to statutory exception and to the provisions of relevant collective licensing agreements, no reproduction of any part may take place without the written permission of Cambridge University Press.

First published 2015

Printed in the United States of America

A catalog record for this publication is available from the British Library.

Library of Congress Cataloging in Publication data
Markus, Stanislav, 1977–
Property, predation, and protection : piranha capitalism in Russia and Ukraine / Stanislav Markus.
    pages   cm
Includes bibliographical references and index.
ISBN 978-1-107-08834-4 (hardback)
1. Privatization – Russia (Federation)   2. Privatization – Ukraine.   3. Right of property – Russia (Federation)   4. Right of property – Ukraine.   5. Political corruption – Russia (Federation)   6. Political corruption – Ukraine.   7. Russia (Federation) – Politics and government.   8. Ukraine – Politics and government.   I. Title.
HD4215.15.M364   2015
338.947′05–dc23   2014025985

ISBN 978-1-107-08834-4 Hardback

Cambridge University Press has no responsibility for the persistence or accuracy of URLs for external or third-party Internet Web sites referred to in this publication and does not guarantee that any content on such Web sites is, or will remain, accurate or appropriate.

Contents

List of Tables and Figures		*page* vi
Acknowledgments		ix
1.	Introduction	1
2.	Agent Predation and Secure Ownership	18
3.	Not Too Petty: Disorganized Threats beyond Corruption	47
4.	Mini-Beasts versus Sovereign: Ownership Threats beyond "The System"	86
5.	Commitment Dissolved	120
6.	Firm Stakeholders versus State Predators	168
7.	Firm Stakeholders and Rule of Law	201
Bibliography		219
Index		239

Tables and Figures

TABLES

2.1.	Summary Statistics for Variables in Regressions	*page* 45
3.1.	Average State Threats on a 1–4 Scale	76
3.2.	Effect of Ownership and Income Threats on Predictability of Future State Threats	81
4.1.	Effect of Blame Attribution to Local Versus Central State on Business Propensity for Predation	112
4.2.	Average State Threats to Property Rights in Eastern and Western Ukraine	116
6.1.	Effect of Alliances on Security of Property Rights in Russia and Ukraine	191
6.2.	Substantive Impact of Alliances on Discrete Threats (Ordered Probit First Differences)	197

FIGURES

2.1.	State Threats to Property Rights	28
3.1.	GDP % from Privately Owned Enterprises, 1991–2010	51
3.2.	State and Private Threats to Property Rights on a 1–4 Scale	78
3.3.	State Threats to Property Rights in Russia and Ukraine, 2002–9	84
4.1.	Average Responses to the Question, "On a scale of 1–4, how important are these factors for the protection of entrepreneurs'	

Tables and Figures vii

right to legally manage their property and derive legal income from it?" 110

4.2. Regional Variation in State Threats to Property Rights across Federal Districts in Russia 115

5.1. Political and Economic Freedoms in Ukraine, 2000–10 152

Acknowledgments

No author is an island; the lucky ones rely on the intellectual, logistical, and emotional support of others. This is the story of my exceptional luck.

This book would have been impossible without stellar professors in college who encouraged me to pursue a PhD in political science. Stephen Whitefield's tutorial in Russian Politics at Oxford University literally changed my life. Rudra Sil at the University of Pennsylvania fanned the flames of my incipient interest, inviting me to accompany him on a research trip to Moscow. I was hooked.

As a graduate student and junior professor, I continued to have phenomenal mentors. Peter Hall at Harvard University and Dan Slater at the University of Chicago commented on numerous drafts while providing invaluable professional advice. Some of the best metaphors in this book are Dan's. Peter's suggestion to move beyond the narrow issue of "corporate governance" and focus on the more important topic of "property rights" changed the course of my research. Both intellectually and personally, these mentors represent what is best in the discipline.

My dissertation committee was nothing less than ideal. Tim Colton, Peter Hall, Yoshiko Herrera, and Torben Iversen: as a group, these scholars provided both feedback and encouragement while letting me explore freely, always trusting that I would find my way. I am deeply grateful to them for caring.

Many others at Harvard and MIT made my intellectual journey an exhilarating challenge. I am particularly grateful to Rawi Abdelal, Jim Alt, Jorge Dominguez, Grzegorz Ekiert, Jeffry Frieden, Gary King, Beth Simmons, Michael Piore, and David Woodruff.

Several colleagues affiliated with the Max Planck Institute cheered me on with enthusiasm and helpful tips. I would like to thank Margaret Levi, Sven Steinmo, and Wolfgang Streeck for their encouragement.

The book morphed into its current shape after an extremely helpful manuscript conference generously sponsored by the Harvard Academy. For their tough love, I am immensely indebted to the participants: Bob Bates, Scott Gehlbach, Peter Hall, Dan Slater, Kathy Thelen, and Dan Treisman.

The Department of Political Science at the University of Chicago has been a stimulating and nurturing place to develop ideas and write. As department chairs, Cathy Cohen, Bernard Harcourt, and Lisa Wedeen have ensured that administrative responsibilities do not stymie research, while also helping me through some medical issues at the start. Like other colleagues in the department, my fellow comparativists are a wonderful and supportive group of people who made my book better while also making it more fun to write. I am grateful to Mike Albertus, Gary Herrigel, Ben Lessing, Monika Nalepa, Tianna Paschel, Alberto Simpser, Dan Slater, Paul Staniland, Lisa Wedeen, and Dali Yang. I also thank our graduate students; in my courses on Business and State, Economic Development, and Plutocracy, I benefited tremendously from the discussions, and so did the book.

The list of people at various institutions in the United States and abroad who have provided feedback or helped with fieldwork is long, and I am afraid I will not be able to repay all. I'd like to make a start by expressing my deep gratitude to Anders Åslund, Harley Balzer, Bat Batjargal, Lisa Blaydes, Martin Dimitrov, Jordan Gans-Morse, Peter Gourevitch, Sergei Guriev, Masha Hedberg, Terra Lawson-Remer, Ed Malesky, Melanie Manion, Cathie Jo Martin, Gerald McDermott, Harris Mylonas, Simeon Nichter, Jean Oi, John Padgett, Jessica Pisano, Heiko Pleines, William Pyle, Mark Roe, Andrea Rutherford, Jefferey Sellers, Andrei Shleifer, Konstantin Sonin, Bill Tompson, Kellee Tsai, Sergey Tsukhlo, David Vogel, David Weimer, Andrei Yakovlev, Jin Zeng, and Alexei Zudin.

I acknowledge gratefully the input of two anonymous reviewers for Cambridge University Press as well as two reviewers for Oxford University Press and, while we are at it, five reviewers for *World Politics*. These reviews have guided me in streamlining the argument and presenting the data, and I thank the reviewers for their time and advice.

Parts of Chapters 1, 2, 6, and 7 have appeared previously in my article "Secure Property as a Bottom-Up Process: Firms, Stakeholders, and Predators in Weak States," in *World Politics* Volume 64, No. 2, April 2012, pages 242–77. Copyright © 2012 Trustees of Princeton University Press; used with permission. Portions of Chapter 5 appeared in my article "Capitalists of All Russia Unite! Business Mobilization under Debilitated Dirigisme," in *Polity* Volume 39, July 2007, pages 277–304. Parts of Chapters 6 and 7 appeared in my article "Corporate Governance as Political Insurance: Firm-Level Institutional Creation in Emerging Markets and Beyond," in *Socioeconomic Review* Volume 6, No. 1, 2008, pages 69–98.

A special *spasibo* is reserved for my interviewees in Russia and Ukraine. Without any reward, these officials and entrepreneurs, journalists, and politicians have shared their experiences and ordeals. I owe this project to them.

Acknowledgments xi

My research required many trips to the region and the implementation of a survey. These undertakings were supported by fellowships and grants from several Harvard institutes, including the Center for European Studies, the Davis Center for Russian and Eurasian Studies, the Weatherhead Center for International Affairs, and the Ukrainian Research Institute. I am also grateful to the Institute for Humane Studies and the University of Chicago for their research support.

My family has given me everything. My mother enabled me to pursue my dreams, despite the hardships of our immigration from the Soviet Union to Germany. My sister is the most caring person in the world. My grandmother, to whom this book is dedicated, began to teach me English when I was a kid; she was the most devoted friend I will ever have. With them at my side, I've been lucky indeed.

I

Introduction

"What was the purpose of your visit to Russia?" The year was 1995, and I was on a Moscow-Kyiv train carrying mostly Ukrainian *chelnoki* or "shuttle-traders," a common phenomenon in the destitute 1990s. The man asking this question had just burst into our compartment with three bulky pals, all dressed in black leather jackets. The train had barely left Moscow, and the man's official-sounding inquiry was strange. The customs inspection at the Ukrainian border was still hours ahead, and the men resembled bandits more than state officials. They *were* bandits. The enterprising gentlemen made us an offer: either to show them all the cash we had, in which case they would take half of it, or to let them search us forcibly, in which case they would take all the money they could find. Being a teenager with no luggage at the time proved a blessing for me. My not-so-lucky neighbor saw himself rough-handled, his suitcases emptied, and his money confiscated; the men then proceeded to "clean" the next compartment. Half an hour later, the train made an unscheduled stop in the middle of a wheat field. Still in shock, I looked outside and saw the band get off, after which the train promptly resumed its journey. That the train conductors were in cahoots with the gang had been obvious; that the locomotive engineer was, too, surprised me. This incident may not have sowed the germs of my interest in property rights, but I stopped finding train robbery scenes in the Westerns amusing.

Fifteen years later, as an assistant professor, I received a phone call from a British law firm seeking an expert in Russia's recent business history for the upcoming 6-billion-dollar battle between two Russian oligarchs at London's High Court. (Full disclosure: I did not testify.) Once the lawsuit became public in 2011, unforgettable tragicomedy ensued. Putin's exiled nemesis, late Boris Berezovsky, accused the Putin-friendly oligarch (and Chelsea Football Club owner), Roman Abramovich, of forcing him to sell certain assets below their fair value in the beginning of the 2000s. Not to be outdone, Abramovich denied

I

that Berezovsky had ever owned these assets, asserting that his payments to Berezovsky were intended as a reward for political protection rather than asset purchase – protection which Berezovsky could no longer provide after Putin came to power. Billed by the media as the biggest personal lawsuit in history, the proceedings proved an embarrassment to Russia and a windfall for the British legal profession. Of course, the lawsuit was "personal" in *de jure* terms only. *De facto*, Putin's Kremlin was implicated as the main threat to Berezovsky's property rights, having allegedly presented Berezovsky with the dilemma of a cheap sale today (to Abramovich) versus an inevitable expropriation tomorrow (by the state).

These two stories capture a common – but only partly correct – view of what jeopardizes the security of property. On the one hand, *state absence* allows private thugs to rob citizens and business owners. On the other hand, *state dominance* raises the specter of sovereign threats to tycoons' property rights. The conventional story of Russia's post-communist (d)evolution, accordingly, views the 1990s as the reign of private mafias and the post-2000 period as one defined by the Kremlin's threats of expropriation. As the two anecdotes here suggest, there is much truth to the "absence-dominance" view of the state's role in undermining property rights. However, this book argues that in the new millennium, it is state *weakness*, conceived as the inadequate control of the sovereign over his bureaucratic apparatus, that constitutes the main threat to property rights (PR) in countries such as Russia and Ukraine. The conceptual shift from state absence or dominance to state weakness in PR theorizing generates profound implications for available paths to secure property.

The book advances three logically connected arguments. First, the *conventional diagnosis* of what makes property rights insecure in modern developing states is incomplete. I argue that the most pervasive threats to PR arise less from the unchecked strength of the state ruler and more from state weakness: less from the executive center and more from the bureaucratic periphery. Importantly, my argument is that the low-level bureaucrats jeopardize not only the income rights of entrepreneurs, as per the literature on corruption, but the *ownership* itself; I conceptualize this process as "agent predation" and juxtapose it with the expropriation by the ruler as well as petty corruption. It is not the bully in the penthouse but the termites in the basement that often undermine the edifice of secure property.

Second, the *conventional solution* to insecure ownership fails in the context of such disorganized, low-level threats to property rights. Specifically, institutional constraints on the state principal do *not* improve the security of property rights because the ruler cannot "commit" on behalf of his staff. This argument strikes at the core of the PR literature preoccupied with modeling the ruler's commitment to PR. Principal-agent dilemmas in the state apparatus decouple the much-praised sovereign commitment from ownership security.

Third, the *novel solution* to insecure property rights involves firm-level strategies rather than macro-institutional design. In particular, alliances with stakeholders such as labor, adjacent communities, and foreign actors can be employed by firms facing weak states to secure property rights. Furthermore, I argue that these bottom-up, non-state solutions may facilitate the development of rule of law; this argument complements the existing narratives of "political will" and "legal reform" as the main paths toward rule of law.

Overall, this volume urges a reconceptualization of the emergence of secure property rights as such. The literature tends to view conflicts over property as epic elite battles whose institutionalized outcome determines national PR security for generations. Yet the significance of agent predation as well as firms' bottom-up "voice" strategies imply that PR conflicts resemble guerilla warfare in which local alliances matter and victory is incremental.

THE MAGIC OF SECURE PROPERTY RIGHTS

Property rights' security fundamentally determines economic growth by influencing investment, worker productivity, credit availability to the private sector, stock market development, as well as the extent of risk-sharing and division of labor in economic life.[1] The consensus on PR security as the key determinant of economic development is not limited to the academic community; the well-respected mammoth World Bank study "Where is the Wealth of Nations?" highlights the security of PR as far more important than the availability of man-made capital or natural resources.[2]

At the political level, PR security constitutes a key ingredient in the elusive ideal of "rule of law." Liberal[3] and conservative[4] thinkers alike have argued that protected private property provides a primary check on governmental discretion by granting dissidents independent bases for existence (and resistance). Using the example of seventeenth-century England, North and Weingast treat political liberties as historically contingent on PR security.[5] As in the case of economic growth, the link between PR security, democracy, and rule of law has found support among policymakers.[6] Overall, empirical evidence suggests that secure property rights promote both economic growth and democratization.[7]

Even *more* fundamentally, PR security influences the processes of state formation and state failure. Machiavelli, no friend of nonsense, argued that secure hereditary property rights are the basis of a strong republic, incentivizing citizens to produce more future soldiers (babies) who in turn will have a stake in

---

[1] E.g., Acemoglu et al. 2001; Johnson et al. 2002; Baumol 1990; Keefer and Knack 2002; Hall and Jones 1999; Malesky and Taussig 2008; Asoni 2008; Claessens and Laeven 2003.
[2] World Bank 2006.
[3] Schlesinger Jr 1997, 7.
[4] Friedman 1962.
[5] North and Weingast 1989.
[6] Hutchison 2005.
[7] E.g., Acemoglu and Johnson 2005; Leblang 1996; North and Thomas 1973; Rosenthal 1992; Stulz 2005.

4 *Introduction*

defending the state.[8] State formation, Margaret Levi argues, is firmly associated with the imperative of defining and defending property rights lest the society remain in the grip of Hobbesian predatory nightmare.[9] Empirically, predation writ large has been shown to trigger wholesale state failure in Africa[10] and state obliteration in the case of the USSR.[11]

FAILED STATES, DOMINANT RULERS, AND CREDIBLE COMMITMENT: CONVENTIONAL WISDOM

The scope of secure property rights' impact and the robustness of pertinent findings in numerous studies grant an almost magical quality to these institutions. It may seem that PR-related literature has settled into a consensus, if not complacency, now limiting itself to robustness checks.[12]

However, two fundamental debates still rage. One debate concerns PR *allocation*. Although the superiority of private over state or community ownership for economic outcomes was long taken for granted,[13] the post-communist transition has shaken this axiom. "Hybrid" public-private property rights seemed to achieve superior results in the Chinese countryside as well as in the East European industrial settings, while rapid privatization in the absence of supporting market institutions brought questionable benefits to polities such as Russia.[14]

The second debate – which this book focuses on – addresses the *determinants* of PR *security*. For while there is accord that PR security rivals the proverbial apple pie, less agreement exists on how to bake it. That, in turn, cannot be answered without addressing the logically prior question of *what threatens* PR. Ownership claims remain unsettled in much of the developing world. The

---

[8] Machiavelli 1998, II.2–II.3.

[9] "The state is a response to the Hobbesian dilemma, that it is in every individual's interest both to make a contract and then, at the first advantageous opportunity, to break it. The state changes the calculation of advantage by socializing people to uphold contracts and by punishing people who break them. More precisely, the state defines property rights, without which there would be no economic growth of production." Levi 1981, 435.

[10] Bates 2008.

[11] Solnick 1999.

[12] This is *not* to say that such studies are unimportant, particularly when they correct hugely influential prior findings. For a successful example questioning Acemoglu and Robinson's work on colonial-era property rights and development, see Fails and Krieckhaus 2010.

[13] Boycko et al. 1997.

[14] Some of the best literature on hybrid PR follows the tradition of economic sociology by stressing the "embeddedness" of economic actors in their sociopolitical context. Unlike the institutionalist approaches in political economy, the embeddedness-based frameworks tend to view the joint state-private ownership of assets, and state-private networks more generally, as a *positive* phenomenon in the developing world. In contrast to the embeddedness literature, the framework in this volume (1) focuses squarely on the *post*-privatization issues of PR security and (2) emphasizes the *non*-consensual "voice"-based strategies of firms vis-à-vis the state actors. Oi and Walder 1999; McDermott 2002; Schoenman 2014; Post 2014.

specter of forceful interference with property rights ruins legitimate businesses, triggers revolutions, and drains the global economy of immeasurable riches. The problem of how societies end up in – and might escape from – the equilibrium of insecure PR has emerged as the crux of "interpreting recorded human history."[15]

Orthodox answers to the core questions of this study – what threatens property rights, and how can they be secured? – boast a long intellectual pedigree. Hume and Hobbes, in particular, offer critical early insights. (Not to spite Locke, but he was rather concerned with ethical justifications of private PR *allocation* in the context of original appropriation.)

For Hume, people have been at war over property since the dawn of time. This quasi-permanent struggle or the possibility thereof, Hume argued, denies the option of stabilizing any particular distribution of property by referring to the ideal of fairness. Instead, hope is in the *self-interest of private predators* who, being fairly equal in their capacities, see the promise of peace.[16] PR security for Hume is essentially a social convention "enter'd into by all the members of the society to bestow stability on the possession of ... goods."[17] Only much later does the state reinforce these informal understandings.

Hobbes likewise ascribes the chaotic violence in the state of nature to people's intrinsic desire to possess (and their readiness to act on it). However, as far as hope goes, *sovereign authority* is the *sine qua non*: embodying the collective will, the Leviathan leads people out of their predicament by allocating and enforcing property rights. The sovereign possesses "the whole power of prescribing the rules whereby every man know what goods he may enjoy.... For before constitution of sovereign power ... all men had a right to all things, which necessarily causes war."[18]

Contemporary literature descends, to a large extent, from these two classical approaches. Studies focusing on stateless tribes and societies tend to follow Hume by examining how private actors achieve predictability in property relations. Inquiries into PR security in states, conversely, echo Hobbes by inquiring how Leviathans secure property in their respective domains.

Neither approach, I argue, is well-suited for the settings in which, on the one hand, state institutions penetrate society and control private violence but where, on the other hand, these institutions do not form a coherent "Leviathan." Severe principal-agent dilemmas may plague the state apparatus even after the government has monopolized the use of violence. In fact, it is the combination of state agents' control of coercion *and* the lack of the state principal's control

---

[15] North et al. 2009.
[16] "I observe that it will be for my interest to leave another in the possession of his goods, provided he will act in the same manner with regard to me.... When this common sense of interest is mutually express'd, and is known to both, it produces a suitable resolution and behaviour." Hume 1978, 490.
[17] Ibid., 489.
[18] Hobbes 1958, 148.

6   *Introduction*

of state agents that gives rise to the phenomenon of agent predation, shifting the primary locus of state threats to PR down the administrative chain of command. This shift in our understanding of PR *threats*, in turn, forces a revision of the axiomatic institutionalist *prescriptions*. Before elaborating this revision, let us review the contemporary scholarship on PR security.

Threats to Property Rights

What threatens PR in modern developing states? The literature stresses two sources of threats. First, *state failure* involves the privatization of violence leading to widespread plunder. Africa's "warlord politics" in the resource-rich Liberia, Sierra Leone, and the Democratic Republic of the Congo furnishes a prime example of top-down predation by strongmen and the associated militias.[19] In most failed states, predation is accompanied by "the militarization of civic society below."[20] In Russia, the government's withdrawal from law enforcement in the 1990s resulted in violent PR disputes, including midday assassinations of business rivals, leading scholars to conclude that "the hidden hand of the market in post-Soviet Russia has its index finger on the trigger of a Kalashnikov."[21] The marauding gangs of New Orleans in the wake of localized state collapse following the 2005 hurricane Katrina remind us that the connection between state failure and looting is not limited to the developing world. Overall, the literature castigating state vacuum has effectively countered what Margaret Levi calls "one of the most nefarious effects of the neoliberal revolution [which] is to disguise how much we depend on government infrastructure, both physical and social."[22]

Second, excessive power of the state over economic subjects substitutes *expropriation by the ruler* for private PR threats. In Weingast's canonical formulation, "a government strong enough to protect property ... is also strong enough to confiscate the wealth of its citizens."[23] In settings as diverse as those of Sparta after the Peloponnesian War, medieval Europe, Mamluk Egypt, and, more recently, Mexico, Russia, Bolivia, the Philippines, Ecuador, Indonesia, Venezuela, and other developing economies, the state ruler – also referred to as "the sovereign" – emerges as the key PR threat.[24] Edward I confiscated the wealth of the Jews, and Phillip IV confiscated the wealth of the Templars. The communist and, to a much lesser extent, fascist regimes of the twentieth century expropriated whole layers of their populations. In the developing countries, foreign investors have often been the target of full-scale state nationalization:

---

[19] Reno 1998; Kaiser and Wolters 2013.
[20] Bates 2008, 9.
[21] Fish 1998, 95.
[22] Levi 2006, 8.
[23] Weingast 1993, 287.
[24] De Mesquita et al. 2003; Winters 2011; Greif 2006; Haber et al. 2003; Guriev et al. 2011; Rajan and Zingales 2003.

Failed States, Dominant Rulers, and Credible Commitment

1960–80, for example, was a particularly nerve-rattling phase for the foreign corporations whose assets were expropriated in seventy-nine countries.[25]

The *ruler-centric concept of the state* defines the core of the literature examining such PR threats. Consider the seminal works of Levi and Olson which focus on the ruler as the main source of PR threats. Olson's "stationary bandit" symbolizes none other than the state ruler, "the bandit leader" whose rationality leads him "to seize a given domain, to make himself the ruler of that domain, and to provide a peaceful order ... thereby obtaining more in tax theft than he could have obtained from migratory plunder."[26] While Levi recognizes that state agents present one of the constraints on the ruler's ability to maximize wealth and power, this constraint is radically de-prioritized relative to others.[27] In a similar vein, Bueno de Mesquita et al. conceptualize the challenge of kleptocracies as one of "reining in the Prince."[28] (In *A Theory of the State*, Barzel similarly refers to "tying the Protector's hands."[29]) The main conclusion of *The Logic of Political Survival* – that policies undermining PR are driven by state rulers, whose political support derives from small winning coalitions – echoes powerfully through the three influential volumes by North, Weingast, and Wallis as well as Acemoglu and Robinson.[30] All of these works proceed from the assumption that abuses by predatory state rulers are the key problem of PR security.

Property rights' abuse by the state rulers, the literature notes, is not necessarily conducted for the narrow purpose of self-enrichment. For North et al., for example, selective predation is a political tool employed to *co-opt elite rivals,* the main concern being the problem of endemic violence. In the "limited access orders," which the authors treat as typical of contemporary developing economies, the engine of predation is the collusion of the ruling elites.[31] The assumption underlying this model is one of relatively small, centralized governments in which the issue of *hierarchical intra-governmental control is assumed away*: "the leaders ... [have] the ability to ... organize and discipline the members of each leader's group."[32]

---

[25] Among these countries, ten were "mass expropriator" states where PR attacks had a frequent, cross-sectoral, ideologically driven character: Algeria, Angola, Chile, Ethiopia, Indonesia, Mozambique, Peru, Tanzania, Uganda, and Zambia. Kobrin 1984.

[26] Olson 1993, 568.

[27] Among six types of constraints (such as foreign actors, elite power rivals, etc.), the principal-agent problem is listed *last* and in reduced form as the imperfect ability to monitor agents. Levi, 448–57.

[28] De Mesquita et al., 3.

[29] Barzel 2002, 138.

[30] Acemoglu and Robinson 2012; North et al. 2009; North et al. 2013.

[31] More specifically, violence specialists commit to peace in exchange for economic rents from other elites (politicians, priests, etc.). Because of their direct control over parts of the population, these other *non*-violent elites can help the violence specialists collect rents without the costly fighting. North et al.

[32] North et al., 4.

8 *Introduction*

Overall, whether the goal of the ruling elites is self-enrichment or the prevention of violence, it is the *coordinated, ruler-sanctioned nature of predation* that conceptually unifies this literature. The scholars typically (but prematurely) treat Russia and other post-communist states with a strongman at the helm as cases of such predation. North et al. add "modern Russia under Putin" to Mesopotamia in the third millennium BC and Britain under the Tudors as examples of limited access orders.[33] De Mesquita similarly suggests that Russia's "egregiously ineffective governance, particularly in the law enforcement" is, in fact, *a part of Putin's strategy* to remain in power.[34]

In addition to stressing the role of the ruler, this literature emphasizes the difference between threats to *income* rights and – significantly more devastating – threats to *ownership* rights.[35] Indeed, this is what distinguishes Olson's "roving bandit," who threatens *ownership* rights through peripatetic plundering, from the "stationary bandit," who merely targets *income* streams through sedentary taxation.

Securing Property Rights

How can property rights be secured? The answer to this question derives naturally from the ruler-centric conception of PR threats discussed earlier. Constraining the upper level of the state executive is the solution to the problem of PR insecurity, according to the literature. However, scholars disagree on *how* to bind the state principal's hands. Two paradigms describe the ways property rights are secured through constraining the ruler's discretion.

First, the "reputational restraint" paradigm puts faith in the self-enforcing effects of strategic interaction: To raise tax revenue tomorrow, governments will abstain from expropriating businesses today, so as to encourage economic activity.[36] A felicitous outcome of strategic interaction between the ruler and economic actors depends on the time horizon of the potentially predatory government: If the survival of the regime is at risk, the sovereign may expropriate,

---

[33] North et al., 31.

[34] "He [Putin] is doing this successfully ... an ineffective economic system, from the viewpoint of a cynical dictator, turns out very effective politically ... you constantly underpay the law enforcers which creates corrupt incentives. Although they cannot be jailed for being disloyal, they can be jailed for corruption. Then you tell them: I can forgive you corruption if you remain loyal.... Politically, this is very effective. Besides, he does not need to spend much money on the repressive apparatus: they can collect all necessary resources through bribes." De Mesquita 2012.

[35] E.g. Kobrin, 330; Winters, 6–7.

[36] For Olson (1993), the ruler may forgo present predation so as to motivate the private owners to increase output and the ruler's revenues in the long run. For Levi (1989, 95–121), war is a catalyst for such strategic interaction because it raises the fiscal needs of the state principal while *also* increasing the willingness of the asset owners (whose welfare depends on military victory) to pay taxes. See also Diermeier et al. 1997; Timmons 2006; Sened 1997; Luong and Weinthal 2004.

Failed States, Dominant Rulers, and Credible Commitment

hence wasting her accumulated reputational capital.[37] Overall, the literature on PR security is rightly skeptical about the sovereign's concern for the future tax revenue as the *only* mechanism to safeguard against predation. Instead, the logic of reputational restraint is often used to explain the emergence of PR security in the face of *private* expropriation in the tightly knit communities where the state is largely absent; in this post-Humean literature, culture and the logic of repeated games between private agents serve as strong behavioral constraints.[38]

Second, the "state commitment" paradigm, by far the dominant school of PR research, extols the virtues of mechanisms that drastically increase the costs of predation for the sovereign or make such predation impossible altogether.[39] This post-Hobbesian literature proceeds from the premise of a profound power imbalance between state and business, the former possessing coercive resources and the latter exposed to their arbitrary use. To reassure private owners, the literature argues, the state must be constrained. But how? Like the paradigm invoking reputational restraint, this tradition relies on the *rationality of the fiscally dependent sovereign*; to signal its benevolent disposition to prospective investors and tax payers, the state binds its own hands:

> During a fiscal crisis, the states desperately sought additional revenue. Often they were willing to make fantastic promises in exchange.... The problem was ... that not all promises are credible.... Each state, therefore, had to find some means of making credible promises.... *The state ... sells constraints on its future behavior in exchange for revenue today.*[40] [my emphasis]

The core debates in the literature discuss various ways in which the states can commit.[41] Some accounts point to policies that can act as bridge-burning tactics: For the post-communist countries, shock therapy, voucher privatization, WTO membership, and EU trade agreements have all been treated as "commitment devices."[42] Other accounts argue that informal state-business ties can also help the rulers to commit.[43] In modern China, for example, company CEOs who are children of the top party officials (the so-called Princelings) "have played a role in securing informal property rights ... [by] in effect act[ing] as ...

---

[37] Olson (2000, 28) argues that "if the king anticipates and values dynastic succession, that ... lengthens the planning horizon and ... increases confidence and thus investment, income, and tax receipts even in the present." Yet the history of Britain, one of the most durable dynastic monarchies, casts doubt on Olson's logic. Out of thirty-one British monarchs who ruled between 1066 and 1702, eighteen saw their succession plans sabotaged by the family members, suggesting that even in dynasties, reputational restraint is prone to break down. (Shleifer and Vishny 1998, 51.) See also Dixit 2004.

[38] E.g. Ostrom 1990; Ensminger 1997; Ellickson 1989; Bates 2001.

[39] E.g. Acemoglu and Johnson; Frye 2004; Firmin-Sellers 1995.

[40] Weingast 1990, 92–3.

[41] E.g. Weimer 1997.

[42] Tompson 2002, 952; Frye 1997; Przeworski 1991.

[43] Haber et al; North et al.

10 *Introduction*

hostages – the children of the monarch placed in the hands of those who need to rely upon the monarch."[44] The state may also choose to selectively enforce property rights for particular industries or elites in exchange for rents or political support.[45] The examples of commitment strategies listed so far involve policies and informal understandings that – albeit at a great personal cost – could still be potentially undone by the ruler.

The state commitment framework emphasizes two types of the more formalized constraints as being *most* effective as a safeguard against governmental expropriation. On the one hand, *formal business associations* uniting the bulk of a country's producers, creditors, or traders can resolve the problem of collective action among property owners, creating a formidable platform for retaliation against the ruler, should he decide to expropriate. In *Institutions and the Path to the Modern Economy*, Greif argues that in medieval Europe, "securing property rights from the grabbing hand of the state" was achieved through "merchant guilds" that shared information about PR abuses, coordinated retaliatory responses, and held the sovereigns in check.[46] By protecting property rights, the literature asserts, national business associations have proved critical for trade, investment, restructuring, and growth in the twentieth-century economies of South Korea, Mexico, Chile, Taiwan, Brazil, Thailand, Hungary, the Czech Republic, and elsewhere.[47] The modern incarnations of the medieval merchant groups "resolve the strategic dilemma of government-business cooperation. By creating opportunities for repeated interactions, such institutions lengthen time horizons and create trust."[48]

On the other hand, an array of *institutional constraints on the discretion of the executive* is expected to enhance PR security. Chief among these constraints are electoral institutions, political parties, and macro-level checks and balances, such as the separation of the legislative and executive branches, the independence of judges and market regulators, "market-preserving federalism," and so on.[49] The goal of this vast literature is to "explain how checks on executive discretion improve the government's commitment to property rights."[50] The positive impact of parliaments is celebrated as a particularly strong determinant of PR security (especially when parliaments "represent the wealth holders in society"[51]), so much so that even in authoritarian settings, legislatures are

---

[44] Gilson and Milhaupt 2011, 267.

[45] Razo 2008.

[46] Greif, 91.

[47] McDermott 2004; Maxfield and Schneider 1997; Doner and Schneider 2000; Root 1989; Bruszt and Stark 1998.

[48] Haggard et al. 1997, 41.

[49] E.g. Acemoglu 2012; Jensen 2008; Li 2009; Acemoglu and Johnson; Gehlbach and Keefer 2011; Bertelli and Whitford 2009; Humphreys and Bates 2005 ibid.; Cox 2011; Feld and Voigt 2003; Qian and Weingast 1997; North and Weingast.

[50] Weymouth 2011, 212.

[51] Weingast, 93.

Of State Piranhas and Business Stakeholders: Toward a New Theory

seen as shackles on the sovereign's grabbing hand.[52] Overall, parliaments and encompassing sovereign-supported business associations are lionized as some of the most effective PR-securing commitment devices.

OF STATE PIRANHAS AND BUSINESS STAKEHOLDERS: TOWARD A NEW THEORY

The next chapter develops a theoretical ideal type of "agent predation," which involves disorganized state threats to ownership rights. Building on the conceptualization of the state as predator by Levi and Olson, I point out that many works in their tradition overemphasize the role of "the ruler" in predation. While the literature recognizes the corruptibility of state agents, the latter appear as little more than an administrative nuisance: State agents "demand both higher salaries and reduced work loads" and in some settings may be "pocketing an unwarranted share of the taxes for themselves," but overall, the ruler is the ultimate predatory machine: "All rulers are predatory in the sense that they ... design property rights and policies meant to maximize their own personal power and wealth" while state agents merely pose the dangers of "free riding, shirking, and venality."[53]

The relationship of state agents and the state principal in orthodoxy resembles that of the cleaner fish and the shark. A zoological note: The cleaner fish eats food remnants literally out of the shark's mouth; since the amount of prey lost to the cleaner fish is miniscule, the shark tolerates this "theft" (and, in fact, benefits from having its teeth cleaned). By engaging in petty corruption, state agents may jeopardize some income streams that would otherwise benefit the state principal, but attacks on the more fundamental ownership rights are the prerogative of state rulers.

Agent predation elaborated here provides a theoretical counterpoint to the predatory symbiosis of the shark and the cleaner fish. To venture another aquatic metaphor, state agents in my framework appear as piranhas: voracious mini-beasts as lethal in groups as the shark, but also more vulnerable individually. Unlike sharks, piranhas never coordinate their attacks and habitually attack creatures larger than themselves. Predation in modern developing states is often conducted by high-powered mini-beasts: policemen, party functionaries, local administrators, directors of state-owned enterprises, tax collectors, or the agents at any of the myriad of departments with the power to halt productive activity (sanitation, fire safety, social security, etc.).

A key difference between the ideal types of state threats to PR concerns the nature of the main state conflict. Generally assuming expropriation on behalf of the ruler, the literature on PR security emphasizes *horizontal political* elite

---

[52] Boix 2003; Wright 2008; Gehlbach and Keefer 2012; Olson 2000, 36–40; North and Weingast.

[53] Levi, 440, 57, 38.

rivalry between the potential state principals.[54] Such emphasis allows for elite pacts as the way to secure property rights. Conversely, "agent predation" prioritizes the *vertical administrative* principal-agent conflicts between state principals and their subordinates. In this approach, elite pacts do not automatically result in secure PR.

As an aside speculation, three reasons stand out for why political science has neglected to fully integrate the principal-agent framework into theorizing the state threats to PR. First, principal-agent models have migrated into political science from economics of organization[55] mostly by way of American politics,[56] applied to a setting in which predation is not acute. (Barry Weingast, in fact, extended the conventional principal-agent model to explain the surprising *success* with which the U.S. Congress controls the American bureaucracy.[57]) Second, principal-agent models traditionally address organizational *genesis* involving a "structural choice" between establishing a new organization, such as a firm or a government agency, and outsourcing production to existing suppliers.[58] At the same time, questions about the *ongoing* (dys)function of executive hierarchies are reduced in theoretical significance to issues of bureaucratic inefficiency, known as "drift" or "slack."[59] Third, the institutionalist wave has downgraded organizations as such, shifting the focus from the "players" to the "rules of the game," as North's famous organization-institution distinction has it.[60]

Crucially, our conception of PR *threats* shapes our understanding of what makes PR *secure*. The ideal type of "agent predation," as the next chapter argues, creates the conceptual space for a non-state pathway toward PR security. Pace orthodoxy, I argue that non-oligarchic companies *can* hold the state accountable through alliances with their stakeholders, including foreign actors, local communities, and labor. Stakeholder networks increase the company's power to deter or resolve an attack on its PR because stakeholders can impose costs on the aggressor on behalf of the targeted firm. A firm's allies can punish state predators through negative publicity, local electoral pressure, labor strikes, and other mechanisms. Stakeholders can employ financial, political, physical, or framing strategies that dramatically increase the costs of a potential expropriation from the aggressor's viewpoint. More generally, I argue that property rights in weak states are secured through a *process* with substantial *bottom-up* initiative by the potential victims of PR violations, rather than a single *top-down act* by the state executive.

---

[54] E.g. Albertus and Menaldo 2012; North et al.
[55] Williamson 1983; Grossman and Hart 1983.
[56] E.g. Epstein and O'Halloran 1994; Shipan 2004.
[57] Weingast and Moran 1983.
[58] Kiser 1994; Moe 1995.
[59] Wyckoff 1990; Epstein and O'Halloran 1994.
[60] North 1990.

Methodology

The theoretical framework elaborated in the next chapter also enriches the discourse on developmental versus predatory states. The most recent permutation of this discourse includes the historicized analytical narratives of "natural states" versus "open access orders" by North, Wallis, and Weingast, as well as the contrast between "inclusive" and "extractive" state institutions by Acemoglu and Robinson.[61] On the one hand, in its focus on *state* institutions, this discourse has sidelined non-state actors as potential remedy-providers for the scourge of state predation. On the other hand, major differences *within* the category of "predatory" states – and, in fact, important distinctions between the *types* of state threats to PR within a *given* state – warrant more scholarly attention. This volume differentiates conceptually and empirically threats to income rights from threats to ownership rights, as well as threats that are coordinated by the state principal from those that are not. In doing so, this book goes beyond the mere *extent* of predation as the main conceptual lever for analyzing PR security.

METHODOLOGY

The data from 152 open-ended interviews, conducted between 2003 and 2012, as well as an original survey of 516 firms, implemented in 2007, form the empirical backbone of the study, supplemented by the analysis of regional media and government documents. The appendix following Chapter 2 provides details on the implementation of interviews and the survey.

This investigation integrates qualitative and quantitative methods, whereby the former predominate. The aim is to capitalize on the promise of the "post-KKV era" by acknowledging that "both theory development and theory testing may take place during each phase of a qualitative-quantitative iteration."[62]

Process tracing in carefully selected cases offers crucial advantages to my inquiry. On the one hand, it questions the causal mechanisms presumed by orthodox theories while demonstrating novel mechanisms at work. Firmly rooted in game theory and too often relying empirically on historical narratives, the state commitment paradigm of PR security has been less successful at showing the step-by-step mechanism linking ruler behavior to PR-related outcomes in modern developing states; meanwhile, the ideal type of agent predation elaborated here suggests that a distinct bottom-up process may lead to PR security. On the other hand, concept validity remains a surprisingly acute challenge in conventional treatments of PR security (discussed later). A combination of qualitative evidence and original survey data here hopefully offers a way forward.

Russia and Ukraine provide an ideal testing ground for my theory for two reasons. First, the addition of Ukraine ensures that the findings are not

---

[61] Acemoglu and Robinson; North et al.
[62] Mahoney 2010, 142.

driven by many of Russia's idiosyncrasies that could influence the political economy of property rights, including its extremely rapid privatization, an economy based on natural resources, the Kremlin's expropriation of Yukos as precedent, unusually strong constitutional protections of private property (by post-Soviet standards), and so forth. Second, the Russia-Ukraine dyad is particularly promising for testing the "state commitment" paradigm, given the emergence of distinct commitment devices in these countries in the 2000s. In Russia, the first years of Putin's presidency saw unprecedented business institutionalization, with several federal business associations emerging as important high-profile actors; these associations represent the best-case scenario of modern "merchant groups," which, according to the state commitment paradigm, should improve the security of ownership. Ukraine exemplifies a different mechanism of sovereign commitment. The 2004 Orange Revolution created an empowered parliament representing the previously sidelined wealth-holders and entrepreneurs and, in doing so, placed stringent institutional constraints on the presidency.

Together, these countries constitute the "most likely" cases for conventional wisdom and, as such, "crucial" cases for our purposes.

Concept validity constitutes a particular advantage of my survey instrument. Consider first the problematic nature of three proxies for PR security – risk indices, behavioral proxies, and surveys – as they are currently used in the literature. Risk indices, prepared by Political Risk Services, the Heritage Foundation, and other organizations are problematic because they (a) rely on the subjective opinions of relatively few experts; (b) are compiled according to a non-transparent methodology; (c) estimate the probability of ruler-coordinated expropriation ignoring the threats from unaccountable lower-level bureaucrats or private actors; (d) do not vary at the subnational level. In addition to these conceptual issues, a severe problem with causal inference arises when risk indices are used to support theories of state commitment. Because the formal constraints on the executive are taken into account by experts assigning a risk rating to a country, the use of the resulting indices as an *outcome* variable by theorists of state commitment comes dangerously close to a tautology.

Behavioral proxies typically measure financial or capital investments by private actors. They are problematic because: (a) like the risk indices, these proxies do not differentiate between various public and private sources of predation; (b) investment is contingent on macroeconomic, product-specific, and psychological factors unrelated to PR; (c) behavioral proxies are often self-reported and suffer from the dissembling bias.

Finally, some instruments (e.g. the early rounds of the World Bank's BEEP surveys) use the actual term "property rights" in questionnaires; this term, as the testing in my own survey shows, is likely to be interpreted very differently by the respondents, resulting in a serious concept misidentification. My questionnaire clarified this problem by asking the respondents to *define* "property

Organization of the Book

rights."[63] Twenty percent of respondents did not include the right to manage assets in their definitions of property rights, 40 percent did not include the right to derive income from assets, and 65 percent did not include the right to ownership transfer in their definitions. All three rights are the definitive parts of the PR bundle in the academic discourse. (Meanwhile, some respondents included in their definitions "the right to receive loans for property acquisitions" (18 percent) and "the right to a qualified labor force" (27 percent), neither of which fall under the rubric of "property rights" in the literature.) An additional common problem with survey instruments is that they omit some of the key PR threats, such as "raiding."

Overall, despite its theoretical super-status, PR security remains an empirical black box. To provide a better measure, my survey fielded questions on eleven specific PR infringements (of which nine are infringements by *state* actors) as experienced by the respondents. I used my informal interviews throughout the region to establish the list of PR infringements. The resulting *Threat* variables are discussed at length in Chapter 3. My proxies (1) differentiate between various sources of PR threats and allow for subnational variation; (2) reduce incentives to dissemble since no self-reporting of sensitive activities by the respondent is involved, as in the case of investment-related questions; (3) ensure inter-firm comparability via detailed easy-to-understand questions, as opposed to an ambiguous question on "property rights." One of the conceptual strengths of my approach is that I take the standard definition of PR seriously and unpack it empirically, whereas much work[64] in the political economy of "property rights" investigates phenomena that have a rather tenuous connection to the concept.

ORGANIZATION OF THE BOOK

Chapter 2 critiques the literature surveyed in the introduction and elaborates my key premise of state weakness into a theory of PR predation and protection. Building on previous scholarship, I conceptualize four ideal types of state threats to property rights. I argue that by neglecting one of these ideal types, namely "agent predation," existing scholarship has also failed to identify one important solution to the problem of insecure PR. On the one hand, state weakness makes it difficult for the ruler (or state principal) to commit to PR security on behalf of state employees (or state agents). On the other hand, a weak state can be disciplined by business actors at the local level more easily than a unified Leviathan presumed by much existing theorizing. The contribution of my

---

[63] The respondent could select multiple answers among a menu of six suggested PR components, only three of which described the actual parts of the PR bundle.

[64] For example, one typical study of PR security does not define "property rights" and proceeds to measure their presumed "protection" in 127 countries via the citizens' foreign currency holdings: in other words, via a placeholder for any and all economic risks. Weymouth.

framework is established both vis-à-vis the general literature on the political economy of property rights and the area-specific scholarship on Russia and Ukraine.

Chapter 3 argues that low-level bureaucrats target more than the income rights of firms by fundamentally undermining their ownership. A detailed case study of the "raiding" phenomenon in Russia and Ukraine, in which low-level state actors partly or fully expropriate firms, illustrates the point. Beyond raiding, the chapter discusses other cases of agent predation involving tax inspectors, law enforcers, regulators, and so on. I exploit my survey of firms to quantitatively compare the *intensity* of different types of state threats, as well as the *impact* of different threats on the risk perception of firm owners and on the predictability of future threats. Finally, I use the BEEPS (World Bank) data to establish the longitudinal change in state threats throughout the 2000–10 decade. Overall, the chapter establishes that agent predation was at least as serious and harmful as petty corruption in the examined countries in the first decade of the new millennium.

Chapter 4 shows that agent predation is different not only from bureaucratic corruption but also from ruler-coordinated expropriation. Many state threats to ownership occur *contrary* to the will of the state principal. This point is substantiated in three steps. First, I show how agent predation has undermined *the priorities* or the self-interest of the respective state principals in Russia and Ukraine. Such priorities include military security, state budget, and popular support, as well as effective electoral manipulation and various pet projects. Second, I detail *the efforts* that the state principals have exerted to crack down on agent predation. The administrative reforms undertaken to rein in the bureaucracies of Russia and Ukraine are discussed, as well as the comprehensive anti-raiding legislation adopted in Russia at the end of the 2000s. Third, I exploit my survey data, zooming in on blame attribution for insecure PR and on the sub-national variation in threat intensity. I find that firm owners often implicate the local state agents rather than the national government, and that the sub-national variation in state threats is more consistent with *disorganized* agent predation than with the narrative of systemic expropriation on behalf of the state principal. I also examine the impact of both threat types on the incentives of firm owners, finding that when firm owners are exposed to disorganized threats, they are more likely to behave in predatory ways themselves.

Chapter 5 shifts the discussion from PR *threats* to PR *security* by evaluating the commitment paradigm of PR security "on its own turf" via longitudinal case studies. These country studies trace the implementation of specific and distinct constraints on the upper executive emphasized in the literature, namely the encompassing sovereign-supported "merchant groups" that emerged in Russia in 2000–1 and the empowered parliament, along with other institutional constraints on the presidency, that materialized in Ukraine in 2004. Counterintuitively, ownership rights did not become more secure in either country over time. The chapter explains these puzzling outcomes, capitalizing

Organization of the Book

on the theoretical potential of the Russia-Ukraine dyad as a testing ground for conventional wisdom.

If constraining the state principals institutionally does not protect firms from agent predation, what might? Chapter 6 explores the potential of firms to improve PR security *at the company level*. I argue that state principals are but the grand façade behind which the real politics of PR security takes place. Such politics is rooted in alliances connecting business owners with various stakeholders around their firms. Multiple case studies from Russia and Ukraine are used to analyze the alliance-based defense mechanisms. Survey data further tests my argument. The incremental, bottom-up, non-state, alliance-oriented aspects of my theory complement the orthodox focus on the grand-scale, unilateral, state-driven events responsible for secure property rights.

The book concludes by discussing the relationship between the firms' stakeholder alliances and the rule of law. Chapter 7 outlines three specific mechanisms through which stakeholder alliances might be conducive to the rule of law taking hold. These mechanisms involve restraining the oligarchs, institutionalizing transparency, and counteracting the political apathy of small business owners. These mechanisms are contrasted with the conventional narratives of "political will" and "legal reform," as well as the putative importance of a diffuse middle class in holding state actors accountable. Finally, this chapter provides a comparative perspective for the key arguments in the book. As dynamics in other parts of the world suggest, a bottom-up theoretical framework for our understanding of secure property and the rule of law is long overdue.

2

Agent Predation and Secure Ownership

BACKGROUND AND DEFINITIONS

As institutions, secure property rights constitute an important subset of the humanly devised constraints on behavior; they shape expectations about ownership and determine the fundamental trajectories of civilizations by constraining governmental and private predation and enabling capital accumulation.[1]

"Property rights" are defined as a bundle of rights containing: (1) the right to derive income from assets; (2) the right to use and manage assets; and (3) the right to transfer the assets to someone else.[2] Political economists often distinguish between the rights to income from assets and the more fundamental rights to the usage or transfer of assets.[3] Accordingly, this book defines (1) as *income* rights, while (2) and (3) are referred to as *ownership* rights. Property rights encompass income rights and ownership rights.

This notion of property rights as abstract and transferable claims dates back to ancient Roman law and stands in contrast to the emphasis on physical control over assets in vogue among legal realists in the early twentieth century. The modern reference to a "bundle" of discrete rights has been reinforced by the increasing complexity of property-related laws, particularly in the Western world.

My inquiry focuses squarely on the rights in *tangible assets that generate income streams* (shops, factories, real estate, etc.). Intellectual PR are fundamentally different and are outside of my scope of inquiry.[4]

---

[1] North and Thomas.

[2] Barzel 1997.

[3] E.g., Olson; Winters.

[4] For one, it is substantially more difficult for any given state actor to profit from threats to an entrepreneur's intellectual PR: the state may neglect to enforce intellectual PR, but it is typically private pirates who profit most from such neglect. For an excellent study of intellectual PR in the postcommunist context, see Dimitrov 2009.

18

Critique of the Literature

A study of rights can focus either on their allocation (who has the right) or enforcement (how the right is secured).[5] The dependent variable of my study is the *enforcement* or *security* of the property rights of firms and individual entrepreneurs: private allocation or assignment is taken as a given. The conceptual distinction between the allocation and the enforcement of property rights is paramount. More than clarity is at stake; as the work of de Soto unintentionally demonstrated, failure to grasp this distinction can lead to harmful policy advice.[6] Whereas the first wave of research[7] on postcommunist property rights addressed privatization – the reallocation of property rights from the state to individuals – this volume addresses the subsequent stage. Now that most property in Russia and Ukraine is legally private, it is the security of formal claims to this property that is our concern.

CRITIQUE OF THE LITERATURE

State Failure and Ruler Dominance as Threats?

Existing literature on PR security, surveyed in Chapter 1, fails to capture some of the most important dynamics in Russia, Ukraine, and the developing world more broadly. To begin, the frameworks of state failure and ruler dominance as the key approaches to PR *violations* are theoretically incomplete.

The concept of the state appears curiously bifurcated: the government is either omnipotent or atrophied. On the one hand, the program on ruler dominance assumes a strong state that is both relatively autonomous in its goal formulation and possessed of sufficient capacity to carry out the formulated policies. On the other hand, the literature on state failure and mafias assumes an incapacitated government. (The less violent paradigm of "state capture," in which oligarchs or thugs usurp the process of rule-making, still sees the government as virtually privatized.[8])

While the "strong vs. nonexistent" dichotomy of state subsets provides analytical value in terms of ideal types, its conceptual and empirical limits must also be recognized. Conceptually, the state bifurcation in the literature often produces a similarly dichotomous treatment of firms, which are theorized as

---

[5] Weimer 1997.

[6] De Soto (2003) advocated the distribution of formal property titles to slum-dwellers and squatters expecting that the poor of the Third World would use this legalized property as collateral, triggering (in the ideal case) a virtuous cycle of capital infusion and growth. The formal *allocation* of property rights was assumed to be synonymous with their *enforcement*. (I raise a similar critique of the work by Shleifer and Vishny later in this chapter.) After the World Bank allocated millions of formal titles in Cambodia, the naiveté of this assumption became clear: the shantytowns of the politically powerless formal owners experienced massive "fires" (read: arsons) and forced evictions, as the local government officials and investors scrambled to profit from grabbing the assets. Gravois 2005.

[7] E.g., Goldman 2003; Boycko et al. 1997; Shleifer and Treisman 2001; Aslund 2007, 143–78.

[8] Hellman et al. 2003; Sonin 2003.

either politically irrelevant (in a "strong" state) or oligarchic (in an atrophied state). Empirically, the largest set of transition states, for example, falls in neither the strong nor the nonexistent subset, as evidenced by the annual Freedom House Nations in Transit reports. More broadly, failed states constitute less than 10 percent of the world's countries, that is, only a small portion of the developing economies.[9] For countries in which the government retains its monopoly on coercion, the "failed state" approach to PR threats is inappropriate.

The "sovereign threat" school, for its part, assumes that *nominal rulers are, indeed, sovereign* – that from a ruler's perspective, the administrative challenges from bureaucratic subordinates are insignificant compared to the political challenges from rival elites. This assumption is often incorrect, as the literature differentiating between "despotic" and "infrastructural" state power – between the ability to order and the capacity to implement – has shown.[10] The literature on sovereign threats, however, sees implicit infrastructural power where despotic power is on display; in doing so, it tends to treat predation as the exclusive prerogative of the state principal. Crucially, the ruler-centric concept of the state common to this literature neglects the role of state *agents* as PR threats in their own right.

Attacks on PR may be agent-driven rather than ruler-organized. The scholarship on corruption has acknowledged this possibility, but only to the extent that *income rights* are concerned. In particular, the principal-agent[11] framework has been fruitfully employed to differentiate between the top-down or systemic corruption and the bottom-up or disorganized corruption.[12] At one extreme, the different levels of the bureaucratic hierarchy collude to maximize the *joint* bribe intake that can then be claimed by the principal. The state principal acts as a price-setting monopolist, while the bribe-paying firms are modeled as *customers* who enjoy the relatively secure delivery of "government services," including permits, licenses, and so forth.[13] At the other extreme, the low-level bureaucrats act as independent agents maximizing their own bribe revenue. In this scenario, the bribe levels depend on whether the goods, such as licenses, that are provided by various bureaucrats are substitutable in nature.[14]

---

[9] Bates, 2.

[10] The postcommunist set of states, in particular, has seen a divergence between these power types. Easter 2012.

[11] Principal-agent problems refer to the difficulty of hierarchical control resulting from information asymmetries between the administrative superior and her subordinates. These asymmetries undermine both the initial selection of effective agents by the principal and their subsequent monitoring. These problems of adverse selection and moral hazard decrease organizational efficiency.

[12] Rose-Ackerman 1978; Becker and Stigler 1974; Aidt 2003; Klitgaard 1997; Klitgaard 1991; Bardhan and Mookherjee 2006; Mishra 2006; Shah 2007; Guriev 1999; Waller et al. 2002; Arikan 2004; Mushkat and Mushkat 2012.

[13] Shleifer and Vishny 1993, 604.

[14] If there is bureaucratic competition for the right to provide a license, for example, bribe levels may decrease; conversely, if a bureaucratic agency has monopoly on a particular type of license, bribe levels rise.

Critique of the Literature

The scholarship on corruption is a helpful – but only marginal – corrective to the literature on "sovereign threats" to PR; it stops short of a true revision because it addresses *only the income rights* within the PR bundle. Disorganized or agent-driven corruption is typically treated as "a way for business to get around illegitimate and inefficient state rules and regulations ... [or] to avoid legitimate laws."[15] The insecurity of *ownership* rights can devastate a country's investment flows and its overall developmental trajectory, but the insecurity of *income* rights is not nearly as catastrophic.[16] Accordingly, the literature conceptualizes disorganized corruption as one

involving low-level officials extracting small bribes for performing their duties (speed money), or for not harassing the innocent by deliberately misinterpreting ... regulations.... *Although these types of corruption are very irksome, they are not necessarily the most damaging ... for the economy.... Indeed ... some corruption of this type could be efficiency enhancing.*[17]

Disorganized corruption is generally referred to as "petty, administrative, or bureaucratic."[18]

To the extent the literature on corruption does address ownership rights, it treats them akin to the "sovereign threat" literature discussed so far. For Rose-Ackerman, ownership rights are violated by "the strong kleptocrat [who] runs a brutal but efficient state limited only by his own inability to make credible commitments," while "corrupt low-level officials" merely "introduce inefficiencies in the form of additional delays and red tape and cross-agency interference."[19] For Shleifer and Vishny, the "security of property ... focuses attention on the power of the ruler to appropriate private wealth for his own benefit, whether through arbitrary confiscation or ruinous taxation."[20] While the literature on corruption has a nuanced approach to state capacity, it does not treat the security of *ownership* as its dependent variable.[21]

Overall, the conventional diagnosis is straightforward: it is state *rulers* who undermine the ownership rights of private actors. Yet, the principal-agent dilemmas of real, existing bureaucracies in the non-OECD world profoundly impact predation. As Chapter 3 shows, this impact goes well beyond inflated budgets, time waste, and petty corruption that helps firms cut through red

---

[15] Rose-Ackerman 2006, xxx.

[16] Hough (2001) argues that while capital flight was the scourge of Russia's development in the 1990s, disorganized corruption was possibly *useful* in creating trust between bureaucrats and the entrepreneurs.

[17] Khan 2006, 220–1 (emphasis added).

[18] Shah, 235.

[19] Rose-Ackerman 1999, 119–21.

[20] Shleifer and Vishny, 30.

[21] For a detailed overview of the literature in which corruption or state capacity appear as independent variables, see Gingerich 2013. The typical *dependent* variables in this literature are the quality of public projects (relating to education, health, and infrastructure), the size of the unofficial economy, and the volume of tax revenue.

tape. The threat of expropriation by lower-level bureaucrats is the rule in weak states. Such threats may include a municipal court issuing an injunction paid for by a competitor; a policeman shutting down some retailers to intimidate others; a local official pressuring a firm to give a job to his relative lest the company lose its operation license; and so forth.

By jeopardizing the very livelihood of entrepreneurs, such low-level threats can trigger profound sociopolitical shifts. In December 2010, a Tunisian street vendor, Muhamed Bouazizi, immolated himself after the confiscation of his wares and the extortion by a municipal official; the subsequent events became known as the Arab Spring. To describe the subversion of PR security, including ownership rights, by bureaucratic agents as slacking or drifting is an analytically misleading euphemism at best. As Russia's federal ombudsman for the protection of entrepreneurs put it in July 2012, "the main problem is predatory pressure on business. Today, property takeovers through the use of the criminal code and the threat of jail sentences are the norm, and this is mostly done by the agents of power structures [*silovykh struktur*]."[22] By 2013, 13,600 entrepreneurs were behind bars in Russia, while 240,000 had been convicted of "economic crimes."[23] Not too petty.

State Commitment as Panacea?

In modern states with the monopoly on coercion, the problem of insecure PR is alleviated when the sovereign is subjected to a "credible commitment" via institutional limits on the ruler's discretion, particularly through empowered parliaments or encompassing business associations – several fundamental objections can be raised vis-à-vis this scholarly consensus.

To begin, the dynamics in Russia and Ukraine present a puzzle. According to conventional wisdom, *systemic PR security should have tangibly improved* in Russia soon after 2000 and in Ukraine soon after 2004. In both countries, state capacity increased relative to the fiscally disastrous situation of the 1990s, marginalizing private violence as a concern. More importantly, the rise of sovereign-supported encompassing business associations in 2000–1 in Russia and the 2004 Orange Revolution in Ukraine provided precisely the institutional constraints on the presidential administration that the "credible commitment" framework emphasizes. Counterintuitively, the abuse of private property rights by the state remained unaffected in both countries.

In general, there is a chasm between the *theoretical emphasis on the role of the state* in securing PR and the *data on the actual characteristics of most developing states*. While the government can, theoretically, protect private property more efficiently than private actors themselves can, few states resemble the

---

[22] *Kommersant* July 10, 2012.
[23] Article 159 of the criminal code ("fraud") is the one most often abused by the bureaucrats in this context. *Kapital Strany* August 1, 2012. *Grani* May 25, 2013.

Critique of the Literature

rational, power-wielding sovereign with long-term horizons that would allow effective self-restraint on predation. Betting on elites to turn their states "developmental" à la Singapore (a common theme in Russia's political discourse on *modernizatsiia*) means ignoring the evidence of just how *exceptional* modern developmental states are, arising typically under the conditions of profound systemic vulnerability with elites facing *concurrent* geopolitical, fiscal, and revolutionary threats.[24] Meanwhile, the sovereign of the state commitment framework resembles Ulysses: fearing his own fallibility, the ruler imposes institutional shackles on himself to resist the temptation of expropriation. In reality, however, state officials from Moscow to Mogadishu are driven by short-term private gains that barely overlap with long-term "state interests" in tax collection or investment. In much of the world, Olson's state "bandits" are "stationary" in the physical sense only – conceptually, they are very much "roving."[25]

A further objection targets the very notion of commitment: by subsuming a bewildering array of institutions, policies, and behavior patterns, the concept of commitment is stretched beyond plausibility, which clouds causal inference. Over time, the intellectual elaboration of "state commitment" presents an arc running from formalism to functionalism. At its genesis, the paradigm tended to associate de jure checks and balances with de facto constraints. This approach could not explain anomalies (notably China) where tremendous growth and investment proceeded in the absence of constraints on the central executive; furthermore, it neglected the fact that "it is not the formal institutions that constitute the true check on executive discretion … [but] the threat of being deposed."[26] In reaction, the concept of commitment became, quite sensibly, more inclusive. By now, however, the problem is the opposite of formalism, namely the tendency to explain *any* action by a ruler halfway competent at staying in power or preventing economic collapse as providing credible commitment to *some* constituent group. The problem is common throughout the literature.[27] The abundance of commitment-based models in theories of PR security generates quasi-tautological propositions. For example, both the ruler's adoption of democratic institutions[28] and her institutionalization of authoritarian parties[29] have been interpreted as commitment. Both the separation of

---

[24] Doner et al. 2005.

[25] Dimitrov; Allina-Pisano 2008.

[26] Haggard et al. 2008, 215.

[27] Consider the influential volume by North, Wallis, and Weingast (2009). In limited access orders, the authors' description of ongoing personal elite exchange clearly lends itself to the logic of reputational restraint, yet the term "credible commitment" is still used, with reference to violence specialists of all parties (p. 19). In open access orders, third-party enforcement of contracts allows actors "to precommit" (p. 16) to diverse arrangements; what exactly *precommitting* means remains unclear. The authors arguably infuse their version of "recorded human history" with commitment-oriented logic too generously.

[28] North and Weingast.

[29] Reuter and Remington 2009; Gehlbach and Keefer.

politics from business through privatization[30] and their fusion through informal ties[31] point to commitment. Finally, expropriation per se has been interpreted as signaling commitment, namely by the expropriating ruler to the rivals of the expropriated group.[32] Overall, the paradigm of credible commitment all-too-easily posits explanatory connections between diverse sovereign policies and the (presumed) systemic imperative of commitment; demonstrable agency and causal mechanisms are not always this literature's fortes.

Business Owners as Mere Policy-Takers?

Another puzzle concerns the relative roles of state and private actors in *securing* PR. If the only party able to enhance PR security legitimately is the upper executive, then private actors can do little but hide their assets or move them abroad if the state fails. That is precisely what the literature argues. In their seminal article "Unbundling Institutions," Acemoglu and Johnson write: "When property rights institutions fail to constrain those who control the state, *it is not possible to circumvent the ensuing problems* [for private actors] ... to prevent future expropriation, because the state, with its monopoly of legitimate violence, is the ultimate arbiter of contracts."[33] Logically, we should also observe little variation in PR security *within* states across similarly positioned private actors. Yet reported levels of PR protection vary widely across firms of the same size and sector within countries and within regions, even though these firms are exposed to the same sovereign threats stressed in the literature. Why?

My final – and crucial – objection to conventional wisdom is rooted in the inherently political nature of property rights: their design determines the distribution of wealth and power in a society. Yet, ironically, both the reputational restraint and the state commitment perspectives on PR enforcement miss the *ongoing politics* through which PR become secure.

The reputational restraint perspective downplays the necessity of politics as such. Sovereigns, driven by their long-term interests, voluntarily abstain from expropriation in the short run. The studies focusing on private conflicts in traditional communities sans state, in turn, may be appropriate for the whaling industry of the eighteenth century or the Kenyan rural clans, but they miss the presence of relatively extensive, potentially predatory governments in many developing countries.[34]

---

[30] Frye.

[31] Gilson and Milhaupt.

[32] Albertus and Menaldo.

[33] Acemoglu and Johnson 2005, 951 (emphasis added).

[34] Furthermore, this literature focuses on the *common-pool resources* where clear win-win strategies exist. (If the goal is to prevent the overdepletion of the commons, everybody can win.) Hence, the role of conflict is downplayed. This does not apply to *private assets* whose ownership

Critique of the Literature

The state commitment paradigm does allow for some state-business interaction. However, the latter is typically limited to the elites and, moreover, too focused on one-shot events, as exemplified by the famous narrative of seventeenth-century England in which the Crown accepts constraints on its discretion under the pressure from the Parliament. The notion of *pacts* between the ruler and a winning coalition or the selectorate forms the core of this scholarship.[35]

However, the shift from predation to rule of law through such *acts* of commitment by the Crown corresponds poorly with reality even in medieval Europe, the empirical context from which New Institutional Economics draws the bulk of the analytic narratives[36] undergirding the state commitment model. Although their findings remain unappreciated by political scientists, economic historians have begun to question the link between the king's institutional commitment on the one hand and secure PR and growth on the other.[37] At the same time, multiple historical studies show that PR threats from unaccountable royal agents were widespread at the time in England, the Low Countries, France, and various states comprising modern Italy, Germany, and Austria, that is, throughout the putative cases of effective "commitment" by the king.[38] Addressing the PR security in various European states, Gelderblom shows that, relative to the danger of crime or expropriation by the Crown, "misbehaving public officials" such as "bailiffs ... town clerks, legal officers" were sometimes "a bigger threat to the foreign merchant communities."[39] Indeed, the more trade-dependent local authorities at times clashed directly with the unaccountable agents of the king: "Amsterdam even rented the bailiff's office from the sovereign lord to prevent corruption by this officer whose income depended on revenues from fines."[40]

If the shifts toward rule of law occurred through *gradual processes* rather than acts of sovereign commitment, the nature of such processes remains a mystery. The central way in which the state commitment framework neglects the ongoing politics of PR security is this: property owners are denied the possibility of *unilaterally* improving the security of ownership rights. Some of the literature rules out such possibility at the conceptual level through deductive reasoning.[41] Other accounts recognize that bottom-up demand for secure PR

---

is a zero-sum game: either the predator succeeds in expropriating or the target succeeds in defending its property rights.

[35] De Mesquita et al; North et al.

[36] E.g., North et al., 148–89; North and Weingast; Greif; Greif et al. 1994; Levi 1989; Weingast.

[37] Clark 2007; Gelderblom and Grafe 2010; Murphy 2013.

[38] Duindam 1995; Zmora 2001; Duindam 2003; Aylmer 2002; Blockmans 2002.

[39] Gelderblom 2013.

[40] Ibid.

[41] Acemoglu and Johnson (2005, 951), for example, conceptualize "property rights institutions" as being "vertical" in the sense that their failure cannot be rectified through private, non-state initiative. Barzel (2002, 115) similarly rules out a priori the possibility of effective private solutions

from the owners exists. However, such demand is treated as a latent factor, a constant rather than a variable; what explains the actual timing of PR institutionalization in these accounts is either the initiative of the sovereign or an exogenous shock (e.g., a ruinous war) weakening the ruler vis-à-vis the private sector elites.[42] Finally, the literature on business associations assumes that these organizations are *supported or even initiated by the sovereign*, providing the latter with a commitment device: "A powerful party might find it advantageous to help weaker parties organize themselves ... in order to allow itself to commit to ... mutually beneficial arrangements."[43] An in-depth study of state-business cooperation in China, Pinochet's Chile, and South Korea under Park Chung-Hee concludes that "the ruler's need to credibly commit to growth ... explain[s] the presence of business groups in each [country].... One way to secure credible commitment is through repeated interactions ... each of the regimes in our studies ... helped create business groups as partners."[44] The rich accounts of the "merchant guilds" throughout medieval Europe,[45] the "corporate institutions" of pre-revolutionary France,[46] and the politically integrated investor "coalitions" in Porfirian Mexico[47] reach the same conclusion. The ruler institutionally organizes business to help the latter retaliate against the ruler's transgressions, hence securing the cooperation of business on economic priorities of the ruler. While this literature uncovers the incentive compatibility behind PR-securing business associations, it neglects the process through which individual asset owners join the struggle for secure PR, as well as the fact that such struggle may fundamentally clash with the priorities of state actors.

Overall, the paradigms of reputational restraint and state commitment imply that firms cannot improve PR security if the state fails to restrain itself. Faced with an unruly sovereign, firms must collude with state actors or hide.[48]

to the problem of PR insecurity in his reconstruction of an incentive-compatible contract between asset owners and "protectors" (violence specialists) underlying the modern state: "To protect themselves from confiscation by their specialized protectors, clients must organize their collective-action mechanism *prior* to initiating relationships with those protectors." Unless asset owners had *historically* formed a cohesive group before the emergence of the modern state, any subsequent attempts at confronting the "protectors" are doomed. According to Barzel, a successful contract arises only when the *initially empowered* asset owners "hire" protectors while limiting the latter's discretion, akin to the shareholders' employment of managers in a firm.

[42] For North (1990, 113–14), it is not the Magna Carta that symbolized the demands of the barons at Runnymede vis-à-vis the ruler, but the much later "fiscal crisis of the state" that actually "forced rulers to make bargains," leading to "Parliament's triumph [that] betokened increased security of property rights." See also Olson, 37–8.

[43] Greif et al., 773; Haber et al.

[44] Gilson and Milhaupt, 276.

[45] Greif et al.

[46] Root.

[47] Haber et al.

[48] Unless the "non-elites" have a powerful state patron, they "have no way to obtain or enforce property or security." North et al., 35.

Agent Predation and the Bottom-Up Path to Secure Ownership

Bribes, capital flight, or the resort to mafias' enforcement services are the coping strategies of non-oligarchic[49] firms faced with the threat of expropriation.[50] In the remainder of this chapter, I elaborate an alternative theory of PR threats and PR security and relate this theory to the literature on postcommunist property rights.

AGENT PREDATION AND THE BOTTOM-UP PATH TO SECURE OWNERSHIP

Ideal Types of State Threats to PR

In my conceptualization of the state, I take Levi's work as my point of departure. The state "is a complex institution ... that control[s] sufficient force to tax, police, and defend the population of a given territory"; this institution is staffed by a self-interested set of actors that "promulgates and enforces the laws of a society, of which the most important are those governing property rights."[51] At the same time, I recognize the distinctness of the postcommunist state-building project which is "(1) rapid, taking place over decades rather than centuries, and as yet has not reached a stable outcome, [and] (2) dominated as much by informal structures and practices as by formal institutions, which are used to varying degrees by both actors seeking to establish their authority and those seeking to resist this authority."[52]

My conceptualization of state threats to ownership rights, however, diverges from that of Levi, Olson, and their followers – which brings us to the ideal type of agent predation. Agent predation involves stationary bandits who have not succeeded in monopolizing theft: state principals who are rational and may well possess long-term horizons, as per Olson, but face serious principal-agent problems vis-à-vis their staff. The bureaucracies in such states do, for the most part, protect the state territory from foreign invaders and domestic militants. The anarchic violence of warlords is not the issue; these are not failed states.[53] Bandits who are stationary but weak constitute a crucial blind spot in PR theorizing.

[49] Not all firms are victims, as the research on oligarchy and state capture argues: the best-positioned companies can change the rules of the game to their advantage or even jumpstart movements aimed at regime change when their property rights are jeopardized. Such strategies, available only to a few elite players, are typically counterproductive from the systemic viewpoint. Overall, the literature agrees on the state's exclusive capacity for protecting private property in a legitimate, predictable fashion. E.g., Hellman et al; Gehlbach et al. 2010; Winters; Radnitz 2010.

[50] Volkov 1999; Svensson 1998.

[51] Levi, 438.

[52] Grzymala-Busse and Luong 2002, 531.

[53] Another point conceptually differentiating agent predation from the roving banditry of failed states is the boundary between the public and private sectors. Such a boundary is much less pronounced in failed states, where the means of violence are privatized.

Type of Threats / Type of Rights	Organized	Disorganized
Income Rights	SKIMMING	SIPHONING
Ownership Rights	PRINCIPAL EXPROPRIATION	**AGENT PREDATION**

FIGURE 2.1. State threats to property rights.

Figure 2.1 visualizes this blind spot in terms of a two-by-two matrix capturing diverse state threats to property rights. "State threats to property rights" are defined as any actual or, from the viewpoint of private owners, highly probable transfers of monetary resources or capital from private owners to the state through the intentional activity of state actors. This conceptualization has two advantages. First, while the literature often limits its conceptual efforts to the actual "extractions" or "takings" by the state,[54] my focus on threats includes the *expectations* of asset owners to acknowledge the importance[55] of stable expectations for the PR regimes. Second, by specifying that threats are *intentional*, my inquiry achieves better construct validity by focusing on a subset of a quasi-infinite number of state activities that could (unintentionally) impact property rights.

Figure 2.1 combines two theoretical dimensions to conceptualize the ideal types of state threats to property rights. The first dimension of the matrix distinguishes between *income* rights and *ownership* rights; this distinction is prominent in the existing literature on property rights, whose works can be placed in the first column of the matrix. The second dimension distinguishes between *organized* state threats and *disorganized* state threats; the literature on corruption, whose works fall into the first row of the matrix, has clarified this difference. The theoretically consequential "hole" is in the lower right quadrant of the matrix, representing disorganized state threats to ownership rights.

[54] E.g., Levi; Olson, 25–43.
[55] Weimer.

The distinction between income rights and ownership rights is analytically important. While threats to income streams generally do not jeopardize the continued operation of a firm, even if they reduce its profits, threats to *ownership* rights fundamentally restrict the ways in which the owners can manage their firm, at the extreme jeopardizing the very existence of the enterprise. Meanwhile, some, although not all, threats to *income* rights are perfectly predictable from the asset owners' point of view and may increase the value of their assets in the long run; consider the examples of stable tax rates levied to provide public goods, or petty corruption allowing firms to do business despite suffocating regulations.

Another conceptual point is due regarding the income-ownership dimension; it is a spectrum. Extremely severe threats to the revenue streams of asset owners can jeopardize their ownership rights either through their sheer *volume* or through their extreme *unpredictability*.[56] When the burden of bribes regularly exceeds the firm's revenues (volume), the firm is pushed into bankruptcy; the owners' rights to manage or transfer their assets are severely impaired or eliminated. At the same time, when corruption payments fluctuate so strongly over time that financial planning becomes impossible (unpredictability), ownership rights are also threatened.

The spectral nature of the income-ownership dimension implies that while some activities of state actors can be classified as "ownership threats" (rather than income threats) based on their difference *in kind* (e.g., raiding), others can be classified either as "income threats" or "ownership threats" based on their *intensity* (referring to their volume or their predictability).[57] Chapter 3 explores these dynamics empirically.

The organized-disorganized dimension refers to the degree of *coordination* by the state principal. As mentioned previously, *organized* threats (the first column of the two-by-two matrix) can serve a variety of purposes for the state principal. The economic rationale for organized threats consists in maximizing the volume of extraction in the pocket of the state principal, that is, at the top of the executive hierarchy. Political rationales for organized threats are more diverse. For Olson, democratically accountable principals with an "encompassing interest" will extract at a relatively low volume so as to be reelected, as the electoral majority's livelihood depends not only on redistribution but also on market productivity.[58] The rich literature on clientelism and property rights goes beyond the ideal type of a functional capitalist democracy

---

[56] Olson (2000, 113) recognized the volume-related part of this statement by noting that "the tax-theft rate" of the sovereign can reach a "confiscatory level" if the future is discounted heavily.

[57] The discussion here pertains to the perspective of firm owners. From the perspective of state actors, their predatory activity shifts from an income threat to an ownership threat (1) in the case of *collectively unintended* "overgrazing" akin to the "tragedy of the commons" but also (2) when the *individual* bureaucrats face a highly uncertain environment, leading them to discount the future and *deliberately* threaten the firm's existence.

[58] Olson, 15–17.

and is hence more relevant for our purposes.[59] Organized threats can help the state principal stabilize elite relations and prevent violence, co-opt rivals, or secure the political support of his subordinates. The notion of *ruler-endorsed exchange* conceptually glues the diverse political rationales behind organized threats. By deliberately abstaining from enforcing the property rights of the non-privileged asset owners, the state principal grants an implicit predatory license to the privileged groups, typically parts of the administrative apparatus, in exchange for their loyalty and support. Fascinating studies document such exchange in Stroessner's Paraguay, Mobutu's Zaire, Duvalier's Haiti, Marco's Philippines, General Zia's Bangladesh, Italy until the 1990s, and so forth.[60] (Whether *all* state threats to property rights in these settings are in some way coordinated by the state ruler, however, is an open question.)

Disorganized threats, conversely, lack coordination; they are not subject to control by the state principal. Serious principal-agent dilemmas in the state apparatus torpedo the benefits associated with coordinated threats from the state principal's viewpoint. Predatory revenues are not channeled toward the executive leadership; nor does the leadership benefit from the political stabilization associated with clientelistic exchange.

In light of these theoretical dimensions, four ideal types of state threats crystallize: skimming, siphoning, principal expropriation, and agent predation.

The organized threats to income rights are referred to as *skimming*. The skimming metaphor conveys a process of removing a well-specified layer of a liquid without draining it altogether. In the case of cash flows, skimming means a systematic, predictable removal of a limited portion of income streams. Some types of skimming, such as organized corruption, are illegal, while others, such as taxation, are not.

Siphoning involves threats to income rights that are disorganized. Contrary to the systematic nature of skimming, siphoning suggests independent agents withdrawing discretionary amounts from a flow, just as bureaucrats do when they request bribes for various government services without coordinating their actions or sharing the intake within the administrative hierarchy. Unlike skimming, siphoning is always illegal, as it refers to the sale of public services by the individual state actors or "bureaucratic corruption" as discussed by others. Because of its uncoordinated nature, siphoning typically removes a larger volume of income streams as compared to skimming, although, like skimming, siphoning does not stop the generation of future cash flows altogether.

Organized threats to ownership rights are defined as *principal expropriation* – these state threats constitute the primary focus of the literature on PR security. How may the state principal carry out such threats? "One possibility is the confiscation of the capital of his subjects. Another possibility is that the ...

---

[59] E.g., North et al; Medard 2002; Chabal and Daloz 1999.
[60] Montinola 2013; Khan ibid.; Nickson 1996; Wedeman 1997; Grafton and Rowlands 1996; Chubb 1996.

Agent Predation and the Bottom-Up Path to Secure Ownership

[state principal] can start taxing real money balances by printing money for his own use in such amounts that unexpected inflation results. Another alternative is that he can borrow money and then refuse to pay it back."[61] The state principal may also set taxation at the expropriatory level or endorse predatory clientelism, as mentioned earlier. As with skimming, some instances of principal expropriation may be legal, while others are not. (Given the power of the state principal to define law, the issue of legality is less relevant in the case of organized PR threats. A gutsy pirate once confronted Alexander the Great at trial: "Because I have only one rickety ship, I'm called a bandit, and because you have a large fleet, you are called an emperor."[62])

The literature offers nuanced analyses of skimming, siphoning, and principal expropriation. Yet *agent predation*, on which this book focuses, remains undertheorized. Such predation involves disorganized threats to ownership rights. Two quotes from regional observers capture forcefully the distinct nature of this ideal type.

The first quote is from Valerii Morozov, one of the few people intimately familiar with predation in Russia's governing apparatus who speaks about it on record. (As an obstreperous real estate developer for the Kremlin, Morozov has worked with, and often against, Russian law enforcement to combat predation.)

> Although many consider the ruling group [in Russia] an organized mafia, the behavior of Putin's group reveals that it never resembled a classical mafia or a serious bandit gang. A mafia has its own laws that imply responsibility, discipline: those who screw up or overreach [*prokolovshiesia ili zarvavshiesia*] are punished up to their destruction. Putin's group, however, acts more like a *bunch of hooligans* [*shpana*]. These hooligans go through "their" neighborhood, and if they spot a victim with an expensive cell phone ... they beat him up and rob him. The hooligans *may listen to their leader, but they often decide themselves, spontaneously, whom to attack....* If Putin remains the leader of a regime of hooligans ... he will remain their hostage.[63]

Morozov's quote suggests that *even when* the ownership threats emanate from *the governing elite,* such threats need not be sovereign-sanctioned or organized. The notion of independently acting "hooligans" – at any level of the executive hierarchy – is what differentiates agent predation from principal expropriation.

Agent predation is also distinct from siphoning. Consider the analysis of street-level business inspections in Ukraine by Volodymyr Dubrovs'kyi, a senior economist at the Center for Social and Economic Research in Kyiv:

> Inspections are a method of a direct takeover of property rights [*sposob priamogo ot"ema prav sobstvennosti*]. What do they threaten when they ask for their 30% cut

---

[61] Olson, 113.
[62] Augustine 1888.
[63] Morozov 2011 (emphasis added).

[during inspection-based extortion]? Very rarely is it about physical threats to the person. Instead, they say 'if you don't give [us the cut], we will kill your business' [*ne otdash', ub'em biznes*]. And they have all possibilities to make good on that threat.... As a result, the number of private entrepreneurs has declined by half within the last two years, according to DerzhKomStat [governmental statistical agency].[64]

At this point, "piranha capitalism" can be defined as a system of economic relations in which (1) the bulk of property rights is formally allocated to private actors and (2) agent predation constitutes a major, although not the only, state threat to property rights.

Varieties of Agent Predation

Theoretically, agent predation can manifest itself in three ways: annexation, extortion, and intervention. *Annexation* occurs when the firm or assets in question are captured in their entirety by specific state actors. While principal expropriation may involve phenomena such as nationalization in which the asset is transferred into the ownership of the "state" as a legal entity (sometimes for purposes serving the public good), agent predation exclusively refers to state employees acting on their own behalf qua individuals while using the leverage afforded to them through their public office.

Extortion occurs when the state actors, rather than assuming ownership in toto, bleed the firm of its revenues through confiscatory "sharing" arrangements, as in the scenario outlined by Dubrovs'kyi in the previous section. (Principal expropriation, conversely, may also proceed via confiscatory taxation, which – unlike extortion – is predictable, stable, and legal; under the communist planned economy, for example, the state principal "restructured its revenue base to gain direct access to societal wealth" by setting the implicit rate of taxation at the confiscatory level.[65])

Extortion, as one manifestation of agent predation, is analytically distinct from siphoning. Predatory extortion works through state agencies that are high-powered *and* opportunistic. High-powered state agencies can shut down the firm for violations of various statutes regulating tax payments, contributions to social funds, environmental compliance, product safety, fire safety, labor standards, compliance with architectural or land codes, and so forth. Opportunism is often rampant among state actors who actually conduct business inspections on behalf of these high-powered agencies. Opportunistic state agents who are high-powered (either *de jure* via their mandate or *de facto* thanks to poor monitoring by their administrative superiors) can intimidate business owners through the implicit threats of firm shutdowns, which are sometimes carried out. Bureaucrats' actions can lead to the *extinction* of an enterprise through multiple channels: bankruptcy via the imposition of prohibitively costly fines;

[64] Author's interview, Kyiv, December 18, 2012.
[65] Easter, 5.

Agent Predation and the Bottom-Up Path to Secure Ownership

production shutdown (e.g., through the cutoff of electricity, forcible property arrest, blocking of bank accounts, etc.) based on diverse regulatory or tax-related violations; provision of unfair administrative assistance to a firm's business rivals; creation of administrative barriers to the firm's obtainment or transfer of real estate or production equipment; sentencing the main owners to prison; and so on. The *implicit threat* of such actions gives bureaucrats the power to extort businesses.

How does such extortion differ from bribe requests for government services (siphoning)? Consider the difference between being robbed at gunpoint and being illegally charged for parking in a free zone; in both cases, one is forced to part with money, yet the aggressor's leverage, the victim's potential monetary losses, and the impact on the victim's future behavior are strikingly different. One may accept or even welcome the illegal charge for the convenience of quick parking, just as entrepreneurs accept reasonable bribes for cutting through regulatory red tape (siphoning), yet nobody accepts extortion in the shadow of one's extinction (predation). It is the latter dynamic that interferes with entrepreneurs' property rights *beyond* their right to receive legitimate income from their assets.

Besides annexation and extortion, *intervention* constitutes the third way state actors can threaten the ownership rights of private actors in a disorganized fashion. Intervention occurs when state actors illegally interfere with the decision-making process of the asset owners, such as through the forceful placement of relatives or associates on a company's management bodies, informal prohibitions on labor dismissals, irregular inspections outside of the legal schedule, and so forth.

State Actors and Agent Predation

Within the executive branch, four types of state actors can engage in agent predation: administrators, enforcers, gatekeepers, and inspectors. The subset of administrators refers to elected or appointed positions with a broad governing or policy-setting mandate, ranging from a village mayor to a minister. Enforcers are distinguished by their direct access to legitimate violence and include members of the police force, the secret service, and the military. Gatekeepers are the bureaucratic cadres who decide *ex ante* whether a given firm's activity is legal; an array of generic permit-issuing agencies as well as the industry-specific expertise-issuing departments fall into this category. Finally, inspectors are the bureaucrats who monitor *post hoc* the firms' compliance with regulations.

While this book mostly discusses the executive branch, the legislative and judiciary branches can also engage in agent predation. The local assemblies, for example, can vote to reassign the ownership rights over particular assets to their associates without providing the private owners fair compensation, hence abusing the "eminent domain" provisions. The courts, can legitimize annexation by issuing paid-for verdicts in favor of the expropriating parties.

What is the role of the state *principal* in agent predation? The degree to which the state threats to PR are principal-organized (i.e., the horizontal dimension of the two-by-two matrix) is a continuum. At one extreme, threats are actively coordinated by the ruler; at a somewhat lesser degree of coordination, the ruler passively tolerates the bureaucrats' interference with private property rights because such interference serves the ruler's interests. Importantly, in both these cases, state threats *are* "organized," whether by the explicit commission or by the conscious omission of the ruler's supervision. Agent predation, conversely, refers to the opposite end of the coordination spectrum at which the bureaucrats' activity does *not* serve the purposes of the state principal. Such a situation arises when agent predation rattles at least one of the pillars on which the state principal's power and wealth rest – administrative control, political support, or material resources.

Principal-agent problems in the bureaucracy, for example, may allow state agents to expropriate the state principal. In one of my interviews, a top official from Ukraine's State Property Fund complained about "local governments expropriating the [central] state" by unilaterally and illegally reassigning rights over the central state's locally situated real estate (sanatoriums, etc.).[66] The example of China, where Beijing has been unable to control land seizures by local state actors, demonstrates that even in developing states traditionally viewed as strong, the state principal may be exposed to agent predation. In addition to material losses and the collapse of administrative control, agent predation imposes political costs on the state principal; by targeting large layers of the population, agent predation delegitimizes the state and, by extension, the state ruler. The single biggest political fiasco for Putin since 2000, for example, has been the successful rebranding of United Russia as the "party of *crooks and thieves*" by the opposition in 2011. While the majority of Russians did not withdraw their support from Putin personally, the machinery of the state-sponsored media could not whitewash the fact that Putin's subordinates are predatory; the Kremlin's party of power was, at least in part, killed by agent predation, and the state principal's support began to decline after a decade of remarkable stability.[67] More generally, the extent to which ownership threats are coordinated by the state principal should be a matter of empirical inquiry, not a priori assumption.

While the state principals are likely to crack down on agent predation when it reaches extreme levels, such efforts to "(re)organize" the state threats *need not be benevolent* and may signal an attempted shift toward principal expropriation

---

[66] For similar dynamics in Russia, see Shlapentokh 2007, 136–7.

[67] Shortly after Alexei Navalny created the memorable moniker in 2011, 31 percent of Russians agreed that United Russia was a "party of crooks and thieves." By April 2013, according to the Levada Center, more than 51 percent of Russians agreed with the statement. In May 2013, 24 percent of Russians supported the slogan "Russia without Putin," an increase of 5 percent over April 2012. *Vedomosti* May 7, 2013; *Vedomosti* April 29, 2013.

Agent Predation and the Bottom-Up Path to Secure Ownership

rather than toward skimming. Whether the state principal succeeds in either case is, of course, a different issue.

Ideal types merely capture the analytical essence of phenomena; in reality, multiple types of state threats in Figure 2.1 can occur simultaneously. This book empirically focuses on agent predation in Russia and Ukraine to demonstrate the theoretically important implications of this ideal type, *not* to deny that in both countries principal expropriation also exists.[68] My approach takes into account "the level of analysis problem" common in the studies of governance: as Gingerich demonstrates, the variation in state capacity and corruption is generally larger within the bureaucracies of a given state than across states.[69] It is generally more useful to compare the four types of PR threats in any given state than to assign states as a whole to the quadrants of Figure 2.1.

From Agent Predation to Property Protection: Three Arguments

The literature theorizes the state principal as predator – I theorize predation as principle. Ownership threats, I argue, often do not proceed "by design" but "by default," driven by the narrow uncoordinated self-interest of individual state agents throughout the administrative hierarchy. Using this theoretical framework as its starting point, the book advances three arguments.

First, agent predation can be *empirically* distinguished from siphoning and principal expropriation and, furthermore, agent predation is at least as intense as siphoning and principal expropriation in Russia and Ukraine. This argument addresses not only the distinct nature and the level of agent predation but also its *consequences*. In particular, I argue that agent predation imposes greater damage on firm owners than siphoning and that agent predation also generates worse incentives for firm owners as compared to principal expropriation. Chapters 3 and 4 provide empirical support for agent predation as empirically distinct, relatively intense, and relatively harmful compared to the adjacent ideal types of state threats in Figure 2.1. The novel conceptualization of PR *threats* offered here calls for a new approach to PR *security*, which is the focus of the remaining arguments.

The second argument of the book is that conventional solutions to insecure ownership rights fail when agent predation is widespread. Specifically, the state commitment paradigm is inappropriate in the context of agent predation because *the state principal cannot "commit" on behalf of state agents.* The lack of effective intra-state control structures weakens the much-praised commitment by the upper executive since it does not translate into commitment "on the ground." Ideally, this argument could be tested via longitudinal

---

[68] In Russia, Putin's attack on Yukos and the rumors of Putin's secret private fortune provide an example. For Ukraine, see the disclosure of incriminating documents from the Mezhyhirya estate following the ouster of President Yanukovych.

[69] Gingerich 2013.

case studies that trace the implementation of specific constraints on the upper executive emphasized in the state commitment paradigm. I argue that Russia after 2000–1 and Ukraine after 2004–5 offer precisely such cases. In Russia, the first years of Putin's presidency saw unprecedented business institutionalization with several "encompassing" business associations emerging as important high-profile actors. Having enjoyed the Kremlin's support from the outset and, moreover, having been directly involved in policy-making, these associations represent the best-case scenario of modern "merchant groups." Ukraine exemplifies a different mechanism likewise celebrated by the theories of state commitment. The 2004 Orange Revolution created an empowered parliament representing the previously sidelined wealth-holders and entrepreneurs and in doing so placed stringent institutional constraints on President Yushchenko, who also personally committed to secure ownership rights through multiple initiatives. Chapter 5 follows both cases to examine why the respective versions of state commitment in Russia and Ukraine have not improved the security of ownership rights. The secret cables from the U.S. diplomats in Russia, made public by WikiLeaks, indicate the flavor of the argument: "While Mr. Putin enjoys supremacy over all other public figures in Russia, he is undermined by an unmanageable bureaucracy that often ignores his edicts."[70] Agent predation severs the link between sovereign commitment and ownership security. But if state commitment cannot secure ownership from agent predation, what can?

Third, I argue that business actors can *directly* improve the security of their ownership rights through firm-level stakeholder alliances. Under principal expropriation, in line with conventional wisdom, individual firms can do little against the state principal. The perspectives of reputational restraint and state commitment, as discussed previously, are both elite-based; the fate of PR security is determined by the central executive and the private oligarchs. Agent predation, however, implies that elite dynamics notwithstanding, most firms in weak states interact with the relatively independent lower-level state agencies; these interactions directly shape PR security. State principals and the biggest tycoons are the proverbial tip of the iceberg – the politics of PR security occurs below water level. And if PR security varies because of the institutions created by firms, then the fundamental puzzle of PR theorizing must be: What are these institutions?

To address this puzzle, I apply Hirschman's[71] categories of exit, voice, and loyalty to firm's behavior under threat. In choosing "exit," the company throws in the towel; it reduces its operations in the official economy by investing abroad or by shifting funds to the illegal shadow economy. In selecting "loyalty," the firm appeases the aggressor; it may offer monetary payments or an equity stake in the firm to the state, for example, hoping to retain most of

---

[70] *The New York Times* November 29, 2010.
[71] Hirschman 1970.

Agent Predation and the Bottom-Up Path to Secure Ownership

its ownership rights and continue business.[72] Both exit and loyalty have been widely used by companies as the data on capital flight, underground economy, and corruption demonstrates.

However, the "voice" option – under which the firm *resists* the aggressor – has received little attention. What, indeed, can a beleaguered firm do against unruly state agents? Does the hide-or-collude dilemma exhaust the options? No, I argue; firms can resist such ownership threats through alliances with stakeholders, who can impose costs on the potential trespassers on behalf of the firm. Often extending beyond a firm's boundaries, such alliances engage diverse groups, pool resources, and effectively outsource the task of PR enforcement to third parties.

To secure their rights, majority owners can build alliances with the following stakeholders: (a) neighboring communities, (b) labor, and (c) foreign actors, such as investors, media, NGOs, governments, and so forth. I define "alliances" as groups of members with common interests of which they are aware. Such groups can be institutionalized or informal. Stakeholder alliances can emerge for a variety of economic, political, or social reasons; it is the shared interest in the continuation of the firm as a going concern that unites the firm's owners and stakeholders. Consider, for example, the alliance between majority owners and foreign creditors; the latter have a clear financial interest in supporting majority owners' struggle against ownership threats because the financiers' investments become progressively "sunk" as the threats intensify. Labor and the neighboring communities may protect the firm owners' rights if the material benefits the company has provided to its employees and the region would cease after annexation, extortion, or intervention by the state agents. Such benefits include the financing of regional development and charity projects, environmental initiatives, firm-sponsored insurance and benefit packages for labor, and so on. (In larger firms, some of these benefits are anchored through the "corporate social responsibility" programs.)

How can alliances secure a firm's ownership rights? Depending on their resources, alliance members can impose financial or political costs on the potential aggressors. Accordingly, a firm's defense can make the PR threat itself, or its consequences, more expensive and hence less profitable for the aggressors. For example, foreign investors as allies of the target enterprise can impose financial costs on state agents through withdrawal of investment from projects benefitting the state agents. Political costs, in turn, decrease the power of the aggressor, that is, her menu of feasible options; this process can involve

---

[72] Hirschman focuses on *individuals* – qua citizens or customers – in his conceptualization of responses to organizational decline. When applied to *firms*, Hirschman's notion of loyalty loses its emotional component (as patriotism or brand loyalty in its original formulation) but retains its analytical rationale as continued participation in the official economy without counter-measures *despite* deteriorating conditions. The firms' acceptance of PR aggressors' terms enables such participation.

electoral pressure, public protests, or behind-the-scenes lobbying by the allies of the target firm. State agents below the top executive level are also sensitive to negative publicity, as the latter can trigger their demotion in the bureaucracy. The threat of public protests, for example, is particularly important for non-democratic countries, such as China.

Whenever the predatory state agents are less than omnipotent, battles over property rights are also battles over public relations. This is particularly true in the postcommunist states, where the legitimacy of private ownership is, at times, questioned. Stakeholder alliances allow the firm owners to bridge the gap of popular distrust that sometimes separates the new capitalists from the public. When state agents can no longer resort to the rhetorical frame of "taking back from the thieves," they can no longer expect the public to remain indifferent toward (or even supportive of) agent predation.

In addition to the financial, political, and framing fronts, battles over ownership can turn physical. If everything else fails and the state agents hoping to transfer juicy assets to their associates show up at the enterprise door with a fabricated court order and a police unit in tow, the owners' last resort is often the workers physically present on the premises. Will these employees let the state agents conclude the takeover or will they form a human fence around the enterprise, forcing media presence, a public discussion, additional lawsuits, and so on? By winning precious time for the asset owners, such responses by labor can save the day by logistically delaying the takeover while also publicizing and delegitimizing it.

As a final conceptual point, a distinction should be made between the *presence* of alliances and the *motivation* behind their creation. While some alliances emerge explicitly because firms seek to protect themselves against ownership threats, many alliances materialize for unrelated reasons. Important exogenous sources of alliance variation may include levels of trust, the presence of civil society institutions, the socialist legacies of welfare provision often inherited by enterprises, and so on. My argument focuses on the *impact* of alliances, allowing for the possibility that ownership protection is an unintended consequence of alliance formation.

Chapters 6 provides case studies and survey evidence for the effectiveness of stakeholder alliances against agent predation. This volume also explores the possibility that, as "second-best institutions,"[73] stakeholder alliances may contribute to the development of the rule of law, whose emergence remains the million-dollar puzzle across the social sciences. The mechanisms gradually translating firm-level alliances into the universally applicable rules predictably enforced by the state involve (a) restraint of the oligarchs by their stakeholder alliances; (b) institutionalization of corporate transparency; and (c) transformation of the political apathy of small business owners into the confidence to

---

[73] Rodrik 2008.

Property Rights and Postcommunism

confront a predatory state. Chapter 7 elaborates the promise of stakeholder alliances along these lines.

The policy implications of my approach diverge from the top-level efforts to institutionally straightjacket the state principal or to engineer a Weberian bureaucracy; ideal-case scenarios yield quixotic advice. More realistically, actors aiming to improve the security of ownership rights in a given economy should start with the owners. Activities aimed at broadening and deepening the networks of stakeholders around a given firm enhance the security of its ownership rights.

To sum up, I argue that firms with stakeholder alliances will have more secure ownership rights than firms without such alliances. My bottom-up approach to PR security departs significantly from available discussions of the role of business in PR enforcement. The state commitment paradigm points to the state principal's role in facilitating collective action by businesses as a commitment device; conversely, I relax the assumption that firms' strategies must benefit the sovereign in order to succeed. The literature on state capture concludes that business oligarchs subvert PR security by undermining the state; I elaborate the strategies of non-oligarchic firms enhancing PR security.

PROPERTY RIGHTS AND POSTCOMMUNISM

Beyond contributing to the theories of PR security, this book complements existing regional scholarship. Two partly overlapping directions of research on post-Soviet economies pertain to this volume.

First, some scholars have prioritized PR *allocation* over PR security as the key issue related to property rights in postcommunism. This research focuses on the process of privatization, although the reasons for deprioritizing PR security vary. Scholars who had advocated rapid privatization saw PR allocation to non-state actors as a switch that would, in due time, activate PR security: "Privatization ... offers an enormous political benefit for the creation of institutions supporting private property because it creates the very private owners who then begin lobbying the government [for PR security]."[74] The expectation that privatization *per se* would trigger collective action among the millions of new owners which, in turn, would transform a predatory state into an effective third-party enforcer has, to put it mildly, not materialized. Other scholars have critically examined the implementation of privatization, making the opposite argument about the link between PR allocation and ownership rights; in these studies, poorly monitored, inequitable, or rigged privatization triggers asset stripping by the interim owners.[75] Whether driven by the ex ante theoretical expectations of privatization's impact, or its post-hoc evaluations, the issue of PR security in its everyday manifestations in these studies

---

[74] Shleifer and Vishny, 10.

[75] E.g., Roland 2001; Goldman; Woodruff 2004.

takes a back seat to (or is entirely derived from) the issue of *PR allocation* as a matter of top-down state reform. Other studies have connected PR allocation to the security of *income* rights, assessing post-privatization corruption levels.[76] Timothy Frye offers a different treatment of PR allocation in *Building States and Markets after Communism*. The author fruitfully distinguishes between "economic" reforms – such as privatization – which can be easily manipulated for rent-seeking, and "institutional" reforms, which can limit such manipulation and promote state-building. It would appear that institutions supporting PR security should fall into the latter category; yet, unfortunately, Frye's empirical analysis omits institutions related to PR security. The "state-building" foreshadowed by the book's title is reduced to *market regulation* (as proxied by the regulatory overhaul of corporate governance, securities, banking, competition, and other policy areas), while the deeper problems[77] of PR security and the principal-agent dilemmas in the state apparatus are bracketed. Poor state capacity as an explanatory variable "is easily taken too far" (p. 13), according to Frye.

Studies of the postcommunist privatization (on which the next chapter elaborates) provide the necessary starting point for any inquiry into PR security, yet they stop short of addressing the issue directly. The problem of insecure ownership rights cannot be reduced to imperfect privatization processes or to the sequence of initial market reforms.

The second stream of regionally focused research inquires more directly into PR security but follows the general literature by focusing on *organized* PR threats while at the same time treating state commitment and reputational restraint as the key remedies for insecure ownership rights.

The postcommunist scholarship has made a great contribution to our understanding of organized state threats to PR. In *Capital, Coercion, and Postcommunist States*, Gerald Easter analyzes tax reforms accompanying the state-building project in Russia and Poland. In terms of Figure 2.1, Easter's fiscal sociology distinguishes between two types of "skimming" – one legitimated by a state-society contract, and one that lacks such legitimacy because the state principal was able "to smash the constraints of the state-elite revenue bargain by demonstrating the capability and willingness of the central state to use unbridled coercion against the elite."[78] Putin's Russia is seen as emblematic of the second type of skimming. Anna Grzymala-Busse dissects a different quadrant of the PR threat matrix, namely that of "principal expropriation," by showing important variations in the elite-coordinated strategies of informal extraction

---

[76] E.g., Brown et al. 2009.

[77] Institutions related to PR security restrain the executive branch at all levels and guarantee the impartiality of courts. Regulatory institutions, conversely, *empower* certain parts of the executive to restrain market participants who "engage in fraudulent or anti-competitive behavior." Rodrik 2007, 157.

[78] Easter, 82.

Property Rights and Postcommunism

across the postcommunist space as well as the impact of these variations on state formation. Here, Putin's Russia presents a case of the "fusion" strategy "exemplified by the fusion of party and state ... [in which] rulers ... politicize state structures ... [while] the ruling cohort distributes rents contingent on societal acquiescence and lowers its probability of exit by resolutely eliminating the opposition."[79] In 2012, Putin's resumption of the presidency cemented the experts' view of PR threats in Russia as shaped and controlled by the state principal. Lilia Shevtsova goes as far as claiming that "the personalized power system" of modern Russia was "built not by Putin or Yeltsin ... but by Stalin," and has been continually "strengthening the corrupted state's monopoly and control over the economy."[80] Alena Ledeneva offers a meticulous book-length ethnography of "Putin's *sistema*," under which "the 2000s saw the return of a more customary and historically predominant model of governance in Russia, whereby the state captures business."[81]

Meanwhile, Ukraine under Kuchma is conceptualized as a case of a "blackmail state" in Keith Darden's memorable phrase, that is, a setting in which PR threats are encouraged by the state principal as tools of administrative control.[82] This top-down nature of PR threats, analysts argue, proved path-dependent and survived the 2004 Orange Revolution: Yushchenko, who replaced Kuchma, "inherited rather effective mechanisms of the 'blackmail state' ... [and] did not replace this informal mechanism of state domination."[83] The central role of the presidency in state predation has, according to scholars, continued unabated (or strengthened even further) after Yanukovych took over from Yushchenko as president in 2010. The logic of such principal-sponsored PR threats, writes Kuzio,

particularly affected the outcomes of the 2004 and 2010 elections as outgoing corrupt presidents sought immunity ... from incoming presidents.... [Expropriation] makes leaders fearful of being out of power because they and their families lose immunity from prosecution. Such fears either lead to election fraud, as in 2004 ... backroom deals between Yushchenko and Yanukovych in 2010 or devising ways of remaining in power indefinitely.[84]

The expert prognosis for Ukraine until the 2014 ouster of Yanukovych explicitly referenced Russia's state principal, forecasting "creeping *Putinization* marked by ... attempts to ... *undermine independent businesses*."[85]

The focus on the postcommunist state principal has identified crucial distinctions *within* the universe of organized PR threats, yet it has also created

---

[79] Grzymala-Busse 2008, 642.
[80] Shevtsova 2012, 1–3.
[81] Ledeneva 2013, 198.
[82] Darden 2001.
[83] Gromadzki et al. 2010, 21.
[84] Kuzio 2012, 7.
[85] Kudelia ibid., 11 (emphasis added).

theoretical blind spots suggested by the previous discussion. Too often, the process of "pulverizing political constraints"[86] by the state principal is identified with the creation of effective administrative controls. However, as a Russian political commentator insightfully put it, the bureaucrats "who have turned into Mafiosi have dissolved Putin's power like sugar in a glass of water."[87] It is the resulting "solution" and its toxic interaction with ownership rights that is our main concern.

As for PR security, scholars of postcommunism have decisively advanced the studies of reputational restraint and state commitment, adding much-needed empirical flesh to the analytic skeletons while updating the narratives of yore for the post-industrial age. The framework of reputational restraint has been extended to model dynamic games between dictators and oligarchs around the issue of property rights in Putin's Russia and beyond.[88] In *Representation Through Taxation*, Scott Gehlbach highlights the impact of strategic interaction on property rights through the state treasury: the post-Soviet space of the 1990s saw "politicians and factory owners settle into a relationship of mutual dependence" as tax systems were devised to target large, visible enterprises that could not evade taxes easily, giving such enterprises disproportionate political influence in return.[89] State commitment to PR security has been explored through the analysis of reforms that are costly to reverse, including privatization and the institutionalization of various checks on the executive branch.[90]

Contrary to the thesis presented here, scholars of postcommunism are skeptical about the ability of private non-oligarchic asset owners to secure ownership rights; accordingly, such owners appear as helpless victims of state abuse.[91] As for the enterprise stakeholders, their role appears *counterproductive* as far as property rights go. In *Without a Map*, for example, Daniel Treisman and Andrei Shleifer conceptualize the stakeholders as short-term oriented actors benefitting from inefficiently allocated property rights and derailing the necessary reforms.[92] In the Chinese context, Martin Dimitrov argues that interference by domestic or foreign stakeholders decreases the chances for rationalized procedural PR enforcement by the state, because such interference forces the state principal into low-quality campaign-style enforcement to placate the stakeholders.[93] In the case of Russia's Yukos, which Chapter 6 examines, Vadim Volkov contends that "foreign pressure in the company's defense only made matters worse for the company."[94]

---

[86] Easter, 81.
[87] *Novaya Gazeta* December 3, 2012.
[88] Guriev and Sonin 2009.
[89] Gehlbach 2010, 17. See also Luong and Weinthal.
[90] E.g., Boycko et al; Diermeier et al; Frye; Frye; Dobek 1997; Bruszt and Stark; Hendley 2006.
[91] E.g., Frye.
[92] Shleifer and Treisman.
[93] Dimitrov.
[94] Volkov 2008, 262.

Appendix: Interviews and Survey

This book builds on existing postcommunist scholarship but argues that state commitment is less important for secure ownership than traditionally assumed. Meanwhile, the role of private asset owners and stakeholders in my account is inverted by 180 degrees; instead of being victims or reform spoilers, firm owners and stakeholders appear as effective activists for secure ownership rights.

Finally, the structured comparison between Russia and Ukraine in this volume goes beyond studies that focus on Russia per se or in conjunction with a diametrically opposed case, such as Poland or the United States.[95] My case selection assures that the findings are not driven by Russia's many peculiarities – including oil, rapid privatization, the legacy of Soviet-wide governing apparatus, *siloviki* authoritarianism, the Yukos expropriation as precedent, and so on – while also exploiting the distinct ways in which "commitment devices" were deployed by the Russian and Ukrainian state principals. Just like the Russia-specific literature, many accounts of Ukraine overemphasize Ukrainian uniqueness – in particular, the fact that Ukraine is starkly split in sociopolitical terms along its East-West dimension. Here, the comparison with Russia helps put such unique "determinants" of Ukraine's trajectory in perspective, suggesting that the institutional weakness of the state apparatus may override sociopolitical geography, at least to the extent PR security is concerned. One of the most striking findings of this volume is how similar the situation was in Russia and Ukraine between 2000 and 2012 regarding the nature of agent predation, the failure of conventional solutions to insecure PR, and the efficacy of stakeholder alliances.

APPENDIX: INTERVIEWS AND SURVEY

Interviews

All of the semi-structured interviews were conducted by the author in Russian or Ukrainian. Out of 152 interviews, 66 percent were conducted with business owners and executive management, 15 percent with local experts (from NGOs, think tanks, media, and academia), 14 percent with state actors (deputies of local and national parliaments, party functionaries, ministry officials of various levels), and the remaining 5 percent with the administrators of business associations. Among interviewed business actors, three quarters represent small enterprises; the remaining quarter come from diversified business holdings or multinational corporations. The skewedness of the qualitative sample toward SMEs balances the survey data (see next section).

I used purposive sampling and chain-referral sampling to select interviewees.[96] Purposive sampling was particularly appropriate for the staff of business

---

[95] E.g., Woodruff; Volkov 2008; Easter; Gans-Morse 2012; Ledeneva; Barnes 2006; Kapeliushnikov et al. 2012; Luong and Weinthal.

[96] Tansey 2007.

associations and local experts, that is, populations that are visible, accessible, and possess well-defined expertise. The interviews of business and, to a lesser extent, state actors had to rely more on chain referrals due to the sensitivity of questions; at the same time, conscious effort was made to keep the sample sufficiently diverse. Attendance of multiple business and policy-related events[97] allowed me to establish an initial sample of pertinent contacts; my presence at these non-public events, in turn, conveyed a token of trustworthiness to the contacts.

I used several strategies to encourage honesty during the interviews in addition to my reliance on referrals by people whom the respondents trust. First, I emphasized that the use of a recording device and by-name citations are optional. While many interviewees agreed to being recorded, they typically requested anonymity. Second, I established my credentials in advance by providing a link to my website and the invitation to confirm my identity with my home institution.[98] Third, I used well-known approaches to the phrasing of sensitive questions (normalization of wrongdoing; third-party perspective; etc.). Finally, I made an effort to triangulate responses by asking multiple interviewees the same question.

Survey

I designed and piloted a survey of firms that was implemented in Russia and Ukraine between February and May 2007. In Russia, the data was collected by the Institute for the Economy in Transition (IET) through a mail survey. In Ukraine, the data was collected by the Institute for Economic Research and Policy Consulting (IERPC) through face-to-face interviews. IET and IERPC count among the most reputable business survey organizations in the region. Both organizations rely on representative panels of firms constructed via stratified random sampling. The analysis here represents a one-year slice of the panel. There are 800 firms in the Russian panel and 300 firms in the Ukrainian panel. The important advantage of using a relatively stable set of companies is data quality. Over the years, substantial trust has developed between these firms and

---

[97] Particularly useful among these events were: (1) business forum "AntiReider" in Kyiv, March 2007, bringing together top Ukrainian policymakers, Russian anti-raiding specialists, and a wide sampling of mid-size business executives; (2) "Russian Corporate Governance Roundtable," a collaboration of the OECD and the Russian government, in Moscow, December 2006, bringing together policy experts, corporate directors and lawyers, as well as representatives of the Committee on Property of State Duma, Ministry of Economic Development and Trade, Presidential Administration, Ministry of Industry and Energy, and Federal Commission on Security Markets; (3) "Council on Entrepreneurship Annual Meeting" in Kyiv, November 2006, gathering representatives of small business from across Ukraine and Rada deputies responsible for promoting SME growth.

[98] I abstained from using introductory letters from the home institution, as I found that such documents trigger unwanted formality on the part of the respondent.

Appendix: Interviews and Survey

TABLE 2.1. *Summary Statistics for Variables in Regressions*

Variable	Mean	SD	Min	Max
Aggression: Perception of poor PR protection as opportunity	2.16	0.97	1	4
BusinessAssociation: Participation in any business association	0.60	0.49	0	1
CentralBlame: Insecure PR blamed on central government	0.43	0.49	0	1
Community: Very significant support of community and labor	0.06	0.25	0	1
ContractSecurity: Effectiveness of contract enforcement by state	3.42	1.08	1	5
Financial: Current financial performance (Russia only)	2.89	0.57	1	4
ForcedFunding: State pressure for community support	0.31	0.46	0	1
Foreigners: Foreign creditor or foreign investor	0.03	0.17	0	1
IncomeThreat: Administrative pressure for informal payments	1.98	0.79	1	4
LocalBlame: Insecure PR blamed on local government	0.31	0.46	0	1
Loyalty: Attitude toward "loyalty" strategies	1.88	0.55	1	3
MerchantGroup: Participation in federal business association	0.28	0.45	0	1
NonPrivatized: De novo firm not previously privatized	0.17	0.37	0	1
OwnershipThreat: Average of six threats to ownership	2.36	0.59	1	4
PropertyThreat: Average of nine threats to ownership and income	2.33	0.66	1	4
TaxShare: Firm's share of local tax revenue	2.26	0.69	1	3
ThreatPredictability: Predictabilty of state threats for next year	2.37	0.81	1	4

the organizations surveying them, reducing dissembling and non-disclosure. It is also noteworthy that the respondents consist almost exclusively of top management (92 percent). While regionally representative, the panels are restricted on size and sector; they are somewhat skewed toward medium and large enterprises and include industrial sectors only. Hence, the results may apply less to the service sectors or to very small firms.

The overall response rate is 47 percent, which is reasonably good for business elites.[99] In Russia, responses were collected from 396 firms out of 800 contacted firms. The respondent firms cover sixty-eight regions out of Russia's eighty-three federal regions. In Ukraine, the interviews were conducted with 120 firms from five regions out of Ukraine's twenty-seven regions, including two Eastern, two Western, and one central region. Of the fifteen sectors in

---

[99] For comparison, a McKinsey survey of top managers in fourteen OECD countries plus China and India in 2003 obtained a 44 percent response rate.

the sample, the largest are machinery (34 percent of firms), food processing (13 percent), light industry (12 percent), construction (11 percent), and wood processing (5 percent). An average firm in the sample employs 1,150 workers (sample minimum: 2 employees; maximum 20,000 employees). Firms in the sample are owned by individuals (51 percent), a board of directors (22 percent), a group of other firms (13 percent), the state (8 percent), managers (5 percent), employees (3 percent), foreigners (1 percent), and banks (1 percent).

Table 2.1 lists summary statistics for all variables used in regressions throughout the book. The details on the coding of all variables are provided in the relevant chapters.

3

Not Too Petty

Disorganized Threats beyond Corruption

PRIVATE OWNERSHIP AND ITS LEGAL PROTECTIONS:
A BRIEF HISTORY

An inquiry into the security of property rights must start with property rights' *allocation*. How has property become private, and what ownership arrangements did it replace? In much of the developing world, assets and resources are either held in communal ownership (of tribes, villages, etc.), or in an open-access regime (i.e., free for all). The mechanisms through which *private* ownership replaces these arrangements have been explored by institutional economists such as Ostrom, Demsetz, and De Soto.

The genesis of *postcommunist* private property is different. Unlike the communities whose main property are natural resources, such as forests, or the housing stock of shanty towns, the societies of communist Eurasia by the end of the 1980s boasted immense, if often decrepit, productive and industrial assets created under the planned economy. The formal owner and benefactor of these assets was the communist behemoth of the state. Accordingly, the challenge of young post-Soviet states was whether, to what extent, and how to reallocate hundreds of thousands of shops, factories, and farms[1] from public into private ownership. For Russia and Ukraine, these decisions had to be made in a similar context – one of creeping anarchy at the enterprise level. Gaps and contradictions in the existing legislation facilitated the "spontaneous" and semilegal conversion of state property into private assets. In particular, the 1989 decree of the Supreme Soviet "On Leasing" allowed for the private leasing of state enterprises with the possibility of a final buyout; since such a buyout could be financed by the profits of the enterprise in question, it often amounted to a privatization free of charge for the enterprise directors and bureaucrats at

---

[1] This overview omits the dynamics of agricultural privatization, as they are tangential to the book's focus. For excellent treatments, see Allina-Pisano; Wegren 2003.

47

the industrial ministries. By 1992, the theft of factory assets by managers was widespread; labor discipline and output collapsed; the supplies of goods dried up. While looted factory assets flooded the black markets, shortages of food and consumer goods in the shops sparked popular outrage. In this setting, reformers such as Yegor Gaidar in Russia argued that *formally* privatizing productive assets would return discipline to the shop floor in the short run while creating efficient incentives for owners and managers in the long run. The supporters of voucher privatization also hoped that the requisites of fairness and justice could be satisfied through a free distribution of assets to the public, albeit at the expense of budget revenues and capital investment in the firm, as the proponents of privatization via sales pointed out. In addition to the economic and equity-based criteria, privatization held a political promise: It was to make, many argued, the communist defeat irreversible through the creation of a wide stratum of property owners with a stake in a market economy.

Ukraine tackled privatization much slower than Russia in the beginning of the 1990s. Yet two decades later, their privatization trajectories have largely converged: Both Russia and Ukraine went through two stages of privatization defined by similar political conflicts with roughly comparable results.

The first stage involved significant concessions to the firm insiders, resulting in the old management's ownership of newly privatized firms. In both countries, this stage was implemented through voucher privatization of medium and large enterprises and management-employee buyouts of small shops and firms in the service sector. In Russia, voucher privatization began in 1992. Although the voucher method was originally designed to transfer shares to the general public, (acting prime minister) Gaidar's government ultimately compromised with the "red directors" of state-owned enterprises. As a result of this compromise, the insiders had the right to purchase shares in their firm, up to a controlling stake, at a discount *before* any equity was offered to the general public. The public could then use the freely distributed vouchers (nominally valued at 10,000 rubles) as "payment" for equity that had not been claimed by the insiders. While the vouchers were successfully distributed to 150 million Russian citizens, an active class of small stockholders did not emerge.[2] Much of Russia's voucher privatization was completed within two years, an astounding record considering that almost 14,000 medium and large firms were transferred into private ownership. In Ukraine, privatization did not take off until 1995 despite the parliament's 1992 passage of the State Program for the Privatization of State Enterprises. The delay resulted for both ideational and organizational

---

[2] Only 15 percent of the recipients exchanged their vouchers for equity in firms, while 45 percent sold or gave away their vouchers, often to the intermediaries controlled by enterprise managers, to state functionaries with access to budget funds, or to bankers. The remaining part of the population invested vouchers in special funds (Khoper, OLBI, etc.) designed to pool equity and exercise control on behalf of the stockholders. These funds were poorly regulated, often defrauding the investors (e.g., in the infamous scheme by the MMM fund). Tambovcev 2009.

Private Ownership and Its Legal Protections: A Brief History

reasons.[3] Hence, until 1995, privatization largely proceeded through the continued abuse of the lease-to-buy provisions in the legislation by the incumbent management. In 1995, the privatization of more than 16,000 firms began in earnest, 80 percent of which were small firms that were quickly privatized through employee buyouts, typically for a token amount. Vouchers were also distributed to the population in 1995 but generated even less enthusiasm than in Russia, partly due to important differences[4] in the design of privatization: 45 percent of the 50 million entitled Ukrainians did not bother to pick up their vouchers. Still, around 7,000 enterprises were privatized through voucher auctions before 2000. By 1998, insiders controlled 64 percent of stocks in privatized industrial enterprises in Ukraine, a higher share than in Russia.

The second stage of privatization, which began in 1995 in Russia and in 1997 in Ukraine, involved for-cash sales to outsiders, promising budget revenues as well as the imposition of discipline on enterprise management. In both countries, however, the realization of this phase was marred by corruption resulting in the exclusion of competitive bidders, pitiful treasury intake, and popular anger. While the voucher stage saw the state unburden itself of thousands of small shops and large loss-making SOEs, it was during the second stage of privatization that many highly profitable jewels of the Soviet economy – often from the natural resource sector – were privatized. And if the red directors triumphed in stage one, stage two gave rise to the post-Soviet oligarchs who were not always tied to the communist nomenklatura, and tended to be younger and more daring.

Political conflict surrounding privatization shaped its path similarly in both countries. Intense parliamentary opposition to privatization throughout the 1990s ensured that the presidential decrees of Yeltsin and Kuchma, as opposed to consensus-based legislation, guided the privatization process. In both countries, the presidents chose strong personalities among the reform-minded technocrats to implement the privatization: Anatoly Chubais assumed the task in Russia; Yuri Yekhanurov in Ukraine. Finally, in both countries, popular disappointment with the privatization of the 1990s facilitated its partial rollback in the 2000s. In Russia, Putin's Kremlin applied political pressure on enterprises

---

[3] The economic policy of newly independent Ukraine explicitly aimed to distance the country from Russia, including the disinclination to mimic Russia's attempt at "shock therapy." However, the professed gradualism of Ukraine's policymakers often masked the lack of organizational resources and clear strategy; the State Property Fund of Ukraine, for example, was vastly inferior to Russia's GKI (both state bodies were charged with privatization) in terms of its mandate, financing, and presidential support.

[4] The key difference between voucher privatizations was the fact that Ukrainian vouchers were "named" (*imennye*) and could not be sold on the market unlike the anonymous Russian vouchers, although, as in the Russian case, Ukrainians could transfer their vouchers to an investment fund. Furthermore, there were two types of vouchers in Ukraine: privatization property certificates (*pryvatyzatsiini mainovy sertyfikaty*), of which close to 90 percent were received by the population, and compensation certificates (*kompensatsiini sertyfikaty*), of which only 30 percent were received.

in the strategic industries (media and natural resources in particular) to sell controlling stakes to the state, while legislating preferential treatment granted to "state corporations."[5] In Ukraine, the high-profile corrupt privatizations under Kuchma added to the popular support of the 2004 Orange Revolution, one of whose leaders, Yulia Tymoshenko, attempted to re-nationalize the assets in question in early 2005.

Apart from privatization, the emergence of private ownership in Russia and Ukraine was driven by "de novo" start-ups. By 2012, around 3 million officially registered entrepreneurs were running small and medium-size businesses in Russia, and 1 million in Ukraine.[6] From the Carpathian Mountains to Kamchatka, the growth of entrepreneurship has been on an upward trajectory since the 1990s, albeit at a glacial pace.

Together, privatization and de novo start-ups provide the story of property rights' allocation in post-Soviet Russia and Ukraine. A good proxy for the extent of privately allocated property rights is the GDP share of private enterprises. Figure 3.1 provides this share for both countries in the 1991–2010 period; the substantial gap of the 1990s (with Russia's private sector constituting a larger share of the economy) was erased by the mid-2000s, with both countries' private shares of the economy stabilizing around 65 percent of the GDP. This share is somewhat lower than the 75 percent in countries such as Poland or Lithuania, but it is remarkable when compared to the shares in state-managed post-Soviet economies, such as Belarus (30 percent) or Uzbekistan (45 percent).

Overall, at least in terms of its *extent*, the allocation of property rights to private owners has been a success in Russia and Ukraine. While the process was patently unfair and continues to be debated on the grounds of efficiency,[7] the more narrow *political* aim of privatization has been achieved; a return to communism, the specter of which still haunted both countries in the 1990s, is unimaginable today in large part because of the widespread private ownership of productive assets.[8] In the post-Soviet space more generally, the extent of privatization has also been linked to the colored revolutions in the wake

---

[5] In 2007, a fundamental revision of the law on state corporations granted these conglomerates tax preferences, wide-ranging regulatory exemptions, and operational independence from local state bodies. The legal ownership form of "state corporation" is distinct from "joint-stock companies" in which the state holds a controlling share (*gosudarstvennye AO*), as well as from the "state unitary enterprises" (GUP).

[6] GEM 2012 Global Report, Global Entrepreneurship Monitor.

[7] According to Brown, Earle, and Telegdy (2006), privatization raised the productivity of enterprises in Ukraine by only 2 percent while actually lowering it in Russia by 3 percent (compared to the increases of 15 percent and 8 percent in Romania and Hungary). At the same time, Guriev and Rachinsky (2005) find that oligarchic ownership is more efficient than state ownership in Russia.

[8] The narrow goal of creating a bulwark against backslide into communism should be distinguished from the more ambitious political goal of creating an active constituency for liberal democracy and rule of law. This latter ambition has failed, partly because the process of

Private Ownership and Its Legal Protections: A Brief History

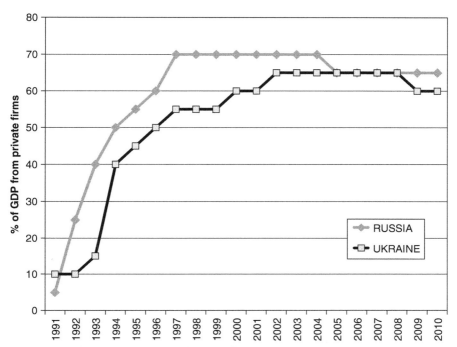

FIGURE 3.1. GDP % from privately owned enterprises, 1991–2010. (*Source*: European Bank for Reconstruction and Development.)

of fraudulent elections in the 2000s; such mass uprisings tended to occur in countries with large concentrations of private capital (Georgia, Ukraine, and Kyrgyzstan), but were absent in countries that had abstained from privatizing their economies.[9]

While private ownership has become the norm in Russia and Ukraine, making this ownership secure against trespass is a daunting task, which the rest of the book examines.

To begin, let us consider the legal basis for the protection of privately allocated property rights in both countries. Although the Soviet Union legally recognized and formally protected *personal* (lichnaia) property since the 1936 Constitution, the scope of such property was restricted to "the income and savings from labor, residential housing and auxiliary facilities, household items, and items for personal use and comfort."[10] Conversely, *private* (chastnaia) property,

---

privatization itself diverged starkly from the criteria of rule of law, infusing large layers of the population with deep distrust toward "the reformers."
[9] Radnitz 2010. Russia's protest movement in December 2011, even if it did not live up to the expectations of a "snow revolution," also fits this pattern.
[10] Article 10, Constitution of the USSR (1936).

52   *Not Too Petty*

including productive assets – Marx's "means of production" – remained largely illegal until the final days of the USSR when the Leviathan under Gorbachev relented.[11]

After the Soviet demise, the protection of private property rights came to occupy a central place in the constitutions and civil codes of both countries. The following rights are declared constitutionally in both Russia and Ukraine: equal recognition and protection of private, state, and communal forms of property; the inviolability of private property; the right to entrepreneurial activity as well as the rights to use and transfer private property; the obligation of the state to protect private property; the rights to a court decision as well as fair, ex ante compensation in the case of eminent-domain expropriation ("forced alienation by the state").[12] Although important differences[13] in the constitutional treatments of private property exist, the big picture is similar: When it comes to the *formal* protections of private property, both countries have left their Soviet past behind. Around one hundred articles in the respective civil codes of Russia and Ukraine elaborate these constitutional guarantees, covering definitional issues of private property as well as the mechanisms of PR acquisition, entrepreneurial usage, transfer, termination, and protection.[14]

While some PR scholarship building on the British case celebrates the formal institutions described earlier, area specialists have long been skeptical about "parchment" rules regulating property rights.[15] Why are constitutionally guaranteed property rights regularly violated today? After 2000, when Putin assumed power in Russia and Kuchma (allegedly) masterminded the kidnapping and murder of a journalist in Ukraine, the discussion shifted from private predation under a state vacuum to the danger of unaccountable central executives. (For scholarly literature, see the preceding chapter.)

Bill Browder, a high-profile American businessman who pioneered investing in Russia as a minority shareholder during privatization and battled the Russian majority owners afterward, personifies this shift in attitudes. Describing the

---

[11] The 1987 Law on State Enterprises curtailed top-down planning, allowing the enterprises to set their own output targets. The 1988 Law on Cooperatives permitted limited, small-scale private and cooperative ownership of firms. The 1990 amendment of the Soviet Constitution replaced the notion of "personal" property with a wider definition encompassing productive assets.

[12] In the Russian Constitution, see the articles 8(1); 34(1); 35; and 114(1.f). In the Ukrainian Constitution, see the articles 13; 41; 42. (The discussion here excludes the rights to land ownership as well as intellectual property.) One difference is the later adoption of the Ukrainian Constitution (in June 1996) compared with the Russian Constitution (in December 1993).

[13] Unlike Russia's, Ukraine's constitution underscores the social aspect of property usage: "Property entails responsibility. Property shall not be used to the detriment of the individual or the society." (Article 13). At the same time, Ukraine's constitution allows for post hoc eminent-domain compensation of private owners by the state "under conditions of martial law or a state of emergency." (Article 41) Finally, the Ukrainian constitution is silent on the right of inheritance (which is guaranteed by Article 35(1) in the Russian constitution).

[14] In the Ukrainian civil code, see articles 316–417; for Russia, articles 209–306.

[15] E.g., Pistor et al. 2000; Allina-Pisano.

1990s as "an orgy of stealing unprecedented in business, with dilutive share issues, transfer pricing, asset stripping and embezzlement," Browder first embraced Putin as the man who put a stop to private predation.[16] After the Russian authorities raided Browder's own investment fund Hermitage in 2005, however, Browder became the most vocal critic of Kremlin-sponsored predation in the international arena. If in 2003–4 Browder cheered on – "who's next?" – as the Kremlin expropriated Yukos in a political retribution campaign, by 2012 Browder saw the fate of Khodorkovsky's assets as a watershed event: "Putin tasted the forbidden fruit."[17] Some of Putin's own former advisors, such as Andrei Illarionov, had similar 180-degree shifts in perception.

Overall, conventional wisdom has emphasized "principal-sponsored" attacks on the ownership rights of Russian and Ukrainian firms since 2000. It is also well-recognized that corruption undermining the income rights of citizens and entrepreneurs has been rampant in both states. While both of these threat types to property rights exist and are, indeed, serious, this and the following chapters argue that a distinct type of state threats has been given short shrift so far, namely the "agent-driven" attacks on ownership rights, attacks which are uncoordinated and unsanctioned by the respective state principals.

AGENT PREDATION BEYOND "CORRUPTION"

The sale of formally "public" goods by individual state actors is pervasive in Russia and Ukraine. Since Transparency International added Russia in 1996 and Ukraine in 1998 to its Corruption Perception Index, which aggregates survey data into a comparative metric, both countries have doggedly languished near the bottom. Out of 176 countries in 2012, Russia ranked 133rd and Ukraine 144th in terms of perceived government "cleanness." Bribes are regularly sought in the education system, medical services, army draft, traffic control, and other areas of everyday life. The emergence of private enterprise has, unsurprisingly, become a magnet for money-minded bureaucrats; both the frequency and the volume of bribes are considerable. According to the 2008 BEEEP survey by the EBRD and the World Bank, between 22 and 27 percent of firms in Russia and Ukraine reported frequent "unofficial payments." In both countries, circa 1.5 percent of companies' annual sales go into bureaucrats' pockets, while the firms bidding for government contracts pay 4 to 5 percent of the contract value in kickbacks to state officials.

While bribe-seeking bureaucrats inflict clear damage on both economies, the theoretical preoccupation with bribes is reductionist. Illegal, disorganized aggression by state agents is not limited to nibbling away at the income streams of enterprises, but often affects *ownership rights* as well.

---

[16] *Financial Times* July 27, 2012.
[17] Ibid.

Annexation

Raiding (*reiderstvo*), which became pervasive in both countries in the 2000s, is a case in point of state aggression compromising ownership rights. Raiding subsumes various state-driven or state-assisted practices that target ownership rights in firms in a non-consensual fashion. As such, raiding is critically different from "hostile takeovers" as they are known in the West, in that (a) state actors play a key role in raiding, and (b) raiding proceeds against the wishes of the majority owners. As an interviewed Russian expert on raiding quipped, "hostile takeovers in the West are just a bit friendlier than our *friendly* takeovers."

The following two vignettes, based on my case studies, illustrate how raiding transgresses a narrow understanding of corruption.[18]

In Kharkiv, a city in Ukraine's Northeast, a limited-liability firm "Khar'kov-Moskva" signed a land lease agreement with the municipal authorities in 2009 that authorized the firm to build an ambitious business center, which would include a hotel and a helipad. The agreement transferred a swath of downtown land to the firm for twenty-five years, subject to subsequent renewal. Having secured all relevant permissions and attracted the necessary investors, the firm launched the construction. In 2010, a new mayor assumed power in Kharkiv. Immediately, the firm came under attack from the authorities. Based on damning reports from a multitude of inspecting agencies, the municipal court annulled the lease, after which the Procuracy opened nine administrative cases and one criminal case against the firm and its director and imposed an 840,000 hryvnia ($103,000) fine on the firm for the "unlawful use of land." According to the firm's director, the new mayor did not mince words when he met with him in March 2011: "He [the mayor] said, 'Let go of the site, or I will take it anyway!'" According to the firm's representative, "We have not received a single answer when we asked the Procuracy representatives during the court proceedings: 'how exactly did the company Khar'kov-Moskva violate state interests?'" Some of the newly launched state investigations targeted projects by Khar'kov-Moskva that had been completed years before and were unrelated to the current land dispute, yet the sudden interest of local state actors in these past projects appeared suspect. As the sweeping investigations of the firm unfolded, the firm's director also began receiving anonymous phone threats against himself and his family. As for the land at stake, the city's Commission on Emergencies claimed that the 16-meter ditch dug by the firm for the construction was unsafe for the adjacent subway lines; this, however, contradicted independent expertise from Kharkovmetroproekt, a foremost authority on tunnel construction in post-Soviet states, which concluded that the construction posed

---

[18] Media references used for both cases include *Ukrains'ka Pravda* September 28, 2011; *Most Kharkov* September 26, 2011; *PRiZ* November 23, 2011; *Podrobnosti* October 5, 2011; *FLB. ru* April 1, 2012.

Agent Predation beyond "Corruption"

no danger. In fact, the chief inspector of the government's own county-level agency, State Inspection for Architecture and Construction (GASK), admitted that the attack had little to do with infrastructure: "You can build there, yes, but for that you need serious project documentation and, above all, *a serious investor*" (emphasis added). According to investigative reports, the new mayor had just such an investor in mind: a local businessman who happened to be the mayor's friend. After Kharkiv's independent TV station, ATN, reported this, the mayor's office blocked the ATN channel. A private agency in Kharkiv that provides consulting services to the targets of raiding shared:

> Depriving people of their businesses has become a tradition ... even if violent methods such as "mask shows" [referring to the deployments of hooded and armed law enforcement agents at companies] are losing their topicality. Now it's "lawful raiding" which is in the foreground.... [The authorities] simply squeeze out the entrepreneurs, forcing them to abandon their property. The ditch on Pushkinskaya Street [the site of Khar'kov-Moskva's construction] is such a tasty morsel: that's why they hunt down the firm owners with their investigations.

According to the same agency, if the city cannot secure a court ruling annulling the lease, and cannot pressure the owners into a deal, "then the 'heavy artillery' is deployed – they declare void the decision of the session of the city council (*gorsovet*) upon which the lease was based." In other words, when the municipal authorities cannot manufacture a semblance of the legal process, they proceed with blunt unilateral annexation. According to a Kharkiv lawyer, such precedents "put a juridicial bomb under any contractual agreements between the city and the entrepreneurs.... People won't be sure that by concluding a lease agreement in full accordance with law, tomorrow or a few years later this agreement won't be annulled based on a protest by the Procurator or on an arbitrary decision of some power-holder." The practice of administrative cancellation of land designations (*zemleotvody*) was pioneered in Kharkiv under the old mayor in 2007 and has been used en masse against small entrepreneurs, according to interviewed experts. As a large firm, Khar'kov-Moskva had the resources to endure for a while, but after the municipal authorities sustained their attack for two years, the investors abandoned the project, de facto acknowledging the sums poured into construction as expropriated capital.

In the case of Moloko, a grocery store in downtown Moscow and also a limited-liability firm, the raiders were private specialists but could not have executed the takeover without the complicity of the local tax inspection office. Situated on prime real estate, Moloko was a Soviet relic whose questionable charm continued to attract customers who, as in times long gone, first paid for goods at the cashier's and then presented the check to the specific unit of the store where requested goods would be fetched by the staff. Through the mid-2000s, the shop's owners had received offers to sell the firm to companies intending to open a jewelry store or a fur salon in the building, but the owners refused. In 2007, Moscow's tax inspection office #46 received a visit from three individuals who presented documents about the sale of Moloko to a different firm. The documents were forged. Without much "inspection," the tax inspectors allowed the raiders to (a) rename the store using Moloko's tax registration number, (b) alter the firm's charter, and (c) appoint a new general director, Mr. Olekhver. Based on the founding documents signed by the tax inspectorate, Moscow's registration chamber gave the newly registered firm a certificate identifying it as the legal "owner" of the building in which Moloko's unsuspecting "former" owners were still selling groceries. The new bogus firm immediately resold the building to one of the three raiders, creating a "bona fide acquirer" (*dobrosovestnyi priobretatel'*) which provides a legal buffer against potential appeals of the deal. Moloko's original owners still appealed. In the court of arbitration, the involved tax inspectors referenced "vague instructions," and asked the court to confirm the raiders as the legal owners. To its credit, the court did the opposite, but the firm was nevertheless worn down in legal battles; Moloko stopped submitting financial documents to the Tax Service in 2007, and shut down in 2011. (In 2012, Olekhver was shot dead in a contract killing, which the media attributed to his raiding activities.)

The process through which state agents of various ranks, unsanctioned by the state principal, directly threaten the ownership rights of businesses varies along several dimensions. Sometimes, the lowest-ranking officials who personally inspect the business premises or the pertinent documentation act on behalf of their immediate *local* superiors (the case of Khar'kov-Moskva), while at other times, predation proceeds without such local coordination (the case of Moloko). Furthermore, state actors may act on behalf of private predators (Moloko) or in pursuit of their own agendas (Khar'kov-Moskva). Finally, raiding may target ownership rights to specific assets or lead to the annexation of the firm as such; for example, Khar'kov-Moskva "only" lost its rights over the construction site, while Moloko ceased to exist as a legal entity.

The expropriatory practices in the vignettes earlier were common in both countries in the second half of the 2000s. The practice of municipal state organs expropriating private investments, as demonstrated by the Ukrainian vignette, was rampant in Russia in 2009. According to the president of OPORA, Russia's main association of small businesses:

> We receive daily emergency calls about ... the transfer of real estate [built by private entrepreneurs] into MUPs [municipal unitary enterprises], about the revocation of agreements with the leaseholders of state and municipal property, about fixed auctions [privatizing expropriated property to favored investors] ... according to OPORA's monitoring data, such violations of property rights ... exist in 36 regions, including Krasnoyarsk Krai and Tula, Kaliningrad, Volgograd, Pskov, Smolensk, and Ulianov oblasts.[19]

The practice of private raiders employing state officials to expropriate other businesses, as demonstrated by the Russian vignette, "became a national

---

[19] *Moskovskaya Pravda* February 27, 2009; *Moskovskii Komsomolets* February 9, 2009.

catastrophe in Ukraine by 2006," says the executive director of Anti-Raiding Union of Ukrainian Entrepreneurs, adding that because "powerful business groups order ... raiding activities leading to the redistribution of property ... the institution of property rights guaranteed and protected by the state is practically absent in Ukraine today ... [and] the very existence of [independent] small and medium businesses becomes questionable."[20]

In the 2005–11 period, *successful* raiding attacks proceeded at a *yearly pace* of more than 10,000 firms in Russia and 1,300 firms in Ukraine (expert estimates, averaged)[21]; whatever the precise form of raiding in a given case, the role that the state raiders play clearly transcends the mere targeting of income rights via requests for bribes.

Note that the lack of an appreciable change in state ownership statistics (Figure 3.1) during this period suggests that state officials or their affiliates become the new owners of expropriated assets in their *private* capacity as individuals. In other words, raiding does not constitute a de jure state nationalization (which would be a subset of principal expropriation). According to Yuri Borisov, one of the leading experts on raiding in Russia, "in this sphere [of raiding], *the 'state' is a passive player, but the bureaucrats are very active.* You'll remember what Karl Marx said long ago – the private property of the bureaucrat is the state."[22] The qualitative sociological study by Russia's Center for Political Technologies based on thirty in-depth interviews with experts from the Duma, think tanks, law firms, business press, and anti-raiding organizations underscores that "according to the overwhelming majority of respondents, *the most widespread type of raider now is precisely the government bureaucrat.*"[23] Unlike in the early 2000s, when raiding was the tool of the oligarchs seeking to consolidate their empires, by 2008 "lone [private] raiders were extinct as a class," and, instead, it is the "representatives of government agencies who appear as raid initiators [*zakazchiki*], who accumulate property by using their official mandates [*dolzhnostnye polnomochiia*]."[24] According to a Duma deputy, "what is happening now is state racket, and honestly, I am ashamed on behalf of the state."[25]

---

[20] Semidid'ko 2007, 27.

[21] Precise data does not exist, partly because the criminal codes of both countries do not treat "raiding" as a distinct crime. For expert estimates, see *Rossii'skie vesti* May 14, 2012; *Kommersant Den'gi* October 10, 2011; CPT 2008, 46; Zerkalov 2011, 219; *Ekspert Ukraina* July 2, 2007; Rosrazvitie 2007; *Literaturnaia gazeta* January 28, 2009.

[22] *Faktor Riska* August 13, 2006.

[23] The non-state raider types, according to the study, run the gamut of entrepreneurial professionals, particularly lawyers and businessmen who were too young to participate in the privatization rounds of the 1990s and criminal professionals whose skills range from violence to forgery. CPT 2008, 6 (emphasis added).

[24] Ibid., 19.

[25] Ibid., 11.

My interviews and the analysis of regional press suggest some analytical commonalities behind the bewildering diversity of raiding attacks on the ground.[26] A successful attack goes through five stages, some of which may be skipped and some of which may be mind-bogglingly sophisticated, depending on whether the target is a small kiosk or a multi-billion-dollar corporation:

1. Intelligence acquisition:
   The following information about the target company is critical to the raiders' preparatory stage: ownership structure, detailed financial situation including outstanding debts, track record of company's legal violations, information on industrial relations within the target firm, personal information about company executives, and so on. State employees of regulatory, taxation, or law enforcement agencies are entitled to request most of the relevant information during the routine business inspections. If the target is a larger enterprise with the adequate data protection systems and lawyers, the law enforcement agents may come with search warrants based on suspected "economic crimes"; such warrants allow them to bypass the legal restrictions placed on routine business inspections. Finally, in the case of open-stock companies (OAO), law enforcers can approach the so-called registrar (a private firm licensed to carry out registration functions in the stock market) for details on shareholders. For example, in 2010, the police ordered the registrar in Kholmsk, a remote small town in Russia's Far East, to hand over information about the firm "Sakhalinskoe Morskoe Parokhodstvo," as part of a raiding attack by local state actors including a parliament deputy and a county-level judge. Raiders may also resort to hiring detectives, eliciting information from the company staff or, in the case of open-stock companies, buying a nominal stake in the company to gain privileged information via minority shareholder protections.

2. Asset fixation:
   If raiders target specific assets of the enterprise, such as buildings, land, or machines, they aim to make it impossible for the victim to transfer or alter these assets once the attack becomes apparent. The courts often play the main role during this stage by issuing temporary property arrests (*obespechitel'nye mery*) pending the outcome of ongoing civil or criminal cases against the enterprise or its owners. For example, in the Simferopol district of Ukraine's Crimean peninsula in 2008–10, state employees and former managers of collective farms used courts

---

[26] For Russia, see *Rossii'skie vesti* October 22, 2012; *Nezavisimaia gazeta* May 24, 2012; *Pravda* October 22, 2009; *Vedomosti* July 20, 2011; *Vedomosti* April 25, 2007; *Kommersant* April 16, 2007; *Rossiiskaya Biznes Gazeta* October 13, 2009; *Ekspert Volga* May 14, 2007; *Ekspert* July 12, 2010; *Ogoniok* May 16, 2007; and *Novy Region* July 7, 2008. For Ukraine, see *Ekspert Ukraina* 2007; *Rossii'skie vesti* 2012; *Dzerkalo Tyzhnia* October 19, 2012; *Dzerkalo Tyzhnia* August 10, 2012; and *Ukrains'ka Pravda* November 8, 2011.

to temporarily arrest privatized land plots while recapturing ownership rights to these plots by folding them into new legal entities.[27] Often, a rapid "cascade" of such cases is generated by raiders against the target: the purpose is not to win the cases but to safeguard the assets until the raid is completed. Regional state prosecutors and law enforcement agencies may initiate such cases, while employees of the regulatory inspection organs can help with the "discovery" of new circumstances in the opened cases to protract the court proceedings.

3. Neutralization of main owners:
    Raiders strive not only to freeze the target assets but also to restrict the decision-making powers of the assets' owners, anticipating the latter's defense efforts. State inspectors on the ground are critical in this phase: the sanitation agency, the fire safety department, and a few dozen other regulators can legally shut down a firm based on code violations. It is through such regulatory pressure, for example, that the former mayor of Samara (in Southwestern Russia) together with the Samara county public prosecutor and affiliated business structures could expropriate more than 238 entities in the region, including a variety of shops, a river port, and a sports complex in 2005–7. Courts can be important in the case of stock companies, for example by arresting an equity block and suspending its voting power at the general shareholder meeting.[28] Raiders also aim to deplete the cash reserves of the owners, which could be used for defense; employees of the regional taxation agencies play a key role here because they can either conduct investigations that lead to crippling fines or freeze the bank accounts of an enterprise if the latter's tax arrears are substantial. Acquiring a company's debt may also be used for the purposes of "cash draining" during this stage.[29] Finally, raiders can

---

[27] The rationale for land arrests was based on outdated Soviet-era legislation, a situation aided by the continuing legal vacuum regarding land privatization in Ukraine. The former state-farm managers created new private firms with the same name as the former Soviet state farms, arguing that these new firms were the "juridicial successors" of the Soviet state farms and hence were entitled to the plots that, although legally privatized, seemingly contradicted Ukraine's moratorium on land privatization at the time of the raid.

[28] Private raiders also use various tricks to prevent some owners from physically appearing at shareholder meetings, such as announcing a meeting in an obscure locale on short-term notice and ensuring that the invitation to the key owners gets lost in the mail. In the past, violent methods of temporary neutralization, including kidnapping, also took place.

[29] In the beginning of the 2000s, given unreformed bankruptcy legislation in both countries, buying up a company's liabilities allowed raiders (both state and private) to force the firm into bankruptcy and seize its assets. Today, such scenarios are too cumbersome for the aggressors. Still, the accumulation of debt serves other functions. Calling in debts before an attack deprives the target firm of funds. On the basis of accumulated debts, the aggressor can also seek the arrest of property pending the resolution of legal claims. During the call-in process, raiders have free access to the target firm's premises, which can be used for a violent takeover or document theft. By calling in a particular debt, the aggressor often triggers an avalanche of call-ins from bona fide creditors – a process from which the target may never recover.

60 *Not Too Petty*

generate a cascade of lawsuits against the target to disorient the owners and distract them from the main attack on assets.[30]

4. Asset seizure:
Most often, owners who are intimidated or exhausted by the previous attack stages ultimately sell their assets to the aggressor "under duress," typically at 10–20 percent of the assets' fair value. The seizure of assets through blunt criminal methods, such as the forgery of registration documents or through a violent takeover, continues to be an issue, although it has declined since 2007 in Russia and since 2009 in Ukraine. In 2011, the city hall of Ukraine's city Odessa on the Black Sea let masked law enforcement agents occupy the premises of two popular canteens while changing the locks and escorting out the owners. Similarly, in Russia's city of Sochi in 2008, a spa resort was taken over by an armed group supported by the police; the intruders claimed to represent the new owners, forcing the staff to sign documents about property transfer, while the status quo owners blamed the takeover on enemies in the city administration and in the local organs of internal affairs (*OVD*). The prize for the audacity of local officials, however, goes to the head of the local government in Tuva, a federal republic in Russia's Siberia: In 2011, he oversaw a criminal takeover of the regional communications provider "Tuvasviaz'inform," whose expropriation involved both document forgery and the violent occupation of premises.

5. Asset anchorage:
No matter what legal transgressions are used during the attack, the raiders aim is to conclude the annexation within the legal field so as to make the obtained property rights irreversible. Assets may be resold countless times through aggressor-controlled firms, which are immediately eliminated; at the end of the chain of defunct intermediaries stands a bona fide buyer whose rights are protected by law. The concealment of the raiding entity through offshore legal structures can make seeking redress by the victim a logistical nightmare. Finally, raiders may file a lawsuit *against themselves* through a technically separate but de facto affiliated entity; this lawsuit ("vaccination" (*privivka*) in raiders' jargon) is then intentionally lost by the plaintiff, reinforcing the legal claims of raiders to the disputed property. For example, in the case of Odessa's canteens mentioned earlier, a private firm affiliated with the mayor successfully contested the canteens' ownership by filing a bogus lawsuit against "the

---

[30] Complex lawsuits are often launched against the firm in the name of nonexistent entities, aggressor-controlled shareholders, or even the executive managers of the target firm themselves (as plaintiffs). Along with the smoke cloud created by these and other measures, raiders may unfurl a powerful public relations campaign aiming to discredit the target firm in the eyes of its partners, state organs, shareholders, employees, and the general public. Amusingly (not for the real owners), the target firm may itself be presented as the raider in the campaign unleashed by the aggressor.

city," which the city hall intentionally lost. Beyond aiming to legalize the annexation of property, raiders may seek to make the reversal of this process financially costly. For example, raiders may apply expensive "permanent improvements" to captured property; should the victims succeed in restoring their legal claims to assets, they would have to compensate the aggressors for such improvements. Alternatively, raiders may saddle the newly expropriated firm with debts, decreasing the desirability of the asset (whose net worth decreases in proportion to newly assumed liabilities) to its prior legitimate owners.

Raiding continues to be an acute problem in both Russia and Ukraine. In 2010, a mid-level commander of Russia's Special Purpose Police Unit (OMON) confessed:

Ours is a profitable business.... The task is usually simple: we storm in, break in the door, remove all people from the premises [of a firm]. Regarding computers and equipment: sometimes we simply trash it, sometimes the employees of the firm take it. After that we control the premises until the new owner arrives. This is the manner in which we took over a plant in the Fili-Davydkovo district [of Moscow]: we kept watch over a plant from September to February until all property-related issues were settled.[31]

A special website (www.zahvat.ru) serves the needs of the raiding industry, connecting state officials with finance providers and lawyers. One ad, for example, reads "Wanted: analyst-scout with a creative mind, possessing his own administrative resource [i.e., government connections].... Main responsibilities: extraction of firms' equity registers [i.e., illegal obtainment of corporate records].... About us: we plunder whatever moves."[32] State and private raiders actively seek financing by making tempting offers to capital holders (e.g., "acquire a $10 mil firm for $2 mil at acceptable risk"). In 2011, Ukraine's Anti-Raider Movement, a civil society initiative, launched www.zahvat.net, a site which aims to provide the opposite type of service, to expose the cases in which "the pressure of state organs" and "the illegal actions or inaction of state power" have led to annexations, while coordinating the owners' resistance efforts (the domain extension ".net" is a pun on the Russian word for "no," while "zahvat" means capture or takeover).

Meanwhile, the central governments in Moscow and Kyiv continued to issue alarmist statements regarding state raiding through the early 2010s. Signing a law designed to combat raiding in July 2010, Russia's ex-president Medvedev exhorted the heads of the Interior Ministry and the Federal Tax Service to pursue "raiders in epaulets," stressing that "raiding is a complex and extremely dangerous crime that is basically choking our economy.... We must beware

---

[31] *Novoe Vremia* February 1, 2010.
[32] Available at: http://www.zahvat.ru/index.php?pg=job&section=vacsingle&id=69. Accessed on October 27, 2010.

of those [state officials] obligated to protect firms who join raider brigades."[33] A year earlier, Putin had elaborated on the raiding issue during the carefully orchestrated annual Q&A on state television. In Ukraine, the deputy chief state prosecutor, Viktor Zanfirov, after the meeting of an interdepartmental anti-raiding commission at the Ukrainian government in February 2012, shared that "to expropriate business in our state is sadly cheaper than to acquire it, and that's the economic basis of raiding for you ... one of the key problems is corruption in courts, law enforcement, and the organs of the state executive."[34]

The distinct role that corruption plays in raiding should be noted here. As discussed in the literature, corruption largely amounts to bribe extraction by state officials for various government services; the targeting of entrepreneurs' cash flows (income rights) is *per se* the raison d'être of corruption. In the case of raiding, however, corruption is merely an instrumental step toward a bigger goal: the capture of entrepreneurs' ownership rights. Consider, for example, the following "price list" (in thousands of dollars), which served as a guide for Russian raiders acquiring additional "administrative resources" for the purposes of expropriation in the second half of the 2000s:[35]

Inspection of target firm by taxation agency: $4 K
Amendment to the government's register of enterprises:[36] $1–10 K
Obtainment of the property sale contract filed at the registration chamber:[37] $5–30 K
Court decision on property arrest / injunction against a shareholder meeting: $10–30 K
Opening of a criminal case against target owners: $50 K
Closure of a criminal case through Ministry of Internal Affairs: $30 K
Closure of a criminal case through General State Procuracy: $1,500 K
Confiscation of shareholder register: $20 K
A commercial court verdict against the target firm: $10–100 K
Arrest of a business competitor through Ministry of Internal Affairs: $100 K
Forcible office takeover: $10–30 K

When private raiders pay their accomplices in the government to help expropriate enterprises, the analysis cannot stop at the level of corruption;

---

[33] *Rossiiskaya Gazeta* July 2, 2010.
[34] *Ukrains'ka Pravda* February 9, 2012.
[35] *Kommersant* 2007; *Novoe Vremia* 2010.
[36] The Single State Register of Legal Persons (*Edinyi Gosudarstvennyi Reestr Iuridicheskikh Lits*) is administered by the Federal Tax Service and records all changes in the legal status of firms, including changes to ownership, the legal form of organization, the headquarters' location, company charter details, liquidation procedures, and so forth. Unsanctioned changes to the Register create faits accomplis that are difficult to reverse.
[37] Regional registration chambers record transfers of private property that involve real estate. These chambers are subordinate to the Federal Service of State Registration, Cadaster, and Cartography.

Agent Predation beyond "Corruption"

while the latter clearly takes place, it is merely a catalyst for a more ominous dynamic, namely the targeting of ownership rights by state employees, either on request from private raiders or on behalf of state employees themselves.

As already mentioned, the evolution of raiding in both Russia and Ukraine has been toward the latter type of raiding, in which the government staff become the new private owners of expropriated firms. According to the vice president of the National Institute of Systematic Research of Entrepreneurship Problems (NISIPP), a reputable Russian think tank devoted to the problems of entrepreneurship, "raiding takeovers are now [in 2012] primarily driven by the law enforcement organs.... The times when [private] businesses squeezed their competitors through state power structures are already gone. Today employees of these [state] structures are business owners themselves."[38] For Ukraine, the in-depth 2012 analysis by *Dzerkalo Tyzhnia* describes "yet another total property redistribution (*cherhovyi total'nyi peredil vlasnosti*) conducted by the current state authorities ... for whose completion the main law enforcement forces are deployed. Instead of searching for economic crimes, operatives are searching for economic targets which are of interest [for annexation]."[39] To better understand how raiding has changed, I interviewed the local executive of Forensic Services at PricewaterhouseCoopers (PwC); this unit, with offices in Moscow and Kyiv, investigates corporate fraud and internal corruption through undercover audits and business surveys. According to the executive I spoke with:

> In 2005–06, business had it hard, particularly in Ukraine where the judicial branch ran completely amuck: the state [executive] simply distanced itself from the problem.... After 2010, judges have not become better, and questionable [court] decisions still exist. However, the takeovers are now [in 2012] executed through law enforcement. *Before, people who conducted these raids had no need to belong to state organs*; they did everything through the courts. *Now, people outside of the state organs won't get into raiding, because it could end badly for them, while people who do belong to the state organs don't need the courts for raiding.* [emphasis added]

Note that the change in the raiding dynamic described here applies primarily to *big* business (PwC's clients are large firms). For small and mid-size firms, however, "nothing has changed in principle. To say that private business was ordering these raids is incorrect: the state bureaucrat himself has always been the organizer and the beneficiary" – so says the director of the Property and Freedom Institute, a Ukrainian think tank supporting small entrepreneurs through legislative lobbying and the coordination of a network of business associations.[40]

What little discussion of raiding exists in Western scholarship has so far been limited to Russia, relating its raiding problems to the quirks of

---

[38] *Sliyaniya i Pogloshcheniya* October 9, 2012.
[39] *Dzerkalo Tyzhnia* January 20, 2012.
[40] Author's interview, December 18, 2012. See also the Institute's website for data and legislative proposals regarding property rights' protection: http://www.pfi.org.ua/.

Russia's legislation (in the spheres of bankruptcy, corporate governance, and administrative accountability), the country's oil abundance, or the relative influence of the oligarchs and the Putin-aligned state forces. Yet raiding is also a pressing problem in Ukraine – as well as Belarus, Kazakhstan, and other post-Soviet states; indeed, China is not immune either.[41] The president of Kazakhstan, Nursultan Nazarbayev, for example, acknowledged the "conquest of country by raiding in which state officials often participate" at the closed meeting of the Security Council in October 2006. In 2009, following an outcry from the entrepreneurial community, Nazarbaev admitted in a live TV address: "Raiding is a curse. The state must absolutely guarantee the inviolability of private property ... [yet] the state bureaucrat is always one of the participants in raiding."[42] (During the address, Nazarbaev was connected via phone to the General Prosecutor, who took a verbal beating and reported on planned counter-measures.) The literature's narrow focus on Russia's peculiarities in discussing raiding seems to have crowded out the larger theoretical takeaway: In modern developing states, government employees attack ownership rights in ways that transcend existing conceptualizations of corruption.

Intervention and Extortion

Although an extreme case of agent predation, raiding is only one of its manifestations. To be classified as "raiding," the asset in question must be fully confiscated. Much of agent predation, however, involves intervention or extortion rather than annexation.

To visualize such interference with ownership rights by lower-level state agents, let us return to the example of Russia's OMON. As mentioned before, this police unit has engaged in outright annexations via raiding. However, OMON has also interfered with the ownership rights of private firms in more subtle ways. According to a detailed 2010 analysis by *Novoe Vremia*, Russia's leader in independent investigative journalism, OMON "has been turned into a money-making structure."[43] For example, OMON directly controls privately owned markets through ongoing extortion. This control is based on an implicit threat of force that can be readily carried out, as in the case of OMON's shutdown of several retail markets in Moscow in 2008–9. OMON also provides security services to crime-connected firms, indirectly undermining the property rights of these firms' counterparties. One known "thief in law" (*vor v zakone*), that is, a criminal authority with a history behind bars, has expressed delight at the fact that while he was pursued by OMON in the 1990s, he has now cut a deal with a colonel, receiving, in exchange for cash,

---

[41] *Sovetskaya Belorussiya* November 21, 2012; *Delovaya Pressa* October 31, 2006; *The Economist* February 23, 2013.

[42] KT news agency, November 13, 2009. http://www.kt.kz/

[43] *Novoe Vremia* 2010. Unless stated otherwise, this is the source for the OMON case study.

Agent Predation beyond "Corruption"

two OMON jeeps complete with professional officers who shadow him as he goes about his business.

Statistical analysis supports the insights from the OMON case. In 2010, St. Petersburg's Institute of Law Enforcement Issues at the European University published a remarkable analysis of the skyrocketing investigations of "economic crimes" in the mid-2000s.[44] The authors compare the relationship between the *launches* (by the employees of Ministry of Internal Affairs) and the *completions* (through a judicial verdict) of investigations across different types of crimes. For crimes featuring a low predation potential for the individual state agents, such as rape or murder, the rate of investigation completions moves in tandem with the rate of investigation launches. However, for crimes offering a high potential for agent predation, such as the violations of "economic" articles[45] of the criminal code, investigation launches increased significantly while investigation completions remained unchanged. Interpreting their findings, the authors argue that the increase in the registration of economic crimes since 2002 "did not lead to the activation of the law enforcement system as a whole, but to the activation of its subcomponents, particularly those tasked with investigations and operative deployment, [whose agents] began working more for their personal interests.... [Up to] 85–90% of activity [related to the investigations of economic crimes] represents ... administrative pressure on entrepreneurs to receive informal income or other private benefits."[46] A different study by the respected Levada Center, based on a large-N survey of Russian police officials, found that more than 80 percent of the police staff "moonlight" on the side and that explicitly predatory activities are particularly common among the more experienced and qualified officers at the county-level [*raion*] departments and investigative organs.[47] In another survey, conducted by the Higher School of Economics in Moscow, 30 percent of Russia's law servants admitted to frequent police extortion and another 30 percent to offering "services to suspend or drop [criminal] cases."[48]

Beyond police, consider the attacks on ownership rights by tax inspectors. An entrepreneur from southern Ukraine remarked in an interview with me:

> Usually, it is the municipal or county [*raion*] agents who are shaking us down, but sometimes also oblast-level [roughly equivalent to U.S. state] agents. The local tax police don't even know the oblast guys, and when the oblast agents come, *many businesses in town close for the day out of fear.* But sometimes oblast folks come to the local bureaus first, and the local [agents] supply them with targets to hit.... We work on top of a volcano. [emphasis added]

[44] Volkov et al. 2010.
[45] According to expert interviews cited in the study, the following articles of the Russian Criminal Code are most often cited in investigations: 22 ("Crimes in sphere of economic activity"), 159 ("Fraud"), 160 ("Embezzlement or misappropriation"), 174 ("Money laundering").
[46] Volkov et al., 3, 20.
[47] Gudkov and Dubin 2006.
[48] Kolennikova et al. 2004.

The quote suggests both that arbitrary tax inspections adversely impact the way in which owners manage their assets and that the lack of coordination across different levels of inspectors enhances this adverse impact. According to Sergei Zelenov, of Russia's small-business association, "tax organs can simply block [bank] accounts, allegedly because some of company's records are missing." Such a mandate, according to Zelenov, allows tax inspectors "to participate in firm takeovers."[49]

Often, high-powered mandates are combined with low professionalism and perverse incentives. In my semi-structured interviews, small business owners in Ukraine complained that the municipal tax police officials "are 'professionals' with purchased diplomas ... [who] call you up and say 'come on, give us something' [*tos' dai nam shos'*]." Such extortion proceeds on a regular basis. A director of a large supermarket chain observed that "although it is easier for the tax folks to harass smaller businesses, they [the tax officials] must also fulfill a plan for sanctions: that's why we get anxious when our documents are all in order. Looking clean is an invitation for trouble." Tax agents uncovering crimes connected to "particularly large tax non-payments" (*neuplata nalogov v osobo krupnom razmere*) are entitled to a bonus from the state budget, which ratchets up predatory behavior, given the legacy of near-universal tax evasion by firms. "In a silent process of property redistribution ... former tax sinners can be torn to pieces," according to a Ukrainian analyst.[50] The practice of value-added tax reimbursement offers another example in which "a whole system of ambiguous regulations is set up to extort bribes and allow practically unlimited discretion of public officials in treating business," according to the European Business Association, with offices in six Ukrainian cities.[51]

Tax inspectors and police are not alone in undermining entrepreneurs' ownership rights. Says the owner of several pharmacies in central Ukraine, interviewed by the author in 2010:

There's a myriad agencies: fire safety, sanitation, quality control, social funds, tax police – there aren't enough fingers on both hands to count them! They all want to grab money, and it's not like they care about law compliance. Take the quality control agency. During the last inspection, they knew the amount they wanted to fine us before they walked in: 50,000 hryvnia. All they asked was: "what do you want to be written up for?" *These people figure out the maximum [amount] they can take based on your estimated turnover, and then they take it.* At least the quality control folks can only visit us once a year, as per law. The tax agencies, on the other hand, have the mandate to drop by at any time: whenever they need money, in other words. [emphasis added]

Extremely high volume or unpredictability of bribe demands from state actors transform petty income-threatening corruption into fundamental ownership-threatening extortion. The pharmacy owner showed me an excel spreadsheet

[49] *Sliyaniya i Pogloshcheniya* 2012.
[50] *Dzerkalo Tyzhnia* 2012.
[51] European Business Association 2009, 86–7.

Agent Predation beyond "Corruption"

in which he budgets his expenses, including those on various regulatory government agencies. According to his outlays in 2003–9, the total costs of government predation fluctuated by up to 300 percent from year to year. On the one hand, this indicates very little if any "optimization" of predatory revenues *across* government agencies. On the other hand, it becomes impossible for the business owners to conduct day-to-day asset management and planning when bribe demands turn into financial time bombs with unpredictable triggers. When this same pharmacy owner was re-interviewed in 2012, his yearly informal expenditures on "government relations" (excluding regular tax payments) constituted HR 23,000 ($2,875) for a single pharmacy; this sum was roughly one half of his total monthly cost of operating the same pharmacy (including expenses on inventory, energy, labor, etc.). Considering the monetary volume at stake, it is little surprise that many entrepreneurs complained that *extortion by state employees can force business closure.* A licensed cab driver in a small town in Western Ukraine, whom I interviewed in 2012 and who subcontracts with a radio dispatcher but owns his car, would hide the checkered sign atop his taxi even as he was cruising the streets looking for hails, so as to evade costly street pullovers by state agents. As he explained:

Licenses are not problematic anymore, because you only have to get it once now. But the taxes, the pension fund folks, etc! Look, I make HR 3000 a month – if they see me on the streets, they'll keep stopping me, and at the end of the month, I'll have more than HR 1000 in their so-called fees and fines – how can I work? They basically charge as if we were in Kiev, but this is a small town, there's no way I can make up in revenues what they ask in illegal charges [*pobory*]. I have to hide [*maskirovat'sia*] or get out of the game. Many cabbies have just shut down.

The earlier discussion suggests that state agents' extortion of entrepreneurs can approach the theoretical scenario of the "tragedy of the commons," and when "overgrazing" by various agencies potentially leads to business closure, it is the firm's ownership that is jeopardized. The sheer quantity of threats to income transforms their quality. Extreme corruption undermining ownership rights and business development was particularly evident in western Ukraine with its tremendous, but so far hypothetical, potential for tourism given EU proximity and the natural beauty of Carpathian Mountains. As one significant local investor told me in 2008, "people here live in poverty on a mountain of gold. When founding a new business, after you go through all the stages of hell, you usually arrive without a kopek [left] in your pocket.... Bureaucratic predation [*chinovnichii bespredel*] leaves little possibility even to the medium-sized [as opposed to small] businesses to invest and work."

Not only the entrepreneurs, but also the independent experts and government employees I interviewed testified to the critical impact of street-level bureaucrats on ownership rights. Volodymyr Dubrovs'kyi, a senior economist at a Kyiv think tank that conducts regular studies of Ukraine's business climate for the World Bank, the United Nations Development Programme, and

68 *Not Too Petty*

various domestic government agencies, had much to say about state inspectors in particular:

The Ukrainian state and business? Think of it as the cattleman [*skotovod*] and the herd. What does a cattleman do? He allows the herd to procreate, to grow, to gain weight, so that he can fleece it ... and butcher it. At the official level here, they stress the creation of conditions for business to emerge and to "gain weight," but at the same time, *the problem is that on the ground, their method of fleecing and butchering is through the inspections* [proverki]. The real cost of inspections has grown incredibly, even if their nominal number may have dropped. In 2008, the ratio of the cost of regulatory compliance including expenditures on equipment [*pereoborudovanie*], staff training, etc. to the cost of inspections was such that the latter comprised 40% of the former, which is a lot if you think about it; in 2010, it was 80%; today [in 2012], it is over 100%, and the situation is worsening. [emphasis added]

Indeed, Mykhailo Brods'kyi, the head of the State Committee on Regulatory Policy and Entrepreneurship, describes the situation in similar terms:

The first penalty fine [in the course of a business inspection] must not lead to the entrepreneur's bankruptcy. The fine should discipline, not destroy [*shtraf maie dystsyplinuvaty a ne znyshchuvaty*] [unlike] today [when] inspectors from our tax service, sanitation and epidemiology service, the fire fighters, the customer rights' protection ... immediately fine you. Bang, and you are bankrupt. Bang, and they shut you down [*Odrazu babakh tobi shtraf i ty banrkut. Babakh i tebe zakryly*].... The responsibility for these decisions is with the unaccountable bureaucrat [*samoupravnyi chinovnik*].... Fines can be ... a form of struggle against the competitor [if the state agent himself is affiliated with another business] ... or an attempt at extortion.[52]

In elaborating the planned response of his department, Brods'kyi raised the strategy of routing every imposed fine through the court system for review, a questionable move at best, considering the level of judicial corruption.

Administrative Wars and Agent Predation

The pharmacy owner mentioned earlier further complained that "the authorities abruptly create laws on dangerous substances that forbid entire ranges of medicine, and then tell the [inspection] organs 'fetch!,' and the organs just make money. Whenever any of these laws is annulled in Kyiv, *the organs on the ground never announce it, and just continue to harass* [us]" (emphasis added). This disjuncture between the central government's actions and their (non-) implementation on the ground suggests that principal-agent problems in the state apparatus are in part responsible for continuing predation.

In the sphere of formal law, such problems extend beyond low-level nonimplementation and include the conscious creation of *local* "regulatory acts," which grant the local power holders opportunities for predation while contradicting the national legislation. In 2011, Ukraine's Cabinet of Ministers

---

[52] *Dzerkalo Tyzhnia* January 20, 2012.

Agent Predation beyond "Corruption"

ordered a revision of 54,000 such acts, which mostly included "decisions" (*rishennia*) and "orders" (*rozporiadzhennia*) passed at the level of town councils (*mis'krada*) and their executive organs (*vykonkom*); according to a state official who participated in the review, only one third of these local acts was found to be in accordance with national legislation.[53] "The *regions['authorities] above all* spew forth regulatory acts which contradict the principles declared by the state ... this is the basis for corruption that works under any [central] power or any regime," so the official.[54]

Although state predation is far from nationally optimized from the state principal's viewpoint (see next chapter), the degree of unity among state actors *in a given region* certainly varies. In some regions, for example, it is the clans composed of local government actors who are responsible for agent predation. Says Brods'kyi, the czar of Ukraine's deregulation campaign:

> The [national] government is adopting measures to deprive state inspectors of legal instruments to pressure business.... But the problem of deregulation is also with our local princelings [*mistsevykh kniaz'kiv*]. The head of the county-level administration has the state prosecutor as the godfather [of his children], the chief of police as his son-in-law, etc. One gang [*odna banda*]. And after his appointment, this [county] head is not thinking about the need to create jobs ... to check how much money is coming into the local pension fund from business and compare it with what the pensioners are paid.... The mentality instead is "after me, the flood." The clans are thinking like this: "Bring to me that Liapkin-Tiapkin [i.e., a subordinate state employee, referring to a character in Gogol's play]! Who is "the businessman" in our county?" That businessman is immediately visited by the [county head's] relative, and with him the fire inspectors, the chums from the tax inspection, the chums from the police. The entrepreneurs start running to the princeling, to the state prosecutor's office – and thus the livestock is corralled [*i pishov zahin*]. "You [have to] build this for us; you [have to] transfer to the charity fund so and so much; you [have to] transfer to the special-purpose fund; and you want to build for yourself? – atta boy! –, then pay into my pocket 100 thousand [*a ty khochesh buduvatysia? – molodets', todi zaplaty meni v kisheniu sto tysiach*]."

Russia offers a similar picture of bureaucrats undermining company owners' property rights and the central state's deregulation efforts. Consider the country's uneven progress through the 2000s in reducing a panoply of state inspections of businesses. The adoption of the Law on Protection of Legal Persons and Individual Entrepreneurs during Administrative Inspections (Federal Law 134-FZ) in August 2001 was considered an early triumph for Putin's de-bureaucratization campaign. However, a closer look shows that it is the "Tax Agency and other fiscal control bodies" that "won the victory against the government by ensuring that budget, currency and tax control would be excluded from the framework of the Law".[55] Only eight years later did Russia's sovereign manage

---

[53] *Krymskaya Pravda* December 29, 2012.
[54] News portal of Independent Bank Rating Agency, http://ibra.com.ua/; *Dzerkalo Tyzhnia* 2012.
[55] Pryadil'nikov 2009, 108.

to push through a fundamentally revised law (294-FZ) curtailing the powers of the most abusive agencies. In 2010, the Ministry of Economic Development and Trade (MEDT) issued a 300-page report analyzing the implementation of both laws through the decade.[56] Triangulating the data reported by dozens of government agencies, the Procuracy, a leading think-tank, and a business association, this report constitutes a comprehensive analysis of principal-agent problems of the modern Russian state. At stake are the 1.2 million business inspections conducted in Russia every year[57] by federal agencies charged with consumer protection, safety standards, employment, and so forth; since such agencies often have the power to halt the operations of a given business, shut it down entirely, or exact massive fines, any illegitimate use of their powers undermines the security of ownership.

The MEDT report delivers a scathing assessment of the implementation of the original law in 2002–7 outlining "severe violations of the requirements of Law Nr 134 ... by state organs without any real accountability for such violations" (p. 5). Among the reasons for rampant predation by bureaucrats, the Ministry lists "general ineffectiveness of the existing system of state control (monitoring)," and the "non-implementation of the Law Nr 134 by discrete federal organs of the executive (for example, the Ministry of Internal Affairs)." (p. 4). The analysis of the implementation of the law's reformed version in 2009–10 leads to the same conclusions. A radical innovation in the new law, for example, requires a case-by-case permit for the "unscheduled visit-based" inspections[58] that proved to be particularly conducive to predation in the past; state agencies must now apply to the Procuracy for a permit, based on explicitly regulated reasons, before carrying out such an inspection. (The Procuracy has, in fact, declined 47 percent of received applications for such inspections [p. 24], suggesting that the process is not pro forma and that the state principal is exerting an effort to control his agents.) Yet federal agents had obtained the Procuracy's permit in only 3.8 percent of relevant inspections that took place during the examined period, inspecting businesses *unlawfully* in the rest of the cases. So far, the MEDT report underscores (a) the persistence of principal-agent problems through a decade of administrative reforms and (b) the ubiquitous character of such problems across the territory of the Russian Federation.[59]

The report also suggests that *differences in the state agencies' predation potential may be driving the interagency variation in the agents' resistance to the state principal.* The leading agency in the percentage of unscheduled

[56] MEDT 2010.

[57] Ibid., 10. Based on 2009–10 data.

[58] Russian law differentiates state inspections along two dimensions: scheduled vs. unscheduled and visit-based vs. document-based. The first dimension separates regularly conducted inspections (e.g., once a year), expected by businesses, from unannounced ones: 54 percent of all inspections of small and medium-size enterprises are currently "unscheduled." Ibid., 16.

[59] The agencies in question, while present on the ground throughout the country, are directly subordinated to the *federal*, not local, state departments.

Agent Predation beyond "Corruption"

inspections (from the total number of inspections conducted) is the Federal Anti-Monopoly Service, which conducts 76 percent of its inspections outside of a regular schedule and whose jurisdiction includes monitoring such lucrative spheres as foreign investment, state procurement, and competition in goods and financial markets (p. 16). Similarly, the Federal Service of State Registration (Rosreestr) ranks first in the proportion of applications for inspections declined by the Procuracy (78 percent) as lacking legal basis (p. 25); Rosreestr registers property rights to real estate and pertaining transactions and made headlines in 2010 for pervasive (by Russian standards) predation.[60] By contrast, the Federal Migration Service featured the lowest percentage of declined applications for inspections (28 percent); not coincidentally, its mandate is primarily oriented toward individual citizens, offering little scope for predation on enterprises.

As in Ukraine, the connection between unstable, complex regulations and the potential for biased, selective enforcement was prominent in Russia through the 2000s. According to Andrei Yakovlev, an expert on state-business relations at Moscow's Higher School of Economics:

> By the summer of 2004 the political pendulum made a full swing to absolute dominance of the state over business.... This dominance is held by the means of *keeping "the rules of the game" obscure*, mainly in such fields as tax legislation and privatization laws. This kind of *"game around the rules" is widely played at lower levels of administrative hierarchy* ... within the scope of competence of ... agencies ... acting on behalf of the state.[61]

A different expert from the Russian Academy of Sciences observed that nothing has changed by 2012: "Juridicial simulation ... is explained by the fact that state representatives do not grasp the substance of law at all. For them, law serves to provide for their own security, or to expropriate the property of others [*iz"iatiia chuzhoi sobstvennosti*]. In principle, law for them is inextricable from the idea of self-interest."[62]

Russia and Ukraine Compared

The Russian business owners interviewed by the author sounded just like their Ukrainian counterparts when it came to bureaucratic extortion and intervention. Illegal administrative barriers to obtaining licenses and operating permissions provoked particular outrage. The owner of a wood processing plant in Siberia noted that "they won't [openly] deny you [your rights], but *your documents may languish somewhere for months or years....* You need a pusher [*tolkach*].... So you take your purse and go. Not because you need anything illegal but because you need it done ... so you must share. Earlier, this could

---

[60] *Izvestiya* April 27, 2010.
[61] Yakovlev 2005, 25 (emphasis added).
[62] *Novaya Gazeta* February 1, 2012.

be settled with a bottle of cognac; today it's about figures" (emphasis added). While the quote describes corruption, its impact clearly transcends income rights: A forced delay in business operations "for months or years" fundamentally undermines ownership rights as such. Operating a typical mid-size plant also requires the ownership or long-term lease of land, which keeps many business owners hostage to local bureaucracies. Referring to the speculation on agricultural and urban land, the owner of a resort complex in southern Russia put it this way: "It's a gold rush.... People try to grab land while they can, [but] this business is in bureaucrats' hands.... *You can attach state officials' names to all the best land plots.* To get land legally, you must traverse the illegal terrain spending a fortune on the poor, destitute, needy bureaucrats, to support their family budgets."

The discussion so far has stressed parallels between Russia and Ukraine. However, there were also some differences between the two economies regarding state interference with ownership rights. My qualitative interview sample contains fourteen businesspeople with extensive business experience in both countries. According to this subsample, *smaller* enterprises were somewhat better protected in Russia, while *larger* firms as well as fully foreign-owned subsidiaries of *multinational corporations* enjoyed more secure PR in Ukraine. A Ukrainian producer of communications equipment employing nineteen people remarked,

I have to say, compared to Russia's FSB, SBU [a security service of Ukraine combining FBI-like and CIA-like mandates] is really on the loose here. Most FSB officers have higher education: they will not break the law if they can help it. And here? Well, in our fine town, SBU personnel are the graduates of the agricultural community college. So what can they do with that education, except for "let's eavesdrop on Sidorov, and see how much money he makes, maybe he can pay up."

Other entrepreneurs with experience in both countries emphasized a provision in Russia's law Nr. 134 that affords new small businesses a breathing space of three years before they can become the subject of inspections as advantageous relative to Ukraine. This contrasts sharply with feedback from big business. A CEO at a large beer company with plants across Ukraine and Russia said,

In 2001, I had the impression that Ukraine was underdeveloped Russia; corruption in Ukraine was much worse. Now [in 2006], the reverse is true. There is more freedom of speech in Ukraine. The country still has idiotic laws, but at least the possibility of a boundless dictate of [political] power over business is gone. Totally "anti-business" decisions [by state elites] are impossible in Ukraine but not in Russia. They [Russian authorities] also have lots of leeway because of the stabilization fund [that accumulates oil revenues]; Ukraine, luckily, does not have such luxury.

The owner of a large, diversified business in central Ukraine downplayed the threat of state inspections, saying: "Inspections are not excessive at all. [State agents] certainly are shaking down small businesses; but I have grown out of these diapers.... I'm on a ship now, not an inflatable boat." In Russia,

Private Threats 73

conversely, even ships seemed exposed to the waves of predation. Not only my interviews but also available survey data reflect the differences in state threats related to firm size between the two countries.[63]

PRIVATE THREATS

Of course, threats to a firm's property rights stem not only from state actors, and, in fact, *private* rackets exploded in post-1991 Russia and Ukraine. In the 1990s, the withdrawal of the state from law enforcement (partly as a result of the neoliberal ideology of reformers in the Russian case, but mostly because of a deep fiscal crisis in both countries) led to an explosion of primitive theft as well as organized protection rackets. The number of criminal groups active in Russia grew from 50 to 14,000 between 1988 and 1995; in Ukraine, the year 1995 saw the most crimes committed in the 1991–2012 period (based on Derzhkomstat data), which, according to veteran police members, was largely connected to protection rackets.[64] In my own experience, it was not unusual in Ukraine and Russia to see burned-down buildings in the bustling commercial districts and in town markets; protection rackets used arson as a payment reminder to particularly forgetful clients. In one of my interviews, Gregorii, a successful internet entrepreneur from St. Petersburg told me that one evening, after he started openly advertising his business in 1998, the bell rang in his luxury apartment on Nevskii Prospekt. He opened the door to see a group of thugs with iron bars – "all they said was that in five minutes I would be a cripple." (It did not come to that, but Gregorii's apartment was emptied of its valuables and equipment, and his garage of its BMW.) Given the comparatively low levels[65] of crime in the Soviet Union, the Hobbesian atmosphere of the 1990s felt surreal: One cab driver in Ukraine in 1996 spontaneously boasted

[63] Panel data from three BEEP surveys in the 2000s show that in Ukraine, firms employing up to nineteen people paid 2.6 percent of total annual sales in bribes to state officials, while firms employing at least 100 people paid only 1.5 percent. In Russia, this relationship was reversed with the smaller group paying 1.7 percent and the larger group paying 2.0 percent. (Thresholds of 19 and 100 employees are based on BEEPS coding for "small" and "large" enterprises.) Furthermore, my own survey is skewed toward large firms (median size of firms in the sample: 400 employees) and shows that most state threats are significantly higher in the Russian Federation than in Ukraine: see Table 3.1 in text. The BEEPS data is more representative of small and medium-size firms (median size of firms in the sample: twenty-five employees) and presents a more balanced picture. According to three rounds of BEEPS, (a) the threats stemming from "business inspections" or administrative barriers to "licensing and permits" are statistically indistinguishable in Russia and Ukraine; (b) the threat stemming from "tax administration" is higher in Russia (significant at the 0.1 level); (c) the threat of "corruption" is higher in Ukraine (significant at the 0.01 level).

[64] Gilinsky 1996, 77; *Segodnya* June 11, 2012.

[65] According to official statistics, crime accelerated rapidly during perestroika (since reporting procedures on crime did not change, this cannot be accounted for by greater openness). While the number of registered crimes increased by 30 percent in the 1985–90 period, the number of unsolved crimes rose by 65 percent. Smirnov 1995.

74   *Not Too Petty*

to me that his friend "just *stole* an awesome foreign car." (Were congratulations in order? I just mumbled in response.) Overall, the 1990s were an era during which the number of property owners skyrocketed while the state's monopoly on the use of force temporarily collapsed. As Gambetta notes, comparing nineteenth century Sicily to the post-Soviet space, "the consequence [was] ... a phenomenal increase in the fear of losing property and of being cheated"[66] – a fear that was profoundly justified.

According to my interviews in both countries, however, the threat of relatively primitive violence-supported extortion by thugs unaffiliated with the state is a thing of the past. The last cases of car explosions, shops burned to the ground, and similar disciplinary measures for non-payments are reported to have taken place in 2000. Most racketeers have transformed themselves into legitimate and largely successful businesspeople (subject to survivorship bias, literally). Interestingly, their prior connections in criminal circles serve them well in the brave new world as some of their former "colleagues" have moved into positions of power, while others have become trusted business partners, suppliers, or clients. According to Viktor, a former extortionist (he prefers the euphemism of "nimble guy" [*shustryi paren'*]) from central Russia, who has meanwhile committed to religion and established himself in the real estate business: "My previous buddies have chosen different paths, but there is still respect.... Not everybody can be a deputy. But some of the people are now in power who used to be very far from it." Unlike some other interviewed ex-gangsters who downplayed their employment histories as "indiscretions of youth," Viktor contemplated the wild 1990s with what may count as professional pride:

In the 1990s, people who came to you were very qualified [*ochen' gramotnye*]; they were economists. They didn't just randomly charge you a fee, they calculated how much you make first.... And they very really solved your problems. Nobody could touch you: not the fire inspection, not police ... if you had any problems with bureaucrats, they could solve them. It doesn't matter what kind of pressure they [racketeers] applied [on state organs], let us not get into that now.... The real mayhem [*bespredel*] came from the police personnel, those were the real bandits.... Anyway, the private defense from state officials is gone now. You don't have to pay anybody [in the private racket] now. But what existed before was economically justified.... Now it's just a trough [*kormushka*] for state folks.

Two caveats must be made regarding the relative insignificance of private threats versus state threats. First, such insignificance relates to *purely* private threats such as rackets, not to hybrid threats, whereby private entities collude with state actors to target rivals' businesses. Second, among the purely private threats, it is the *external* threats from aggressors unaffiliated with the firm that are, indeed, low. However, the *internal* threats arising from incumbent

---

[66] Gambetta 1996, 252.

management or partial owners remain serious; such internal private threats can manifest themselves as asset theft or the provision of assistance to outside raiders. According to the Economic Crime Surveys conducted in 2009 and 2011 by PricewaterhouseCoopers, internal asset theft was perceived to be as serious as external bribe requests in Russia and Ukraine: 60 percent of respondents identified both of these threats as "very important," ranking them above cyber-crime, manipulation of accounting, unfair competitive practices, and violations of intellectual property rights.[67] PwC identifies mid-level management as the most typical perpetrator of asset theft in Russia and Ukraine. Furthermore, in Russia, the 2009–11 trend involved an increase in internal private threats both in absolute terms and relative to perceived external corruption (as a threat), according to PwC.

SURVEY EVIDENCE: AGENT PREDATION OR SIPHONING?

The qualitative evidence on state threats suggests that not only people with guns, such as law enforcement agents, but also the bureaucrats working for various regulatory and taxation agencies threaten ownership rights either by engaging in full-scale annexation or in more subtle ways. (Nota bene, even in the case of raiding, the relative role of "unarmed bureaucrats" appears to be more important than that of the police or the security services.[68]) But how serious are the different types of infringements on ownership rights relative to each other, and relative to the infringements on income rights?

Income Threats and Ownership Threats Compared

To untangle the web of state threats to income and ownership rights, I designed a survey, which was implemented in Russia and Ukraine between February and May 2007. The survey fielded questions on the extent of specific types of PR infringements. Informal interviews throughout the region helped establish a list of typical PR infringements. The entrepreneurs evaluated the seriousness of each infringement for their business on a 1–4 Likert scale: 1 means "no threat at all"; 4 means "very high threat". Table 3.1 presents threat intensities for nine types of *state* threats to PR in Russia and Ukraine. (Additional questions probed the intensities of purely private non-state threats.) Among these nine state threats, the general "administrative pressure for informal

---

[67] PricewaterhouseCoopers 2009; PricewaterhouseCoopers 2012.
[68] On the eve of the 2009 anti-raiding legislative reform in Russia, a detailed analysis was prepared by a dozen of governmental, commercial, and academic organizations. The document analyzes twenty-two articles of the Russian criminal code that can be violated by state agents engaged in raiding; of these, eight articles are typically violated by law enforcers (articles 137, 163, 179, 183, 330, 294, 303, 327), while fourteen articles are more often violated by mere pen-pushers (articles 138, 159, 170, 195, 196, 197, 199, 201, 285, 286, 291, 290, 292, 293). Krasnov et al. 2009.

76 — Not Too Petty

TABLE 3.1. *Average State Threats on a 1–4 Scale*

Russia	Threat (Type)	Ukraine
2.92	Extortion by taxation agencies (income or ownership)	2.75
2.80	Illegal inspections by regulatory agencies (ownership)	2.29
2.72	Illegal administrative barriers to obtaining licenses, operating permits, etc. (ownership)	2.06
2.47	Illegal administrative barriers to purchase or sale of land, real estate, assets, etc. (ownership)	2.23
2.51	Hostile use of state resources by competitors (ownership)	1.52
2.39	Raiding, illegal ownership capture (ownership)	1.73
2.13	Administrative pressure for financial contributions to various social funds (income or ownership)	2.33
2.04	Administrative pressure for informal payments (income)	1.86
1.63	Illegal administrative interference with hiring or firing of labor, including top management (ownership)	1.48
2.40	AVERAGE	2.03

Based on a 2007 survey of 516 firms in Russia and Ukraine. The seriousness of a given threat was reported on a 1–4 scale from least to most serious. Numbers show averages for all firms in a given country. Threats are listed in the decreasing order of pooled averages across both countries.

payments" represents the threat to entrepreneurs' *income* rights. Two more specific types of bribe threats – namely "extortion by taxation agencies" and "administrative pressure for financial contributions to various social funds" – may target income *and/or* ownership rights.[69] The remaining six threats target *ownership* rights, covering raiding, illegal inspections, administrative barriers

---

[69] The reason why pressure for bribes from taxation agencies and social funds may jeopardize *ownership* rights is that these agencies are both high-powered and most rapacious in terms of requested bribe amounts (as already argued, beyond a certain threshold, income threats jeopardize ownership per se). According to the president of Ukraine's Association of Business Incubators and Innovation Centers, "[social] funds in the regions can inflict anything they want upon enterprises [*tvoriat s predpriiatiiami chto khotiat*]: They launch investigations and lawsuits, they demand arbitrary penalties.... Regional authorities dictate to entrepreneurs that unless they pay up into the social funds, their [entrepreneurs'] problems will not be resolved." (author's interview, Kyiv, February 14, 2007).

Survey Evidence: Agent Predation or Siphoning?

to assets' transfer or use, illegal interference with labor practices, and illegal administrative support of business competitors.

A comparison of threat types reveals that ownership threats are at least as intense as income threats. The classification of threats from taxation agencies and social funds as either "income" or "ownership" determines whether average income threats are higher or lower than average ownership threats (since the threat from taxation agencies is the single most intense threat overall).[70] For a cleaner comparison, let us leave these two threats aside and consider how the "pure" income threat ("administrative pressure for informal payments") relates to the average of six "pure" ownership threats. At the pooled level, the average state threat to ownership rights (2.33) is higher than the state threat to income rights (1.98), a difference that is statistically significant at the 0.01 level. The significance of this difference derives from the Russian subset (where threats to ownership and income measure 2.39 and 2.04 respectively); in Ukraine, the two types of threats are not significantly different (measuring 1.89 and 1.86 for ownership and income). Figure 3.2 summarizes these differences and also includes threats from *private* rackets for comparison. As indicated by the figure, extortion by rackets is significantly lower than state threats to either income or ownership; this holds for both Russia and Ukraine.

The inference of relatively severe threats to ownership, as compared to income, is further supported by additional questions from the Ukrainian part of the survey.[71] In particular, when respondents were asked to select one threat as "the single biggest obstacle to your business," 11 percent of firms identified *raiding* as the biggest obstacle; only extortion by taxation agencies was identified by a higher share of respondents (44 percent) as the most harmful.[72] Meanwhile, not a single firm out of 120 in the Ukrainian subsample considered "administrative pressure for informal payments" to be their #1 concern.

Could it be that the state threats to ownership and income, while conceptually separate, are empirically indistinguishable? To address this, I examine the "high-threat firms," that is, companies that gauge the state threats to be high or very high (3 or 4 on the 1–4 scale). If the categories of ownership and income threats are a figment of PR theorists' imaginations, then companies facing high threats to ownership should look very similar to firms facing high threats to income. However, the data suggests that the two subsets of high-threat firms

---

[70] If threats from taxation agencies and social funds are classified as "income," then the average of all income threats is 2.41 as compared to the average of 2.33 for all ownership threats. Conversely, if threats from taxation agencies and social funds are classified as "ownership," then one remaining income threat measures 1.98 as compared to the average of 2.39 for all ownership threats. (In both classification cases, the differences between ownership and income threats are significant at the 0.01 level.)

[71] While the questionnaires for Russia and Ukraine were largely identical, some questions were fielded in one country only.

[72] Raiding was followed by pressure to contribute to social funds (8 percent), as well as illegal state inspections (7 percent) and barriers connected to licenses and permits (7 percent) as threats selected by the highest percentage of respondents.

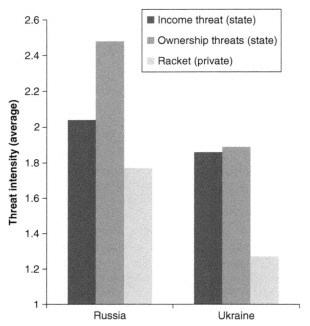

FIGURE 3.2. State and private threats to property rights on a 1–4 Scale. (*Source*: Markus, 2007. N=516.)

are very different. First, firms facing high threats to ownership are significantly smaller in terms of employed labor (by 19 percent) than companies facing high threats to income. Second, firms experiencing high threats to ownership are significantly more likely (by 83 percent) to have highly fixed assets – as proxied by metallurgy, construction, and chemical sectors – than companies facing high income threats. Third, companies facing high ownership threats are significantly less likely (by 71 percent) to find themselves in regions where the public regards substantial private wealth favorably, as compared to firms dealing with high income threats.[73] Theoretically, such stark differences only make sense if threats to income and ownership capture distinct, if interrelated, phenomena. Bureaucrats may find it easier to threaten firms' ownership – as opposed to just income streams – when the company is smaller (less repercussions from disgruntled or fired labor); when it is hostage to immovable assets (less danger of the firm relocating from the region); or when the firm is surrounded by a citizenry that perceives wealthy business owners as fat cats (less public outrage

---

[73] The survey question inquired whether the firm owner believes that the public in his region (1) approves of successful and wealthy entrepreneurs, (2) sees them as role models, (3) regards them with envy, or (4) considers them a symbol of injustice. The constructed dummy for *Legitimacy* equals 1 if the firm chose options (1) or (2).

Survey Evidence: Agent Predation or Siphoning?

over expropriations). Naturally, these associations need not imply causation (Chapter 6 explores the determinants of threat intensity). Our more limited goal here is to confirm that threats to income and ownership do differ in theoretically meaningful ways.

Impact of Distinct Threat Types

Even if threats to ownership are distinct in terms of their substance, and relatively serious in terms of their intensity when compared with income threats, ownership threats need not necessarily have a more *deleterious* impact on the firm. Consider, for example, what a high-ranking (and highly frank) officer at Ukraine's Ministry of Internal Affairs shared in one of my interviews:

> Look, there are two types of state officials in Ukraine: thieves and grafters [*vory i vziatochniki*]. I am a thief. A long time ago, I stole from a [state] tender – [with that money,] I built a business for my wife, but now I don't reach for the pot anymore. But ninety percent of officials are grafters, and they are the most horrible, because they are like drug addicts on bribes.

In other words, to the extent outright annexation constitutes a one-shot transfer of ownership, it may establish better long-run incentives than the opportunity for the ongoing embezzlement of legitimate income streams.[74] While intriguing, this hypothesis is not supported by the survey data.

My survey measured deleterious impact in two ways. First, the companies were asked: "Considering all risks connected to your production, what should be the minimal annual rate of profit from additional investments into your business for these investments to make sense?" This question taps into the fundamental link between risks and profits: firms faced with higher risks – including income and ownership threats from state actors – will demand higher profit rates in order to invest. Our question is whether firms exposed to ownership threats would demand higher compensation as compared with firms exposed to income threats. It turns out they do.[75] The rate of compensation demanded by firms faced with high income threats (as compared with low income threats) is 1.4 percent. The rate of compensation demanded by firms faced with high ownership threats (as compared with low ownership threats) is 5.8 percent. Ownership threats inflict substantially more pain on firms – a difference of more than 4 percent of *expected profits* – as compared to income threats.

---

[74] This must be differentiated from a similar argument used by the early proponents of privatization, namely that even if semilegal, privatization would establish proper long-term incentives for the new owners. The point here is not to compare asset allocations (state vs. private) but threat types (ownership vs. income).

[75] The average compensation required across the whole sample is 26.4 percent; the variable ranges from 3 percent to 101 percent. The analysis proceeds by separating firms into low/high subsets based on the intensity of perceived threats to income and ownership respectively. (Low/high separation is at the midpoint of the threat intensity scale for the respective threat measures.)

The "pain" that state threats inflict on firms, however, is not limited to foregone profits. Theoretical work has identified the *predictability of future state interference* as a separate channel through which PR regimes affect the firms' operations.[76] The firms' ability to predict the level of state threats in the future, whether such a predicted *level* is high or low, should allow company owners to plan their business development accordingly. But how do *current* state threats affect the predictability of future state threats? Furthermore, do current state threats to income rights affect the predictability of future state interference more or less than current state threats to ownership rights?

Empirically, these relationships have not been tested to date. The reason for this omission is the literature's focus on *institutionalized* predictability, as proxied by policy volatility or various government-restraining commitment devices. Conversely, the predictability of state interference *as it is subjectively perceived by asset owners* has been understudied, although it presents a critical causal link between state institutions and firm behavior.

To fill this gap, my survey instrument featured this question: "For the next year, how predictable is the level of state interference with the right of the owners to manage your enterprise and receive legal income from it?" This is the second way in which the deleterious impact of state activity on firms' property rights was measured. The dependent variable, *ThreatPredictability*, is ordinal and ranges from 1 ("completely unpredictable") to 4 ("completely predictable"). (For the summary statistics on all variables used in regressions, please see Table 2.1 in the methodological appendix.)

Table 3.2 presents the results of an ordered probit regression with robust standard errors. The main independent variables include measures of current threats to ownership and income. *OwnershipThreat* is an average of six ordinal variables capturing diverse threats to a firm's ownership rights, as specified in Table 3.1 (threat type: "ownership" only). *IncomeThreat* is an ordinal variable measuring "administrative pressure for informal payments."

I also include controls that may impact the predictability of state threats, as well as current threats, according to the literature. These controls include a dummy for a firm's membership in a business association (*BusinessAssociation*); a firm's estimate of the legal system's effectiveness in protecting contracts with private counterparties (*ContractSecurity*); a dummy for de novo, that is, non-privatized firms (*NonPrivatized*), as well as additional dummies for size categories, sector, ownership structure, and region.

The main result is this: Current state threats to ownership drastically decrease the predictability of future state interference, while threats to income do not. Ownership threats inflict more harm on businesses than do income threats by subverting future-oriented planning. While the *OwnershipThreat* coefficient is negative and highly significant, *IncomeThreat* is positive and insignificant. In substantive terms, the *OwnershipThreat* coefficient implies that when a firm

---

[76] Weimer, 7–8.

Survey Evidence: Agent Predation or Siphoning?

TABLE 3.2. *Effect of Ownership and Income Threats on Predictability of Future State Threats*

Threat	Predictability
OwnershipThreat	−0.48*** (0.16)
IncomeThreat	0.13 (0.13)
BusinessAssociation	0.28* (0.16)
ContractSecurity	0.30*** (0.07)
NonPrivatized	0.04 (0.20)
SizeMedium	0.35 (0.24)
SizeLarge	0.32 (0.23)
N	258
$P > \chi^2$	0.000
Pseudo R^2	0.12
Dummy Variables	Sector
	Ownership
	Region

* $p < 0.10$, ** $p < 0.05$, *** $p < 0.01$. Ordered probit model with robust standard errors (in parentheses). The dependent variable is respondents' estimate of how predictable state threats are "for the next year" on a 1–4 scale.

perceives a relatively modest hike in its *current* ownership threats from level 2 to level 3, the probability that the firm will consider state interference *in the future* as "predictable" or "completely predictable" decreases by 18 percent.[77] For the maximum possible hike in the current level of ownership threat (from level 1 to level 4), this probability drops by 44 percent.

Membership in a business association improves the perceived predictability of state interference (significant at the 0.1 level), which may be due to better communication channels with the state, allowing member firms to estimate future interference. More interestingly, the perceived effectiveness of the legal system to protect contracts also has a positive effect (significant at the 0.01 level and substantively larger than the effect of association membership): Companies experiencing the effectiveness of the legal system in resolving *private* disputes may be projecting such competence onto the state writ large in matters concerning the *state's* future interference with property rights.[78] Finally, the firm's privatization history or size have no impact on the perceived predictability of state interference.

[77] Stata's Clarify package is used for the simulation of first differences to translate ordered probit coefficients into substantive quantities of interest. All control variables are held at their median values in the simulation.

[78] Theoretically, this finding belies the stark contrast drawn in the literature between the security of property rights and contractual rights. See Acemoglu and Johnson; Frye.

The survey evidence presented so far underscores that (a) state threats to ownership and income are distinct empirical phenomena, (b) the level of ownership threats is at least as high as that of income threats, and (c) threats to ownership harm companies more than do threats to income.

Dynamic Trends and the Broader Postcommunist Region

The cross-sectional data discussed earlier cannot illuminate dynamic trends. For that purpose, I use the data from the BEEP Survey implemented by the World Bank and the EBRD over three rounds in 2002, 2005, and 2008/9.[79] (For Russia and Ukraine, N = 4,271.) While the BEEPS instrument works magic for broad comparisons, it has important shortcomings for examining threats to ownership and income rights in Russia and Ukraine.[80] Still, in the absence of more granular longitudinal data, BEEPS serves several purposes by providing a robustness check for the data presented so far, establishing a time trend, and verifying the extent to which Russia and Ukraine are representative of the wider postcommunist region. Three insights emerge.

First, the BEEPS data verifies that ownership threats stemming from the bureaucrats on the ground are as serious as income threats. Consider the BEEPS questions about "obstacles to the current operations" of the firm, whose seriousness the respondents evaluated on a 0–4 scale.[81] Among the obstacles listed, "corruption" most closely represents threats to income, while "business inspections," "tax administration," and "licensing and permits" most closely represent threats to ownership. The differences between the first three threats are statistically insignificant; across 2002–9, firms in Russia and Ukraine estimated the severity of corruption as an obstacle at 1.95 on a 0–4 scale, exactly the same level as that of tax administration; the severity of inspections as an obstacle was slightly lower at 1.81. Obstacles related to licensing and permits measured 1.51 and were significantly (at the 0.01 level) lower than those related to corruption.

Note, however, that "corruption" may impact both income *and* ownership threats, depending on the volume of bribes siphoned off by the bureaucrats; as argued previously, beyond a certain threshold the volume of informal payments

---

[79] The last round of the decade was implemented in 2008 in Ukraine and in 2009 in Russia; other rounds were implemented in 2002 and 2005 in both countries.

[80] BEEPS omits some of the key threats to ownership rights in these countries, including raiding, hostile use of state resources by competitors, as well as administrative barriers to transactions involving real estate, land, and machinery (BEEPS's far narrower question is about "access to land" and "zoning"). Very few questions allow a direct comparison between income threats and ownership threats. Furthermore, in some years, the BEEPS instrument used the actual term "property rights," which is too vague to be interpreted consistently across the respondents (see the discussion of methodology in Chapter 1).

[81] Earlier rounds of BEEPS used a 0–3 scale. For the entire analysis here, variables were rescaled across survey rounds to 0–4 when necessary for consistency.

Survey Evidence: Agent Predation or Siphoning?

requested by bureaucrats may simply bankrupt an enterprise. The BEEP survey helpfully allows us to *distinguish* between corruption as an income threat and corruption as a threat to ownership by asking the enterprises to estimate the volume of corruption as a "percent of total annual sales paid in informal payments." My own interviews suggest that when such volume approaches the 5 percent mark, ownership rights are inevitably jeopardized.[82] Across 2002–9, the volume of bribes as reported by Russian and Ukrainian firms averages at 2 percent of annual sales, with a range of 0–60 percent. In line with qualitative evidence,[83] this data shows that some firms are regularly pushed to the brink of extinction by bureaucratic greed, but how many? Out of 2,414 firms responding to this question across three survey rounds, a sobering 17 percent (or 411 firms) report bribe volumes equal or above 5 percent of annual sales. In other words, for more than one in six firms, "corruption" means a fundamental threat to ownership rights rather than an income-related nuisance. Incorrectly judging the level of income threats by identifying them with "corruption" overestimates income threats and underestimates ownership threats. Further strengthening the inference of serious ownership threats from the bureaucrats is the BEEPS question on the single "most serious obstacle affecting the operation of this establishment" (only available for the 2008/9 round); while 9 percent of firms in Russia and Ukraine selected "corruption," 16 percent of companies considered "political instability" to be the single most pressing concern. Across all fifteen options respondents could choose, "political instability" was the third most frequently selected one, while "corruption" ranked fourth.[84] To the extent political instability affects firms' operations through ownership rights, as per the literature,[85] the level of ownership threats appears to be at least as serious as that of income threats.

Second, through the 2000s, there was no appreciable improvement, from the firms' perspective, in the level of income and ownership threats, and in some cases the severity of these threats worsened. Figure 3.3 captures the main time trends.[86] From 2002 to 2009, licensing and permits as an obstacle

---

[82] Assuming a 10 percent rate of profitability and a 30 percent effective tax rate, more than *two thirds* of post-tax profits are lost to bribery at this threshold. (Bribes are typically paid out of retained profits.)

[83] According to Dmytro Oliinyk, the deputy chair of Ukraine's Federation Council of Employers, "depending on its type of activity, business in recent years was forced to surrender up to 50% of its revenues as bribes ... entrepreneurs are often singled out as targets for extortion by the bureaucrats." *Ukrains'ka Pravda* February 26, 2014. The Federation Council's experts estimated in 2014 that "at the very least HR 160 billion [$19.2 billion] has been channeled annually from the legal turnover into the bureaucrats' pockets." Ibid.

[84] "Tax rates" and "access to finance" ranked first and second respectively. Most options did not focus on income or ownership threats addressing instead logistical problems connected to infrastructure, human capital, etc.

[85] E.g., Svensson 1998.

[86] The question on "business inspections" was included only in the 2008/9 round of BEEPS and is not in the figure.

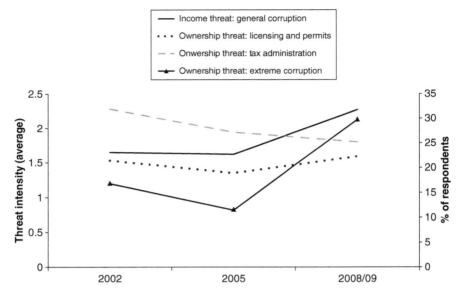

FIGURE 3.3. State threats to property rights in Russia and Ukraine, 2002–9. (*Source*: BEEP Surveys, World Bank; author's calculations. N=4,171.)

remained virtually unchanged, while corruption as an obstacle became much more severe (an increase from 1.7 to 2.3 on a 0–4 scale). As a percentage of annual sales, the volume of corruption more than doubled, rising from 1.8 percent in 2002 to 4.1 percent in 2008/9. The same is true for the share of firms exposed to ownership-threatening corruption; in 2002, 16.9 percent of firms spent at least 5 percent of their annual sales lining the bureaucrats' coffers; in 2005, this share dropped to 11.6 percent; in 2008/9, however, it skyrocketed to 29.8 percent. More promisingly, interference stemming from tax agencies has decreased during the decade, from 2.3 to 1.8 (0–4 scale). At the same time, however, the *frequency* with which "unofficial payments or gifts" were used by firms "to deal with tax collection" did *not* change[87]: presumably, the perceived alleviation of threats stemming from tax collectors captured the *lower volume* of bribes demanded by these particular state agents. The more general trend across state agencies beyond tax collectors, however, was the opposite: a much higher volume of bribes (as indicated by the percentage of sales) exacted at a

---

[87] On a 1–6 scale, this frequency was 2.2 in 2002 and 2.1 in 2008/9 when averaged across both countries.

Survey Evidence: Agent Predation or Siphoning?

somewhat lower frequency.[88] The bottom-line? Russia and Ukraine remained a business-hostile environment through the 2000s, and firms operating in these economies were overall no better protected against state threats to income and ownership by the end of the decade than they had been at its outset.

Third, the numbers on Russia and Ukraine are only somewhat higher than regional averages, suggesting that this country dyad is not an outlier. The BEEPS data contains observations from twenty-eight postcommunist countries,[89] including fourteen post-Soviet states (all except Turkmenistan) and fourteen East European nations. Through the decade, all four relevant state threats mentioned earlier are somewhat higher in Russia and Ukraine than across the region; however, these differences are minor. Across the region, the averages for the perceived obstacles of corruption, inspections, tax administration, and licensing/permits are 1.65, 1.31, 1.82, and 1.29 respectively; across Russia and Ukraine, these averages are 1.95, 1.81, 1.95, and 1.51. The modest magnitude of differences (only in the case of inspections more than a third of one standard deviation) suggests that Russia and Ukraine are not outliers.

The data on corruption volume also shows a divergence: As a percentage of annual sales, bribery comprised only 1.5 percent across the region in the 2000s as compared to 2 percent across Russia and Ukraine. Once the time trend is taken into account, however, the gap not only disappears but is *reversed*; by 2008/9, corruption comprised 4.93 percent of annual sales across the region, compared to 4.11 percent across Russia and Ukraine. The same reversal holds for ownership-threatening corruption. Across the entire decade, the regional average of 13.8 percent – for firms whose corruption expenditures amount to at least 5 percent of annual sales – appears lower than 17 percent in Russia and Ukraine. However, this divergence derives from years 2002 and 2005; by 2008/9, the regional average was 37.2 percent, compared to "only" 29.8 percent in Russia and Ukraine. Overall, the intensity of state threats to ownership and income in Russia and Ukraine through the 2000s, while closer to the upper end of the spectrum, is still fairly representative of the postcommunist region.

---

[88] The general frequency with which "firms like you pay additional payments / informal gifts" to "officials," fell from 3.0 to 2.6 (on a 1–6 scale) between 2002 and 2008/9.

[89] The BEEPS also includes Turkey; for theoretical consistency, regional averages in this paragraph omit Turkey.

4

Mini-Beasts versus Sovereign

Ownership Threats beyond "The System"

Evidence presented so far suggests that state agents often threaten not only firms' income but also their very ownership. Yet even if the bureaucrats commonly thought of as mere grafters actually engage in raiding, bankruptcy-inducing extortion, or self-serving business shutdowns, *such predation may still be encouraged by the sovereign.*[1] If the ideal type of "agent predation" captures the ongoing messy conflicts over property rights, then the state agents should be able to threaten ownership without the blessing of the state principal.

In terms of the conceptual two-by-two matrix (Figure 2.1), we have so far distinguished agent predation from siphoning; this chapter will argue that agent predation also differs from principal expropriation. The argument is developed in three steps. First, I demonstrate how agent predation has undermined the *priorities* of the respective state principals in Russia and Ukraine, as they relate to military security, state budget, popular support, and so forth. Second, I detail *the efforts* that the state principals have undertaken to rein in agent predation, including administrative reforms in Russia and Ukraine as well as the comprehensive anti-raiding legislation in Russia. Third, I use my survey data to examine *blame attribution* for insecure PR and the *sub-national variation* in threat intensity, finding that firm owners often implicate the local state agents rather than the national government, and, more importantly, that the sub-national variation in state threats is more consistent with agent predation than with principal expropriation.

---

[1] As a reminder, the literature refers to "the sovereign" or the state principal in two related ways. First, the principal is "the ruler" in charge of the executive branch (e.g., the president, the chancellor, the prime minister, the dictator). Second, the principal is "the system" that is, the entire state machinery that follows a particular systemic logic (of tax or investment maximization, of geopolitical survival, etc.) The literature on the security of property rights uses these two ways of referring to the principal interchangeably, the assumption being that state machineries behave rationally as if they were directed by a rational individual.

86

Expert Opinion and Bureaucrat behavior

To be clear, principal expropriation, that is, predation designed or sanctioned by the respective countries' leaders, exists in both Russia and Ukraine. The argument here is *not* that the state principals are benevolent. Rather, I argue that the state principals in both countries *failed – miserably – to control or monopolize agent-driven predation* through the 2000s.

EXPERT OPINION AND BUREAUCRAT BEHAVIOR

The leaders of Russia and Ukraine failed to transform piranha capitalism into shark capitalism, in which principal expropriation would predominate. The experts from the region have recognized this point well. In 2002, Vladimir Pastukhov (a keen Russian political commentator, Oxford fellow, and advisor to the Constitutional Court) observed that in "attempting to solve the problems characteristic of a contemporary postindustrial society," Russia has been "relying on a bureaucratic machine of the preindustrial age ... irrational and not subject to genuine control ... the kind of machine ... with which the two great reformers – Peter the Great and Vladimir Lenin – were forced to put up."[2] In 2012, when Putin had long lost the cachet of a "reformer," Pastukhov admitted:

Putin ... was able to give back bureaucracy its power, but incapable of making it work in a methodical ... way. Moreover, he allowed bureaucracy to get even more out of hand than had Yeltsin, who knew how to keep his apparatus in check through fear. Russia's new bureaucracy ... attacked the country like a swarm of locusts ... Putin has brought a horde to power ... letting greedy ... bureaucrats run amok. The temporarily tamed external chaos ... [of] the "bad 1990's" was soon resurrected in the form of an outrageous mess in the state apparatus and uncontrolled bureaucratic lawlessness that spilled into the outside world. Putin brought the horse out of the stable but wasn't able to saddle it and let the unbroken horse gallop out into the world, crushing everyone in its way.[3]

With respect to raiding, the already quoted sociological study by a Russian think-tank concludes that the main problem is *disorganized predatory rivalry*:

What we have is a keen competition among various state departments [*vedomstvami*] and within discrete state departments: as a result, while one enforcement agency is combating raiding, another agency is, in fact, conducting it. It is simply a ... *struggle dictated by the desire to intercept loot* [*perekhvatit' dobychu*], not a struggle ... for the purpose of law enforcement.... The problem is that *the state does not exist*. It has been privatized by various bureaucrats, clans of bureaucrats ... who under the guise of national state structures pursue their own ... material interests.[4]

Russia's high-profile activists fighting corruption among the elites concur with this view. Asked whether Russians face a well-oiled predatory machine, Alexei

---

[2] Pastukhov 2002, 74.
[3] *Novaya Gazeta* 2012.
[4] CPT, 35–8, (emphasis added).

Navalny, a lawyer turned star corruption fighter, sharply observed in 2011 that "the people who work in business ... can tell you that *there's no machine at all. It's all a fiction*. That is, they [the central state] can destroy a single person, like Magnitsky or me or Khodorkovsky. But, *if they try to do anything systemically* against a huge number of people, *there's no machine. It's a ragtag group of crooks* unified under the portrait of Putin."[5] Consider feedback from Alexander Lebedev, the tycoon owner of Russia's opposition newspaper *Novaya Gazeta*, who has repeatedly embarrassed the top government cadres, including the FSB, by disclosing their wealth. Asked about his ongoing conflicts with certain Russian law enforcers who have raided his business, Lebedev says: "the hatred of power agencies towards me ... is mostly about my anti-corruption investigations of very specific affairs of specific people. *Their tales of "Putin ordered to tear apart this traitor* [i.e., Lebedev] *with his measly newspaper" are fabrications for the sake of convenience*."[6] Navalny and Lebedev's broad opposition to the Putin regime adds credibility to the activists' key point: Even much elite-level predation is a nonsystemic, disorganized phenomenon.

Predatory bureaucrats and law enforcement agents themselves are typically aware of the unsanctioned nature of their activities, suggesting that such predation cannot be properly conceptualized as "organized." The study of Russia's OMON by *Novoe Vremia* (introduced in the last chapter) offers three insights to support this. First, there is abundant evidence of lower OMON units executing "missions" that run counter to orders from above. For example, in 2009, the Cherkizovskii market made headlines for its unsanitary conditions, and the Moscow administration made a legal decision to shut it down; however, OMON was *hired privately to protect* the confiscated goods, which, instead of being destroyed as officially mandated, were safely transported to a supermarket for resale. OMON's commanders cashed in 100,000 rubles per container thus saved. This prompted a public outcry and a protest at the supermarket: OMON, again, was hired privately (by the supermarket administrators) to disperse the protesters. According to an OMON participant,

when we arrived, a guy dressed in civilian clothes came to us and said "I'm the head of security here [at the supermarket]. Guys, some local residents are now approaching to protest.... Your task: destroy the posters; don't touch women and children; as for men, drag them right onto our territory here." *No papers, no orders, no official instructions whatsoever....* Typically, when we are dispatched to a protest, we have a written [order] saying "Unsanctioned protest. So-and-so many people expected." (emphasis added)

Instead of dispersing the protesters, the lieutenant in charge of the dispatched OMON unit called local police and procuracy to verify the mission, unintendedly disclosing the predatory venture of his commander to other law enforcement agencies. Because of the intervention of these other agencies

---

[5] *The New Yorker* April 4, 2011, (emphasis added).
[6] Lebedev 2012, (emphasis added).

Sovereign Priorities and Agent Predation

on site, OMON fighters were promptly removed from the premises of the supermarket. The hapless lieutenant lost his job the next day. His commander's explanation for the dismissal? "You ruined such money, idiot."

Second, OMON commanders running predatory business ventures take *extensive precautions against potential discovery and sanctions from their own superiors.* For example, commanders sending OMON officers on a private mission make them sign a waiver stating that the officers were "warned about the inadmissibility of commercial activity." In addition to the waivers, officers sign an undated resignation form. These resignations are stored in the commander's safe: should OMON's moneymaking missions be exposed to the superiors, resignations can be dated retroactively, thus releasing the commanders from responsibility for the actions of the technically "former" OMON employees. Commanders sending their employees on predatory ventures have also stopped giving these employees service weapons (*tabel'noe oruzhie*), since any use of such weapons would have to be officially explained; employees are furthermore asked to change their telltale blue uniforms before going on such ventures.

Third, inquiries and punishments from superiors – including state principals – do occur, although clearly not to the extent that would be sufficient to root out OMON's moneymaking. Two weeks after the investigation by *Novoe Vremia* was published, President Medvedev fired the implicated OMON commanders.[7]

SOVEREIGN PRIORITIES AND AGENT PREDATION

The OMON case militates against the theoretical models of carefully controlled expropriation systems in which the state principal grants economic rents in exchange for political support. More generally, the hypothesis that the bulk of the ongoing predation in Russia and Ukraine represents such systemic collusion is questionable because agent predation undermines the top priorities of state principals. The argument in this section relies on a straightforward counterfactual: *If* predation *were* conducted mostly on behalf of the state leaders, it would not undermine their most fundamental interests.

Power Retention

The most basic priority of any sovereign is to attain or retain power. In semi-democracies and soft authoritarian regimes, such priority is often achieved through a combination of genuine popular approval as well as the leaders' capacity to manipulate elections through clientelistic arrangements or fraud. In

---

[7] The dismissals of seventeen high-ranking bureaucrats from the Ministry of Internal Affairs were outlined in an opposition (Kasparov) leader's online newspaper. Available at: http://www.kasparov.ru/material.php?id=4B7D57B31B85A

Russia and Ukraine, agent predation seems to have hurt *both* of these routes to leaders' power retention.

Regarding power retention through popular approval, predation by local state actors makes this priority more difficult to achieve by antagonizing *wide layers* of the population. My interviews suggest that the problem extends far beyond business owners.

In both Russia and Ukraine the elderly, for example, face the danger of having their apartments annexed by the "caretaker" state agents. The problem is particularly severe in large cities where real estate is expensive. The bureaucrats from the department of social welfare withhold assistance, including medical care, unless the elderly person in question bequeaths his apartment to the unscrupulous bureaucrat. In any country, there is fraud against the vulnerable. In the case of piranha capitalism, however, the vulnerable may easily constitute the majority, while the fraud is centered on property and perpetrated by low-level state agents – a dynamic that discredits the state principal.

Consider further a case from Ukraine involving the theft of public property by individual state actors. According to a former SBU employee interviewed by the author:

> If you drive through Ukrainian villages today, you sometimes hear "don't go there, it's the forest of deputy so and so." Villagers say that in all seriousness, because if they go there to pick mushrooms, for example, certain people in jeeps will arrive and throw them [the villagers] out or beat them up. But constitutionally, forests and other natural resources are the property of the Ukrainian people. In reality, that forest is leased by some "OOO Romashka" [i.e., obscure limited liability firm] which is registered in Cyprus, and is basically run as the private terrain of the [local council] deputy.... For the people, the perception is one of feudal private ownership by state employees.

SBU is well-positioned to comment on the phenomenon, considering the agency's involvement in the high-profile arrest of Viktor Lozinsky, the Rada deputy who shot dead a villager in 2009 on the territory of "Lozinsky's" forest. The press has uncovered Lozinsky's "active interference with the local self-governance" of the Golovanevsk county (in Kirovohrad oblast); according to investigative reports, Lozinsky was the "de facto owner [*khoziain*]" of the county through commercial intermediaries managing two collective farms as well as 3,900 hectares of forests.[8] Whether on the day of the killing Lozinsky and his assistants engaged in "human hunting" for recreation, as some reports suggested, is unclear. The clear point is this: Local predation by state agents discredits the sovereign in the eyes of the population. In 2004, Lozinsky was the county-level trustee (*doverennoe litso*) of Prime Minister Yanukovych when the latter ran for president in the run-up to the Orange Revolution. In 2007, Lozinsky jumped horses and joined BYuT, the party of Yanukovych's nemesis,

---

[8] Media references for the Lozinsky case include *Tema* June 26, 2009; *Ukraina-Centr* June 24, 2009; *Korrespondent* June 23, 2009.

Sovereign Priorities and Agent Predation

Yulia Tymoshenko. As the killing scandal erupted in 2009, both the president and the prime minister, despite their ongoing intra-executive feuding, resolutely disowned Lozinsky, forcing a detailed investigation into Lozinsky's business and property-related dealings and the lifting of Lozinsky's parliamentary immunity.[9] (In 2011, Lozinsky was sentenced to fifteen years in prison.) While extreme, Lozinsky's case distills a key theoretical point: For state principals who cannot ignore popular legitimacy in their power retention calculus, predatory state agents present a liability.

Indeed, even when popular legitimacy is *not* part of the calculus, as in the case of electoral manipulation by the state principal, agent predation can still upset the equation. Consider Russia's 2011 parliamentary elections. As the chairman of United Russia and the candidate in the upcoming presidential elections, Putin needed his party to win at all costs. The elections featured numerous well-documented violations, yet the Western verdict on the Russian elections missed the state principal's perspective. To the OSCE observers parachuted for several weeks to Russia, elections to the Duma "were marked by the convergence of the State and the governing party"[10]; unfortunately for Putin, however, that was far from the truth as a result of agent predation, which *dramatically reduced the effectiveness of electoral manipulation.* Consider the analysis by Valerii Morozov, a self-proclaimed watchdog with access to the Kremlin:

This was the most expensive and … least effective electoral campaign by the party of power in Russia's modern history. The supernatural ineffectiveness of our economy due to the uncontrolled theft of budgetary funds pales in comparison to the ineffectiveness of the political machine, above all the campaign headquarters of United Russia.… Before, Putin had a fear syndrome about unmanaged [*nepodkontrol'nye*] elections. Now, he has acquired a fear syndrome about the possibility of failure of managed elections. In all Russian electoral campaigns, kickbacks [*otkaty*] and the theft of funds allocated for the campaign have typically amounted to circa 50%. This time … the corruption component [*korruptsionnaia sostavliaiushchaia*] has reached the peak of what we see … in construction business and the equipment procurement for the office of Presidential Affairs Management, i.e. beyond 70%. Simultaneously, the same phenomenon happened which had occurred in the economy and state service: the most talented and independent [party cadres] were displaced by the loyal, at least superficially, who were ready to steal and to safeguard the stealing by other mediocrities. The mentality of a peculator [*kaznokrada*] represents … the mass of the ruling party.… The campaign headquarters fabricated reasons for the tremendous campaign expenditures [which were] funds stolen from the budget. Actual work was minimal, just enough to conceal theft.… They all relied on the administrative resource. [President] Medvedev's phrase on the day after elections – "but where is that resource?" – deserves its place in history.[11]

Resorting to the administrative resource on the day of elections, after millions of dollars in party funds were pocketed by the "superficially loyal," meant

---

[9] *Tema* 2009; *Ukrains'ka Pravda* July 3, 2009; *NEWSru* June 26, 2009.
[10] OSCE 2011, 1.
[11] Morozov 2011.

blunt fraud and the subjection of the sovereign to unwanted uncertainty. United Russia lost 15 percent of its vote share compared with the previous elections in 2007, while the runner-up Communist Party gained 8 percent. Yulia Latynina, a widely respected journalist, agrees. Commenting on the fate of Vladislav Surkov (a charismatic Kremlin puppeteer who for eleven years was to Putin what Machiavelli had been to the proverbial Prince), she described the aftermath of the 2011 anti-Putin protests:

All the while [through the 2000s] Surkov was provoking discontent among the public, nobody fired him. As soon as it turned out that Surkov cannot guarantee the "Party of crooks and thieves" [United Russia] a high result and that they could assemble a mere 5,000 people for the pro-Putin demonstration and not 25,000 as promised ... [because] *four fifths of the allocated funds were stolen* – that's when Surkov was kicked out.[12]

Social scientists may have been too rash in conceptualizing United Russia as a successful "commitment device" for managing the principal-agent problems between political elites and bureaucracy, as well as between the central and regional executives.[13] As for Surkov, his stepwise dismissal by the state principal traces closely the politically consequential cases of agent predation. After being fired from his position as the first deputy of the chief of presidential administration in 2011 (to which Latynina's quote refers), Surkov migrated to the post of the deputy prime minister in the cabinet. More than a year later, in May 2013, Surkov lost that position as well when Skolkovo, a high-profile innovation hub for which Surkov had become responsible, was caught in an embezzlement scandal.

Meanwhile, Ukraine's newly semi-authoritarian sovereign faced similar issues to his Russian counterpart. After Yanukovych's 2010 presidential comeback, elections to the Ukrainian Rada lost any remnants of the Orange democratic glow; many feared direct SBU involvement in the elections. Commenting on this danger, the outspoken Rada deputy from the opposition and former vice chair of the SBU himself, Gennadii Moskal', says:

In every opposition party, there are integrated [*vnedryonnye*] SBU agents.... We [in the opposition] know who all these [agents] are, but we do not expel them. We simply isolate them from any serious information. We do not fire them because at least we know them, and that's easier than trying to filter out new [SBU agents] later.... Our president has some memories of the KGB and by habit perceives SBU as an analog. But that's a myth. *If I were president, I would not entrust SBU anything.* Because the day after they open an ORD [acronym for "covert investigation"] on anybody, the target will know about it. *Because whoever sits in the same office as the initiator of the investigation will sell him [the target] this information....* I would not exaggerate their [SBU's] role in the electoral process. Whatever tasks they receive – they'll botch them.[14]

---

[12] Latynina on the radio program "Kod Dostupa" at Ekho Moskvy, December 31, 2011, (emphasis added). Transcript available at: http://echo.msk.ru/programs/code/844324-echo/

[13] Reuter and Remington.

[14] *ORD* September 7, 2012, (emphasis added).

Sovereign Priorities and Agent Predation

When the state cadres responsible for the sovereign's power preservation instead prioritize self-enrichment, predation does not sustain but undermines "the system." In his blog, Morozov brilliantly captures the crux of the issue: "The important part is that *the leader depends more on the hooligan group than the group depends on him.* He cannot toss or liquidate the group and replace them with others."[15]

Sovereign priorities, of course, extend beyond narrow power preservation. Military security and economic stability, if undermined beyond a certain threshold, will adversely affect the state principal. More idiosyncratically, state leaders often have personal pet projects they desire to see implemented. On all these fronts, agent predation has thwarted the sovereigns in Russia and Ukraine.

Military Security

Predation in the defense industry, for example, has sapped military security in both states. During the 2008 hearings at Russia's Civic Chamber, the FSB presented materials documenting ongoing raid attempts at 200 defense factories, including tank plants, rocket makers, and so on; according to the presenters, these conflicts "are no longer disputes between economic subjects but a real danger to national security."[16]

Consider the case of the state-owned Bazal't, a producer of bombs and grenade-launchers.[17] In May and June of 2006, investigators from the state procuracy conducted six searches of the factory and confiscated computers and accounting documentation. The local tax agency froze Bazal't's accounts. The official rationale for the proceedings cited embezzlement charges against Bazal't's CEO. However, the personal pressure exerted by law enforcers on the CEO, including illegal arrests and consignment to a psychiatric ward, as well as the strangely low sum of alleged embezzlement, suggested alternative motivations. As the state inspections paralyzed Bazal't's production, its premises – 1.5 hectares of land near a subway stop – were frequented by Moscow businessmen who helpfully offered to buy out the enterprise; according to Bazal't's senior management, the plan was to build elite condominiums on the site. Meanwhile, to oversee the elimination of a profitable, strategically important enterprise, a local law enforcer (with the long-winded title of the deputy prosecutor of Moscow for overseeing the implementation of laws in the "special regime entities") aimed to capture the CEO position at Bazal't for himself. The raiding attack ultimately failed, but the damage was done; *the orders by Russia's defense ministry went unfulfilled for months*, while a sizeable *arms contract*

---

[15] Morozov, (emphasis added).
[16] *Moskovskii Komsomolets* April 11, 2008.
[17] *Russky Kur'er* December 3, 2007; *Moskovskie Novosti* March 30, 2007.

negotiated by Putin and the king of Jordan was canceled by the Jordanians, who grew concerned about Bazal't.

Given the continued seriousness of attacks, the Duma's Security Committee formed in 2010 a working group charged with protecting strategically important enterprises against raiding.[18] More generally, the non-raiding types of agent predation in the Russian defense industry are subtle and widespread. According to military experts, "in the structures conducting procurement for the army, a group of military bureaucrats has formed that has learned how to game the price formation mechanism in defense orders."[19] The problem is with the "mid-level commanders ... who represent the link connecting the Ministry of Defense to the military-industrial complex and the Ministry of Trade and Development": by "overseeing the documentation connected to orders and prices," these people generate personally profitable price gaps between the weapons sold to the Russian armed forces and those exported abroad, de facto stealing substantial budget streams earmarked for national defense.[20]

Ukraine did not fare any better. Strategic enterprises in which the state owns the controlling share (e.g., Saturn, the producer of long-distance reconnaissance equipment) have faced raiding attacks, leading Aleksandr Dichek, chair of the economic security commission, to conclude in 2012 that "raiding has become a threat to national security comparable to economic terrorism."[21]

A series of investigative articles by *Dzerkalo Tyzhnia* uncovered three main predatory schemes perpetrated by the Ministry of Defense employees.[22] One scheme involved the sales of fuel to the armed forces through commercial intermediaries linked to the Ministry's employees, based on four contracts signed in 2008. Despite the wholesale volumes, the Ukrainian army was charged a 20–30 percent premium relative to the retail gas prices; the scheme led to a collapse in the number of in-flight hours for fighter jets and the reduction of operability for navy ships and other vehicles. (According to the reporters' analysis, this scheme alone imposed an unnecessary loss on the army which was the equivalent of fully equipping, motorizing, and maintaining for a year a 1,500-man brigade of land forces.) Another scheme targeted the provision of food to the soldiers, again through the intermediaries aiming to satisfy the bureaucrats', not the motherland defenders', hunger. While the predatory margin here was somewhat slimmer (15–20 percent) than in the fuel-related scheme, the scope for new entrants was also much larger. The bureaucrat-controlled "OOOs" (limited liability organizations) successfully evaded quality controls while plundering the budget; in 2009, the Ukrainian army was

---

[18] For discussion of the working group's activity, see Transcript of the Meeting of the Social-Conservative Club "Civic Platform" of United Russia, May 13, 2010. On file with author.

[19] *Moskovskie Novosti* 2007.

[20] Ibid.

[21] *Rossii'skie vesti* 2012.

[22] *Dzerkalo Tyzhnia* May 15, 2009; *Dzerkalo Tyzhnia* August 20, 2010; *Dzerkalo Tyzhnia* November 12, 2010.

Sovereign Priorities and Agent Predation

rocked by food poisonings throughout the country, immobilizing hundreds of soldiers. The third scheme involved real estate. As a legacy of Soviet hyper-militarization, the Ukrainian army holds vast but unnecessary properties under the so-called military townships (*voennyi gorodok*). In 2007, the Ukrainian Cabinet of Ministers signed off on a list of 250 such townships whose land was to be auctioned off to the highest bidder, with the projected revenue earmarked for desperately needed military housing.[23] Despite the potential for a massive cash infusion, considering hundreds of hectares were at stake (including in the prime coastal areas of Crimea), the reporters' analysis shows that by 2009, the military bureaucrats gave away most of these lands *for free*, at least on paper, to the towns and counties in which the lands were located; through the legal-istic charade of formal "renunciation letters" (*otkaznye pis'ma*), well-placed military employees shed unwanted assets while receiving informal kickbacks from local authorities who then sold the properties privately.

State Budgets and Pet Projects

Apart from undermining military preparedness, agent predation blows massive holes in the state budget, undercutting various projects prioritized by the sov-ereign. For many specific schemes used by the state agents, the hypothesis that such schemes were sovereign-sanctioned appears untenable.

Putin's reign in Russia, for example, was propped up by high oil prices through most of the 2000s. Meanwhile, a sophisticated analysis by *The Economist* shows that a state-linked Russian oil trader, Gunvor, was regularly driving *down* the price for Urals, a Russian export oil mixture, for *private* profit.[24] Gunvor trades vast volumes of oil (annual revenue: $80 billion) and is headed by a Putin loyalist, Gennadii Timchenko. In the aforementioned "regime of hooligans," however, nominal loyalty yields to predatory temptations. *The Economist*'s analysis of Gunvor trading strategies from 2005 to 2009 con-cludes that "[because] Gunvor caused the Urals price to fall ... a benchmark for crude has been distorted and the Russian taxpayers ... have seen a lot of money depart to Geneva [where Gunvor's main trading office is located]." To paraphrase, one of Putin's hooligans has been assiduously nibbling away at one of the pillars of Putin's power (high oil prices).

In Ukraine, my 2011 interview with an SBU officer from a unit that traces budgetary theft discloses a different scheme:

Tymoshenko [in her capacity as the Ukrainian prime minister] signed a 10-year contract with Putin [in 2009] for us to buy gas. Because we could not afford gas at those prices, we had to borrow from banks in the EU.... That's where our bureaucrats found a way to make money for themselves. They offered the EU banks even higher interest rates under

---

[23] Approximately the same number of townships had already been vacated by the military by 2007, bringing the total number of townships to be auctioned off to circa 500.
[24] *The Economist* May 5, 2012.

the condition that these interest payments would go through certain intermediaries registered in Luxembourg. Of course, these were shells, and they were charging fees that went straight into the pockets of our official state representatives [*predstavnyky vlady*]. Everybody benefitted: the banks, the bureaucrats.

Economic crisis and empty state budget notwithstanding, the Ukrainian state employees offered to overpay the EU banks for the loans, on taxpayers' dime, as long as the extra proceeds would be split with the specific Ukrainian bureaucrats involved. As with Russia's Gunvor case, it is unlikely that this scheme would have been tolerated, much less designed, by the Ukrainian state principal. The year 2009 in Ukraine saw the tensions between Yushchenko (president), Tymoshenko (prime minister), and Yanukovych (presidential candidate) boil over, as the acting and aspirant state principals battled for public support and international legitimacy under the conditions of upcoming presidential elections, free-falling economy, and harsh mutual recriminations. It is unlikely that any of these state leaders would have risked it all for a scheme that not only drained the budget but also risked international humiliation by disclosing its predatory nature to Ukraine's EU partners.[25]

When state principals are saddled with predatory agents, their pet projects suffer. Consider some of the unquestionable priorities of Vladimir Putin through the 2000s: the increase of Gazprom's share on the European gas market; the development of the Shtokman gas field to harness the Arctic's hydrocarbon potential; the launch of the South Stream pipeline to transport Russian gas to Europe without relying on Ukraine or Belarus; the completion of the Nord Stream pipeline through the Baltic Sea following the 2005 agreement with Western partners; the rebuilding of Chechnya's destroyed capital Grozny to pacify the secessionist republic; the successful preparation of the 2012 Asia-Pacific Economic Cooperation Summit in Vladivostok and of the 2014 Sochi Winter Olympiad. All of these projects aimed to increase Russia's – and Putin's – international prestige, geopolitical weight, and domestic stability. Of these, only the rebuilding of Grozny can be considered a qualified success. Gazprom's share in the total imports of OECD states in Europe was dropping continuously from 39 percent to 27 percent between 2000 and 2010, despite favorable market conditions and before shale gas became a factor; according to the German intelligence service BND, Gazprom's economic and political clout in Europe collapsed by 2013, due in large part to Gazprom's internal theft (detailed by Gazprom board candidates), which has tripled the cost of Kremlin's gas-related projects compared to those of rivals.[26] Development of the Shtokman field, dubbed as "the gas project of the century," stalled completely despite a 2008 agreement between Gazprom, Statoil (Norway), and Total (France); according

---

[25] SBU uncovered the scheme after Yanukovych assumed the presidency in 2010, without suggesting that Tymoshenko (whom Yanukovych later jailed on unrelated charges) was responsible for it.

[26] *Der Spiegel* February 1, 2013; *East European Gas Analysis* September 14, 2010; Kleiner 2005.

to intelligence from the U.S. State Department disclosed in 2011 on WikiLeaks, Shtokman screeched to a halt when Statoil, "one of Gazprom's most valuable and uncomplaining business partners," realized the extent of corruption at Gazprom linked specifically to Shtokman, and Statoil's CEO predicted that this "corruption risk" would grow.[27] Indeed, "after Statoil abandoned the project, Gazprom had little choice but to shelve it."[28] The planning and construction of Nord and South Stream pipelines, as well as the preparations for the APEC summit and the Sochi Olympiad were marred by delays, failures, and astronomical costs resulting from relentless theft by state agents; the coverage of these projects in the independent media has mostly embarrassed the Kremlin.[29] Overall, the reason for the "striking ineffectiveness of Putin's bureaucracy at executing its very own tasks" is "the situation in which there is no power vertical, but there are bureaucrats each of whom behaves *as a cancer cell in an organism, multiplying uncontrollably*," according to Latynina.[30]

In theoretical terms, the discussion so far implies that a key assumption behind conventional wisdom on principal expropriation is unfounded – namely the assumption that predation by state employees, once unleashed, *can be limited and managed by the sovereign* in ways that benefit him. The dynamics in Russia and Ukraine suggest that once the gloves are off, the bureaucrats' hands may not stop at the pockets of private entrepreneurs but could reach for the sovereign's throat as well.

SOVEREIGN EFFORTS TO CONTAIN AGENT PREDATION

The argument presented here would be strengthened if the state principals exerted efforts to limit agent predation and to control their agents more broadly; evidence of such efforts would suggest that an implicit license to engage predation is not being used as the primary tool of control by the principal and that much of predation is disorganized.

Administrative Reform

To begin, the bureaucrats indeed seem to be "multiplying uncontrollably," despite the sovereigns' efforts to the contrary. Roughly 1 million people were servants of the Russian Federation in the early 1990s. By 2005, their ranks increased to more than 1.4 million and on to 1.7 million by 2009. The number of bureaucrats as well as their salaries continued to grow rapidly in 2011, according to Rosstat's data (which excludes "power agencies," such as the

---

[27] *Reuters* January 7, 2011; *ArcticWay* January 13, 2011.
[28] *The Moscow Times* September 27, 2012.
[29] Nemtsov and Milov 2010; Morozov 2012; Lebedev 2012.
[30] Latynina on the radio program "Kod Dostupa" at Ekho Moskvy, December 31, 2011, (emphasis added). Transcript available at: http://echo.msk.ru/programs/code/844324-echo/

interior ministry and the FSB).[31] Granted, Russia's civil service is not huge by international standards, and part of its growth since 1991 can be explained by the bureaucracy's assumption of the functions previously fulfilled by the Communist Party.[32] Yet the growth of bureaucracy is theoretically paramount because it occurred despite the persistent attempts of the sovereign through the decade to effect the opposite, that is, to decrease his staff.

Immediately upon assuming power, President Putin declared in March 2000 that the number of state employees (*gosapparat*) should be cut by 10 percent.[33] In April 2002, in his address to the federal assembly, Putin called the state apparatus too "bulky, clumsy, and ineffective," ordering Prime Minister Kasyanov to identify areas for cuts. In a matter of months, Putin confirmed via decree the hastily drawn up program on the "Reform of State Service of Russian Federation" which explicitly foresaw the reduction ("optimization") of civil service. In July 2003, Putin signed another decree "On Measures Aimed at Administrative Reform," which prominently included the "elimination of duplication of functions and mandates of federal executive bodies." A government commission duly examined 5,634 functions carried out by the federal organs, finding 5 percent of them "duplicative," 15 percent "in need of correction," and 26 percent simply "superfluous." Out of 18,983 departments examined (*uchrezhdeniia*) under a federal mandate, 36 percent should be "liquidated or reorganized," according to the commission's report. The overall effort, however, moved little beyond taking inventory. While the number of ministries was cut from twenty-three to fourteen, the overall number of federal administrative bodies actually *grew*, as did the number of employed bureaucrats. With Medvedev's assumption of the presidency in 2008, the number of ministries grew to eighteen, while sixty brand new upper-level administrative bodies (*vedomstva*) were created. All the while, both Putin and Medvedev were forcefully advocating de-bureaucratization. During his annual televised Q and A with citizens in December 2009, Putin appeared peeved and overwhelmed when asked about the bureaucracy, affirming that "No matter what [setbacks], I will continue this work on cuts [in the apparatus]." In June 2010, Medvedev put a number on this aspiration: 20 percent of the country's bureaucrats would be sacked, according to the ex-president (whose instruction was echoed in the detailed project drawn up by the ministry of finance). Importantly, the Kremlin repeatedly tried to back words with aggressive action. In 2010, for example, the Russian police (*militsiia*) experienced a purge unprecedented in its ninety-three-year history; Medvedev fired seventeen generals in charge of the regional interior offices, two deputy ministers at the Ministry of Internal Affairs, and

---

[31] *Argumenty i Fakty* May 26, 2011.

[32] For a policy argument against the reduction of the bureaucratic apparatus in Russia's circumstances, see the article by Gehlbach and Earle in *Vedomosti* February 17, 2011.

[33] Speech at the meeting of the government presidium. For quotes and statistics in this paragraph, see: RF 2005; *Vremya Novostey* July 30, 2010; *Vedomosti* December 21, 2011.

Sovereign Efforts to Contain Agent Predation

10,000 regular staff.[34] Furthermore, as Russia's low-level police officers shared in a survey conducted by the Higher School of Economics, possibilities for moonlighting began to decline after 2009 because of stronger internal controls.[35] However, despite the cuts, in 2012, Russia's police force was 1.7 times larger than that of six West European countries (in all cases relative to the population size), while its productivity was up to 8 times lower.[36] More generally, the data on bureaucracy growth throughout the decade contrasts sharply with the initiatives of state principals. Overall, there were 79.5 bureaucrats per 10,000 citizens in Russia in 2000; by 2010, the number was 115.

The thrust to cut the bureaucracy, far from being driven by laissez-faire ideology, constitutes the Kremlin's admission of bureaucracy's power to undermine the sovereign. Putin, the statist, bent on reducing the state! The oxymoron is resolved by recognizing the statist's failure to subjugate his staff. Addressing business representatives in 2003, Putin thundered "We realize what resistance these [administrative] reforms arouse in officials used to giving their powers a broad interpretation, who only know how to authorize, distribute, restrict and decide for others.... Any excessive bureaucratic powers must be viewed as abuse."[37] By the end of the decade, Putin sounded desperate. In an unprecedented, one-hour tirade, Putin elaborated the results of the investigation he had ordered into the offshore schemes used for theft by the state employees (among whom many unfortunates were mentioned by name) in the energy sector: "Look at the sums [of stolen budget funds]! ... It's all about personal profit.... Not even concern for self-preservation stops them. [State employees] have become completely cocky [*sovsem oborzeli*].... Sorry, there are no better words."[38] In 2011, the sovereign's acknowledgement of bureaucratic *bespredel* went viral when all state-controlled television channels showed the chair of state audit management (*kontrol'noe upravlenie*), Konstantin Chuichenko, imparting on President Medvedev that "in the sphere of state procurement for federal and municipal needs ... the economic effect of 'cleaning' corrupt purchases, based on the most conservative estimate, could exceed 1 trillion rubles."[39] One trillion rubles constitutes around 20 percent of the total state budget funds allocated to state procurement (a process involving 10 million annual contracts between the state and 260 suppliers and contractors). The

---

[34] Cheloukhine and Haberfeld 2011, 131–2.

[35] The survey was conducted in 2011 and included 450 officers in seventeen towns throughout Russia. Of respondents, 32 percent thought that possibilities for moonlighting had declined, while 7 percent disagreed. For details, see Kosals and Dubova 2012.

[36] Based on the comparative analysis by Moscow's Higher School of Economics. The West European countries comprised Austria, Germany, France, the UK, the Netherlands, and Switzerland. Productivity was measured as the number of convicted criminals who pass through the hands of an officer, as well as the probability of arrests per 100,000 citizens. Strebkov 2012.

[37] XIII RUIE Congress Address, November 14, 2003

[38] *Kommersant* December 19, 2011; *DV-News* December 19, 2011.

[39] *Novaya Gazeta* November 9, 2011; *Pravo* October 29, 2010.

size of the hole in the budget bucket was not lost on Russia's president who gasped, "You mean, to put it in simple Russian language, the volume of theft could be decreased by 1 trillion rubles."

The dynamics in Ukraine parallel those in Russia.[40] The Ukrainian sovereign's effort at controlling the bureaucratic apparatus began to manifest itself by the mid-2000s, when Tymoshenko's government ordered an extensive background study for administrative reform in 2005 (to examine the correspondence of state organs' purposes to their de facto functions). Once conducted, the study detailed the extent of Soviet legacies in the Ukrainian state apparatus, underscoring an abundance of agencies with overlapping mandates. After the 2010 presidential elections, Yanukovych declared that, by June 2011, the executive apparatus would be cut by 50 percent, appointing Brods'kyi, a self-proclaimed "anti-bureaucrat," to head the deregulation effort. However, over a dozen ministries and a similar number of province-level administrations explicitly sabotaged the deregulation reform from getting off the ground in 2010, according to Brods'kyi. In 2012, Brods'kyi admitted that "we barely managed to cut the apparatus by 20%. People [i.e., state employees] have lost a sense of fear and are unwilling to give up their departmental interests [vidomchykh interesiv]." Brods'kyi's interview further conveys some of the department-specific pains involved:

In January we conducted a reform of the sanitation and epidemiology service. They had 53,000 people working there! ... We immediately fired 24,000 bureaucrats ... but even that [the remaining staff] is a lot – imagine all these employees on a [monthly] salary of 1,200 hryvnia [$150] who must every day "earn" something [on the side]. So the people are groaning – they are being robbed [narod stohne – iogo hrabuiut'] ... During the second phase of personnel reduction we should get the staff of the sanitation and epidemiology service down to 6,000 as it is in Poland.... In the taxation agency we have 60 thousand people working. Such a huge army is just sitting there and thinking throughout the day how to procure money for the state – and for themselves. It's abnormal. I think 40,000 of tax folks [podatkivtsiv] must be fired. And [Deputy Prime Minister] Boris Kolesnikov believes that the taxation agency should be reduced by 90%.

While the post-2010 staff-cutting in the legions of Ukrainian bureaucrats is impressive, the numerous setbacks in the preceding decade are even more so. Consider that the funds for the 2005 study commissioned by Tymoshenko were not released by the responsible state agencies until 2007 under the cabinet of Yanukovych. Indeed, an additional $70 million in funding from the EU "for the urgent horizontal reform of state management in Ukraine" remained unclaimed for years (a sensation in its own right). Furthermore, even while many of the predatory agencies were clearly overstaffed, regional bureaucracy

---

[40] For this and next paragraphs: *Dzerkalo Tyzhnia* October 23, 2010; *Dzerkalo Tyzhnia* February 27, 2010; *Dzerkalo Tyzhnia* February 11, 2011; *Dzerkalo Tyzhnia* January 20, 2012; *Krymskaya Pravda* 2012.

Sovereign Efforts to Contain Agent Predation

has refused to staff the new bureaus introduced by Kyiv to simplify local business regulation and root out predation; for example, the 2010–11 "one window" initiative was hampered when the regions of Donets'k, Zhytomyr, Poltava, and Cherkasy claimed that they "did not have enough cadres" to participate (which is ironic, since the one-window bureaus by design require little staff). The interdepartmental variation in bureaucracy growth through the 2000s, that is, before Yanukovych's 2010–13 deregulation efforts, is noteworthy: While some bureaus were cut drastically, *agencies directly related to the private-sector regulation managed to more than triple their staff.* These burgeoning departments included the State Property Fund, Tax Service, Anti-Monopoly Committee, as well as a wide range of agencies charged with business inspections. Courts and the Prosecutor's Office, which continue to figure prominently in property takeovers have increased their employment 2.7 times. Overall, the number of bureaucrats in Ukraine has increased by 76 percent since the country became independent from the Soviet Union.

Manual Control

Given the resounding victory of bureaucracy in its battles against the sovereign over the administrative reform throughout the 2000s, the presidents of Russia and Ukraine changed their tactics and attempted to *personally* control their bureaucracies.[41] In November 2011, Medvedev signed a law allowing him to fire state employees because of "loss of trust," a legal formula intended to inspire fear in corrupt bureaucrats and, according to experts, aimed primarily at the renegade *siloviki* members.[42] In a more populist way, Prime Minister Putin ordered monitoring cameras to broadcast directly into the Kremlin the rebuilding process after the 2010 forest fires across Russia, "otherwise, all [state budget] money will be stolen," according to the presumably almighty Putin.[43] In June 2012, upon returning to presidency, Putin instituted the office of a "federal ombudsman for the protection of business people," appointing a well-known business leader to the job – a development that is phenomenal for two reasons. On the one hand, the ombudsman is accountable to the president only, has impressive investigative and sanctioning powers vis-à-vis the "power ministries," and is tasked exclusively with rooting out state-sponsored expropriation; this implies that the state principal clearly understands the severity and negative impact of agent predation. On the other hand, the ombudsman's involvement is based on individual complaints received from the entrepreneurs;

---

[41] *Versiya* July 11, 2011; *Dzerkalo Tyzhnia* 2011.

[42] In 2000–10, three regional leaders (most notably Moscow's mayor, Luzhkov) were fired based on the "loss of trust" formulation before its explicit legal status. The legalization of the formula and the institutionalization of the accompanying procedures were expected to boost administrative discipline.

[43] *Novaya Gazeta* 2011.

this institutionalization of the "go to the tsar to punish the boyar" approach implies the utter failure of systemic solutions to the problem of agent predation. (Chapter 5 relates the ombudsman institution to the disappointing impact of sovereign-supported business associations in Russia.)

In Ukraine, meanwhile, Yanukovych's empowerment of Brods'kyi is strikingly similar in its underlying logic. Brods'kyi almost comically appealed to one million Ukrainian entrepreneurs in 2012 to post complaints about bureaucratic predation on his Facebook page or to call him or the prime minister: "Talk to us, don't be afraid. Then there will be a result."[44] More broadly, President Yanukovych offered law drafts in 2010 allowing him to personally appoint and fire the staff of all "organs of central executive power" (of which, together with ministries, there are more than seventy) and introducing the institution of "entrustments" (*porucheniia*), which are oral or written instructions below the status of a direct order by the president to anybody in the executive branch. These tactics drew fire from Ukraine's liberal opposition. In my interview, Dmytro Liapin (a Ukrainian think-tank leader who received the title of "distinguished economist" from president Yushchenko in 2009) noted:

> The reform of the central executive organs of December 2010 via decrees [by president Yanukovych] is senseless.... Instead of creating a minimally logical system where ministries manage certain agencies, committees, etc.... instead of such a pyramid, it all boiled down to the president *personally appointing everybody*.

While these initiatives of the Russian and Ukrainian state principals may in part be driven by authoritarian ambitions, they are not aimed at civil society, other branches of power, or the regions.

Aimed at the executive itself, these initiatives signal a dynamic that is more complex than the sovereign's personal lust for power. A parallel to state ownership of assets, pervasive in weak states, is instructive. As Chaudry illustrated, state ownership of property in the developing world is often the *last resort of a weak state unable to regulate* markets and extract taxes.[45] Similarly, the sovereign's drive to "own" his bureaucracy through personal micromanagement stems, inter alia, from his failure to "regulate" the bureaucracy through the institutional channels.

Anti-Raiding Reforms and Sovereign Intentions

The state principal's efforts to control agent predation can be *serious* while not *benevolent*, that is, not, in the first place, aimed at benefitting the citizens or the property owners. Consider the case of Russia's anti-raiding laws adopted in 2009–10 in parallel with the rise of a new law enforcement agency, both sponsored by the state principal.

---

[44] For the entire paragraph: *Dzerkalo Tyzhnia* January 20, 2012; *Krymskaya Pravda* 2012.
[45] Chaudhry 1993.

Sovereign Efforts to Contain Agent Predation

The need to close legal loopholes and to stiffen penalties for raiders had been discussed in the Russian expert community for years. Then, in July 2009, the Duma fired a loud salvo in the fight against raiding by adopting exhaustive amendments to the existing legislation (Federal Law 205-FZ). The list of amended legislation included the tax code, the code on administrative violations, the code on arbitration procedures, as well as the federal laws "On joint stock companies," "On limited liability companies," "On securities markets," "On state registration of juridicial persons and individual entrepreneurs," and others. These interrelated amendments aimed to prevent collusion between judges and raiders by clarifying the jurisdiction of courts involved in corporate lawsuits, to enhance the safety of equity registries (often stolen or falsified by raiders), and to provide the legitimate owners with timely information on potential attacks. In December 2009, the Duma adopted its second anti-raiding law (383-FZ), amending the criminal code to eliminate pretrial detention during tax investigations while allowing tax offenders to escape criminal prosecution if the tax arrears are paid off within a reasonable timeframe. The purpose of this law is to reduce raiding based on extortion by tax and law enforcement agencies. In April 2010, the Duma adopted two additional laws. One law (62-FZ) was specifically designed to prevent "merchandise raiding" (*tovarnoe reiderstvo*); such raiding involves state employees confiscating goods under a legal pretext in order to sell them for private profit.[46] The new law protects confiscated goods by mandating their immediate appraisal by independent experts, by allowing their sale only with the consent of the owner or via court order, and so forth. The other law (60-FZ) amended the criminal as well as the criminal-processual (*ugolovno-protsessual'nyi*) codes to drop criminal liability for "fraudulent entrepreneurship" (*lzhepredprinimatel'stvo*), to eliminate pretrial detention for a variety of "economic crimes" while also raising steeply the fines for such crimes, and to harshen the penalties for state officials "interfering with lawful entrepreneurial activity." In July 2010, the Duma concluded its legislative crescendo by adopting the fifth anti-raiding law (147-FZ), which amended the criminal code, introducing substantial fines and jail terms for the specific types of manipulations and falsifications of equity registries as well as corporate documentation by both state officials and private actors involved in raiding attacks.

The 2009–10 legislative barrage against raiders by the Duma could be naively interpreted as the lawmakers' response to the pressure of legitimate business owners; however, *the self-interest of the state principal accounts better for the timing and the implementation of the reform*. Raiding in Russia peaked in the mid-2000s; in 2006, the representatives of Business Russia, a business association, together with the Ministry of Economic Development and Trade

---

[46] Firms carrying compact high-value products, such as electronics or furs, presented particularly attractive targets; in 2006, for example, state employees confiscated and partly sold 167,500 mobile phones from the firm Evroset' under the pretext of "consumer safety" violations.

(MEDT), submitted a package of legal proposals to the government as a part of their "anti-raiding campaign."[47] Independent experts considered these proposals "uncontroversial," the bare minimum of legislative change needed to halt the raiding epidemic. Despite the acuteness of the problem and the modest nature of the proposals, the legislative initiative withered away; two years elapsed between the Duma's first and second reading of the proposals, after which the lawmakers failed to vote. According to Viktor Pleskachevsky, the head of the Duma's Committee on Property and a high-profile expert on raiding, "the entire process of what we called 'fight against raiding' came apart [*razvalilsia*] ... due to [the disagreements between] three different [Duma] committees."[48] Yet one year later, something galvanized the Duma into forgetting interfactional rivalry and unleashing *pronto* not one but five laws, each more ambitious than the original Business Russia/MEDT package (which had not included any amendments to the criminal code, for example).

The involvement of the Russian sovereign sheds much light on this puzzle. Although raiding was rampant in the mid-2000s, the problem was (a) limited to business owners, a negligible constituency in terms of electoral support for the state principal and (b) mitigated by the fact that the president still enjoyed 80 percent approval ratings. By 2009, the financial crisis threatened to both *extend the fallout from raiding to the wider population* (through salary delays and layoffs) and *sink the approval ratings of the Medvedev-Putin tandem*. Medvedev himself admitted as much when addressing the leaders of the State Procuracy in 2009:

Raiding, [and property] takeovers ... under the conditions of deep economic crisis – these crimes present a heightened public danger because they concern the interests of a substantial number of people. We understand that under the conditions of crisis, this can lead to the escalation of social tensions.... That's why one must harshly prosecute any such violations. We must think *not so much about protecting the owners' interests* but about the interests of *large numbers of people working at the given enterprise*.[49]

Another aspect explaining the timing of the sovereign's initiative was the massive delay of construction work for the Sochi Olympiad resulting from raiding attacks on the involved firms.[50] Medvedev repeatedly signaled his determination to the lawmakers, at one point noting bluntly at the Federation Council: "Somehow I do not recall anybody being jailed for raiding."[51] Through United Russia and affiliated legislators as well as through the Civic Chamber, the reform envisioned by the presidential administration was "dragged through" (according to Pleskachevsky) the Duma speedily.

[47] *Kommersant* October 26, 2006.
[48] Transcript of the Meeting of the Social-Conservative Club "Civic Platform" of United Russia, May 13, 2010. On file with author.
[49] *Ekspert* February 25, 2009, (emphasis added).
[50] *Advisers.ru* September 22, 2010.
[51] *Izvestiya* November 6, 2009.

Sovereign Efforts to Contain Agent Predation

In the media, the laws became unofficially known as "presidential anti-raiding laws"; the involvement of the business community in the 2009–10 reform was minimal.[52] Indeed, the leader of OPORA, a prominent small-business association whose members were the *primary victims* of raiding during the reform, admitted that "the amendments offered by the President's council ... were quite a surprising document for business ... we were presented with a fait accompli."[53]

The number of criminal cases opened against suspected raiders tripled following legal change.[54] Importantly, the criminal cases enabled by the new legislation targeted *state employees*. Specifically, employees of the state equity registrar (Rosreestr), regional regulators, regional deputies, employees of the Ministry of Property Relations (Minimushchestvo), police operatives, regional representatives of the state procuracy, a former deputy minister of the interior, judges, and others have been charged with participating in various raiding schemes since the legislative reform took effect.[55]

The relatively vigorous implementation has been the result of the sovereign's novel approach: By indicating early on to *both* the Interior Ministry and the State Procuracy that their respective investigative committees may ultimately claim the right to single-handedly prosecute all raiding cases, the state principal successfully pitted two organizational state agents against each other. In their competition for novel bureaucratic turf,[56] the leaders of both investigative committees began diligently reporting on their anti-raiding and anti-corruption efforts.[57]

The competition was won decisively by Aleksandr Bastrykin of the State Procuracy because of higher corruption inside the Interior Ministry itself (several high-profile scandals at the time did not help), the relative professionalism of the Procuracy's investigators, and Bastrykin's willingness to stand up to the FSB and to personally confront intransigent Duma deputies from the Committee on Security.[58] Bastrykin's Investigative Committee not only

---

[52] At this stage, only Business Solidarity and New Course, relatively marginal business movements, were considerably involved. However, Business Solidarity rarely advocated specific amendments, insisting vaguely on a "systemic approach" to the reform, while the amendments suggested by New Course lacked professional expertise and were dismissed. The amendments proposed by the lobbyist heavyweights of the business community – Business Russia and the Chamber for Commerce and Industry – were routed through the Duma's Committee on Security and ultimately dismissed. (The Committee on Security, headed by the *silovik* Vasil'ev, lost out to Pleskachevsky's Committee on Property in terms of the legal reform's content.)

[53] *Kommersant* November 15, 2010.

[54] *Izvestiya* April 12, 2012.

[55] Ibid.; *Kommersant* February 4, 2011; *Bfm.ru* April 7, 2010.

[56] An additional carrot dangled in front of these bodies was the promise of directing "a Russian FBI," a new organization drawing on the resources of the police, the Procuracy, the FSB, and the State Drug Control. Ultimately, the FBI-like agency did not materialize.

[57] Alekseev 2009; *Novaya Gazeta* May 18, 2009; *Interfax* October 13, 2009.

[58] *Kommersant* September 24, 2010; *Vedomosti* March 20, 2009; *Vedomosti* February 12, 2010.

received a monopoly on the anti-raiding mandate but was also detached from the Procuracy into a powerful stand-alone agency, complete with a fifteen-floor modern high-rise, its own special forces, and aviation. People whom Bastrykin had crossed fumed: Aleksandr Hinshtein, a Duma deputy from the Committee on Security, alleged that "having escaped the supervision of the Procuracy, he [Bastrykin] has turned his agency into an uncontrollable machine for chopping heads off."[59] A more dispassionate analysis by *Ekspert*, however, praised Russia's progress in confronting raiding while insightfully noting the sovereign's incentive to *monopolize predation*:

The national government is fighting raiding not because it is hurting the society but rather because it is hurting the government itself. Disgraced are those who are not sharing [with the government] and acting without coordinating with it. That is, *bureaucrats of the highest rank are throwing sand into the wheels of their lower-ranked colleagues and competitors* [i.e., low-ranked bureaucrat raiders].[60]

By the end of 2011, however, Bastrykin's head-chopping machine appeared overwhelmed by "the lower-ranked colleagues" from police and the regulatory agencies. Among other obstacles, a particular problem noted by the analysts was the deliberate obstruction by the lower-level bureaucrats, who receive complaints from entrepreneurs about raiding and "forget" to forward such complaints to the Investigative Committee.[61] Presumably, if all such complaints had found their way to Bastrykin, however, the usefulness of special forces and aviation against thousands of renegade pen-pushers would have quickly found its limits. In the absence of robust civil society and Weberian bureaucracy, the "dictatorship of law" that Putin promised in 2000 is a logistical nightmare. (The fact that Bastrykin's resources were also diverted to investigate Putin's *political* opponents, such as Navalny, suggests that the *rule* of law was, from the state principal's viewpoint, not in the cards to begin with.)

The case of Russia's anti-raiding legal reform underscores two key points. First, the state principal has exerted serious efforts to control predation by state employees, suggesting that much of such predation is perpetrated by unaccountable state agents rather than at the behest of the principal. Second, the state principal's *reasons* for reining in agent predation need not be benevolent and can relate to the sovereign's power retention calculus, his prestige projects, or his incentive to monopolize predation.

Deregulation and Sovereign Intentions

The Ukrainian sovereign's efforts to rein in agent predation have likewise been serious while reflecting the state principal's naked self-interest. (These

---

[59] *Moskovskii' komsomolets* November 19, 2009.
[60] *Ekspert Ukraina* July 2, 2007, (emphasis added).
[61] *Kommersant Den'gi* 2011.

Sovereign Efforts to Contain Agent Predation

efforts were more delayed than in Russia, however, because of the chronic legislative-executive power gridlock in Kyiv until 2010.) In addition to the already noted deregulation and administrative efforts, president Yanukovych pushed through several laws (# 3993-VI, 3994-VI, 3995-VI, 4154-VI) on business permits and licensing in 2011–12. This legislation reduced the number of mandatory permits; consolidated the agencies issuing such permits; allowed business activity when the state agency delays its decision on permit issuance (or denial) beyond the specified timeframe; and transferred the right to issue certain permits (e.g., related to land use) from the local executives to the plenary meetings of the local legislative organs.

Furthermore, the Interdepartmental Anti-Raiding Commission was jolted back to life and began to accept entrepreneurs' complaints while meeting biweekly to work on legislative reform.[62] This national governmental commission was created at the Cabinet of Ministers in 2007 on the initiative of the Ukrainian Union of Industrialists and Entrepreneurs yet remained de facto moribund until it was relaunched in 2011 under the chairmanship of Andrii Kliuev, the secretary of national security and defense (and former minister of economic development and trade).

What about the state principal's rationale for this broad array of initiatives aimed at the predatory officials? According to a Ukrainian executive at PricewaterhouseCoopers in Kyiv, interviewed by the author,

> Before Yanukovych [became president], nobody wanted to deal with raiding, so predation was everywhere. Now they understand that the economy is only a step away from total collapse. Until 2008, there was a boom, so the budget received some money anyway [i.e., despite predation]. Now, however, life is forcing them; Ukraine has no [credit] rating.... While Yanukovych was obsessed with eliminating political opposition, the lower ranks [*liudi na mestakh*] have lost a sense of appropriateness. Now he has realized that factions in his own camp are stealing [from Yanukovych], so they [the Party of Regions] have to jail their own because there is not enough to steal for everybody [*ne khvataet na vsekh vorovat'*]. So they begin to cut off hands. See what happened to Galitskii, for example.... They flush out [*slivaiut*] their own, people who appropriated without sharing.

Vladimir Galitskii, referred to in the interview, was a long-term associate of Yanukovych, a functionary in the Party of Regions, and the head of Ukraine's Employment Agency. In 2011, Galitskii was convicted of spearheading a scheme to extort enterprises in the coal sector, expropriating tens of millions of dollars; according to SBU materials, when "the percentages specified [by Galitskii] were not paid, enterprises were subjected to controlling inspections."[63] In other cases, the state principal's sense of justice vis-à-vis his agents was awakened by the costs related to elections, as shared by a business executive from a Kyiv-based consultancy in my 2012 interview:

---

[62] *Rossii'skie vesti* October 22, 2012; *Argumenty i Fakty* February 9, 2012.
[63] *Vzglyad* March 7, 2011.

Before the elections, they [the clan of Yanukovych] cracked down on customs under the slogan "the Ukrainian Customs Service does not take bribes and must fill the budget," but the subtext was "because we do not have money for elections." They began jailing customs officials caught taking bribes in Odessa [Ukraine's main import hub]. As the country is running out of money, they [the state officials] will continue devouring each other.

An additional incentive for Yanukovych to confront agent predation was regaining international legitimacy after the 2010 politicized trial against his nemesis Tymoshenko. From the beginning, Yanukovych's reforms related to property rights' enforcement were designed and elaborated by McKinsey (a respected Western consultancy), earning Yanukovych reluctant praise from oppositionist think-tanks which juxtaposed the professionalism of Yanukovych's approach with that of his predecessor.[64] According to Dmytro Liapin of the Property and Freedom Institute, the prospect of improving Ukraine's business-related international rankings played a role:

Yanukovych's approach to [structural economic] reforms has been that everything is meticulously declared vis-à-vis the external world, such that the world hopefully says "well, they [Yanukovych's team] are bad guys, but they are trying to be good guys." ... Regarding the reforms in the sphere of entrepreneurship, our government also has the example of Belarus where despite Lukashenka's dictatorship, Belarus has a respectable place in Doing Business [a World Bank ranking]. This tells our leadership that the ranking in Doing Business has nothing to do with [democracy].... Yet *the problem of the executive vertical is where it all comes to a halt.* What is the strength of Lukashenka's dictatorship? It is manageable. The signal issued by the presidential administration there makes its way downward with minimal distortions, in stark contrast with Ukraine where the system distorts such signals beyond recognition.

Between 2010 and 2013, Ukraine did substantially improve its Doing Business rankings in some of the main categories. Most prominently, the number of mandatory tax payments for businesses dropped from 147 to 28; the time needed to file taxes declined from 736 to 491 hours; and the time needed to register property declined from 118 to 70 days.

However, the total *de facto* tax rate on commercial profit remained virtually unchanged from 57 percent in 2010 to 55 percent in 2013.[65] What does this mean? Ukrainian economists see the tax system as still characterized by "the confiscatory principle foreseeing the extraction of tax revenue based on the particular agreements between a specific taxpayer and a specific tax collector [*okremo vziatym podatkivtsim*]."[66] The state principal's initiatives, then, have aimed to cut as many "specific tax collectors" as possible out of the equation, while maintaining the effective tax burden on firms – an effort to monopolize predation, par excellence. Plugging the leaky bucket of tax revenues allows

---

[64] Boyarchuk et al. 2012.
[65] All data can be obtained at http://www.doingbusiness.org/
[66] Boyarchuk et al. 2012, 4.

the state principal to pursue an array of objectives that may or may not be related to society's welfare. Yanukovych, for his part, substantially increased salaries to the repressive apparatus, including the procuracy, law enforcement, and security services, between 2010 and 2013 (the 2013 budget was dubbed as "the budget of the cudgel" in the Ukrainian media) while cutting the benefits to other state employees and a wide range of welfare recipients, including war veterans, Chernobyl survivors, and so on.[67]

SURVEY EVIDENCE: AGENT PREDATION OR PRINCIPAL EXPROPRIATION?

Using surveys of entrepreneurs to test whether state threats to ownership are principal-organized or agent-driven is difficult; the respondents may not know whether the bureaucrats targeting their property rights are acting on their own account or in (tacit) collusion with the state principal. Still, the results from my 2007 survey suggest that the bulk of ongoing predation may be disorganized.

Blame Attribution and Remedies for PR Insecurity: Central Vs Local State

We start with a "naïve" approach; business owners were asked, "Among the reasons listed below, which do you think best explains the insufficient protection of entrepreneurs' right to legally manage their property and receive income from it?" At the pooled level, 43 percent of respondents blamed "incorrect actions by the *national* government," while 31 percent blamed "incorrect actions by the *local* authorities."[68] This difference is significant at the 0.01 level, but is somewhat difficult to interpret. In particular, entrepreneurs attributing blame to the "national government" may imply either that the quality of laws on the books is inadequate – hence blaming in part the competence of the legislative branch – or that the central executive is a predator when it comes to the implementation. The real difference in the attribution of blame between the purely predatory (not lawmaking) activities of the central versus local executives could hence be much smaller. Even if these numbers are correct, however, the implication is that, from the entrepreneurs' perspective, agent predation is at least 75 percent as intense as principal expropriation.

A better question, which skirts the issue of positive law, concerns potential *remedies* for the state threats to PR. In both countries, firms were asked to rate the importance of various factors for secure property rights. As a reminder, in the literature on principal expropriation, credible commitment of the *national* government – most often through democratic checks and balances – is the

---

[67] *Ekonomichna Pravda* December 10, 2012.
[68] Interestingly, the central-local blame attribution was much more polarized in Ukraine, where 64 percent of entrepreneurs blamed the center and 36 percent the local state actors. In Russia, the numbers were 36 percent and 30 percent for central and local state respectively (*not* a significant difference at the 0.01 level).

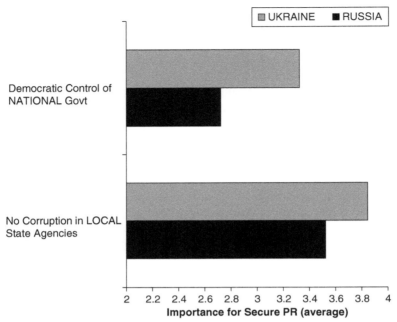

FIGURE 4.1. Average responses to the question, "On a scale of 1–4, how important are these factors for the protection of entrepreneurs' right to legally manage their property and derive legal income from it?"
(*Source*: Markus, 2007. N=516.)

sine qua non of secure property rights. However, as Figure 4.1 shows, Russian and Ukrainian entrepreneurs consider such democratic control of the national government to be *less* important for secure property rights than the incorruptibility of *local* state agents. (For both countries, the difference is significant at the 0.01 level.)

Note that the issue of *remedies* is inextricable from the *sources* of state threats. If entrepreneurs believed that most threats are organized (or willingly tolerated) by the state principal, it is unlikely that they would stress the incorruptibility of state actors on the ground. After all, such honest bureaucrats would still be legally subordinated to the state principal; if the latter is the problem, then the honesty of low-ranked bureaucrats offers no avail. In other words, Figure 4.1 suggests that most entrepreneurs view agent predation as a bigger problem than principal expropriation for the security of property rights.

Impact of Central-Local Blame Attribution on Firm Behavior

Another way to approach the issue is to compare the *impact* of the local versus central blame attribution on the behavior of respondent firms. Not all companies

Survey Evidence: Agent Predation or Principal Expropriation?   III

facing state threats (organized or not) are mere victims: as our discussion of raiding suggested, some firms become predators themselves. Many factors determine a firm's decision which side of the legal boundary to play on when it comes to property rights. One such factor could be the firm's perception of what causes insecure property rights in the first place. Are firms that blame the state center, that is, a unified expropriatory state "machine," more or less likely to engage in predatory behavior than firms that blame insecure PR on the local state, that is, on the unaccountable bureaucrats on the ground?

To obtain relatively honest responses and prevent self-incrimination by business owners, my questionnaire used an attitudinal proxy for firms' behavior. Entrepreneurs were asked: "To what extent do you agree with the following statement: 'the poor protection of property rights presents not only a threat but also an opportunity for business growth'?"[69] My assumption is that respondents who agree more with this statement will be more aggressive in their exploitation of an environment defined by insecure PR. The variable *Aggression* ranges from I to 4 ("completely disagree" to "completely agree"). Of the firms that answered this question, 36 percent agreed or completely agreed that insecure property rights allow for business expansion.

Table 4.1 shows the results of an ordered probit regression in which the dependent variable is *Aggression*. The key independent variables are *LocalBlame* and *CentralBlame*, each a dummy that equals one for companies that see the local authorities or the national government as the primary culprit undermining property rights. (The question on blame attribution had more response options than these two, hence the use of separate dummies.) As in the previous analysis, I include the following controls: a dummy for a firm's membership in a business association (*BusinessAssociation*), a firm's estimate of the legal system's effectiveness in protecting contracts with private counterparties (*ContractSecurity*), a dummy for de novo, that is, non-privatized firms (*NonPrivatized*), and dummies for size categories, sector, ownership structure, and region.

The key finding is striking: Firms that see local state actors as the main culprits exhibit a significantly higher propensity to engage in predation than companies that do not attribute blame to the local state. In substantive terms, companies that view bureaucrats on the ground as the main reason behind insecure property rights are II percent more likely to view insecure PR as a chance to expand business than are firms that attribute PR insecurity to factors other than local bureaucrats.[70] Meanwhile, whether firms view the central state as the key culprit has no impact on the firms' aggressiveness. These findings help disentangle further agent predation from principal expropriation. In particular, to the extent firms perceive state threats to PR as agent-driven, such

---

[69] Since this was one of the most sensitive questions, it concluded the questionnaire. The response rate for this question was 66 percent.

[70] Stata's Clarify package is used for the simulation of first differences.

TABLE 4.1. *Effect of Blame Attribution to Local Versus Central State on Business Propensity for Predation*

	Aggression
LocalBlame	0.32** (0.15)
CentralBlame	−0.01 (0.14)
BusinessAssociation	−0.10 (0.14)
ContractSecurity	0.13** (0.06)
NonPrivatized	0.05 (0.20)
SizeMedium	0.05 (0.25)
SizeLarge	−0.08 (0.21)
N	306
$P > \chi^2$	0.000
Pseudo R^2	0.12
Dummy Variables	Sector
	Ownership
	Region

* $p < 0.10$, ** $p < 0.05$, *** $p < 0.01$. Ordered probit model with robust standard errors (in parentheses). Dependent variable is respondents' level of agreement on a 1–4 scale with the statement identifying insecure property rights with "an opportunity for business growth."

perception is *more likely to prime firms to engage in predation themselves.* Companies believing state threats to be organized, conversely, do not exhibit such aggressive attitudes.

Paradoxically, agent predation is even more harmful than principal expropriation for the incentives of business owners, probably because principal expropriation allows considerably less scope for the entry of new predators compared to agent predation. This finding extends in two ways Shleifer and Vishny's (1993) crucial theory of the pernicious impact of democratization on corruption through the "disorganization" of bribe collection. First, my point addresses threats to *ownership* rights rather than income rights. Second, while Shleifer and Vishny elaborate the incentives of state officials, I address here the incentives of *business* owners.

A few additional insights emerge from Table 4.1. *BusinessAssociation* and *NonPrivatized* are insignificant. *ContractSecurity* is significant and has a positive sign. At the first glance, this is counterintuitive: Why would firms perceiving the legal system as effective in enforcing private contracts regard insecure property rights as a chance to grow business? The likely reason is that much of privately initiated raiding or expropriation through state capture has been conducted through *legal channels that rely on the enforcement of contracts.* This result contributes to an important theoretical debate on the rule of law in Russia. While some scholars see the improved performance of Russia's

Survey Evidence: Agent Predation or Principal Expropriation? 113

"low-level" court system handling private lawsuits as promising for the rule of law (e.g., Hendley 2006), others argue that successful contract enforcement can mask – and *enable* – various forms of predation (e.g., Woodruff 2012). My analysis supports the latter perspective.

Subnational Variation in State Threats

The final way to estimate the relative importance of agent predation versus principal expropriation capitalizes on the subnational variation. The literature on principal expropriation views the system in terms of exchange: The state principal tolerates predation by state agents in exchange for political support. My data allows inferential leverage here because for both Russia and Ukraine, we have reasonable estimates of the *antecedent (pre-exchange) propensity of certain regions to support the state principal politically*. The exchange perspective on principal expropriation implies that if some regions are, *to begin with*, obstreperous vis-à-vis the state principal, the state principal would likely grant such regions a license to engage in predation so as to induce them to support the principal. (Conversely, if a given region is viewed by the state principal as unproblematic or "safe," the state principal should be less willing to share predatory revenues with the regional state actors.) The nature of regional resistance to the state principal differed between Ukraine and Russia in 2007. In Ukraine, the main regional split regarding the support of the state principal concerned the east-west dimension: While the Europe-leaning west staunchly supported the Orange team of President Yushchenko, the Russia-leaning east opposed it (and would later spearhead the electoral defeat of politicians affiliated with the Orange Revolution). In Russia, the end of Putin's second term did not see the state principal (and his doppelganger Medvedev) face serious electoral challenges given the Kremlin's "managed democracy"; however, Moscow continued to deal with the legacy of regional insubordination from the 1990s.[71] The analysis here inquires whether state threats to PR were more intense in these ex ante "obstreperous" regions in 2007, as would be expected *if* such threats were based on a systemic exchange (under principal expropriation).

To identify "obstreperous" regions in Russia, I draw on the work of Katherine Stoner-Weiss. In her book *Resisting the State*, Stoner-Weiss presents a quantitative index of regional noncompliance with federal policy in Russia of the 1990s, arguing that "Putin's administration suffered ... defeats that left the regional structures of the 1990s largely intact" and that "despite what Putin ... purported, the ... capacity of his Russian state in the provinces was not ... that different ... from the Russia of Boris Yeltsin."[72] Out of 396 firms I surveyed

---

[71] Stoner-Weiss 2006.
[72] Ibid., 152–4.

114   *Mini-Beasts vs. Sovereign*

in Russia, 46 are located in the ten regions[73] identified as "top non-compliers" with federal policy by Stoner-Weiss.

Were state threats in these "non-compliers" higher than in the ex ante more compliant regions? It turns out that the average state threat to ownership rights in the two regional subsets was virtually identical: 2.49 in the more compliant regions versus 2.52 in the historically noncompliant regions, a difference that is not significant at the 0.1 level and not suggestive of principal expropriation.

A different way to utilize the subnational variation capitalizes on the regions' distance from the administrative center. In Russia especially, given its enormous territory spanning nine time zones, distance may play a role. In fact, the reason behind Putin's superimposition of seven "federal districts" on Russia's federal system in 2000 was to bring the far-flung corners of Russia under Moscow's control. More generally, the "institutional capacity of a central state ... to penetrate its territories"[74] is a popular theme in the literature on infrastructural power. Taking this into account, the exchange perspective on principal expropriation implies that if (a) state threats are organized, and (b) the furthest regions are hardest to control, *then the state principal may tolerate predation by state agents in such remote regions to incentivize these regions to support the center.* However, my data does not corroborate this. Figure 4.2 presents average state threats to ownership and income in the seven federal districts of the Russian Federation.[75] The districts are displayed in the ascending order of their distance from Moscow; the leftmost bars represent threats in the Central Federal District (with Moscow as its administrative center), and the rightmost bars show threats in the Far Eastern Federal District (which extends along the Pacific). The trend lines indicate the results of a linear regression of threat averages on the ordinal variable indicating distance from the center.

State threats to ownership remain essentially *constant* as one moves from Russia's administrative center toward Kamchatka, 6,000 miles away. (State threats to income show a slight decline.) Such invariance is more likely to reflect agent predation than principal expropriation; while the literature expects the collusive deals between Moscow and the regions to vary with the regions' location, there is no reason to expect such variation if state threats are driven by bureaucratic insubordination. If predation by low-level bureaucrats proceeds *without* a license from the state principal, there is no reason to expect bureaucrats in Magadan to be any less (or more) hungry than their predatory colleagues in Moscow.

While in Russia, the intensity of predation is merely *invariant* to the regional dimensions (which should matter, according to the theories of principal

---

[73] Stoner-Weiss ranks these in the descending order of noncompliance as follows (p. 66): Chechnya, Kalmykiia, Bashkortostan, Tatarstan, Mari-El, Karachevo-Cherkesiia, Sakha, Komi, Udmurtiia, Kemerovo, Primorye. My sample contains firms from all non-compliers except Chechnya.

[74] Mann 1984, 113.

[75] The discussion of Figure 3.2 introduced my measures of ownership and income threats, which are also used here.

Survey Evidence: Agent Predation or Principal Expropriation? 115

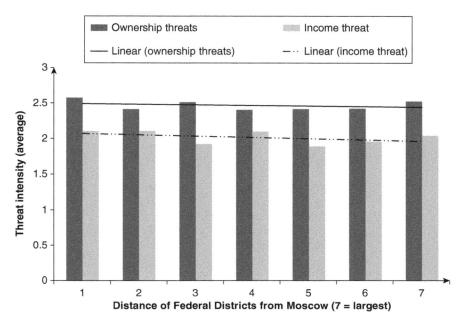

FIGURE 4.2. Regional variation in state threats to property rights across federal districts in Russia.
(*Source*: Markus, 2007. N=393.)

expropriation), in Ukraine, the regional variation in state threats is strongly pronounced in the *opposite* direction of what should be observed under a systemic exchange. In 2007, given the differential antecedent propensities of the east and the west to support Kyiv, one would expect a rational Ukrainian sovereign to do two things. First, a rational state principal would allow some predation in the recalcitrant eastern part of the country so as to sway the regional *state agents* to support the Orange elites in Kyiv.[76] The urgency of such a strategy, from the state principal's viewpoint, was bluntly illustrated by Ukraine's early parliamentary elections of September 2007, in which the *anti*-Orange Party of Regions, affiliated with the east, captured the largest percentage of votes (34 percent) compared to other parties. Second, a rational state principal would limit predation in the western part of the country, where the *voters'*

---

[76] Since the bulk of the country's industrial assets is concentrated in the east in the form of huge, partly state-owned coal mines and factories, the support of regional state actors in the east would be of particular importance to the Orange state principal, because these local brokers could help shape public opinion and voting processes. In the west, conversely, public opinion is much less mediated by local brokers.

TABLE 4.2. *Average State Threats to Property Rights in Eastern and Western Ukraine*

EAST	THREAT (significance of east-west difference)	WEST
2.16	Extortion by taxation agencies (*)	2.53
2.16	Administrative pressure for financial contributions to various social funds (*)	2.50
1.97	Illegal inspections by regulatory agencies (**)	2.43
1.84	Illegal administrative barriers to obtaining licenses, operating permits, etc. (*)	2.18
1.79	Illegal administrative barriers to purchase or sale of land, real estate, assets, etc. (***)	2.34
1.71	Administrative pressure for informal payments (*)	1.95
1.47	Illegal administrative interference with hiring or firing of labor, including top management (*)	1.73
1.31	Hostile use of state resources by competitors (***)	1.90
1.29	Raiding, illegal ownership capture	1.37
1.74	AVERAGE (***)	2.10

Based on a survey of thirty-eight firms from the east and forty-one firms from the west of Ukraine. The seriousness of a given threat was reported on a 1–4 scale from least to most serious. T-test results comparing eastern and western regions for a given threat in parentheses: * $p < 0.10$, ** $p < 0.05$, *** $p < 0.01$.

support for the Orange coalition was deep and could only be ruined by state threats to PR. Such would be our expectations *if* state threats were systemic or "organized" in 2007.

My data directly contests these expectations. I compare the Ukrainian subsamples covering eastern and western regions.[77] Table 4.2 displays the results for both regions, listing individual threats in their descending order and indicating the significance level of the respective east-west differences for each threat. All threats are *lower* in the recalcitrant, anti-Orange east. The average intensity of state threats is 1.74 in the east, while it is 2.10 in the west of Ukraine (significant at the 0.01 level).

While undermining the "principal expropriation" hypothesis, this data also presents a puzzle: Why would Ukraine's western region suffer from higher predation than the country's eastern frontier? To address this puzzle, we begin by adding the survey results from Kyiv, which were not included in Table 4.2 because of Kyiv's special politico-economic status and its geographically central location. State threats to property rights are generally *higher* in Ukraine's capital city than elsewhere in the country: Kyiv's overall threat intensity is

---

[77] In the east, firms were sampled from Sumy and Luhansk *oblasts*; in the west, firms were sampled from L'viv and Khmelnytskyi *oblasts*.

Conclusion: Bespredel, Samodeiatel'nost', and History

2.27 as compared to 1.94 for the rest of Ukraine (east and west combined), a difference significant at the 0.01 level. Out of nine threats in Table 4.2, Kyiv's threat levels are highest relative to both the east and the west for four threats; Kyiv places in the middle on four other threats; and for one threat, Kyiv's levels are lowest.[78] Once Kyiv data is taken into account, the reason behind the east-west difference in threat intensities in Table 4.2 becomes clearer. The explanation that would suit the data pattern, as well as my qualitative interviews from across Ukraine, concerns demographics. Ukraine's eastern regions exhibit high inequality with little trace of a middle class, while the country's west – *as well as Kyiv* – feature a much larger middle class and with it, critically, many more independent small and medium-size enterprises. The latter, in turn, are the life-blood for the state agents qua predators. In the east, "a few people are like Akhmetov [a prominent billionaire], but most are just workhorses, miners.... They have nothing to give," remarked an entrepreneur from the region in my interview. Juicy assets in the industrially concentrated east belong to powerful business empires beyond the reach of most state agents; in Ukraine's central and western regions, conversely, the fruits are smaller but plentiful and ripe for the picking.

Overall, three findings from my survey support the argument that agent predation is a relatively serious state threat to property rights as compared to principal expropriation: (1) Business respondents assign more importance to the incorruptibility of the local authorities than to the democratic checks on the national government as a way to improve PR security; (2) firms exhibit a higher propensity to engage in predation themselves when they see the local authorities rather than the central state as the main culprits; and (3) the subnational variation in state threats to PR in Russia and Ukraine fails to conform to a pattern of "exchange" between the state leader and the local bureaucrats.

CONCLUSION: *BESPREDEL*, *SAMODEIATEL'NOST'*, AND HISTORY

Far from being encouraged by the state principal, much predation in Russia and Ukraine is a symptom of dysfunctional yet high-powered bureaucracies. Indeed, the two most frequent words describing state threats in my interviews with business owners and experts in the region were "bespredel" and "samodeiatel'nost'." *Bespredel* can be roughly translated as "lawless mayhem" or "menacing chaos." *Samodeiatel'nost'* literally means "self-activity" and traditionally describes amateurish grass-roots performances as opposed to the professional acts.

---

[78] Among the four threats that are highest in Kyiv, Kyiv's lead is significant at the 0.01 level for two threats: (1) extortion by taxation agencies and (2) raiding, illegal ownership capture. The only threat lower in Kyiv than in both eastern and western parts of the country is illegal administrative interference in hiring or firing of labor; Kyiv's lag is significant at the 0.01 level.

It would be wrong, however, to label Russia and Ukraine as cases of agent predation as opposed to principal expropriation. Many, and maybe most, cases in the developing world are mixed. Instead, Chapters 3 and 4 have defended empirically the conceptual space we carved out for understanding an essential type of PR threats largely ignored by the approaches stressing disorganized corruption and systemic expropriation.

In conclusion, the prism of history should be briefly pointed at the tragedy of property fights in Russia and Ukraine. For if agent predation has deep roots in the countries' pre-"transition" past, then any arguments assuming principal expropriation must demonstrate just how these path dependencies have been overcome by the postcommunist state principals.

The patrimonialism of the Russian Empire, at its height between the fifteenth and the mid-seventeenth centuries, effectively fused sovereign ownership of property and power. Meanwhile, the vastness of the empire, combined with its poor infrastructure, empowered the bureaucracy, whose creed was "that which I manage, on it I feed [*chto kontroliruiu, tem i kormlius'*]." Although the state's patrimonial control over the economy and noblemen receded during the reforms of the nineteenth century, the 1917 Revolution turned back the clock forcefully. The communist sovereign reasserted his power over property, at least until Stalin's death.

Then, the bureaucrats resumed their feeding, as private wealth – concealed and illegitimate – began to accumulate. Many esteemed Western scholars have mistakenly viewed the Soviet Union in its prime as the epitome of high "infrastructural power."[79] Yet, despite the World War II glory and light-speed industrialization under Stalin, the infrastructural power of Soviet Union was anything but impressive. Far from being a Weberian wunderkind, the Soviet bureaucracy was penetrated at every level by the Communist Party. The resulting politicization of everyday bureaucratic life was exacerbated by the personalization of both recruitment and decision-making, as well as the complex overlapping mandates in the state-party hierarchy: no legal rationality, no public-service ethos, and poor division of labor.[80] In the sphere of property rights, Khrushchev's 1957 reforms, adopted in response to the pressure of regional bureaucracy, devolved the management rights in state-owned assets from sectoral ministries to the regions. The empowerment of local state agents was dramatic and proved resistant to Brezhnev's 1965 backlash (in which management rights were formally returned to sectoral ministries).[81] The economic

---

[79] Huntington (1968, 1) famously observed that in the Soviet Union, just like in the United States, "the government governs," that is, it has "strong, adaptable, coherent political institutions: effective bureaucracies." See also Mann 2008, 356; De Mesquita et al., 6.

[80] Volensky 1984.

[81] For a thorough analysis, including new data, of the evolution in Soviet property rights' system and its ramifications for today's property relations in Russia, see Tambovcev.

Conclusion: Bespredel, Samodeiatel'nost', and History 119

decentralization during Gorbachev's perestroika in many ways formalized *fait accompli* while devolving effective control even further from the region-level to enterprise-level state employees. The communist sovereign may have perished in the Soviet collapse, yet the bureaucracy persisted,[82] and, as this chapter argued, has not lost its appetite.

[82] In both Russian and Ukrainian bureaucracies, the higher-ranked employees, as a group, are predominantly older males who began their service in the Soviet Union. In addition, civil service suffers from adverse selection; while the more qualified mid-career bureaucrats leave for the private sector, many young hires enter the service in order to develop the necessary business contacts and then, too, leave. The resulting high turnover among younger employees contrasts with the greying of the upper ranks, where bureaucrats face no pressure to leave after entering pension age. For an excellent OECD study on Russia, see Tompson 2007.

5

Commitment Dissolved

Our inquiry so far has profiled an important phenomenon jeopardizing the security of property rights in Russia and Ukraine. Agent predation constitutes an underappreciated, widespread, and detrimental state threat to ownership rights. This conclusion raises the question of appropriate *remedies*, the subject of the remaining chapters.

The literature on PR security (see Chapter 2 for an overview) has converged on the notion of *commitment* by the ruler or the central executive as an effective solution to the scourge of predation. Among the long list of commitment devices available to the sovereign, two specific institutions appear as the most promising in allowing the ruler to commit beyond "cheap talk." First, the ruler may commit by supporting or initiating encompassing formal business associations. Second, the ruler's commitment can be facilitated by institutional checks and balances, particularly by an empowered parliament.

This chapter argues that Russia and Ukraine in the 2000s experienced the creation of precisely such commitment devices – encompassing business associations in the case of Russia and an empowered parliament in the case of Ukraine. The *failure* of these developments to improve the security of property rights in these countries (and in Ukraine's case the possible *worsening* of the situation) makes for a puzzle in light of conventional wisdom.

To be sure, one could argue that the executive commitment simply was not credible enough in our two cases. However, such defense of the commitment paradigm would imply tautological reasoning; if "commitment" can only be inferred based on its post hoc effectiveness, then the state commitment paradigm is unfalsifiable and, as a definitional exercise, rather uninteresting. The more fruitful approach is to take the paradigm's key causal argument seriously. Russia's encompassing business associations after 2000 and Ukraine's empowered parliament after 2004 may fall short of ideal-case commitment scenarios, yet by the empirical standards of modern developing countries, these commitment devices deployed by – or imposed on – the rulers of these two economies

Putin's Russia and the Rise of The Business Quartet

are as good as it gets. If such devices fail to improve the security of ownership, then an examination of *why* they failed becomes critical.

I argue that the conventional devices, which are expected to commit the state principal, fail to improve ownership security in the face of agent predation. The reason is that the state principal cannot commit *on behalf of* the state agents. The nets designed to constrain a shark are not sufficiently fine-meshed to constrain piranhas.

PUTIN'S RUSSIA AND THE RISE OF THE BUSINESS QUARTET

Business Institutionalization under Putin

After the Soviet collapse, Russian capitalists took advantage of their new freedom of association. Throughout most of the 1990s, however, the development of formal business associations (BAs) was unsuccessful.[1] While the inter-firm linkages in state-owned industry crumbled because of the abolition of branch ministries, the organizational consolidation of *private* entrepreneurs was obstructed by the state's general imperviousness to independent formal interest groups. Some BAs in new sectors, such as the Association of Russian Banks, developed into effective organizations; however, they faced the problem of leadership as associational competition for the representation of new sectors led to intra-sectoral strife, manifested in the creation of redundant BA structures in the same sector. The absence of threat from organized labor reduced the urgency of employer unification in all sectors. Overall, like other segments of Russia's civil society, BAs failed to develop sustainable organizations in the 1990s.

My research suggests that Russia's business world – once an amalgam of warring and colluding, failing and powerful, but in all cases organizationally disunited firms – underwent an institutional transformation during Putin's first presidency. I focus on four *cross-sectoral* and *federal* associations that have achieved solid membership bases as well as organizational ties with state structures after Putin's assumption of power.

Since 2000, Putin's administration has conducted its interactions with organized business exclusively through four BAs, profiled in this chapter.[2] Two of these BAs (the RUIE and the CCI) existed prior to 2000 but were fundamentally reformed, while two others (the OPORA and Business Russia) were created from scratch.

The Russian Union of Industrialists and Entrepreneurs

Undoubtedly the most prominent association, the Russian Union of Industrialists and Entrepreneurs (RUIE), includes some 328,000 individuals, representing

---

[1] Zudin 1997, 10–13.
[2] Unless otherwise noted, the reference for this entire section is Markus 2007.

more than 5,000 companies and other associations in all of Russia's eighty-three federal regions. The firms in the RUIE account for 60 percent of the GDP.[3] The union's roots go back to 1990, when the Scientific-Industrial Union was formed, a stronghold for "liberal communists" in the enterprise directors' corps, with Gorbachev's market reforms and the "Chinese path" as their guiding vision. The RUIE formed in December 1991 and attempted to ride the wave of industrialist influence during the early 1990s, progressively waning in significance toward the end of the decade. The RUIE's main achievement of the 1990s was Minister of Industry Alexander Titkin's 1992–3 service on the RUIE board. Even this claim to fame, however, was modest; the real heavyweights of the industrialist lobby – Viktor Chernomyrdin, Georgy Khizha, and Vladimir Shumeiko – shunned the RUIE throughout the decade, as did the presidential administration. The RUIE attempted to launch an industrial political party in 1994, but the project never took off. At the end of the 1990s, hundreds of workers were still bussed to the RUIE's congress meetings to create a Potemkin village-like semblance of importance.

In 2000, dozens of Russia's so-called oligarchs joined the RUIE. Unlike the "red directors" of the state-owned enterprises, the newcomers were younger, less likely to have engineering background, and much wealthier, having made fortunes during the rigged privatizations of the 1990s. In less than two years, the RUIE's "native" industrialists were sidelined by reformist corporate capital. In 2002, two of the RUIE's veterans from the state enterprise sector defiantly left the RUIE's Management Bureau to lead smaller BAs in the regions.[4] Meanwhile, the oligarchs divided competencies within the RUIE among themselves,[5] sometimes leading industrialists to cry foul: "The oligarchs now control virtually all committees and working groups in RUIE.... RUIE's Management Bureau makes all main decisions behind closed doors.... RUIE's charter reminds us of the Brezhnev-era constitution with its provision about the guiding role of the party."[6]

Despite the clash of cultures following the oligarchic takeover, the RUIE emerged as a powerful organization. Since 2000, the RUIE has engaged in sustained top-level policy work, achieving considerable prestige in the economic policy community. The RUIE's congress meetings are attended by the president, the prime minister, and key cabinet members. Membership in the RUIE's high-profile "Management Bureau" (biuro pravleniia) carries a $100,000 annual price tag for its twenty-seven individual affiliates. By 2001, the press was referring

---

[3] The RUIE's website, http://www.rspp.ru/.
[4] Vakhtang Koveshnikov of the electronics industry launched the St. Petersburg Business Circle. Vladimir Luzyanin of the aviation industry took over the Nizhny Novgorod Association of Industrialists and Entrepreneurs.
[5] Vladimir Evtushenkov took over issues related to industrial policy; Mikhail Khodorkovsky – foreign relations; Kakha Bendukidze – tax and budget policy; Mikhail Fridman – court reform; Ruben Vardanyan – energy sector reform; Vladimir Potanin – corporate governance.
[6] Vslukh December 10, 2003.

Putin's Russia and the Rise of The Business Quartet

to the Union as a "shadow cabinet" or, less flatteringly, the "oligarchs' trade union." One media analysis, tellingly titled "Who is the master of the house?" concluded at the time, "Having emerged from the ruins of the 'red director' corps, RUIE may not be prepared to seize the power as some analogous organization of army generals would do, but it is ready to explain to the authorities what must be done.... It seems that the government will have to listen."[7]

By 2003, the RUIE boasted an $80 million budget (comparable to an average Russian ministry at the time), two thirds of which was spent on policy projects. While in the 1990s BAs depended on underfunded public institutions for conducting modest economic analysis, the RUIE now relies on its own well-staffed Expert Institute; in advance of the 2004 presidential election, more than 100 professional experts were working on an economic program to be advocated by the RUIE.

The two new formal mechanisms linking the state with the RUIE are President Putin's institutionalized meetings with the RUIE leadership and the latter's access to policy-making. The biannual meetings of the RUIE's Management Bureau with Putin, during which legislative proposals prepared by the RUIE's fifteen policy groups (on taxation, land law, World Trade Organization [WTO] access, etc.) are discussed, became a routine by 2003 and have continued throughout Putin's second term. Furthermore, on Putin's instruction, the RUIE's Management Bureau members were mandatorily included in "consultative commissions and organs at the presidency and the government of the Russian Federation."[8]

The best indication of the RUIE's new status is the list of policies the Union has shaped. The 2002 laws on pensions were based on the RUIE proposals. The Union pushed through the 2002 Law on Employers Unions. The 460-article Code on Customs, laboriously adopted in 2003, resulted from the joint work of the State Customs Committee, the RUIE, and the federal government; the RUIE successfully insisted on the implementation of international best practice in customs procedures and curtailed the ability of the State Customs Committee to amend the law in the future. In 2006, the RUIE and the Federal Antimonopoly Service submitted a proposal to the Duma that was adopted as the Law On Protection of Competition; the RUIE succeeded in increasing the threshold market share that triggers scrutiny from state regulators from 5 to 8 percent as well as in transferring the right to impose sanctions from the Federal Antimonopoly Service to the courts. Perhaps most remarkably, formally organized business with the RUIE at the helm made landmark tax reform possible. Through formal intermediation via the Council on Entrepreneurship, a key agreement was reached in 2001 on the taxation of oil sales.[9] Under RUIE pressure, Minister of Finance Alexei Kudrin agreed in 2003 to the stepwise

---

[7] Goreslavsky 2001.
[8] *Vedomosti* June 27, 2001.
[9] Peregudov 2003.

124   *Commitment Dissolved*

lowering of the value-added tax from 20 to 15 percent over three years.[10] The RUIE pushed through far-reaching amendments to the tax code constraining the discretion of tax police in 2006.[11] The full scope of the RUIE's policy impact includes numerous other issues, such as land leasing, standardization of accounting practices, repatriation of offshore capital, bankruptcy legislation, industrial policy, foreign exchange regulation, reform of natural monopolies, WTO access, enterprises' debt restructuring, banking reform, administrative reform, court reform, and others.

The Chamber of Commerce and Industry

Larger in scope than the RUIE, the Chamber of Commerce and Industry (CCI) has shown even more dynamic growth through the 2000s. Its regional network grew from 155 to 174 regional and municipal centers while its membership skyrocketed from around 20,000 to more than 50,000 companies and associations between 2000 and 2012. The number of the CCI's representations abroad grew from fourteen to nineteen in the same period. The CCI's annual budget grew to $23 million by 2011. While all business categories are represented, small and medium-sized businesses account for 70 percent of the CCI membership and have a strong voice in the organization, a key difference vis-à-vis the RUIE.

Another difference is the CCI's semipublic status, a residue of the CCI's Soviet roots. Created in 1932, the CCI served as "an outlet into foreign commerce for the increasingly isolated Soviet power." Although under the tutelage of the KGB, the CCI cultivated an apolitical profile and became integrated into the global system of trade chambers at the height of the Cold War. Today, the law still instructs state organs "to assist the chambers of commerce and industry in implementing their charter mission" and to provide them with real estate.[12]

In the 1990s, the CCI continued to fulfill state functions connected with economic representation abroad while staying out of politics. For a brief period, the CCI possessed the formal right of legislative initiative under the Law on Chambers of Commerce and Industry in Russian Federation; remarkably, the association had never used this right before it became moot under the 1993 Constitution (Article 104 limits legislative initiative to three branches of state power).

After 2000, the Chamber shed its technocratic inertia and assumed a prominent lobbying role, epitomized by Primakov's leadership of the CCI since December 2001. (Primakov's political resume includes the positions of minister

---

[10] Prime-Tass News Wire, January 29, 2003.

[11] As the Union president notes, "RUIE, as the initiator of all these amendments, first of all achieved the consolidation of business community's position on these issues, and, second, actively articulated this position in all possible public arenas." Shokhin's interview with Gazeta.ru, July 18, 2006.

[12] Article 4.1, Law N 5340–1 "On Chambers of Commerce and Industry in Russian Federation."

of foreign affairs and prime minister.) In 2003, the CCI's chair of the legislation department underscored in his interview with the author that "among the Union's three functions, the representation of business interests vis-à-vis the state is decisive. We also develop basic business infrastructure including peer courts, and offer for-pay services including asset valuation and contacts with foreign investors." The CCI's success in lobbying for a simplification of the Tax Code chapter for small and medium enterprises (SMEs) was most indicative of its new role. Together with the OPORA (discussed in the next section), the CCI has effectively promoted legislation reducing state discretion in registering, certifying, and inspecting small enterprises. By the end of the 2000s, the CCI was organizing around 100 press conferences per year to report on the Chamber's key initiatives, the meetings of its leadership with Russia's president, and new legislation affecting business.

The Union of Business Associations of Russia (OPORA)
Exclusively aimed at SMEs, the Union of Business Associations of Russia (OPORA) – whose Russian acronym means "support" – was founded in 2001 by fifty sectoral and regional associations, uniting 850,000 firms. The number of associations affiliated with the OPORA grew from 50 to 140 by 2012. In 2003, the ORORA opened its doors to individual firms. Rising quickly on Russia's lobbyist horizon, the OPORA opened sixty-four regional centers before 2005; by 2012, the OPORA's eighty-one regional centers were spanning Russia from Kaliningrad to Kamchatka.

Since its foundation, the OPORA has been led by Sergey Borisov, an ambitious entrepreneur who has owned or managed firms in the gas station and transportation sectors and likes to flaunt his executive coursework at the Harvard Business School. Unlike the CCI's Primakov or his successor, Katyrin, both career politicians, Borisov commands the respect of Russia's entrepreneurs as one of their own. Combating the administrative harassment of entrepreneurs constitutes the OPORA's prime mission, according to Borisov (author's interview), along with the improvement of the banking infrastructure. The association also provides expert consultation (on taxation, licensing, etc.) to member firms, participates in drafting legislative proposals, and runs international programs in conjunction with several government ministries.

By 2003, the OPORA had established itself as the prime interface for the exchange between governmental structures and the SMEs. Initially, the OPORA's nine sectoral working groups (services, retail, agriculture, etc.) institutionalized their communication channels with the Ministry of Economic Development and Trade, the Ministry of Finance, and the Committee on Customs. By 2012, a stunning ninety-five committees and councils included OPORA representatives in the government of the Russian Federation, the General Procuracy, the offices of plenipotentiary presidential representatives in the federal regions, the parliament (both in the Duma and the Federation Council), the Highest

126   *Commitment Dissolved*

Arbitrage Court, the Public Chamber, as well as a plethora of federal executive organs (ministries, services, and agencies).[13]

Business Russia *(Delovaia Rossiia)*

Business Russia was created from scratch, like the OPORA, in 2001, but its rise has been more protracted and tumultuous. The association grew out of the eponymous, inter-fraction Duma union of fifty-five medium-sized business representatives who, inspired by the RUIE's success (and initially viewed by the RUIE as its own Duma wing) took up independent association-building and sought ties with the presidential administration in 2001. At the time of its foundational meeting in October 2001 and following a reception by Putin, Business Russia positioned itself as the representative of companies with an annual turnover of $10–500 million. Despite Putin's embrace and the existence of a parliamentary platform, the organization ran into financing difficulties, lacking the OPORA's large and enthusiastic membership base, the RUIE members' wealth, or the CCI's semipublic status. In 2003, Business Russia also suffered from the departure of its enterprising founder, Igor Lisinenko (CEO of Maisky Chai, a tea company, and the Duma deputy of United Russia). For several months, the association was in limbo.

Since 2004, Business Russia has resurrected itself, led to prominence by its new chair, Boris Titov. A former CEO of the chemical financial-industrial group Interkhimprom as well as a "wine-tourism" holding, Abrau-Durso, Titov was also a member of the RUIE's Management Bureau which he left in 2005 to focus on developing Business Russia. From 500 individual members at its founding, Business Russia has built an umbrella organization for sixty sectoral associations that unite entrepreneurs from sixty-four federal regions. The organization has cleverly branded itself as representing mid- to large-size businesses outside of the natural resource sector; this niche has proved extremely effective vis-à-vis the presidential administration. The instability of oil prices after the 2008 financial crisis has reinforced Putin's long-stated goal of moving away from economic dependence on the resource sector. Since the latter is mostly represented at the RUIE, while Russia's small businesses of the OPORA and the CCI continue to be relatively insignificant for the state budget, Business Russia, with its core of mid- and large-size manufacturing firms, has recently emerged as an important interlocutor for the federal government.[14]

By 2012, representatives of Business Russia were included in thirty-seven committees and councils in federal executive organs, the Federation Council,

---

[13] http://opora.ru/organization/representation_in_government.php

[14] In his opening address at the forum of Russian business on May 26, 2011, Putin thanked Business Russia, adding that "the main driver of development is our mid-size manufacturing business … those who achieve success not due to the resource rent or … asset speculation … but above all due to opening effective enterprises, implementing advanced technologies, constantly raising the standards of corporate governance." Full transcript on file with author.

Putin's Russia and the Rise of The Business Quartet

the General Procuracy, the Audit Chamber, and the Moscow city government. While its overall presence in government bodies is less comprehensive than that of the OPORA, Business Russia leaders sit on four committees[15] in the presidential administration (the OPORA is not represented at this level at all). The portfolio of achievements by Business Russia now includes: 2010 amendments to the criminal code aimed at decriminalizing business and instituting harsher punishments for bureaucrats preying on entrepreneurs; the 2009 harmonization of legislation on business inspections, aimed at extending small firms' privileges to mid-size businesses; the 2006 lowering of customs fees on imports of high-tech equipment; 2006 amendments to the Law on Protection of Competition restricting the use of "administrative resources" in market competition; the 2006–7 creation of state-based financing vehicles for innovation and business support, such as Development Bank and Russian Venture Company; and so forth.[16]

The BA Quartet

To sum up, all four BAs after 2000 experienced successful interest aggregation as well as the formalization of the state-business dialogue in which BAs (as compared with individuals or single firms) have come to play an important role. As the vice president of the CCI noted in my interview,

In that period [the 1990s], the entrepreneurial community was just being born.... Organizations per se did not exist; they were formed as monuments and ruins [of defunct state organs], sometimes created by very respected people but not needed by anybody, with wrongly identified missions. Now we witness ... the formation of a civilized entrepreneurial system.

The OPORA's president spoke in my 2003 interview of "a new cultural attitude of government towards business ... the Prime-Minister, the mayor [of Moscow] now consult with business associations." As compared to the 1990s, he added, "business is better organized – and taken into account." The leader of Business Russia summed it up best: "We are talking about the emergence of *business community as such* out of an amorphous mass of entrepreneurs that were split into clans."[17]

The perception that the rules of the game had changed was not limited to the immediate beneficiaries of the process. In my 2003 interview, the chief editor of *Ekspert*, Russia's premier business magazine, remarked:

The situation has changed dramatically.... The first step towards the creation of strong entrepreneurial organizations ... has been made during the last three years. [In

---

[15] These include: the Council on the Realization of Priority National Projects and Demographic Policy, the Council on Assistance in Developing Civil Society and Human Rights, the Council on Developing the Information Community, and the Working Group on Modernization and the Technological Development of Russia's Economy.

[16] http://www.deloros.ru/main.php?mid=188

[17] *Novaya Gazeta* July 5, 2001.

128   *Commitment Dissolved*

the 1990s,] these were social clubs rather than "associations" ... but today they are real, important public organizations that have a relationship with [state] power. It is a systemic phenomenon. Look at the serious discussions being conducted in business associations now, e.g. about Russia's entry into the WTO: what we witness is interest structuration and expression. In the 1990s, there was none of that: there was property redistribution [*peredel sobstvennosti*] ... as in 1917, the state said "steal what had been stolen from you," so that's what business was preoccupied with. Now the situation is different in principle.

Andrei Yakovlev, an expert on state-business relations at the Higher School of Economics, wrote:

In 2000–02, a relative balance of power was maintained between business and the state.... This balance relied on mutual obligations ... implying that the state will refuse to revise the outcome of the 1990s [privatization].... In 2000–2003, when tax, labor and customs codes were being developed ... [the] collective interests [of business] were represented by RUIE, Business Russia, and OPORA.... Business associations will ... give a more effective response to bureaucratic consolidation of the state machine than giant conglomerate holding company groups, which were created by the business in the early 2000s.[18]

The Kremlin views the BA quartet profiled here as the exclusive interlocutors for the presidential administration. These are the only four organizations whose meetings Putin regularly attends, and he has done so for more than a decade in his capacities as president and prime minister (as did President Medvedev in 2008–12), delivering lengthy addresses and engaging in discussions that, unlike Putin's televised question-and-answers with citizens at large, are typically unscripted. There are no cross-sectoral associations outside of the quartet, whose representatives the Kremlin has insisted on including in committees at various levels of the executive, legislature, and the judiciary. Interviewed leaders of all four BAs acknowledged that the presidential administration signaled its readiness for a dialogue with organized business upon Putin's assumption of power.[19] The administration was also clear in its welcoming of size-based (rather than sectoral) associations.[20]

Finally, Russia's post-2000 business institutionalization[21] appears striking not only relative to the Byzantine 1990s but also in a national comparative

---

[18] Yakovlev, 20, 31.

[19] To quote the head of Business Russia, "in the Presidential Administration, the idea was ... to interact with business at three levels, with big business through RUIE, medium business through Business Russia, and small business through OPORA.... The Presidential Administration declared immediately that it would support Business Russia. A meeting with president [Putin] was conducted, he said 'I will support all your positive initiatives,' and in that fashion the highest power showed unambiguously its support of our organization." (author's interview)

[20] As Putin imparted on the delegates of a 2002 CCI congress, "The state very much needs the ... civil activity of entrepreneurs. Unification of business communities is needed – and not only on sectoral basis – but also for the solution of other ... tasks, influencing the total economic situation." Putin's address at the Fourth Congress of the CCI on June 19, 2002.

[21] Business institutionalization is defined as interest aggregation within the entrepreneurial community and the relational formalization of the state-business boundary.

Putin's Russia and the Rise of The Business Quartet

perspective. It may dwarf the level of business organization in Mexico, which is considered *highest* in Latin America.[22] The EU-level of business organization likewise appears weaker than that found in Russia; the "strategic alliances" created by firms to assist the EU Commission with policy-making have been largely informal, policy-specific, unstable, and limited to large corporations.[23]

The Logic of Business Institutionalization: Cooptation versus Commitment

The encompassing nature of the business quartet, as well as its close interaction with the state principal should be auspicious for the latter's commitment to PR security. Still, commitment could be undermined if the quartet were supported by the sovereign for a purpose that conflicts with the logic of commitment. The most plausible commitment-undermining purpose is the cooptation of rivals; rather than binding himself, the sovereign may aim to neutralize his enemies. However, I argue that it is unlikely that Putin institutionally empowered business either to engage in vote harvesting or to dominate private firms.

Business Institutionalization for Vote Harvesting?

The comparative literature suggests that the cooptation logic of business empowerment by the sovereign could manifest itself in two ways. First, the sovereign, facing external political rivals, may institutionally empower third parties, such as business associations, to help him defeat challengers to the throne.[24] Yet this explanation completely misses the timing of the Russian case. When Putin's administration jumpstarted business institutionalization, the state principal's mandate was at its strongest in Russia's history to date. After feeble and utterly discredited Yeltsin resigned, Putin's no-nonsense approach to Chechen rebels and the oligarchs sent his approval ratings into the 80+ percent stratosphere, while the hike in oil prices provided a much-needed cushion to the state budget. Furthermore, Yeltsin's appointment of Putin as acting president on December 31, 1999, months ahead of the presidential election, helped cement Putin's advantage. As business institutionalization unfolded, Putin was cruising to victory, which he assured in the first round with 53 percent of the votes while the Communist runner-up Zyuganov gathered less than 30 percent.

A contrast with *Yeltsin's* attempt at business institutionalization in the years preceding the 1996 presidential election is instructive at this point. With

---

[22] The Consejo Mexicano de Hombres de Negocios, roughly comparable to Russia's RUIE given the cross-sectoral focus on big business, has been hailed as the "single most important organization of the private sector." Yet the Consejo's "core activity," monthly luncheons with non-senior government officials that only occasionally include cabinet members, is but a pale shadow of the RUIE's formalized, multidimensional, well-funded, top-level policy involvement. Schneider 2002.

[23] Coen 1997.

[24] E.g., Polsky 2000, 457; Schneider, 91; Coen, 91–108.

approval ratings in single digits, Yeltsin's prospects against the Communist candidate were so bleak that members of Yeltsin's entourage urged him to suspend elections and impose martial law. Instead, Yeltsin's administration began supporting organized business in a bid consistent with the cooptation theory.[25] The state principal's choice fell upon the Roundtable of Russia's Business, an organization that emerged after the 1993 parliamentary putsch, when the danger of a Communist Duma majority scared business circles into closer cooperation with the incumbent president. Uniting a group of business elites (with Peter Aven as its highest-profile businessman), the Roundtable was led by the charismatic banker Ivan Kivelidi. According to a leading expert who knew Kivelidi personally, the Roundtable "was important not as an organization but as an agreement between oligarchs to stop shooting each other."[26] Still, the meetings of the Roundtable were also attended by high-ranking government officials, and the membership of some popular businesspeople, such as Vlad List'ev (the CEO of First Channel TV, admired by Russians for his journalism) held out the promise of converting the organization into an electoral vehicle for Yeltsin. In addition to its popular appeal, the government hoped to use the Roundtable as a campaign piggybank; a fund was set up at the Roundtable to pool sizeable "membership fees," which were widely seen as political contributions.

The case of the Roundtable could not be more different from business institutionalization in 2000–1. Putin's administration did not attempt to seek donations from the BA quartet or to use organized business in its electoral campaigns at the time. Organized small business presented the largest political temptation to Putin in terms of its electoral appeal. However, in choosing the relatively apolitical OPORA as its preferred interlocutor, the administration *rejected two politically more promising small-business organizations* that were competing with the OPORA for presidential attention at the time: the All-Russian Political Movement "Development of Entrepreneurship," led by a veteran economy expert and Duma deputy, Ivan Grachev, and the small-business wing of the Union of Right Forces party.[27] The cooptation and "development" of these platforms promised real electoral dividends, yet the Kremlin chose otherwise.

Furthermore, the sheer durability of the quartet through the 2000s, regardless of electoral cycles, contrasts sharply with the brief prominence of the Roundtable in the 1990s. Yeltsin's government, in line with the cooptation logic, abandoned the Roundtable once it became clear that the latter could not be an asset in the elections; the wealthiest oligarchs had never joined Kivelidi's Roundtable in the first place, betting their funds on individual politicians rather than organizations. The efforts of Vice Prime Minister Shumeiko to attract the

---

[25] References for this case, in addition to author's interviews, include: *Ekspert* October 22, 2001; *Kommersant* October 30, 1993; *Kommersant* September 2, 1995.

[26] *Novaya Gazeta* February 7, 2005.

[27] *Novye Izvestiya* October 18, 2001.

Putin's Russia and the Rise of The Business Quartet

heaviest money bags to the Roundtable failed, and the government gradually lost interest in the association. The Roundtable soon disintegrated because of both the government's aloofness and the pervasive distrust among the Roundtable members (it did not help that four prominent members were assassinated in a somewhat bizarre fashion[28]). Overall, the case of the Roundtable of Russia's Business shows that business institutionalization was not only fundamentally different after 2000 in terms of its *extent*, but also in terms of the underlying *sovereign incentives*, as compared to the 1990s.

Business Institutionalization for Sovereign Domination of Firms?

The second type of cooptation logic suggests that the sovereign, facing pressure from *individual firms*, may help organize them in order to dominate them more easily.[29] Accordingly, the RUIE's strengthening has been interpreted as part of the state's agenda to control the notorious oligarchs institutionally.[30] Yet the cooptation-for-domination perspective falters once business institutionalization is acknowledged *beyond* the RUIE. Tens of thousands of small enterprises, perennial victims of Russian bureaucracy and fervent supporters of the Kremlin's economic reforms, simply never were a challenge to Putin's administration. It is rather puzzling why BAs, organizationally effete and functionally marginal throughout the 1990s, presented a target for the state's takeover. Even if limited to the RUIE, the domination thesis begs questions. Putin may have brought magnates' blatant politicking under control, but *formal BAs have played no role in the process*. The administration has successfully targeted specific corporations and persons without any recourse to the RUIE. If the latter was intended as a domination instrument, it proved utterly redundant.

Neither is it the case that the sovereign pursued a "divide and conquer" approach to business. In 2004, the RUIE, the OPORA, and Business Russia created the Coordination Council of Entrepreneurs' Unions (*Koordinatsionnyi Sovet Predprinimatel'skikh Soiuzov*), which "was not an independent organization but a platform to coordinate our positions," according to the RUIE's president, and it "worked very effectively for a few years."[31] The state principal supported this inter-BA platform, and the latter has lost its punch recently

---

[28] Vlad List'ev, Oleg Kantor, and Oleg Zverev were assassinated first, in separate incidents. After one funeral, Kivelidi told the Roundtable, "perhaps my death would force you to unite against criminal business?" Kivelidi was prescient, if only about himself: In August 1995, he was poisoned with a hyper-toxic weapons-grade substance sprayed on his phone receiver. (Through macabre accidents, his secretary and the autopsy examiner died from the poison still emanating from Kivelidi's body.) While the *poisoning* did not technically violate the Roundtable's covenant of not *shooting* each other, organization members jumped ship nonetheless, and the organization closed.

[29] E.g., Offe 1981; Silva 1996.

[30] Barnes, 175–7.

[31] Aleksandr Shokhin on the radio program "Dura Lex" at Ekho Moskvy, March 26, 2011. Transcript available at: http://www.echo.msk.ru/programs/lex/759898-echo.html.

132   *Commitment Dissolved*

because of disagreements between BA members, not sovereign subversion.[32] Russia's entrepreneurs themselves, a notoriously cynical bunch, did not view Putin's support of BAs as an attempt to dominate business. As the chief editor of *Ekspert* noted in my interview, "it is not the case that the administration created a pocket organization for itself: *it simply has no need* for such a pocket organization. On the contrary, it wanted to help business self-organize, so as to release new energy."

The discussion so far casts doubt on the cooptation logic behind the sovereign's support for the quartet. Conversely, business institutionalization has been compatible with the logic of commitment in several ways.

To begin, the government's management of the "state-endorsed" BAs became *less* authoritative under Putin. In the 1990s, many BAs were created by the government to fulfill a particular function prescribed by the state (mostly dictated by neoliberal reforms); given such instrumental objectives, the state was unwilling to "let an association go."[33] Frequently, BAs were de facto integrated into their birth-giving state structures. After 2000, however, support for the BA quartet came directly from the presidential administration, not from the functional ministries. Also, BAs were *encouraged* rather than directly created. This was done not via state financing but by promising the entrepreneurs access to policymaking. Curiously, the leader of a major BA related to me that the OPORA's founding members, aiming to increase the association's leverage with the government in the future, asked the presidential administration to delegate a leader for their new organization, yet the administration *explicitly declined to get involved in BA's internal politics*. This approach diverges quite radically from the establishment of nominal structures to execute predetermined state functions in the 1990s.

Until the end of the 2000s (see next section), the state principal's dialogue with organized business was very different from his authoritarian approach both to other sectors of civil society and to individual firms. While Putin did not hesitate to silence or heavy-handedly coopt organizations pursuing an array of potentially sensitive issues, such as media freedom or army draft, his interactions with the BA quartet were defined by extensive dialogue, institutional inclusion, and policy concessions. The divergence between the Kremlin's approach to select BAs and other civil society segments becomes easier to grasp once the fundamental difference between organized capital and other societal forces is acknowledged. Organized business remains *business*; after all is said and done, the goal is to make profit. With his pro-market, statist bent for increasing national prosperity while controlling dissent, Putin was a welcome ally for organized firms. As for individual firms, the Yukos case demonstrated clearly that the BA-supporting sovereign reserved the right to target select

---

[32] Ibid.

[33] Examples of such BAs include the Union of Metal Exporters, the Union of Associated Cooperatives, the All-Russian Association of Enterprises to be Privatized, etc. Zudin 1997.

Putin's Russia and the Rise of The Business Quartet

individuals for political insubordination. Yet, while Putin declined to bargain with the RUIE about Yukos's main shareholder Khodorkovsky, Putin indicated his continuing support for organized business by attending the thirteenth RUIE Congress in November 2003. The exertion of administrative pressure on single magnates and the state principal's support of business associations are not mutually exclusive. Interestingly, while Khodorkovsky's arrest at the time was linked in part to the tycoon's support of Yabloko, an opposition party, the OPORA openly cooperated with Yabloko without triggering any inquiries from the administration.

The cooperative genesis of business institutionalization, radically distinct from presidential feuds with the oligarchs and Putin's suppression of political dissent, was evidenced in the creation of new institutional platforms for state-business interaction. The Council on Entrepreneurship, established in 2000 and headed by the prime minister, provided an arena for interaction between twenty-four businessmen and the government. Since the businessmen were government-picked, including the representatives of medium enterprises along with big business, the latter signaled that it "did not find such format appropriate." On the suggestion of Mikhail Fridman (the head of Alfa Group), Putin, *in a conciliatory response to organized big business*, mandated the inclusion of the RUIE's Management Bureau members in governmental consultative commissions to provide a more exclusive platform for top-caliber business.[34] More than seventy such government-business commissions were plowing through an extensive legislative agenda by the end of 2003.

Business Institutionalization as Commitment

As exemplified by the Council on Entrepreneurship, institutionalized state-business dialogue focused on the *upper* executive branch, that is, on the part of the administrative hierarchy emphasized in the commitment paradigm. In Russia, this hierarchy features three levels: ministries (top), services (middle), and agencies (bottom). Even the OPORA, which is entirely composed of small firms, targeted the upper nomenklatura through its inclusion in bureaucratic structures. By 2012, the OPORA was working at thirty-seven ministry-level councils, twenty-two service-level councils, and only six agency-level councils.[35] These councils featuring the OPORA covered 70 percent of all ministries, 30 percent of all services, and only 20 percent of all agencies. The OPORA was also active at eight councils in the Duma and six councils at the Federation Council.

An inquiry into the *ideational* basis for business institutionalization further supports the commitment perspective. The key ideas were furnished to the administration by the awkwardly named Institute for the National Project "Social Contract." According to an interviewed expert, the Institute

---

[34] *Kommersant-Daily* June 8, 2001.
[35] The OPORA website.

"generated the new ideology of state-business relations at the federal level." A nongovernmental organization, the Institute refers to itself as a "think-and-do tank" and was founded in 1999 by Club 2015, a group of forty-nine businessmen with a progressive vision for a prosperous and corruption free Russian future. The Institute's articulation of a structured partnership between business and government coincided closely with the new administration's agenda.[36] The central mission of the Institute, "to liberate business from bureaucratic shackles," also appealed to the presidential administration; the Institute conducted numerous studies for the administration supplying the requisite expertise for the passage of the landmark 2001 de-bureaucratization laws (on licensing, inspections, and registration).[37] The Institute's president, Alexander Auzan, an internationally recognized figure in civil society movements and a well-published economist, joined the boards and expert councils of the OPORA and Business Russia shortly after their creation. Both associations proved crucial in the adoption of the de-bureaucratization laws in the face of bureaucratic opposition (more on this later). The Institute was also the driving force behind the 2007 Law on Self-Regulating Organizations (Number 315); eagerly awaited by entrepreneurs for years, the law outlined the guidelines for the delegation of regulatory functions away from state agencies to sectoral business associations.

Finally, the case study of Russia's de-bureaucratization laws forcefully demonstrates the compatibility between business institutionalization and the logic of commitment. Under agent predation, laws curtailing the powers of state agents should incite particularly vicious resistance from the state apparatus. That is precisely what happened with the "de-bureaucratization" package, whose implementation Putin entrusted to German Gref. When the package was finally adopted, Russia's *Kommersant* opined that Gref's successful "pushing of the State Duma ... to gnaw away at bureaucracy ... is astounding considering the deputies' negative attitude to his liberal ideas."[38]

It was the OPORA, the CCI, and Business Russia that ultimately came to Gref's rescue, in a process coordinated by the state principal, as described below. Such sovereign-business collaboration aimed at curtailing the discretionary powers of the state apparatus constitutes "commitment" in much of PR theorizing.

---

[36] As *Forbes* noted at the time, "reform [was] set in motion ... when ... Putin asked his minister of trade, German Gref, to produce a ten-year plan for ... economic development. Gref worked closely with members of Club 2015 to produce one with a very ambitious (and wholesome) agenda: the reform of pensions, taxes and customs ... [and] ... the nurturing of a civil society." *Forbes* January 7, 2002.

[37] The list of NPI publications can be viewed on Institute's website: http://inp.ru/ourpub.php. For the list of NPI-lobbied laws, see the Institute's page at the website of the Presidential Civil Society Council: http://www.sovetpamfilova.ru/help/partners/2043/.

[38] *Kommersant-Daily* June 8, 2001.

Putin's Russia and the Rise of The Business Quartet

Gref assumed the ministerial post at the tender age of 36, quickly becoming known as Putin's "reform maker" (*delatel' reform*) in 2000 Moscow. Enjoying the president's trust (both men began their careers as protégés of St. Petersburg's mayor Sobchak), the minister of economic development did not mince words in confronting the bureaucracy; defending the administrative reform against bureaucratic sabotage, Gref attacked the prime minister by describing his boss's apparatus as follows: "Do you know what a camel is? It is a race horse after the completion of all departmental approvals."[39] De-bureaucratization consisted of three law drafts born at the Center of Strategic Planning, a state think-tank and "the headquarters for the preparation of doctrine on the strategic development of the country."[40]

The drafts aimed to cut off the lifeblood of predatory agencies by reducing the number of required procedures as well as the number of state agencies enforcing the procedures regarding (1) state inspections of existing businesses, (2) registration of new businesses, and (3) licensing of specific business activities.[41] All three drafts sparked intense, multistage opposition – first, at the level of the executive agencies, whose approval was needed before sending the package to the Duma, then, at the Duma level, where deputies were trying to drown the legislation in a sea of proposed amendments.

The fight over the licensing legislation proved most vehement. A member of the Duma committee on property commented that the deputies' obstruction was "mainly the work of different lobbying groups from the federal executive agencies [*vedomstva*], those who conduct much of the licensing – these agencies could not protect their turf in the government, so now they are inciting the deputies."[42] Forty-two representatives of these executive agencies formed a long line to address the Duma, each taking the podium to argue that while new legislation was needed, *their* particular agency should be exempt. A representative of Gref's ministry present at the two-day showdown in the Duma (complete with screaming, X-rated language, and walkouts) explained: "Well, it's not easy for the agencies to give up 200 bn rubles [$8 bn] in illegal annual revenue."[43] (A license in the alcohol industry, for example, officially cost $600 while bureaucrats charged $400,000 for it.) The agencies' strategy seemed to be working. Deputies suggested hundreds of amendments to the law draft,[44] sending it back to Gref's ministry.

---

[39] *Argumenty i Fakty* June 18, 2003.

[40] Ibid. Putin appointed Gref to head the Center in early 2000 before announcing the government composition, sparking discussions that Gref may become the new prime minister.

[41] Law on Protection of Legal Persons and Individual Entrepreneurs during Administrative Inspections (134-FZ); Law on State Registration of Legal Persons and Individual Entrepreneurs (129-FZ); Law on Licensing of Specific Activity Types (128-FZ).

[42] *Vedomosti* June 29, 2001.

[43] *Segodnya* May 15, 2001.

[44] At the time, around 500 business activities required a license from federal authorities in addition to 1000 activities requiring a license from regional authorities. (The range of such activities was

136   *Commitment Dissolved*

Meanwhile, a similar dynamic was unfolding with respect to the drafts on registration and inspections, the former undermined by the ministry of justice, and the latter by the ministry of internal affairs, as both stood to lose power and profits.[45] Overall, the analysts concluded:

> The attack on bureaucrats is choking. Heavy battles are raging ... between the united forces of Russian bureaucracy and the representatives of the liberal government wing.... The bureaucrats are fighting desperately.... On their side are representatives of almost all fractions, including the pro-government Unity Party [*Edinstvo*]. Their goal is to fail the government's law draft.... And they are reaching it.[46]

Not all Duma fractions sided with the bureaucracy, however. The interfraction Duma group Business Russia met with Gref in March 2001 at the ritzy Prezident Otel', popular among the Russian state elites. At that point, the leader of Business Russia, Lisinenko, told Gref that Business Russia could help "with organizing the efforts to implement the government program [on de-bureaucratization]. We could become your fulcrum [*tochka opory*] in the Duma."[47] Gref welcomed the prospect, replying "You can count on us. And let us talk about our future interaction." (Seven months later, Business Russia's leaders met with Putin. One day after meeting the president, Business Russia held its founding congress as a business association at the Prezident Otel'.) Lisinenko did not disappoint. Together with the OPORA, Business Russia drummed up support for the government's reforms among deputies. Reflecting on the role of these two BAs during Putin's first tenure, the already mentioned ideologist of business institutionalization, Auzan, said:

> Their key contribution was to the formulation of new rules ... to the de-bureaucratization policy, to Gref's program.... A wide array of laws from the de-bureaucratization package was created with the liveliest participation of medium and small business. *The adoption of this [legal] package would have been impossible without a certain pressure from this side [of BAs].*[48]

Days before the decisive vote in the Duma, the OPORA, the CCI, and Business Russia galvanized business owners from around the country to air their concerns directly to the deputies; at the same time, these BAs launched a massive social advertising campaign on major TV channels and throughout the regions.[49] By the end of the summer, the law package was finally adopted.

---

very broad, including publishing, pipe production, animal control, production of medical equipment, auditing, and so on. For a comparison, the number of mandatorily licensed activities in the OECD countries was 20–150.) Gref sought to reduce the total number of licensed activities tenfold and to replace barriers to market entry ex ante with better control of business activities ex post.

[45] *Vedomosti* December 5, 2000.
[46] *Izvestiya* June 30, 2001.
[47] *Kommersant-Daily* March 21, 2001.
[48] *Novaya Gazeta* 2005.
[49] Pryadil'nikov, 104.

Putin's Russia and the Rise of The Business Quartet

However, amendments to the adopted laws continued to be lobbied over the next two years. Sovereign-supported BAs remained at the frontline. In 2003, under the OPORA's pressure, the Law on Inspections was amended to grant new firms a three-year window free of regular government inspections.[50]

Although sovereign-supported BAs naturally had much to gain from the new legislation, their work was channeled by the sovereign. In the regions from Ural to Siberia, "coordination councils" were set up by the federal organs to monitor the implementation of the new federal legislation on economic de-bureaucratization. Typically, these councils included OPORA or CCI representatives tasked with listing obstacles to entrepreneurial activity created contrary to federal laws by state employees.

The Limits of "Commitment"

More than a decade after business institutionalization spread throughout Russia via the regional offices of the BA quartet, the presidential administration as well as the Ministry of Economic Development and Trade (MEDT) continue to interact exclusively with the quartet on issues of general significance to Russian business.[51] The BA quartet continues to offer the state principal the delivery vehicle for controversial economic policies, most recently Russia's 2012 entry into the WTO after eighteen years of internal dissent and external negotiations.[52] Indeed, the BA quartet is moving closer to becoming a true veto player in the adoption of business-relevant legislation. In May 2010, Putin signed a resolution introducing the mechanism of "regulatory impact assessment" (*otsenka reguliruiushchego vozdeistviia*) to Russia's lawmaking.[53] The MEDT eagerly assumed the burden of supervising the assessment process, vetoing a third of submitted law drafts, decrees, and other regulations concerning business.[54] In line with the dynamic of the 2000s, the MEDT soon turned to the BA quartet for help. In April 2012, the MEDT prepared a resolution according to which the quartet becomes the second filter, after the MEDT's

---

[50] The "unplanned" (*vneplanovye*) inspections were not covered by the amendment, one of the reasons the law was later scrapped and rewritten in its entirety. Still, small business had a reason to celebrate. The OPORA's Borisov said at the time, "Finally lawmakers are listening to entrepreneurs. I perceive these amendments as a big gift." *Gazeta.ru* September 17, 2003.

[51] For the entire paragraph, unless otherwise noted: *Gazeta.ru* April 9, 2012.

[52] Anti-WTO sectoral interests (including producers, Duma representatives, and ministries) sought to use the CCI for lobbying their cause – as did the post-Gref MEDT, in favor of the WTO. While wary of antagonizing some members, the CCI ultimately sided with the reformist ministry. The narrow ratification of Russia's WTO entry in the Duma (238 to 208 votes) underscored the importance of the BA quartet's support for the MEDT. *Moskovskie Novosti* March 1, 2012.

[53] Resolution of Russian Federation Government Number 336, May 15, 2010, "On Introduction of Changes into Selected Statutes of Government of the Russian Federation"

[54] Around 300 drafts were vetoed out of almost 900 submitted between May 2010 and April 2012.

138   *Commitment Dissolved*

own committee, which the new legislation must pass. (Predictably, the Duma is opposed while entrepreneurs push for an even larger mandate.)

The mantle of a legislative watchdog may flatter the quartet's leadership, but it grants little in terms of *selective benefits* to the *members* of these associations. Legislative reforms are a public good; all of Russia's entrepreneurs benefit from BAs' involvement on the legislative front (while only BA members foot the bill).

More pertinently, their lasting prominence notwithstanding, sovereign-endorsed BAs do not offer their members enhanced PR protection. My survey analysis shows that in Russia, membership in a BA affects neither the levels of state threats, nor their predictability.[55] This is puzzling both given the orthodox literature on "merchant groups," and Russia's own dynamics; it would seem that the interests of the state principal and organized business, both confronted with agent predation, would converge on limiting it.

Subversion by State Agents

The wide-ranging cooperation between Russia's state principal and merchant groups has not enhanced PR security for two reasons. First, state *agents* have succeeded in *subverting business institutionalization* beyond the level of formal legislative initiatives. State agents grasped clearly who the real target of business institutionalization was and have protected, with considerable success, their rent-generating domains. Consider the courts; contesting the state's monopoly on adjudication, the RUIE, the OPORA, the CCI, and Business Russia created a system for non-judicial resolution of corporate disputes in which a network of peer courts (*treteiskie sudy*) provides an alternative to the profoundly corrupt state judiciary.[56] Reacting immediately in 2002, the state judiciary pushed through legislation subordinating the verdicts of BA-based courts to revision by the state courts.[57] Experts have hoped that peer courts would unburden the overloaded state courts. Rather than welcoming BA courts, however, the (presumably overworked) state judges through the end of the 2000s continued

---

[55] For more on threat levels, see Chapter 6. For more on predictability, see Chapter 3. (Note that the positive effect of BA membership on threat predictability in Chapter 3 derives entirely from the Ukrainian subsample; for the Russian subsample, BA membership is not significantly related to threat predictability.)

[56] While the verdicts of BA-based arbitration are legally nonbinding, strong pressures exist for companies to comply, according to my interviews. Companies signing the agreement, are expected to abide by the commission's rulings, lest they be blacklisted in their business dealings with other firms. Furthermore, courts at the BA quartet offer firms a chance to win public opinion, or to "practice" before going to a state court.

[57] The law technically endorsed the norm of mere *procedural* supervision of peer courts by state courts, implying noninterference with the *substantive* verdicts reached by peer courts. However, a list of vaguely worded "exceptional situations" diluted this norm, de facto allowing state courts to annul the verdicts of their commercial competitors. Author's interview with the legislation department chair at the CCI.

"the practice of unfounded limitation of peer courts' competencies in a broad range of ... disputes," according to the chair of the RUIE-based court.[58] It just so happened that this practice of subversion most often targeted the most lucrative spheres of adjudication; in 2011, the conflict over whether peer courts could issue judgments in disputes involving real estate and fixed assets reached Russia's constitutional court.[59]

The state agents' subversion of sovereign-endorsed BAs extends to other critical areas, such as self-regulatory organizations. A legal draft on the sectoral nongovernmental associations with state-delegated regulatory functions in a particular industry was part of Gref's de-bureaucratization reforms. The draft was enthusiastically supported by the BA quartet.[60] In December 2007, the Law on Self-Regulatory Organizations (315-FZ) was finally adopted. However, entrepreneurs' hopes for a decrease in predation were dashed forcefully. The analysis of the law's implementation conducted in 2010 by the MEDT outlines how sectorally oriented state agencies have pushed a panoply of amendments to the law, "reorienting the general model of self-regulation in Russia in the interests of one sector."[61] State agents affiliated with the construction industry carried the day, in essence capturing the self-regulatory organizations and turning them into private cash cows. By 2012, the situation was so catastrophic that Minister Elvira Nabiullina, Gref's successor, admitted defeat and called for a fundamentally new law; the OPORA's vice president supported the minister, noting that "self-regulation in the construction industry was created in order to legalize the predatory activity of bureaucrats."[62] More generally, the state principal has been unsuccessful at limiting the state *agencies'* subversion of legislative initiatives; according to the deputy chief of the government apparatus, Andrei Loginov:

The so-called departmental lobbyism [*vedomstvennyi lobbizm*] when the representatives of ministries and agencies ... push down the [Duma] deputies' throats the wish lists of their agencies [*vedomstvennye khotelki*] directly, without standing a chance to get them approved in the government. This is absolutely unacceptable [*ni v kakie vorota ne lezet*]! ... We've been trying to limit this for almost 20 years.... Cases of departmental lobbyism become known immediately as they are conducted through specific deputies. Such cases are typically counteracted by our "legislative triad" – the Ministry of Justice, Ministry of Finance, and MEDT.[63]

---

[58] *Rossiiskaya Gazeta* July 19, 2010.

[59] The constitutional court ruled in favor of peer courts (resolution Number 10-P of May 26, 2011). This does not change the privileged position of state courts according to the 2002 Arbitration Procedure Code (95-FZ), however.

[60] In my interview at the time, the CCI director of legal affairs shared that "upon this law depends the future of organized business."

[61] MEDT, 21.

[62] *Gazeta.ru* April 22, 2012.

[63] *RBK Daily* December 25, 2012.

In addition to subverting the sovereign-supported BAs at the level of implementation and adoption of laws, state agents have also proceeded to capture the merchant groups directly. Current or former state employees have increasingly assumed executive and administrative positions in these BAs, a dynamic that has been particularly pronounced in the regional offices of the CCI (23 percent of which were staffed by state agents, typically high-ranking federal bureaucrats, by 2010); Russian analysts dub the phenomenon the "lateral statization" (*kosvennoe ogosudarstvlenie*) of the BA quartet.[64]

The hostile reaction of Russia's state agents suggests that commitment devices such as encompassing sovereign-endorsed merchant groups can easily malfunction in the context of agent predation. The bureaucrats' powerful backlash underscores just how much has been at stake *for them*, beyond the dynamics of commitment or cooptation that are largely limited to the bilateral *sovereign-business* relations.

Politicization of Business Associations

The second reason for the BA quartet's *de facto* ineffectiveness at securing PR has been its increasing politicization toward the end of the 2000s. By 2008, much of Putin's political capital was wasted on power-grabbing, antagonizing parts of the electorate just when Russia was buffeted by the economic crisis. As the state principal's political future became more uncertain, he began to draw on the quartet to maintain his own power.

On June 20, 2011, Putin met with the new CCI president, Sergei Katyrin. The transcript of their meeting outlines a fascinating negotiation of the terms of the dialogue between a BA featuring massive membership across its 174 regional offices and the state principal facing a politically uncertain transition.[65] After introductory pleasantries, Putin dangles the carrot of delegating some state functions to the CCI at the local level: "Your interaction with regional authorities, does it go beyond petty paperwork? ... Are they listening to you? *Are they delegating any functions to you?*" While much is at stake, given the extent of local predation, Katyrin replies with a seeming non-sequitur underscoring the CCI's political usefulness to the sovereign: "By the way, almost all of our regional chambers have joined 'People's Front' [Putin's non-party electoral vehicle] ... all have responded to your appeal." In response, Putin melts, suggesting that the functions to be delegated to the CCI should go beyond mere investment-attracting activities to include regulation, which leaves Katyrin breathless (the CCI's efforts on this front always failed in the past): "Vladimir Vladimirovich, we butt against legislation which does not allow this. We are not a state organ, so to delegate some functions to us with money [from the budget] and so forth.... All of this runs aground because of legislation." The men end up agreeing that although the CCI is not legally a self-regulatory

---

[64] Zudin 2010.
[65] Transcript of the meeting on file with the author.

Putin's Russia and the Rise of The Business Quartet

organization, it would become a regulator "in the sphere of small business because that is where most problems and sores arise." (The agreement was confined to several pilot regions, after which this practice and the necessary legislative changes would be adopted at the national level.)

The *quid pro quo* involving BAs' political support in exchange for the sovereign's attention has been increasingly on display in Russia since the end of the 2000s. In May 2011, Putin addressed the BA quartet thanking each of the four BAs for joining the People's Front, after which, in a lengthy address, he demonstrated remarkable knowledge of problems facing business, including local predation.[66] Consider also the BAs' cooperation with United Russia, the "party of power." At the beginning of the 2000s, the BA quartet cooperated with United Russia *as well as other parties* on matters of *policy*, working out legislative drafts and providing expert consultation on party programs.[67] Toward the end of the decade, such cooperation was increasingly focused on United Russia while also being used as an *electoral weapon*.[68] The shift in the nature of BAs' cooperation with parties coincided with Putin's assumption of United Russia's leadership in 2008.

Over time, the logic of sovereign-BA interaction in Russia has come to resemble the orthodox perspective on cooptation – there is, however, an important difference. According to orthodoxy, merchant groups are granted secure property rights in exchange for political support – as, indeed, reflected in the rhetorical promises made to each other by Putin and BA leaders. However, while BAs can lend their associations' electoral capacities to the state principal, the state principal cannot deliver his part of the bargain; he may choose to abstain from expropriation himself, but he cannot root out de facto agent predation.

The decline in credibility on the sovereign's part has not escaped Russia's business community. Signaling their demand for better PR guarantees, entrepreneurs have convinced Putin in one of his first acts upon returning to the presidency in 2012 to institute the office of the "federal ombudsman for the protection of business people" at the presidential administration. Boris Titov was deputized to assume this office, relinquishing his position as the leader of Business Russia. His selection among competing candidates was based on demonstrated loyalty to Putin and experience in defending entrepreneurs.[69]

---

[66] Address at the First Social Forum of Russian business, May 26, 2011.

[67] The OPORA, for example cooperated with the Yabloko Party on housing reform while also cooperating with United Russia on innovation and investment in the pharmaceutical industry. Other BAs engaged in similar programmatic collaborations.

[68] Since 2008, regional CCI chambers served as a cadre pump to United Russia. Leaders of the BA quartet became members of United Russia (a dynamic *least* pronounced at the OPORA). In December 2011, Business Russia also created its own political movement "Right Turn," essentially throwing its (modest) weight behind Putin in the upcoming presidential election. For a complete description of this dynamic, see Zudin.

[69] In 2012, Titov approved of Putin as "a strictly democratically elected" version of Singapore's Lee Kuan Yew and Chile's Pinochet. At the same time, Titov was the driving force behind the

Commitment Dissolved

Titov also knows expropriation firsthand; in the early 2000s, his business venture was subject to a competitor's raiding attempt involving the state's security services, forcing Titov to temporarily leave the country and "sit it out abroad."[70] Titov's background, financial independence, and (phenomenally) public support of Khodorkovsky provide hope that Titov will be no ordinary *chinovnik*. So far, he radiates an aggressive stance toward Russia's asset-hungry bureaucracy:

> Today employees of the power structures [*silovykh struktur*] ... are not hiding ... their expropriation of entrepreneurs' property.... The problem has reached the point at which we had to try new methods to resolve it. Business community has suggested the institution of the ombudsman.... *Ombudsman will not only protect but also attack....* Today we are happy to be freeing entrepreneurs from jail, but we have to finish the job – to make sure that "werewolves" [predatory bureaucrats] ... become personally accountable.

Titov has a plan of attack: His office will use article 169 of Russia's criminal code ("interference with entrepreneurial activity") to initiate proceedings against suspects in the state apparatus, a step that entrepreneurs themselves are typically afraid to take. In his capacity as ombudsman, Titov has thirty-five legal consultants as well as access to task forces within the Ministry of Internal Affairs and the Procuracy.[71] During his first two years as ombudsman, Titov has impressively pushed through the amnesty of 2,314 incarcerated businesspeople[72]; this suggests that Putin's attempts at commitment are more than cheap talk. A bona fide businessman has become the sovereign's attack dog on bureaucracy. Whether he will continue to bite, however, is open to doubt, given Titov's political ambitions and the ombudsman's reliance on certain cooperation from the "power structures."

Overall, the story of Russia's business institutionalization underscores three points. First, sovereign-endorsed encompassing "merchant groups" can achieve significant *legislative* breakthroughs; however, the adoption of business-friendly legislation is *not sufficient* to secure property rights. Second, the state principal's support for business associations may signal "*sovereign* commitment," but it does not amount to "*state* commitment" in the context of agent predation, because the state principal cannot commit on behalf of state agents. In Russia, state agents have successfully undermined the BA quartet at the implementation level, despite the near-absolute approval of and the close cooperation with the

---

humanization of Russian legislation with respect to entrepreneurs (adopted under President Medvedev) in which jail sentences based on economic crimes were dropped. Along with Titov, entrepreneurs suggested three other people to Putin for the office of the ombudsman: Borisov (the OPORA's leader), Yurgens (a RUIE Management Bureau member), and Barshchevsky (a prominent lawyer). *Kapital Strany* 2012; *Ekspert* March 12, 2012.

[70] For the entire paragraph unless otherwise noted: *Kommersant* 2012.

[71] *Kapital Strany* 2012.

[72] Website of the Ombudsman Office: http://ombudsmanbiz.ru/2014/02/5410.html

Ukraine's Orange Revolution and Property Rights

quartet by the presidential administration. Third, the logic of the sovereign-BA interaction depends on the sovereign's perception of his political future; as the latter becomes less certain, the logic shifts from a commitment mode into the cooptation mode. As Putin's political prospects declined, he began to draw on the BA quartet to maintain power, in contrast to his previous engagement of the quartet's resources to achieve PR-securing policy reforms.

UKRAINE'S ORANGE REVOLUTION AND PROPERTY RIGHTS

Constraints on the Ukrainian Presidency before and after the Revolution

To appreciate how the Orange Revolution limited the discretion of the Ukrainian presidency, it is worth revisiting the prerevolutionary administration of Leonid Kuchma, Ukraine's longest-serving president to date. Before joining the political establishment in the early 1990s, Kuchma was the consummate red director, having run the world's largest missile factory in Dnipropetrovsk during the Cold War. In 1994, as Ukraine was reeling from the economic collapse, he won the presidency with the slogan "under Kuchma, your plant will work again!" Kuchma's electoral promises notwithstanding, he surprised many with remarkable pragmatism once in power, endorsing critical economic reforms and spearheading the adoption of the Constitution. Although Ukraine had become independent in 1991, it did not have a Constitution until 1996. In the interim, the country was muddling through with the 1978 Constitution of Soviet Ukraine, rubber-stamped in Moscow. As a result, the country was barely governable until 1996; the balance of power between the president and the Supreme Rada was unspecified, rendering both (at least in their own minds) sovereign and, as a consequence, at each other's throats. Kuchma's goal was to enshrine his vision of the Ukrainian state as a super-presidential and unitary system against the political left, which foresaw a parliamentary, federalist republic. Kuchma largely succeeded, paving the way with the presidential decrees of August 1994, which extended presidential powers. The 1996 Constitution – the culmination of Kuchma's efforts – created a unitary state, giving the president the power to appoint the prime minister (as well as all ministers and regional governors) and strengthening executive authority over law enforcement.[73]

Ukraine's slide into authoritarianism during ten years of Kuchma's rule, however, went far beyond constitutional limits. Before mass outrage erupted via the Orange Revolution, Ukraine saw a steep decrease in media freedoms, suspected murders of political opponents and journalists critical of Kuchma, persecution of opposition parties, and explicit presidential pressure on the

---

[73] Still, unlike Russia's truly "super-presidential" Constitution of 1993, Ukraine's 1996 Constitution was technically "presidential-parliamentarian," leaving the parliament with crucial veto powers (e.g., over the appointment of the prime minister).

Supreme Rada (henceforth: Rada) and the electoral commission. As for property rights, Kuchma's administration gave birth to a veritable Frankenstein Pavlo Lazarenko, also known as "the greatest parasite in the history of independent Ukraine"[74] (a notable distinction considering the competition). Hailing from Kuchma's home town, Lazarenko was appointed prime minister in 1995 and devoted his volcanic energy toward regulatory extortion, particularly in the gas and grain sectors. Among other areas, Lazarenko fought vigorously for the supervisory mandate in environmental regulation, albeit with a particular connotation of "green" in mind. Environmental inspectors "extorted the largest bribes because of Ukraine's ... strict Soviet environmental standards, which had been established for show and were never supposed to be applied."[75] After fleeing the country with a Panamanian passport, being arrested in Switzerland, and skipping a $2.6 million bail in 1998, Lazarenko belatedly faced justice (in the form of a nine-year jail sentence) in the United States in 2006, accused of collecting more than $200 million in bribes from Ukrainian firms. Overall, country experts agree that toward the end of Kuchma's reign, Ukraine presented "a model case of competitive authoritarianism ... [where] the combination of authoritarian state structures and oligarchic rule served to concentrate executive power,"[76] and "even when many in parliament became worried about Kuchma's behavior, the parliament was ineffective in checking his power."[77]

Such was the context of the Orange Revolution and the 2004 presidential elections in which the candidate of Kuchma's ancien régime, Yanukovych, faced his liberal nemesis Yushchenko. The regime intervened against the opposition by shutting down media broadcasts, investigating oppositionist financial backers, arresting activists, and channeling all administrative support toward Yanukovych, but to no avail. In November, massive electoral fraud during the second round of presidential elections was the straw that broke the people's patience. Hundreds of thousands of protesters flooded Kyiv's Maidan square. Well-prepared by civil society groups, such as the students' *Pora*, and partly guided by Western pro-democracy organizations, the Orange Revolution galvanized the Ukrainian population like no other event since the country's independence from the Soviet Union. It also led to a split in the Ukrainian government and its armed forces, forcing Kuchma to choose a political settlement over violence. Merely ten days after the protests transformed Ukraine from the global backwater into the darling of the world media, the previously docile Supreme Court confirmed electoral fraud, and invalidated election results. On December 26, Yushchenko won the repeat of the second round, assuming presidency in January 2005.

[74] Åslund 2009, 97.
[75] Ibid., 94.
[76] Way 2005, 131, 37.
[77] D'Anieri 2006, 58.

Ukraine's Orange Revolution and Property Rights

After the Orange Revolution, both the *de jure* limits on the discretion of the Ukrainian presidency and Yushchenko's own *de facto* behavior suggest that the commitment of the state principal to the rules of the game, including those related to property rights, increased dramatically.

Crucially, the political settlement adopted by the Rada on December 8, 2004, involved constitutional amendments that restricted presidential powers in favor of the parliament and, by extension, the prime minister. The Rada would now nominate the prime minister. The president would propose the ministers of defense and foreign affairs, but all other ministers would be appointed by the (Rada-nominated) prime minister. The president's power to dissolve the Rada was constrained. The regional governors, although still appointed by the president, would be accountable to the government. According to my 2012 interview with the director of a Ukrainian think-tank specializing in entrepreneurship, the importance of the constitutional changes from the perspective of property rights was that "the parliament became influential in terms of appointing the highest-ranked government officials such as ministers." In addition to these constitutional changes, "the Orange settlement" involved a new electoral law whose result was to further strengthen the parliament.[78]

The first post-revolutionary parliament, elected in March 2006, was anything but shy in flexing its newfound muscle. Coalitional shifts in the Rada dominated the political news. Once the dust settled, President Yushchenko was pushed by the Rada toward a historic milestone involving Yushchenko's appointment of Yanukovych as the prime minister and the adoption of a broader program of national unity (with specific policy directives on economic reforms, relations with NATO, official state language, etc.) as a sign of Ukraine's East-West reconciliation. The lofty language of official pronouncements aside, Yushchenko was shown his place – an office, not a throne. And if that gesture were not enough, in December 2006, the Rada passed the Law on the Cabinet of Ministers, which further augmented parliamentary powers at the expense of the president.[79] Yushchenko vetoed the law, but his veto was overruled.

The revolution also bolstered the independence of courts vis-à-vis the presidency and the executive branch more generally. In October 2008, embittered Yushchenko attempted to pull the emergency brake, issuing decrees to dissolve the parliament and conduct early elections. The administrative district court of Kyiv, following the claim of the BYuT party, disagreed, putting preparations for the elections on hold and explicitly taking sides against the president

---

[78] Elections to the Rada became fully proportional (before, half of the seats were elected in single-mandate districts), while Rada's term was extended from four to five years. The law had the desired effect of strengthening the party system by reducing the previously bewildering number of parties and elevating the importance of coalitions.

[79] In essence, the law declared the cabinet of ministers the top executive organ accountable to both the Rada and the president. In 2008, a new version of the law was passed further eviscerating the presidential mandate.

and the electoral commission. Despite Yushchenko's pressure (he dissolved the defiant court, which was reinstated by the council of judges), Ukraine was not subjected to another[80] round of extraordinary Rada elections. Meanwhile, in a further sign of courts' strengthening vis-à-vis the upper executive, the number of *senior* public officials brought to administrative liability for corruption increased steadily after the Orange Revolution from 511 in 2005 to 1,369 in 2009.[81]

While constraining the state principal is important from the viewpoint of property rights, it is equally important *on whose behalf* these constraints are implemented. If, for example, the Orange Revolution were an event engineered by the oligarchs or, conversely, a mass uprising of non-owning labor, then it would not necessarily be auspicious for the security of property rights because both revanchist oligarchs and labor may have incentives to engage in expropriatory redistribution. The Orange Revolution, however, was largely a classical bourgeois revolution, not a palace coup or a blue-collar upheaval. The Revolution had the passionate support of entrepreneurs outside of the oligarchic clans, that is, entrepreneurs who had been the main victims of insecure property rights during Kuchma's reign. In my interviews with business owners throughout the Ukrainian regions, this support as well as the financial donations to "Maidan events" were near-universal. A brilliant Ukrainian analysis from a participant deserves to be quoted at length:

What was the Orange Revolution ...? According to the first version, "the masses rose against a criminal power." ... Spontaneous popular riots driven by ... poverty would mean a wave of ... marauding and vandalism. Yet the streets adjacent to the revolutionary Maidan were stuffed with parked and unprotected Porsches and Lexuses, while their owners were there [on Maidan], protesting! ... No, definitely not a riot of the rabble [*niiak ne bunt cherni*]!

According to the second version, "a revolt of the millionaires against the billionaires," a typical palace coup using many movie extras, [but] organized by those who disagree not with the nature of the system but only with their share of the pie.... Yet it is hard to fool the people, and the people are not eager to support the thief from whom another thief had stolen the cudgel [i.e., the second-tier oligarchs who lacked access to the "administrative resource" under Kuchma]. For their own part, the bounty hunters [second-tier oligarchs] would not allow leaving elections at the mercy of the voters ... because that way they really could have lost everything: the restoration of justice is a double-edged sword [*vidnovlennia spravedlyvosti – shtuka dvosichna*].

According to the third version, "a bourgeois-democratic [revolution]." ... Professionals aware of their own worth and especially free entrepreneurs – these are, indeed, the true gravediggers of the system of organized extortion because they can only win from its

---

[80] In 2007, Yushchenko capitalized on popular dissatisfaction with Rada's ineffectiveness and successfully dissolved the parliament. The formal reasons were the illegal formation of party factions as well as the counter-constitutional nature of the Law on the Cabinet of Ministers that had been adopted by the Rada.

[81] The data refers to the civil servants of categories 1–4. Transparency International 2011, 102.

Ukraine's Orange Revolution and Property Rights

destruction. They have nothing to fear from popular wrath, because they really "did not steal anything" – if only because they simply did not have access to the trough.... Such non-privileged business has a chance to convince the more "progressive" [*naibil'sh 'prosunutu'*] part of the population about the honest source of its capital.... However, in our time, because everybody knows how revolutions end, such coalition [of entrepreneurs] was joined in the early stages by the "millionaires" ... [whose] mediation allowed to avert big bloodshed ... but they were temporary travel companions [*poputnyky*].[82]

As behooves a fundamental political breakthrough, the losers took the results seriously. Very seriously, in fact; three important figures of the ancien régime committed suicide or were murdered in the wake of the Revolution, presumably to avoid prosecution or disclosures that would compromise their affiliates.[83] Ukraine's richest oligarch, Rinat Akhmetov, temporarily fled the country, while another oligarch, Ihor Bakai, did so permanently.

Overall, the Orange Revolution ushered in substantial constraints on the office of the Ukrainian Presidency. These constraints were accompanied by media freedom and civil society activity that remain unparalleled in the post-Soviet world outside the Baltics. After authoritarian stagnation under Kuchma, Ukraine surged back to being a vibrant, if messy, democracy; in 2005, Ukraine was for the first time in its history – and as the only post-Soviet state outside of the Baltics – rated "free" on civil and political rights by the Freedom House.

Importantly, it is not only the *general constraints* on the president's discretion that increased following the Revolution but also the Orange president's *actual behavior* with respect to property rights that came to signal loud and clear "commitment."

To begin, Yushchenko's background as a liberal economist and a successful reformer sent, by itself, an important positive signal. In 1999, Kuchma was desperate to avert Ukraine's default amidst economic crisis and surprised many by nominating the liberal Yushchenko as the prime minister. During his brief stint as the prime minister in 2000–1, Yushchenko managed to achieve "a severe break in the rent-seeking society"[84] – in other words, the impossible – through cleaning up corruption in the energy trade, deregulating small firms, defeating barter, balancing the budget, and making the tax system more transparent. Once the default was averted, Kuchma and the oligarchs ousted Yushchenko.

Four years later, *deliberate* commitment to property rights defined the first year of Yushchenko's tenure as the Orange president. Such orientation derived not only from Yushchenko's own convictions but also from the double

---

[82] *Dzerkalo Tyzhnia* January 12, 2007.

[83] Yuri Kravchenko, former minister of the interior, committed suicide on the eve of appearing as the key witness in the murder of a journalist (Gongadze). Yuri Lyakh, a banker oligarch close to Kuchma and his chief of staff, Medvedchuk, was found with a slit throat and a dubious suicide note. Georgy Kirpa, former minister of transportation and a veteran election fixer, (allegedly) shot himself on the day after the electoral rerun; doubt remains about the voluntary nature of his departure.

[84] Åslund, 147.

whammy of post-revolutionary politics. On the one hand, Ukraine's 2004 GDP per capita was below its 1992 level, and Yushchenko's party, Our Ukraine, would be judged in the 2006 Rada elections on his ability to restart growth and attract investment. On the other hand, the Rada that Yushchenko had inherited in 2004 was rife with populist temptations to "restore justice" via revising the results of privatization, alarming investors and threatening to derail recovery.

In this situation, Yushchenko implemented commitment-oriented policies on four fronts. First, important documents were signed that committed the revisionist Rada *and* the president to respect private property rights. On June 16, 2005, Yushchenko convinced the Rada's chairman Volodymyr Lytvyn and Prime Minister Tymoshenko to sign a binding "Memorandum on Guarantees of Property Rights and Provision of Legality during their Realization" (*Memorandum pro Harantii Prav Vlasnosti ta Zabezpechennia Zakonnosti pry ikh Realizatsii*). Among the points to which the signatories committed were the following:

To guarantee the rights of owners and the stability of property regime which are the prerequisites for dynamic economic development. ...

To provide for all-encompassing, unconditional, and law-based realization of property rights by the people ... and achieve on this basis a high standard of living.[85]

The memorandum was signed in the presence of most factional leaders in the Rada, as well as the president, the state secretary (Oleksandr Zinchenko), the secretary of the Council for National Security and Defense (Petro Poroshenko), and other top government officials.[86] Speaking to journalists, Yushchenko noted that "in signing the Memorandum, the executive and the legislative powers demonstrate that the legislation on privatization does not and will not have any retroactive power ... the Memorandum will be ... the key element in creating a modern Ukrainian economy ... [and that] upon the Memorandum depends the fate of repatriation ... of money from the offshore zones."[87]

To extend the Memorandum and provide a step-by-step guide to improving the security of property rights in Ukraine more generally, Yushchenko signed a detailed decree on November 24, 2005, that gave legal force to two prior decisions by the Council for National Security and Defense – "On Measures to Improve Investment Climate in Ukraine" (June 29, 2005), and "On Measures to Establish Guarantees and Raise Effectiveness of Protection of Property Rights in Ukraine" (October 28, 2005).[88]

Second, Yushchenko met personally with the leaders of big business to reassure them that the Orange Revolution would not turn into expropriatory

---

[85] *Ukrainskaya Pravda* June 16, 2005.
[86] Four Rada factions voiced disagreement with the memorandum: the Social-Democratic Party of Ukraine, the Communists, the Party of Regions, and the Socialist Party of Ukraine.
[87] *Ukrainskie Novosti* June 16, 2005.
[88] Presidential Decree Number 1648/2005. Full text available at: http://zakon4.rada.gov.ua/laws/show/1648/2005

Ukraine's Orange Revolution and Property Rights

vengeance. Startlingly, Yushchenko's first meeting was aimed at the *Russian* oligarchs. Top Russian corporations had prospered in Ukraine under the pre-revolutionary Kuchma regime and were most likely involved in financing Yanukovych's (anti-Orange) presidential campaign in 2004. Following the Revolution, Russian capital began to leave Ukraine, fearing retribution. Barely a few months in office, President Yushchenko invited the CEOs of Russia's corporate empires – including Alexei Miller of Gazprom, Anatoly Chubais of RAO UES, Viktor Vekselberg of TNK-BP, Vladimir Evtushenkov of AFK Sistema, Vladimir Potanin of Interros, and a dozen others – to Kyiv in order to personally commit to protecting their capital.[89] The meeting, which took place in March 2005, was unprecedented. As the Russian *Kommersant* noted, "never before had such a high-profile group [of oligarchs] left the country in a coordinated fashion to negotiate abroad."[90] The oligarchs long "equi-distanced" at home from the Putin's Kremlin were now jokingly referred to as being "equi-approached" (*ravnopriblizhyonnye*) by Yushchenko. At the meeting, Yushchenko emphasized that "we value very much the role of Russian business in Ukraine, we welcome capital inflow into Ukraine regard-less of geography." According to Vagit Alekperov, the Russian oil magnate of LUKOIL, "President [Yushchenko] guaranteed that nothing would happen to the property of Russian businessmen that had been acquired in non-criminal ways." The chairman of Vneshekonombank, Vladimir Dmitriev, opined that "Mr. Yushchenko managed to smooth out [*sgladit'*] our negative perception of events in Ukraine." Overall, the oligarchs were impressed, and investment forums were launched in Kyiv by Alfa-Group, Renaissance Capital, and other powerhouses of Russian finance.

On October 14, 2005, Yushchenko conducted an analogous meeting with the Ukrainian tycoons. Both Rinat Akhmetov as well as Victor Pinchuk – the financial pillars of Kuchma's ancien régime – were present, as well as around twenty other top businessmen.[91] During the meeting, Yushchenko demonstrably ordered the prime minister "to remove all problems surrounding enterprises that had been dubiously privatized, and to stop all talk about re-privatization."[92]

On November 29, 2005, Yushchenko met with the representatives of for-eign (non-Russian) business at a roundtable organized by *The Economist* at which he outlined the roadmap to the legally supported "amnesty of capi-tal" within three months. In his remarks at the roundtable Yushchenko noted, "first we must legalize property, then earnings, and then the next step will be the legalization of expenses that will above all concern state employees and politicians."[93] (In a more innovative approach to foreign direct investment, the

---

[89] *Ukrains'ka Pravda* March 14, 2005.

[90] For this and other quotes from this paragraph, see *Kommersant* October 17, 2005.

[91] For a full list of attendees, see *Ukrains'ka Pravda* October 14, 2005.

[92] *Kommersant* 2005.

[93] For the entire paragraph, see *Kommersant Ukraina* November 30, 2005.

president also invited foreigners "to live in Ukraine and to marry Ukrainian girls.") Speaking after the president, Prime Minister Yekhanurov clarified the restitution procedures for overpaid value-added tax and promised "to channel the spirit of freedom from Maidan into the economy."

Third, Yushchenko launched an array of joint state-business policy-making arenas as well as deregulation initiatives, mainly aimed at the small- and medium-sized enterprises. To reward entrepreneurs for their ardent support of the Orange Revolution and to incentivize them to create growth (and jobs and votes), Yushchenko's office organized a series of forums "Business and Power as Partners." The first forum took place in Kyiv on March 11, 2005, and was attended by Yushchenko, the prime minister, Ukraine's top regulators, and business representatives from all regions. The event took the entrepreneurs' breath away; for the first time, the state principal was willing to institutionalize a dialogue with non-oligarchic capitalists.[94] Speaking at the Forum, Yushchenko noted, "the civil organizations of entrepreneurs [*hromads'ki struktury pidpryemtsiv*] must be integrated into the decision-making processes that concern their activity.... They must become an organic component of the executive branch at the state and county levels – a bridge of sorts for the organs of [state] power and business."[95] By the end of September, similar forums took place in all Ukrainian regions. Yushchenko used the second meeting of the Forum to animate a landmark deregulation law that had been passed by the Orange forces in the Rada a year earlier but was not being implemented.[96] Having reinforced the law with a presidential decree, Yushchenko used the forum to outline a strategy for its implementation while ordering the attending ministers to report to him within ten days on the abolition of regulatory norms in line with the Decree.[97] Finally, Yushchenko breathed new life into the "Civic Rada" at the government's main regulatory agency for SMEs (*Hromads'ka Rada pry Derzhpidpryemnytstvi*). The Civic Rada, created in 2000 during Yushchenko's stint as the prime minister, united sixty leaders of business associations, entrepreneurs, and independent experts to provide legislative input on regulatory issues.[98]

Fourth, Yushchenko took a strong stance against the re-privatization campaign by sacking the prime minister, Tymoshenko, and replacing her with the opponent of re-privatization, Yuri Yekhanurov, in September 2005. The action spoke volumes. Yushchenko jettisoned a popular politician and his partner in the Orange Revolution, once it became clear that Tymoshenko

---

[94] See the detailed report on the history of business institutionalization in Ukraine by Vyacheslav Bykovec, the head of the Union of Private and Privatized Enterprises. Bykovec 2007.

[95] Ibid., 20.

[96] Law N 1160-IV, "On Principles of State Regulatory Policy in the Sphere of Business Activity."

[97] Presidential Decree Number 901/2005 "On Liberalization of Entrepreneurial Activity and State Support of Entrepreneurship." Full text available at: http://uspishnaukraina.com.ua/news/372.html

[98] Bykovec, 24–8.

Ukraine's Orange Revolution and Property Rights

would not back down from the re-privatization agenda (more on this later). Yushchenko's choice of Yekhanurov was made, above all, to please business. As a technocrat, Yekhanurov was not well-known to the Ukrainian public and did not necessarily bode well, from Yushchenko's perspective, for the upcoming 2006 Rada elections. But for business – including, notably, small business – Yekhanurov was a godsend.[99] According to Maksym Latsyba, the director of the civil society program at the Ukrainian Independent Center for Political Research, "Yekhanurov canceled re-privatization. He said that 'steal what had been stolen' [*grab' nagrablennoe*] – that's not for us" (author's interview). Instead, Yekhanurov introduced the institution of "peace agreements" (*myrovy uhody*), which allowed the owners of questionably privatized assets to pay additional sums post hoc to resolve the legitimacy of their ownership. In the months leading up to his nomination as the prime minister, Yekhanurov pioneered the peace agreements successfully at the local level as the governor of the Dnipropetrovsk region. At the national level, peace agreements proved largely effective; in December 2005, the Cabinet of Ministers published the list of enterprises with which such agreements had been concluded.[100] Meanwhile, Yushchenko decreed to compensate the (mainly foreign) investors working in Ukraine's free economic zones who had been harmed by the re-privatization campaign.[101]

These four points suggest that Yushchenko did not come to endorse secure property rights reluctantly but acted consistently in support of property rights *even when* such actions were politically disadvantageous.

The 2004 Orange Revolution, for its part, did more than rectify a stolen election; by triggering presidency-constraining constitutional changes and bringing to power a liberal state principal with a market-friendly reputation, it ultimately institutionalized the commitment of the Ukrainian sovereign to the security of property rights.

Whither Sovereign Commitment?

Overall, between 2004 and 2010, Ukraine experienced a dramatic "window" of robust democratic controls on the presidency, yet this window of political freedoms was not paralleled by economic freedoms. Consider Figure 5.1, which plots available country scores from Polity IV, Freedom House, and the Heritage Foundation for the 2000–10 period; for the sake of comparability, all scores

---

[99] In 2000, Yekhanurov helped push through Ukraine's most successful economic reform to date, a simplified taxation system for small entrepreneurs that led around 1 million entrepreneurs out of the shadow economy into the legal sphere. Yekhanurov had also established the Coordinating Expert Center of Entrepreneurs' Unions in December 1998 and presided over the Association of Small, Medium, and Privatized Enterprises of Ukraine.

[100] *Kommersant Ukraina* December 8, 2005.

[101] Presidential Decree Number 1513 of October 28, 2005.

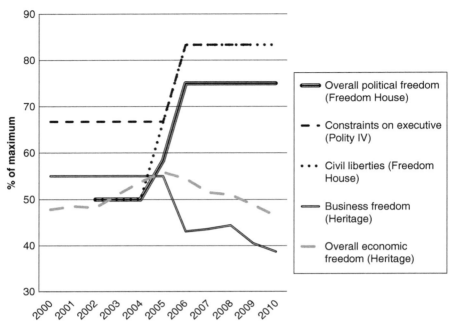

FIGURE 5.1. Political and economic freedoms in Ukraine, 2000–10.
(*Sources*: Freedom House, Center for Systemic Peace, Heritage Foundation; author's calculations.)

are standardized to a 0–100 scale.[102] The graph is curiously scissors-shaped; as general political freedoms and the constraints on the executive soared after the Orange Revolution, economic freedoms plunged.

The World Bank's Worldwide Governance Indicators, based on multiple surveys of enterprises, citizens, and experts, amplify the puzzle behind the scissors-shaped pattern. Within five years of the Orange Revolution, Ukraine's percentile rank (0–100, relative to other countries) developed inversely on two indicators that should, in theory, be positively related.[103] Between 2004 and 2009, Ukraine's rank on "Voice and Accountability" (which measures citizens' empowerment vis-à-vis the executive, freedom of association, and freedom of the media) *rose* from 29.3 percent to 49 percent, and yet, during the same time period, its rank on "Government Effectiveness" (which measures "the quality of the civil service ... the quality of policy formulation and implementation,

---

[102] Given their well-known shortcomings, the data from the rating agencies is used here to illustrate trends, not to replace a substantive discussion.
[103] For details on methodology and data, see http://info.worldbank.org/governance/wgi/resources.htm.

Ukraine's Orange Revolution and Property Rights

and the credibility of the government's commitment to such policies") *fell* from 33.7 percent to 22.5 percent.

The data on economic freedoms in Figure 5.1 also tailgates with the BEEPS data presented in Chapter 3. A comparison between the BEEPS rounds of 2002 and 2008 in Ukraine (N=1,908), that is, three years before and three years after the Orange team assumed power, reveals that ownership threats did *not* decline overall. Threats based on "licensing and permits" did not change significantly, and neither did the frequency with which firms resorted to "unofficial payments" when dealing with tax collectors.[104] Meanwhile, the proportion of firms exposed to ownership-threatening corruption (bribe-related losses exceeding two thirds of post-tax profits) actually skyrocketed from 21 percent in 2002 to 38 percent in 2008, a difference significant at the 0.01 level. Three years after the Orange state principal committed to secure the property rights of Ukrainian entrepreneurs, nearly a quarter of them (23.5 percent) considered political instability the "most serious obstacle" to their businesses among fifteen various obstacles. In fact, Ukraine featured the highest percentage of entrepreneurs who deemed political turmoil their primary enemy across all of twenty-nine countries in which the BEEPS was implemented in 2008. (Even in Georgia, which was being bombed by Russia at the time of survey's implementation, fewer entrepreneurs (20.3 percent) felt paralyzed by political instability.)

Finally, my own 2007 survey also supports the inference of unchanged PR security after the Orange Revolution. In addition to questions about the threats at the time of the survey, my instrument fielded questions on how the entrepreneurs would rate these same threats "2 years ago," that is, just months after the Orange Revolution. Because of the heightened unpredictability of a quasi-revolutionary environment, one would expect PR threats at that time (in 2004–5) to be substantially higher than two years later after the new state principal had a chance to institutionalize commitment. Yet the perceived threat intensity remained virtually unchanged.[105]

Predation in Orange

The dynamics described so far militate against the central tenet of the state commitment paradigm. Despite the serious commitment of (and by) the state

[104] The severity of threats (0–4 scale) based on "licensing and permits" fell somewhat from 1.65 to 1.59 between 2002 and 2008, while the frequency of bribes (1–6 scale) vis-à-vis tax inspectors rose slightly from 2.26 to 2.27 in the same time period. Neither difference is significant at 0.1 level. (For details on all variables, as well as the analysis of the pooled data from Russia and Ukraine, please see Chapter 3.)

[105] While in 2007 state threats to ownership averaged 2.03 (1–4 scale), "two years ago" that is, in 2005, these threats averaged 2.04. The threat of illegal ownership capture (raiding) increased significantly between 2005 and 2007, while the threat of illegal inspections significantly declined. Other threats did not change at a statistically significant level. (Note that while valuable, this data is prone to recall bias.)

154   *Commitment Dissolved*

principal in the wake of the parliament-empowering revolution, the security of ownership failed to improve. The theoretical framework presented in Chapter 2 helps make sense of this development. The Orange state principal's lack of control over the state agents ultimately vitiated his commitment to property rights. Sovereign commitment is no remedy for agent predation.

Did the Orange Revolution make a difference at all? My fieldwork[106] suggests that the Revolution made a difference through its considerable side effects in three related ways.

Impunity and Instability

First, political instability at the level of state agents increased while their oversight by and accountability to their administrative superiors plummeted. The revolutionary transition from Kuchma to Yushchenko at the top triggered a substantial (if uneven across oblasts) replacement of government cadres at the lower levels of the executive hierarchy, directly disrupting existing chains of command. In some regions, for example, up to 90 percent of the police force has been replaced, according to an interviewed official at the Ministry of Internal Affairs. According to official statistics, 18,000 civil servants were dismissed in 2005.[107]

The turnover interrupted established lines of dialogue between state and business, particularly at the lower (agent) levels of state administration. The president of Ukraine's Association of Business Incubators noted in my 2007 interview:

Companies in the regions suffer from the very fast turnaround of mayors ... each [mayor] has his own rules and brings a new team. Very serious processes have begun, especially locally [*na mestakh*].... Whole business structures are being wiped out. How? We hear from our member firms that the local procuracy organs now launch investigations based on some trifle. Then [in the framework of the initial minor investigation], they extract information from the enterprise about its partners and clients. Then they induce [*skloniayut*] one [of the clients] to [falsely] claim that the target enterprise has cashed in [*obnalichil*] on a contract without fulfilling its obligations, which opens the door to a major lawsuit [creating a pretext for extortion or annexation].

In some cases where the previous local administration had established a working relationship with business associations, this relationship was terminated; as one director of a local association complained to me in 2006, "this [municipal] government ignores us completely; it is unprecedented! ... The previous administration at least reacted to our concerns."

---

[106] Each year in the 2005–12 period, I conducted semi-structured interviews with business owners, upper management, and state cadres in Ukraine, including longitudinal interviews with a set panel of entrepreneurs in Khmelnytskyi oblast (central-western Ukraine) and state officials in Kyiv.

[107] EBRD 2005, 194.

Ukraine's Orange Revolution and Property Rights

Kseniia Liapina, a long-term Yushchenko advisor and the head of the Entrepreneurs' Council at the Cabinet of Ministers (a consultative organ lobbying the interests of small and medium business), shared that Oleksandra Kuzhel', her predecessor during the Kuchma administration, was *more successful* in establishing a dialogue between the central state and business in the regions before the Orange Revolution: "Oleksandra received a carte-blanche from Kuchma, and State Committee on Entrepreneurship [*DerzhPidpryemnytstvo*] *had real authority because local bureaucrats knew she would report to Kuchma, that's why their regional strategy was successful*. It's much more difficult now."[108] Gennady Belous, deputy chief of the State Committee on Entrepreneurship, confirmed this interpretation and provided an example:

> I get a lot of emergency calls from entrepreneurs these days particularly from areas like L'viv where there are a lot of small establishments like cafes and restaurants that play music.... Recently, there is massive harassment [*massovye naezdy*] against such entrepreneurs by [state] officials who abuse the Law on Authorship Rights. In 2003, there was a jointly-signed decision by law enforcement bodies [and business] that was mediated by Kuzhel' that clarified the enforcement of this law [regarding the usage of copyrighted entertainment in for-profit establishments]. However, for some reason this system is spinning out of control [*sistema raskruchivaetsia*] today. Entrepreneurs see their entire equipment and property confiscated by state agents.[109]

The unwinding of the state-business dialogue on the ground – Yushchenko's commitment at the level of the state principal notwithstanding – was a systemic phenomenon. A critical issue raised by business leaders at the October 2006 National Congress of the Council of Entrepreneurship at Ukraine's Cabinet of Ministers, for example, was the municipal authorities' *unilateral dissolution* of the so-called local Coordination Councils in the regions. These Coordination Councils were created in 2000 following concerted lobbying by Ukraine's business associations. Although the presidential decree (906/2000) that created these Councils was never abolished, many post-Orange mayors simply dissolved the arrangement.

Paradoxically, the authoritarian Kuchma administration may have been more of a blessing for small entrepreneurs than the democratic Orange team. According to an expert from the Center for Social and Economic Research in Kyiv, interviewed by the author in 2012,

> In his time, Kuchma considered small business harmless for himself because it was no competition to big business which supported Kuchma, so he gave small business an opportunity to grow.... The logic for this was interesting: in order not to redistribute, i.e. not to share, they [Kuchma and the oligarchs] gave possibilities [to small business] which they themselves didn't need anyway. This is a somewhat myopic policy ...

---

[108] Author's transcript of the National Congress of the Council of Entrepreneurship at the Cabinet of Ministers. October 23, 2006 (emphasis added).

[109] Ibid.

because those who received these possibilities asked for more, becoming precisely that force which marched on Maidan. But Kuchma was not afraid, either because of his myopia or his progressiveness.

Of course, the "opportunities to grow" granted by Kuchma, the comrade king, only mattered because he was able to exert reasonable (if far from solid) control over his administrative machine on the ground – control which the Orange Revolution subsequently destroyed. The same expert noted that after the Revolution, "the ministries we work with were reeling from chaos and confusion (*razbrod, bardak, shatanie*). People in the ministries complained that the cadres were leaving; that it was impossible to organize work."

When asked what factors contributed to the explosion of raiding after 2005, the director of the European Bank for Reconstruction and Development in Ukraine, Kamen Zahariev, replied: "The disappearance of the centralized control exercised by the presidential administration under Kuchma, political instability, sense of impunity."[110] While Ukraine is a unitary state, the Orange Revolution exposed its centralized system of governance as a sham. According to the vice president of Ukraine's Institute for Competitive Society, a liberal think-tank:

The country is too big to be unilaterally governed from a single center.... If you analyze the regional administrative dimensions [*upravlencheskie ploskosti*], then our conversations and contacts [with local elites] show that after the [Orange] Revolution, you can no longer talk about the president ... being in charge, as that would assume that his decisions will work their way through to the bottom [*otrabotany do samogo niza*]. In our situation, conversely, decisions are implemented in an unpredictable fashion, and it is unclear what efforts are required at the top to see anything through.... Simply issuing orders won't suffice. [The Revolution] showed the system to be extremely maladjusted [*razbalansirovana*]. The law did not work. Centralized administration did not work. (author's interview)

Such was the post-2005 chaos that some of the older entrepreneurs began to reminisce wistfully about the Soviet system (in whose late stage private cooperatives flourished). According to the owner of a small cable factory in south-central Ukraine interviewed in 2008, "In the Soviet Union, if you had an official seal [on a permit], that was *it*: it was sacred. Now, I get 2–3 bureaucrats in my office arguing in front of me whose permission I really need to go forward with the project. Everybody can tell me that another [bureaucrat's] decision is unlawful [*nepravomernoe*]."

The collapse of the administrative oversight was not a deliberate strategy of the Orange administration. In fact, quite the opposite; Yushchenko's original campaign promised to send "bandits to prison" – state bandits above all – and, in her capacity as the Orange prime minister until September 2005, Tymoshenko attempted to make good on Yushchenko's promise. However,

---

[110] Personal email communication, March 5, 2007.

Ukraine's Orange Revolution and Property Rights

lacking the requisite administrative levers and a coherent legislative framework, her attempts boiled down to rhetoric that, in the long run, backfired. According to a professional business lobbyist in Kyiv interviewed by the author:

In March 2005 Tymoshenko's Cabinet with new ministers and her loud declarations about fighting corruption and so forth paralyzed the country for a certain time. The element of fear kicked in for state officials, and the corruption schemes stopped. However, they stopped in the context of law being not implemented – not just because nobody wanted to implement it, but because it's often impossible to do so when a huge number of acts contradict each other, and there is no motivation for meticulous legislative work to harmonize them [*vylizyvanie i privedenie v sootvetstvie*]. So in this situation where corruption schemes had existed in customs, land relations, etc, when at the upper-most level it was declared that "one must not do this," it all simply stopped. But such situation could not be sustained.... It was on hold for different periods in different spheres, after which all the corruption schemes returned, but the corrupt officials now demanded a premium, a premium for their fear [*korruptsionery potrebovali dopolnitel'noi platy, platy za strakh*]. *The Orange power led to a rise in the price of corruption.*

In terms of the ideal types of state threats, the corruption in question went far beyond siphoning. By abusing the process of tenders (e.g., for state contracts or the long-term leases of municipal land), by helping monopolize markets through their administrative support of affiliated parties, and by participating in illegal ownership capture (raiding), the bureaucrats did not help lift red tape but fundamentally undermined the ownership rights of legitimate Ukrainian entrepreneurs.

Overall, while increasing the accountability of the *state principal* to the *public*, the Orange Revolution dramatically reduced the accountability of *state agents within the executive hierarchy*. This development inflicted harm on Ukrainian business owners by intensifying agent predation. As a well-connected developer from western Ukraine shared in author's interview,

Around eight of my friends served in the municipal administration before the Orange Revolution, and let me tell you, they were trembling with fear when Yushchenko came to power. They all thought it was the time of reckoning [*vremia rasplaty*], that they would go to jail. Who knew that stealing would become much easier instead! ... I remember doing business during Kuchma very well ... if an official really stepped out of line, the guy one step above could fire him, or at least give him a call and reprimand him, which was often enough.... It became worse immediately after the Orange Revolution because everything became permissible [*stalo vse dozvoleno*].... So what has democracy led to? Impunity [*beznakazannost'*].

This sentiment was shared universally by entrepreneurs across Ukraine, from eastern Luhansk to western L'viv, regardless of businesspeople's sharp disagreements about the relative merits of *presidential* candidates. At the 2006 meeting of the Entrepreneurs' Council in Kyiv, the delegate from Sevastopol (Crimea) summed it up thus: "We used to have a 'vertical of power' some years ago; bureaucrats were afraid of something.... Now it's gone, and our main issue is: how to return a token amount of fear to state authorities?"

Incompetence

The second way in which the repercussions of the Orange Revolution undermined sovereign commitment was through the incoming post-revolutionary low-level state cadres who exhibited (even) less experience and professionalism as compared to their predecessors. In Mykolaiv oblast, for example, a business leader shared that "our government refuses to listen to our [business] association when we tell them about the new [deregulation] laws, and simply says that unless we pay into their funds, the government will not resolve any issues.... 'Because that's how we will run things,' the bureaucrats tell us."[111] In other words, the local officials showed business the door (to the officials' coffers) when the business informed them about the new pro-business laws adopted in Kyiv.

On the one hand, administrative incompetence was fueled by corrupt hiring practices, with future predation as their intrinsic component, at the regional level of *oblasts* (states). A confidential interview with the former head of the municipal department of public education (*GorONO*) of a *raion*-forming (county) town in central Ukraine provides insight here. This person has served in his position since the early 1980s, becoming apolitical but high-performing after the Soviet collapse (prior to which he was a member of the Communist Party like all ranking members of the state apparatus). In the early 1990s, the representatives of Ukraine's independence movement *Rukh*, aiming to expose the corruption among the Soviet cadres, visited his apartment to verify that one of the best-known government figures in town was living in a modest two-bedroom flat with his entire family. That was, indeed, the case, and further investigations by *Rukh* did not uncover any wrongdoings. Despite the economic collapse of the 1990s, the town saw a steady rise in the number of new schools as well as its share of prizes in the "academic Olympiads" popular in Ukraine. After the Orange Revolution, GorONO's chief was subjected to administrative pressure to leave his post while at the same time being offered a promotion to become the head of the oblast-level education department for 200,000 Euro. When he replied that he does not have that kind of money, the response of his local "politically correct" Orange colleagues was "don't worry, we'll credit you. You can make it up later." The Faustian bargain is simple: By accepting such a costly promotion, the new officeholder must aggressively seek out predation opportunities to pay back the "loan" (or permanently remain hostage to requests for arbitrary favors). The *oblast*-level job that the interviewee rejected (while losing his municipal job, too) ultimately went to a kindergarten teacher who was egregiously underqualified, a fact that the bureaucrats masterminding the job sale attempted to mask by hastily promoting her to the position of a school principal (in advent of the 200,000 Euro career upgrade).

---

[111] In a different dynamic, other entrepreneurs noted that the local authorities were sometimes genuinely unaware of regulatory changes, continuing to enforce old laws, which suggests critical gaps in principal-agent communication.

Ukraine's Orange Revolution and Property Rights

On the other hand, the ancien-régime cadres who *kept* their jobs faced increased odds of being fired based on political expediency as opposed to performance. In Vinnytsia – where the local administration apart from the mayor largely remained intact – a business veteran (who had started as a citrus fruit trader and within ten years owned a plant bottling mineral water as well as a wholesale trade complex) put it as follows in my interview: "Our authorities now think of themselves as placeholders, as hotel residents who may be evicted any day. Their main purpose is to grab in time."

The problem of short-termism was exacerbated by the fact that many government seats in the local administrations did not see the new permanent cadres appointed for years after the Revolution, relying instead on the intermittent "acting" positions (*vykonuiuchyi obov'iazky*). At the same time, extraordinary elections were planned and canceled routinely in the local parliaments as parties changed strategies based on the latest polls.

In addition to corrupt local hiring and the shrinking time horizons, the drop in professionalism also resulted from the relative poverty and ensuing rapaciousness of the newly appointed regional cadres. One interviewed entrepreneur labeled the newcomer bureaucrats "hungry have-nots" (*golodrantsy*), juxtaposing them with the former regional elites who had accumulated enough personal wealth to focus on the long run: "Bribes became more expensive [after the Revolution]. A man without anything comes to power.... What does he do? As a first step, he creates a piggy bank, the principle being 'once there's money, we'll buy our way forward' [*budut den'gi, kupim dal'she*]. This is the real brake on business development."

In many towns, the new administrative cadres were drawn from relatively recent village migrants who, in addition to their relative privation, were fueled by a sense of entitlement as a result of humiliations endured prior to the Orange Revolution. Vinnytsia, the center of Ukraine's agricultural region 140 miles west of Kyiv, provides a good case here. A member of the city council walked me through a heap of documents detailing how municipal properties have gone to firms controlled by the new regional executives at nominal prices while independent firms were shut out or not informed about the tenders. In his words:

Since the beginning of the 1960s, our region was the most agricultural in Ukraine, and because there was abundant labor, the Soviets built some large enterprises in Vinnytsia. So it's the peasants who moved to the city in the following decades to take these jobs. These people lived in dorms, endlessly waiting for apartments. They fed themselves from their villages. They were enduring all hardships, patiently.... And now that they came to power, it's like a dike has burst.... These people simply had not had time to raise their educational levels, and now it's all about nepotism, relations, connections [*kumovstvo, rodstvo, sviazi*].

To underscore the negative impact on cadres' mentality, a different official noted tin an interview: "In the West, the city has devoured [*poglotil*] the village; in Ukraine, the village has devoured the city." The director of a local business association shared the outrage about Vinnytsia's post-revolution mayor, who assumed office at the age of 27: "He used to sell bananas.... Our mayor graduated from a technical school and then from a pseudo-college without accreditation. Political technologists from Moscow spun his campaign, but he is utterly incompetent.... At least the old mayor would acknowledge mistakes and listen to advice."

In a different manifestation of "not listening," which suggests not so much a lack of technical expertise but deafness to the social context, bureaucrats in post-Orange Ukraine did not bother with attempting to legitimize their extortion. This contrasts sharply with Tsai's findings in China, where local norms provided an informal check on governmental discretion.[112] In 2009, a retail entrepreneur from western Ukraine shared that "one inspector from the agency that controls trade standards and counterfeit wares said *he wanted to buy equipment for his office and needed money.* I offered him 500 hryvnia. The inspector got furious. He told me, 'what is this, charity for the poor? I need five to seven thousand dollars'" (emphasis added). Sometimes, bureaucrats' legitimation attempts are themselves hilariously incriminating. A small shop owner confided that tax inspectors, when asking for cash, "often invent a fable blaming their boss, saying their boss has a birthday, and they have to go to Khmelnytskyi and buy him a present" – to my question as to why tax agents would not at least pretend they need the money for town development, the shop owner exhaled: "Town development? Now *that* would be funny."

As in their predation, so in their consumption did the post-Orange local bureaucrats show little concern for public opinion. Says the CEO of a construction firm in central Ukraine: "From the very first week of coming to power, they begin to build houses for themselves, for their wives, for their children: I got a new wave of contracts right after the [Orange] Revolution." The conspicuous consumption of luxury cars by the local administrators elicited universal dismay across interviewees. In the case of cars, however, local norms seem to have made a difference in at least one case, that of the municipal council secretary in western Ukraine; he started graciously replacing his $100,000 Audi every year with a new Audi of the same make and color, allegedly to attract less attention than he would by getting visibly different vehicles. (People in the know were not amused.)

While the discussion so far has focused on administrators, gatekeepers, and inspectors, the behavior of low-level *enforcers* also complicated the commitment of the Orange state principal. Some departments with a legacy of higher professionalism, such as the SBU (State Security Service), fared better initially, yet several years after the Revolution, even the KGB's successor was a mess. According to a former senior officer who left the SBU in 2009:

Our staff is subdivided into low-level operatives who obtain information, and analysts who constitute the upper level. The analysts evaluate information and can give the

---

[112] Tsai 2007.

Ukraine's Orange Revolution and Property Rights 161

operatives awards if the information is particularly good. I was disgusted with the growing internal corruption and favor trading [after the Orange Revolution]. Some operatives would get favorable reviews [from the analysts] for a bottle of cognac while others just purchased good reviews while submitting empty reports with an "accompanying letter" [i.e., cash in an envelope]... Now [under President Yanukovych in 2012] the practice still continues, except for the new amateurs are now all connected to the Donetsk clan.

During an earlier interview in 2006, the same SBU official acknowledged that "there is now a feudal system in Ukraine in which local police, local power-holders more generally determine how private property can be used."

Ukraine's DSO (State Protection Service) provides another case of deterioration in enforcers' behavior. The DSO is a special police unit officially charged with the protection of particularly important state assets. During the 1990s, because of a lack of state funding, the DSO was set adrift onto a "self-financing" platform. Unlike Russia's OMON, however, the DSO *officially embraced* market principles behind its activity in the 1990s, which led to relatively high professional standards; the DSO was forced to search for private customers, spin off semi-private stock companies, and develop marketing expertise while carving out *legal*, contract-based space for the profit-oriented use of the state's violent resources. Yet, over time, market principles in the absence of Weberian structures gave rise to agent predation, which was amplified in the aftermath of the Orange Revolution. On many occasions in 2006–12, the DSO muscled its way into contracts to guard banks, museums, and other organizations across Ukraine, illegally sidelining private security firms. To win business with banks, for example, the DSO put pressure on bankers, according to Suhonianko, the president of Ukrainian Banks Association: DSO employees "have begun to exceed their mandate illegally assuming regulatory functions [vis-à-vis banks], conducting inspections of branches of several banks, demanding footage of video monitoring contrary to the principle of bank privacy, etc."[113] Such activities directly interfere with the owners' right to legally manage their assets. The DSO has also been implicated in raiding activities. In 2011, the DSO aided the unlawful "privatization" of an insulin-producing factory, Indar, in Kyiv; the raiding takeover directly contradicted the 2007 decision by the Cabinet of Ministers to include Indar in the list of objects that would be exempt from privatization because of the factory's strategic importance for the Ukrainian health market. A DSO employee interviewed by the author in central Ukraine in 2008, after a raiding attempt on a plant producing electrical equipment, proudly shared that "if a raider has procured the documents and is coming with *siloviki*, with our boss, then even if the current plant director has worked his whole life [at the plant], he has no chance." The employee described the conflicting incentives within the DSO by saying that his colleagues "work based on private contracts but are still part of the Ministry of Internal Affairs,"

---

[113] *Den'* February 1, 2012.

162   *Commitment Dissolved*

and that the DSO exists "outside of bureaucracy, outside of state budget" (*vnevedomstvennaia, vnebiudzhetnaia*) while DSO employees "work for the state and for themselves." When asked how the DSO differs from its purely private competitors, the employee dismissed the latter as "just guard dogs," emphasizing that the DSO can launch lawsuits on behalf of the state.

Combined, the heightened impunity and incompetence of the state agents after the Orange Revolution raise the question of why the state principal did not counteract more forcefully this development. The answer is that Yushchenko was consumed by the *political* infighting in the Orange coalition, which exacerbated the *administrative* transition to a more democratic system. Georgia provides a useful contrast here; there, the administrative turnover following the post-2003 democratization under Saakashvili proceeded along clear guidelines directly enforced from Tbilisi. For example, much of the police force in Georgia was fired, as in Ukraine – but *unlike* in Ukraine, the incoming cadres in Georgia had to take a meritocratic exam and pass a lie detector test inquiring into their motivation for joining public service. After Georgia's Rose Revolution of 2003, Saakashvili's popular mandate and hold on power was relatively secure during his first term, allowing him to focus on "cleaning the stables." Meanwhile, in Ukraine, it was the plausibility of the incoming cadres' self-portrayal as "orange" that eclipsed other considerations from the embattled state principal's viewpoint. The loyalty-competence tradeoff among state agents has been theorized from the perspective of dictators.[114] The findings here suggest that such a tradeoff also pertains to nascent democracies and that, furthermore, the state agents' administrative compliance does not necessarily follow from their proclaimed political loyalty vis-à-vis the state principal. Enhanced political competition after the Orange Revolution perversely worsened vertical accountability and the quality of low-level civil servants.[115]

Re-privatization

The third and final side effect of the Orange Revolution concerned re-privatization.[116] Although Tymoshenko's re-privatization campaign originally aimed at only a handful of unjustly privatized oligarchic conglomerates – and was soon aborted altogether by President Yushchenko – it generated predatory repercussions throughout Ukraine with respect to all business types.

The policy of re-privatization as conceived by the Orange revolutionaries would temporarily nationalize largest firms whose privatization involved legal violations, after which the government would privatize them again in a transparent fashion. The plan enjoyed popular support.[117] It was also hoped

[114] Egorov and Sonin 2011.
[115] See also Popova's (2012) brilliant study of declining *judicial* quality as a result of political competition.
[116] Unless otherwise noted, the section on re-privatization is based on an in-depth analysis by Paskhaver et al. 2006.
[117] In May 2005, 71.3 percent of Ukrainians supported the revision of privatization of the biggest state enterprises, while only 10.9 percent thought it "would be best to leave everything as

that re-privatization would help fill the budget (through the revenues from a new round of asset sales by the state). However, while fiscal gaps and the popular desire for justice were often cited in official speeches, the crux of re-privatization from the perspective of the incoming Orange government was to discipline the oligarchs who had financed the Kuchma regime. The "punitive nature" (*karal'nyi kharakter*) of re-privatization explains why the official campaign almost exclusively targeted enterprises connected to Interpipe and SCM, the industrial empires of Pinchuk and Akhmetov respectively.[118] As Yushchenko noted, "we are talking about exceptions ... when the large predominant facilities were privatized in a fashion through which Catherine the Great once used to hand out lands to her lovers.... This is not privatization – it is a humiliation for honest business."[119] Ultimately *only one* enterprise, Krivorozhstal', was successfully re-privatized.[120] All in all, official re-privatization was designed as a "surgical intervention"[121] limited to certain oligarchs, not a war on private business, and, even as an anti-oligarchic procedure, it turned out to be short-lived. Attempts to re-privatize proved a legal nightmare and provoked an outcry among domestic and foreign investors; only months into the process, Yushchenko admitted the government's mistake, sacked Tymoshenko, and declared that formerly privatized property is inviolable.[122]

Despite the quick cancelation of re-privatization at the level of the state principal, however, the campaign continued through the unsanctioned opportunism at the lower administrative levels. As the local experts concluded in 2006,

is and declare an amnesty for shadow capital." The support for such revision was stronger in Central and Western Ukraine (roughly 80 percent) than in the East (53.4 percent). Based on a representative survey by Kyiv Sociology Institute (N=2024).

[118] Paskhaver et al., 26.

[119] *Reuters* October 6, 2005.

[120] This does not include smaller assets re-privatized by the State Property Fund (SPF). Unlike the politically driven re-privatization of Tymoshenko's Cabinet, the re-privatization conducted by SPF had a clear legal basis (non-fulfillment of stipulated investment obligations *after* the completion of privatization itself) and had been ongoing *before* the Orange Revolution. Throughout its existence, by June 2006, SPF had returned 211 objects to state ownership, of which 124 were resold. Of these 211, 61 were returned to the state after the Orange Revolution, of which 45 were resold (by June 2006). The 61 objects returned to the state after the revolution included three blocks of shares, nine operational productive assets (*tsilisnyi mainovyi kompleks*), and forty-nine uncompleted constructions.

[121] CPT 2005.

[122] Speaking at an economic forum in L'viv, Yushchenko said "I realize what harm the policy [of re-privatization] has caused.... The conceptual position of the government is this: we find that the privatization policy of the last 14 years is a policy that satisfied the legislation at the time. It would be a big mistake to conduct a deep revision of privatization history.... Thus we must admit – property in Ukraine has taken shape [*sostoialas'*] in the framework of existing legislation.... [Re-privatization] would amount to a policy of asset redistribution between the old and the new power, would be politically colored, and would end in an embarrassment." *AFN News Agency* October 6, 2005.

The Ukrainian practice has shown that the real danger of re-privatization consists not in a few high-profile cases [*rezonansnykh spravakh*] but in the incentives for its uncontrolled extension ... to all government organs [that] become the initiators of re-establishing 'fairness' in their own spheres of competence at the regional level ... with the help of re-privatization or its threat, one can bankrupt a competitor or expropriate property ... it quickly becomes an all-encompassing redivision of property.[123]

The opening salvo in this process was fired by the Kyiv municipal authorities, who launched a revision of land parcels from the recreational zone of Pushcha-Voditsa that had been allotted to private persons. The local authorities in Crimea and Transcarpathia were quick to emulate the practice.

Once the local administrators showed the way, the enforcers followed suit. Between February and May 2005, employees at the Ministry of the Interior opened 1,700 cases concerning legal gaps in past privatizations, leading "many domestic investors and entrepreneurs of non-oligarchic scale [*neoliharkhich-noho masshtabu*] to experience themselves what re-privatization felt like."[124] After the state principal explicitly ordered an end to re-privatization, the self-serving initiatives of enforcers continued unabated. In addition to filing cases on behalf of the state, individual enforcers also used their information to file lawsuits *as private persons*, covertly operating on behalf of competitors or private raiders, against companies with murky privatization histories.[125] By April 2006, the lower-level employees at the Ministry of the Interior as well as SBU were "massively" (*valom*) engaged in this practice, according to Oleksandr Bondar, the deputy chief of the State Property Fund at the time.[126]

Over time, local courts and judges have become powerful predators in their own right. By the end of 2005, Kostiantyn Stoliarov, a veteran business journalist, was writing:

It is absolutely correct to say that re-privatization is over. In any case, at the level of the executive power.... However, our purely native paradox is that *although there is no re-privatization as a process in Ukraine, and no legal basis for it, there exist informal re-privatizers* [repryvatyzatory-neformaly].... Today one can talk about a complete consensus within the political elites regarding the unacceptability of re-privatization ... [including] the president, the prime-minister, the chair of the Supreme Rada; it is one of the few questions on which the positions of NSNU, SPU, the Party of Regions, the

---

[123] Paskhaver et al., 42.

[124] Ibid.

[125] Kyiv's Pechersky District Court saw a number of lawsuits filed against prominent enterprises across Ukraine by private Kyiv residents in the first months of 2005. Later, the practice spread to smaller courts and smaller firms.

[126] Ironically, the chief of Ukraine's State Property Fund, Valentina Semeniuk, filed lawsuits as a natural person against six enterprises. The practice itself is legal for state employees and in Semeniuk's case was driven by her ideological (socialist) convictions, not by monetary interests. Though in favor of re-privatization, Semeniuk insisted on acting within the bounds of the law, distancing herself early on from Tymoshenko. Semeniuk demonstrably resigned when re-privatization was cancelled. Yushchenko declined her resignation, and Semeniuk went on to oversee an impressive improvement in the corporate governance of state enterprises in Ukraine.

Ukraine's Orange Revolution and Property Rights

People's Party converge. Moreover, big business has de facto made its step towards the president, having accepted the peace agreements.... The disturbing conclusion is that the continuation of re-privatization practices is connected, first of all, with the breakdown of the legal system, to be more precise – its courts [*sudovoi skladovoi*].[127]

The article cites several examples in which a low-level court – in order to facilitate predation – knowingly made mutually contradictory decisions (such as proclaiming a shareholder meeting unlawful while also declaring that the vote taken at the "unlawful" meeting has legal force), or a decision that contradicted a prior verdict of the Supreme Court. As Stoliarov further argues,

The exoticism of decisions made especially by courts of the first instance [i.e., at the lowest level] ... is still perceived as a "bump" of sorts on the way of developing private property ... in Ukraine. However, after a few more successful takeovers, even if local, precisely this way will be considered the highway [by raiders].... All the more so because the precedential basis of "correct decisions" has already been created. Technically speaking, Ukraine does not practice legal precedent ... the precedent here exists rather in the form of the judges' impunity.

Both the head of the EBRD in Ukraine and a senior partner at PricewaterhouseCoopers Ukraine (see Chapter 3) underscored the role of court-based predation as a consequence of the Orange Revolution in my interviews.[128]

More generally, my interviews confirmed the arbitrary extension of re-privatization to the lower administrative levels. According to the director of the Institute for Competitive Society, "all of business felt its vulnerability ... hysteria was quite big also at the local level where only the sum in question [i.e., valuation of property] – the number of zeroes – was different ... *not just business, but also the next layer of middle class* that had invested in high-cost property also felt this threat" (emphasis added). A senior manager overseeing regional portfolios at a Ukrainian investment bank shared in 2006 that

parallel to a political retribution campaign against select big businesses there has been a much broader trend. Every region had its own Krivorozhstal' [a prominent officially re-privatized steelmaker], down to the level of Culture Houses [formerly state-owned entertainment centers] that would be contested following the change of regional government ... and while few enterprises ended up actually re-privatized, there were plenty of destabilizing attempts.

A former government adviser on privatization told me that "at local levels, re-privatization is used as a cover to extract bribes; local procuracy and authorities inflate the issue [*razduvaiut problemu*] to blackmail business." An

---

[127] *Dzerkalo Tyzhnia* December 17, 2005.

[128] On balance, Kamen Zahariev of EBRD opined that the protection of property rights since the Orange Revolution changed "only marginally.... If in the past security services were the main culprits of violations, after the Orange revolution, corrupt courts have been the main problem." Personal email communication, March 5, 2007.

entreprencur from Kharkiv oblast, interviewed in 2006, provides an insight
into how re-privatization sometimes played out in practice:

I bought a complex from the state for my storage facility business. At the time, it was
overgrown with brush, abandoned buildings.... It cost pennies because it was in a terrible shape. It took me a few years to get it in shape. Now the municipal authority tells
me I didn't pay enough, and that today this property costs so and so much – well, yes,
after I built it up, it does [cost that much]. But I bought it yesterday! Anyway, they pressured me into selling the assets.

Importantly, "the initiators of re-privatization [at the state principal level]
did not expect such broad impact themselves, that it would affect all business
sizes in all regions," according to the leading local expert from the think tank
Case Ukraina. The director of Ukraine's state agency for the attraction of foreign capital – itself created after the Orange Revolution – bluntly admitted in
his interview with the author that "bureaucrats made a mockery out of local
power; they did whatever they wanted. At the top, we said 're-privatization.'
At the bottom, they heard that kiosks, shops, cinemas – everything – was up
for grabs."

The predatory unraveling following the Orange Revolution contrasted so
starkly with the sovereign commitment that accompanied it that some international organizations were caught off guard. As the intellectual weekly *Dzerkalo
Tyzhnia* observed,

It is clear that the 'krivorozhstalization of the whole country' has become a reality
[a pun on Lenin's "electrification of the whole country"].... The world, having not
come to its senses after the rapture of the Orange Revolution, simply does not believe
what is happening. Perhaps that is the reason behind the comments of the World
Bank representatives that re-privatization won't affect the attractiveness of Ukraine
for investors? ... Yet the camp of foreign partners of Ukraine's privatized enterprises
is already in turmoil. So, the commercial attaché of Austria in Ukraine tells us that
Austrian companies are contacting the diplomatic mission ... not understanding what
is happening.[129]

Of course, not all foreigners were blindsided by the Orange glow. According
to a joint 2006 study by German and Russian economists, Ukraine sacrificed
2.5 percent of its GDP growth in 2005 due to the "excessive desire of state
employees to conduct a redivision of property."[130]

Conclusion

The Orange Revolution paradoxically negated one of its major achievements –
the sovereign commitment to property rights. By increasing bureaucratic impunity, tolerating administrative incompetence, and allowing re-privatization to
spiral out of Kyiv's control, the aftermath of the Revolution allowed state agents

---

[129] *Dzerkalo Tyzhnia* 2005.
[130] Tambovcev, 287–8.

to violate private ownership rights via annexation, extortion, or intervention, even as threats from the state principal to most firms abated. While principal expropriation was the predominant type of ownership threat under Kuchma, the Orange Revolution also unleashed agent predation on business owners. As the political rights of Ukrainians increased, their property rights became less protected. Parliamentary empowerment failed to act as a commitment device, because it was not only the lawmakers who were empowered vis-à-vis the state principal; so were the predatory state agents.

6

Firm Stakeholders versus State Predators

At this point, the reader can be forgiven for feeling dejected. The story of property rights in Russia and Ukraine reads as a post-mortem on two kleptocracies whose economies the much-praised commitment by the sovereign failed to resuscitate. This chapter shows the light at the end of the tunnel by demonstrating that firms can enforce their property rights through alliances with stakeholders, such as foreign investors, local communities, and labor. The literature treats the state as the only actor able to enforce property rights; firms appear as mere policy-takers that must resort to capital flight, bribing, or asset concealment when faced with predation. This chapter demonstrates the limits of conventional wisdom and offers an alternative.

That property owners may fundamentally contribute to PR security flows logically from the preceding arguments in this volume. Disorganized threats to ownership allow for firm-level defenses; agent predation allows for stakeholder-based protection. If unaccountable low-level bureaucrats constitute the main threat to companies' PR, then certain firm-level strategies can neutralize such threats, although such strategies may fail in the face of threats from the more powerful state principals. Moreover, as will be argued in the case of Russia's Yukos, even if the threat is one of principal expropriation, stakeholder alliances can complicate or even derail the attack.

ALLIANCES IN ACTION: DISSECTING THE MECHANISMS

To illustrate the causal mechanism translating stakeholder alliances into secure property, this section begins with a case study of Oleyna factory, whose owners – thanks to alliances with a foreign bank, labor, and community stakeholders – successfully repelled an annexation attempt by local state actors and private raiders.

Oleyna is a factory producing vegetable oil in the city of Dnipropetrovsk, Ukraine. Founded in 1947, Oleyna was bought out by the employees in

Alliances in Action: Dissecting the Mechanisms

1993, establishing a "closed joint-stock company." In 1995, the company received loans for technological modernization from the European Bank of Reconstruction and Development. In 2001, Oleyna became a certified ISO 9001 producer, the first Ukrainian plant in its sector, implementing an internationally accepted quality management system.

In 2006, the financial-industrial empire Privat Group launched a complex attack on the property rights of Oleyna's majority owners, ultimately aiming to expropriate a 60 percent equity stake in Oleyna by nullifying the 2002 legal sale of this stake to an investor. To do so, Privat Group attacked Oleyna directly as well as through the local state administration. To begin, Oleyna's majority owners noticed that large chunks of shares were changing hands without being officially registered as purchases; Privat Group was buying up shares illegally.[1] Afterward, Privat Group unleashed a "cascade of harassment" on Oleyna through the local government to intimidate the majority owners. Oleyna was swamped with lawsuits and investigations by the local Prosecutor's office, covering issues ranging from alleged environmental transgressions to a criminal case against the CEO. Meanwhile, Privat Group started spreading misleading information about Oleyna to the press in order to discredit the majority owners and the executive management. Some newspapers embarked on a shrill campaign against Oleyna, charging that the firm was "helping ... to plunder the state budget of Ukraine" and speculating that Oleyna's oil, a winner of numerous quality contests, might contain heavy metals and arsenic.[2] After preparing the ground in terms of public opinion and state agencies' readiness (not without financial incentives in the case of the latter), the raiders filed their main lawsuit on behalf of people previously affiliated with Oleyna. Although intimately familiar with Oleyna's affairs, the raiders claimed that they were "unaware" that the firm had a new investor and that the sale of a 60 percent equity stake should be reversed.

What could Oleyna's majority owners do, considering the clout of Privat Group? Because of its prior efforts, Oleyna was blessed with a diverse range of stakeholders whose support it could enlist. The firm had modern standards of corporate governance, that is, empowered shareholders, various labor-supporting programs, a variety of social initiatives in the region (particularly with respect to children), and, as previously noted, a large foreign creditor. Oleyna's reaction to the attack was multidimensional, as the firm drew on the capacities of its different stakeholders. First, the firm called on the European Bank

---

[1] Oleyna's legal status provides for "preemptive rights": Shares must first be offered to existing shareholders before being sold to outsiders. Privat Group abused a gift-giving clause to buy shares surreptitiously. If shares are given as a gift, the ownership change does not need to be registered; corporate raiders often use this clause to buy up shares *illegally* by making concealed payments to "gift-givers."

[2] Both oblast-level *Litsa* and country-level *Komsomol'skaya Pravda* were engaged in the smear campaign. The newspapers were mailed to Oleyna's existing shareholders; such targeting implies that raiders had gained illegal access to the shareholder register.

of Reconstruction and Development (EBRD) for assistance. Together with the EBRD, Oleyna prepared a detailed chronology of the attack and convened a joint press conference. The presence of the EBRD director for Ukraine at the conference guaranteed that the information would be viewed as credible. The conference had a tremendous media response, with more than twenty articles appearing in major national and foreign newspapers. According to the director of Oleyna's press service, "Our elite is very sensitive to the international opinion ... press abroad is very important.... Translated reprints at home ... had impact at the local government level."[3] Second, Oleyna's employees joined to defend the majority owners by writing a letter to the Ukrainian president. The letter was also signed by two thirds of minority shareholders and then disseminated to the press. Finally, Oleyna moved to make its community work visible by spreading Oleyna banners on the playgrounds it had built.

Through its stakeholders, Oleyna created substantial pressure on the local government to stop assisting the raiders. Given the spotlight, if the local politicians, the Prosecutor's Office, and the courts helped Privat Group expropriate the majority stake in Oleyna, it was clear there would be both retribution at the voting booths and likely administrative sanctions from Kyiv. As a result, the fabricated case against the firm was dropped by the Prosecutor's office, due to the lack of a body of crime, a "corpus delicti" clause, practically an admission that the Prosecutor had no reason to open the case from the start. Without political support, the raiders lost interest and did not resort to the criminal tactics they had threatened. According to an Oleyna executive, "we had threats that they will crush our gates with a Kamaz [a large truck], and we're lucky it did not come to this ... we strengthened security but that's not what saved us."

Oleyna's case is not exceptional. Consider the case of EkspoPUL, a factory in Russia's Saratov, whose protection likewise engaged a range of domestic and foreign stakeholders.[4] EkspoPUL offers a particularly harsh test of stakeholder effectiveness because of the inauspicious (from the perspective of PR security) combination of the firm's links to the defense industry and the presence of foreign investment in the firm, which together created a ready pretext for state threats.

EkspoPUL's pedigree goes back to the Soviet plant Reflektor, a star of the Soviet digital industry. After its post-Soviet privatization, Reflektor went bankrupt. In 1996, it was split by its creditors into six independent closed-stock companies including EkspoPUL. In 1998, EkspoPUL's main creditor sold a stake to an American investor, the NSC Corporation, headed by Jimi Hendrix's erstwhile promoter Mike Matthews. Following the investment, EkspoPUL experienced a rare turnaround, becoming profitable, increasing its output

---

[3] Presentation at business forum "AntiReider 2007" in Kyiv, Ukraine (March 29, 2007).
[4] Unless otherwise noted, the EkspoPUL case is based on *Vedomosti* May 12, 2006; *Kommersant* May 23, 2006; *Stereophile* May 20, 2006.

Alliances in Action: Dissecting the Mechanisms

almost fourfold, and employing more than 800 people as one of the largest factories in Saratov.

Although EkspoPUL's post-revival production focused on vacuum tubes and digital lamps used in hi-fi musical equipment, the firm was legally saddled with a special status as a defense-related (*Minoboron zakaz*) enterprise. This status provided the municipal authorities with ammunition to launch an attack against the firm. The attackers' goal was to take over the sprawling territory occupied by EkspoPUL, which the authorities hoped to profitably transfer to Russian Business Estate (RBE), a well-connected developer. After the initial friendly offer to buy the enterprise was declined by EkspoPUL in 2005, the raiders dispensed with civility. In 2006, RBE's director in Saratov ominously suggested that "we have instructions of the FSB [state security service] ... that a military factory cannot exist beside a company with foreign capital.... The FSB hasn't gotten involved only because we haven't gotten them involved.... Writing a letter [to the FSB] would be all ... [that's] needed to shut the factory."[5] (In fact, RBE proved more creative; an RBE affiliate would later produce a forged statement, allegedly from the U.S. embassy, in court stating that Mike Matthews was a U.S. spy.) Municipal crews began using jackhammers on the perimeter of the enterprise, generating dust that rendered the plant's clean rooms inoperable. Finally, municipal fire inspectors provided the official "cover" to cut off electricity to EkspoPUL, paralyzing its production altogether.

The attack by Saratov's municipal authorities and RBE proceeded *despite* the official decisions by Russia's Anti-Monopoly Commission and the Arbitration Court, both of which affirmed the rights of EkspoPUL owners. Among other points, these decisions declared *ex ante* the threatened electricity cutoff illegal, but the cutoff followed nonetheless. The day after electricity was reluctantly restored, the gas supply to the enterprise was severed. EkspoPUL's lawyers may have won symbolic court battles, but the war continued and was ultimately won by stakeholders.

The factory's directors organized the workers to protest in Saratov's main square, where the workers publicly signed a petition to Putin stating that "representatives of the ... [state] organs are handing over Saratov's industry to financial criminals ... escalating social tensions with unpredictable consequences."[6] According to EkspoPUL's deputy director, Sergei Nikitin, "we received significant support from the trade unions. They assumed the main organizational role during the period of mass public protests. We owe them our extreme gratitude."[7] The local trade unions that had benefitted from EkspoPUL's growth helped frame the conflict as an assault on regional labor as such, leading

---

[5] *The New York Times* May 16, 2006.

[6] *Kommersant (Volgograd)* April 7, 2006.

[7] This and other quotes from Nikitin are from the Online Conference with EkspoPUL Management, May 25, 2006. Transcript on file with author.

workers from other enterprises to join the protests in which more than 1,000 (several thousand, according to some sources) workers participated.

Meanwhile, the U.S. investor galvanized an array of foreign stakeholders. The U.S.-Russia Business Council, a consortium of FDI providers, officially signaled its disinclination to invest in Saratov. In April, the U.S. Ambassador to Russia, William Burns, pointedly invited EkspoPUL's general director, Vladimir Chinchikov, to a roundtable discussion of investment opportunities in the Volga region. At the roundtable, which took place in Samara and was attended by representatives from Coca Cola, GM, Marriott, Citibank, and other corporate heavyweights, Chinchikov presented a firsthand account of the deteriorating investment climate in the region. Meanwhile, EkspoPUL's American investor, Mike Matthews, rained fire on the Saratov authorities in his interviews to Russia's leading business paper *Vedomosti* and anybody else who listened, including CNBC, Radio Free Europe, and *The New York Times*. With his trademark panache, Matthews listed the addresses of the governor of Saratov oblast, Russia's general prosecutor, and the presidential plenipotentiary representative for the Volga Federal district, asking readers to write them on behalf of EkspoPUL, adding that "people can also send positive letters to President Vladimir Putin.... The raiders are so pervasive that he needs grassroots support. Putin has ... gotten rid of the daily racketeer-style murders, but white-collar corruption is so widespread that stopping it is like trying to plug up the dikes in Holland.... [But] they [the raiders] are fighting rock'n'roll this time."

Ultimately, the intervention of the oblast [county-level] procuracy and the oblast governor on behalf of EkspoPUL helped counterbalance the predatory municipal forces. The procuracy intervened to finally reestablish the energy supply to the firm, while the governor convened a mediation roundtable between EkspoPUL, Saratov's municipal authorities, and RBE, signaling that expropriation would not be tolerated. In his press conference, EkspoPUL's representative, Nikitin, thanked the oblast authorities while caustically noting that "the city urgently needs a real mayor, a professional ... [to stem] the complete breakdown in the system of city management.... The free-for-all between cadres [*kadrovaia chekharda*] in the city hall and at the municipal enterprises has generated an acute ... crisis." Reflecting on their triumph, Nikitin noted, "We, the workers of EkspoPUL, consider ourselves to be the carriers of the traditions of the Saratov plant [Reflektor], and we are not weak.... We have enough *socio-political* [obshchestvenno-politicheskikh] and legal resources to fend off any takeover attempts."

While the pressure and publicity generated by local labor and foreign investors kept the EkspoPUL ownership intact, all five *other* firms that had split from Reflektor lacked EkspoPUL's stakeholder alliances and were taken over by RBE.[8] This stark contrast between the otherwise comparable firms is suggestive of the causal effect of stakeholder alliances.

---

[8] These firms included PUL-ENERGO, Refenergo, Ref-Optoelektronika, RefSOI, and Reflektor.

Alliances in Action: Dissecting the Mechanisms

Oleyna and EkspoPUL benefited from a *combination* of foreign and domestic stakeholders. However, discrete stakeholder alliances can also be highly effective, as the case study of Vimpelcom demonstrates; this case also highlights the usefulness of foreign investors' connections to their own governments.

One of the leading wireless operators in Russia, Vimpelcom was the first Russian company since 1903 to list its equity on the New York Stock Exchange. The year 2004 proved very tense for the company's relations with the state, even by Russian standards.[9] In January, as a result of an unscheduled inspection, the state regulators for telecommunications informed Vimpelcom it did not have the proper license for its 5.5 million subscribers in Moscow. In February, a criminal case was opened against the company by the procuracy of the Northern Administrative Region; allegedly, the corporation was engaged in "illegal entrepreneurship" with its subsidiary. In the summer, Vimpelcom experienced a deficit of approved phone numbers for its subscribers; the company claimed this was the result of the state organs' intentional blockade. Without any explanation, the firm was also refused a license for the Far East region (necessary for nationwide coverage).

The final note in the crescendo of state threats came in September 2004, when the firm was presented with a $157 million back-tax bill (for 2001) by the Federal Tax Service. Nominally, the company was cited for having neglected to pay taxes owed by its fully owned subsidiary Impuls. Realistically, analysts pointed to the long-standing conflict between the Vimpelcom's controlling shareholder, the Alfa Group, run by Mikhail Fridman, and Russia's minister of communications, Leonid Reiman. The fact that Alfa Group had publicly accused Reiman of corruption seemed to justify expectations of a full-blown showdown.[10] Given this background, *Kommersant* at the time concluded that "the tax persecution of Vimpelcom is related to the conflict of its shareholders with the state regulators of the sector."[11] AC&M Consulting commented that "the company can appeal the demands of tax organs in court, but the ... *probability that the tax authorities will nevertheless obtain the full sum from Vimpelcom is quite high.*"[12] Vimpelcom's shares on the NYSE plunged by almost 25 percent after the announcement of the tax claim, underscoring market pessimism regarding the outcome of the company's clash with

---

[9] *Kommersant* December 9, 2004.

[10] The conflict between the corporation's main shareholders and the state had even deeper roots. In August 2003, Alfa Group purchased a blocking stake in its rival firm, Megafon, which had been under the control of Telecominvest; after the purchase, Alfa Group was able to "fully paralyze the activity of its competitor by applying its veto to all decisions of the board of directors." *Delovaya Nedelya* August 6, 2003. Inauspiciously for Vimpelcom, Telecominvest had been backed by the St. Petersburg power clan. Telecominvest, perceived by many analysts to be still under the personal control of Reiman, challenged the purchase by Alfa Group, and both commercial structures clashed in a series of international lawsuits. *Vzglyad* July 26, 2005.

[11] *Kommersant* 2004.

[12] Ibid (emphasis added).

state structures (which, at this point, ran the gamut from administrators and enforcers to gatekeepers and inspectors).

The denouement of the Vimpelcom drama startled all observers. The authorities scaled down the tax bill to $17 million, that is, *almost tenfold*, although the firm did not turn to courts on this issue.[13] Also, Reiman was temporarily removed from his post, which some analysts tied to the Vimpelcom battle.[14] Reiman's failure to be appointed to the new 2008 cabinet as well as his subsequent departure from the post of presidential adviser, under pressure from Putin and Medvedev, were more clearly the result of Reiman's business predation,[15] laid bare by the Vimpelcom case.

What happened? Vimpelcom's management, it turns out, employed a political strategy relying on the company's image as a modern corporation with transparent accounts and relatively empowered minority shareholders. It is the foreign investors who came to the firm's defense after the tax assault. Through a series of purchases, the Norwegian phone company Telenor came to own 30 percent of Vimpelcom by 2001. Telenor lobbied the Kremlin – successfully – on Vimpelcom's behalf.[16] Dag Vangsnes, Telenor's director, emphasized in an interview to the Russian press that "Vimpelcom is an open, transparent company which is working for the well-being of Russian people. The attempt of the Russian authorities to claim these taxes now ... is an attempt to charge the same tax twice."[17]

The real boon for the Vimpelcom-Telenor alliance was the fact that the Norwegian firm is itself 54 percent owned by Norway's government. The use of political connections by Telenor to defend Vimpelcom against "tax terrorism," as a leading Russian economist Yasin put it, is striking.

It is noteworthy that *until the intervention of Telenor*, Vimpelcom was hardly effective at countering state threats to its PR; earlier in the year, the state gatekeepers had turned down all of the firm's ninety-seven legitimate requests for additional bandwidth. This contrasts sharply with a comparable dispute in 2000 when Vimpelcom fought a move by the Communications Ministry to strip the firm of its frequencies in favor of a competitor. In this instance, Telenor representatives conveyed the problem to Norway's Prime Minister Jens Stoltenberg who asked his Russian counterpart, Kasyanov, "to look into the matter."[18] Vimpelcom retained its frequency spectrum. This within-case comparison between the outcomes of PR threats suggests that the activation of its foreign alliance made a real difference for Vimpelcom.

Overall, foreign alliances usually work through backdoor lobbying. According to the EBRD Director for Ukraine, when affiliated firms face state

---

[13] *The New York Times* March 2, 2005.
[14] *PriMetrica* March 10, 2004.
[15] *Vedomosti* September 10, 2010.
[16] *The New York Times* 2005.
[17] *Kommersant* 2004.
[18] Ibid.

Alliances in Action: Dissecting the Mechanisms

predation, "EBRD support takes the form of official demarches, public support, and unofficial approaches."[19] The CEO of a large beverage company with sizeable investments from Denmark and the UK noted in my interview that "our access to the EU Business Association and the American Chamber of Commerce in Kyiv is a real luxury" when the firm is faced with PR threats: "these organizations are real levers of influence [*rychagi vliianiia*], and our appeals to them often make additional individual lobbying superfluous." The former Ukrainian adviser to the prime minister confirmed in my 2007 interview that

firms with a foreign stake are better protected than pure natives. We have the U.S. Ambassador running to the cabinet of ministers [*kabmin*] based on any trifle, screaming 'an American investor was hurt!' Americans lobby hard. It can be annoying, really, but it works. Germans also create a fuss. Their ambassador is of course calmer [than the American], but they have Frau Rau who is the permanent delegate of German business. These people can easily attract the foreign general public [*zarubezhnuiu obshchestvennost'*] to their cause, too.

Another important mechanism for foreign alliances involves the foreigners' expertise in leveraging Western courts and legal structures against domestic predators, as will be shown in the case of Yukos, discussed later in this chapter.

Alliances with the community and labor often involve pressure on upperranking state officials to sanction their predatory subordinates, as was seen in the cases of Oleyna and EkspoPUL. Consider also the case of Muvakal, a limited-liability firm that opened a grocery store in Moscow's Meshchanskii District. Similarly to EkspoPUL, the attraction of Muvakal's store to the predators consisted in its real estate. Unlike EkspoPUL, Muvakal is a de novo (nonprivatized) firm. Established in 1999, Muvakal acquired the 316 square meters of shop space in 2002 for 1.8 million rubles; by 2007, the space was valued at more than $1 million, a thirtyfold increase, as a result of the completion of a nearby "ring road" and the boom in real estate markets. The attack began when a former co-owner who had sold his stake in 2000 filed a complaint at Moscow's state department for fighting economic crimes; the complaint alleged that no such sale of the equity stake ever took place, despite available documentation to the contrary.[20] As it became clear, the private plaintiff was being used as a Trojan horse by state raiders. Muvakal was swept with numerous investigations, including a simultaneous unannounced illegal visit by the representatives of the Moscow Central Administrative District (*TsAO*), the epidemiological service, fire inspection, the department of building maintenance,

---

[19] Personal communication with author, March 3, 2007
[20] The owners ordered a legal expertise from independent experts and from the Interior Ministry's Expert-Criminological Center, both of which confirmed the authenticity of the document. Curiously, the *local* district police in Moscow, unaware of the federal expertise by the ECC, conducted its own, which disputed the authenticity of the sale document. This suggests that the predatory initiative came from the district-level state agents.

and so on. Although no specific violations by Muvakal were mentioned, the delegation of state officials asked the owners to present the ownership registration papers. The owners declined, fearing attempted forgery (of registration papers) or takeover by the state agents. The owners then received a call from people who introduced themselves as "former law enforcement agents with good connections"; these ex-agents promised to resolve Muvakal's troubles if the owners agreed to sell the firm at a steep discount.

Instead, Muvakal activated its stakeholders. A huge banner was placed in the store's windows, declaring "We are being attacked by raiders." The shop's banner, albeit legal, was cut down several times by state officials. Local newspapers began writing about the conflict. Importantly, it is the identity and the activity of the shop's key stakeholders – the World War II veterans – which made the difference in how the conflict was covered and ultimately resolved. Russian law grants WWII veterans certain shopping privileges by subsidizing select grocery stores. Muvakal had the accreditation of Moscow's municipal government "to serve the veterans of the Great Patriotic War." When the store temporarily closed during the state attack, the veterans from the neighboring communities panicked; to them, Muvakal provided an oasis of affordable groceries in overpriced Moscow. Luckily for Muvakal, the veterans did more than panic; they offered the owners their help and began "going to the offices," (*khodit' po instantsiiam*) widely filing complaints about the mistreatment. The press amped up the volume, rhetorically asking "do they [our veterans] deserve this?" and citing the legal provision that obliges the municipal authorities to ensure the continued functioning of the "social shops." The campaign focused its pressure on Yelena Chernykh, the administrative head of the Meshchanskii District, who gave the order to remove the shop's SOS banner. The success of the campaign materialized within several months; the threatening phone calls stopped, and so did the official investigations.

In addition to potential sanctions from administrative superiors, the financial mechanism can play a role in community-based defenses. As the deputy CEO of Russia's premier anti-raider consulting firm, RosRazvitie, notes "for the aggressor, it's … a business project. *Bribes can triple if officials are afraid of public [protest] campaigns*: when the raider is exceeding his projected costs, that's when the expropriation order is canceled."[21]

Meanwhile, large trade unions may have the resources and expertise to organize a legal defense that some business owners may not be able to realize on their own. Russia's Federation of Independent Trade Unions (FNPR), for example, mounted a legal defense for several businesses in Sochi in 2008, including the sanatorium "Moskva" as well as the stadium "Spartak," ultimately prevailing over the state-assisted raiders in courts. According to Mikhail Shmakov, the chair of the FNPR, "trade unions participate very actively in the fight against raiders. [We] support the employee collectives, draw the attention

---

[21] Presentation at business forum "AntiReider 2007" in Kyiv, Ukraine (March 29, 2007).

Alliances in Action: Dissecting the Mechanisms

of the first persons in the government to the problems of Russian enterprises, suggest our legislative amendments."[22]

Furthermore, organized community and labor can prevent a physical confrontation, as in the case of the Ukrainian plant NZF, where, in 2005, the workers faced down a cordon of special police forces (the latter trying to implement a politically motivated takeover of NZF). As the wider town community of Nikopol' joined the protests, reporting on the conflict invariably mentioned NZF's desirability as an employer: "Last week, Nikopol' was Ukraine's second capital: thousands of protesters, dozens of TV cameras.... The special forces left the territory of the world's largest ferroalloy producer ... [where] the standard salary ... is 1600–2000 hryvnia."[23]

Tavria, a cognac-producing plant in Crimea, provides another case. In 2009, up to 1,000 workers, some with tractors, physically protected the plant from 150 commandos during a night of skirmishes. As a result of the widespread media attention following the standoff, the Ukrainian minister of interior personally intervened to protect the legitimate owners. The chief editor of IA Advisers, Russia's private information agency reporting on corporate conflicts, says: "By far not every armed detachment [*silovoe podrazdelenie*] will want to fight with a crowd of workers in front of cameras. But ... you have to establish a relationship with your employees in advance. You cannot just get ... them to go out there for you on 'ready, set, go': workers usually hate their managers."[24]

That a certain *critical mass* of benefit transfers to stakeholders is required before the latter become effective allies was widely recognized by interviewees; many also emphasized the importance of the *publicity* of such transfers. The owner of a small retail chain in Ukraine, interviewed by the author, noted that "I've done some charity without advertising it, out of my own pocket: to the veterans, to the orphanage, to people who needed a surgery.... If I did this systematically, with a track record, through my company, it would protect my firm from the state. But with the financial crisis, I just can't afford to do more, and, as it is, people are not on my side [*narod ne za menia*]." From the same town, but *with* the "track record" is Oleg, the owner of a small cable factory. Local state agencies were pressing his company for substantial bribes. Oleg's approach: "I came to an agreement with the mayor. Since I had been donating big sums for the purposes of city development – and why not? – my problems were resolved" (author's interview). When asked about the instances in which such philanthropy is useful, Oleg shares that it also helps *in advance* of projects' implementation, that is, as a preemptive measure and not just in instances of *post hoc* PR defense: "I can come [to city authorities] and say: '*I need this and that – and this is what I can do for the city. To you personally I will not*

---

[22] *Tribuna* April 11, 2008.
[23] *Gazeta Po-Ukrains'ky* September 9, 2005.
[24] Presentation at business forum "AntiReider 2007" in Kyiv, Ukraine (March 29, 2007).

give anything [i.e., no bribes]. So you decide.' Since the decision is usually not up to any single person, they tend to decide in my favor." When asked whether his status as a significant local taxpayer offers any protection, Oleg turns skeptical, pointing to the immobile nature of his assets:

> If you come to city's treasury and say, 'I'm a taxpayer and tomorrow I will shut down,' of course it's not profitable for anybody: they understand that, too. On the other hand, whom can they squeeze for money? Manufacturing. Because if it's trade, you can just move your shop out of the region; but if you're a manufacturer, there's no way back ... it would be a very long process [of relocating].

The importance of the connection of charity-related work to *the specific firm* was confirmed by the president of RUIE, Russia's big-business association, Aleksandr Shokhin. For publicly traded corporations, however, this involves a tradeoff because such firms are limited in the amount of resources they can donate. Says Shokhin,

> I have ordered to conduct an inventory of the ... charity funds of the RUIE members.... Almost all [members] route their charity through personal funds, especially in the case of public companies – there, it is inappropriate to conduct large-scale charity through the funds of the firm; the limits are quite harsh there ... so that nobody thinks that money is being divided among the insiders, or being laundered, and so forth.[25]

The firm's organizational form, in other words, may shape its outreach efforts vis-à-vis the stakeholders.

Furthermore, such efforts need to *be seen as voluntary* to be effective; when the government pressures the owners into transferring certain benefits to the stakeholders, it is the state actors rather than the owners who take credit. According to Shokhin,

> Apart from charity there is such a thing as ... corporate social responsibility. Often this ... is not about solving the employees' problems, or solving the problems existing on the territory adjacent to the companies. Instead, it is about satisfying the demands of federal, regional, and local authorities.... Because many [owners] implement this so-called "social responsibility" according to this scheme, they don't have time to engage in normal civilized [i.e., voluntary] charity ... they consider that they have done their part already.

For the asset owners, protection from the state during a PR attack requires some distance from the state *during the preceding stage of alliance-building*. Such distance allows the stakeholders to identify clearly the party whose defense would best serve their interests.

The cases of Oleyna, EkspoPUL, Vimpelcom, Muvakal, NZF, and Tavria as well as the additional analysis so far suggest two general variation vectors. First, the effectiveness of different alliances at PR enforcement may vary.

---

[25] Aleksandr Shokhin on the radio program "Dura Lex" at Ekho Moskvy, March 26, 2011. Transcript available at: http://www.echo.msk.ru/programs/lex/759898-echo.html

Yukos Redux

This *inter-alliance* variation depends on the capability of particular allies to impose costs on predatory state agents. Numerical strength, political connections, financial clout, publicity access, and other factors increase the capability of various alliances. For example, the political links of foreign investors to *their* governments carry a premium for the domestic owners whose PR are under attack, as Vimpelcom's case shows. Second, a given alliance will also vary in its effectiveness across *various subsets of predatory state agents*, since the latter differ in their vulnerabilities; some are more sensitive to the financial costs of expropriation, others to the negative publicity such attempts may generate, and so forth. In this context, the presence of multiple alliances whose members have *complementary capabilities* to punish the aggressors increases the universality of a given firm's PR defense, as illustrated by Oleyna's case.

YUKOS REDUX

Of course, alliances can fail to protect firms. Yukos, Russia's former oil giant whose 2003–4 expropriation has been well-covered in the literature, seems to have been a sensational failure. The Yukos case is important, as it establishes the main boundary condition for my argument: No matter how strong its non-state alliances, business is likely to lose in a head-to-head confrontation with the central executive. However, the key threat to most entrepreneurs in the developing world is not the central executive but local state actors as well as private predators. Previously discussed evidence shows that stakeholder alliances do increase PR security against such threats.

The Yukos case offers more than a boundary condition, however; it also substantiates my argument in two ways. First, Yukos's allies *did support the firm* and continue to do so after its legal demise; in other words, the Yukos case confirms the link between the establishment of alliances and the stakeholders' support in the case of a PR attack. Second – and crucially – once the fates of Yukos's "political" shareholder Khodorkovsky and the rest of Yukos's owners are separated, it is clear that the latter have achieved *important victories against the sovereign due to stakeholders' support*. To describe the impact of Yukos's alliances as "failure" is an incomplete verdict. Let us zoom in on both points.

The *presence* of Yukos's alliances at the time of the Kremlin's attack is beyond doubt. With charitable donations exceeding $50 million annually across a broad range of causes[26] – a truly massive amount for Russia – ex-CEO Khodorkovsky could teach Dale Carnegie a thing or two about how to win friends and influence people. The magnate's lavish spending in Washington gained him access to top-level U.S. policy-makers, including several senators and George Bush, Sr.. As foreigners are barred from donating money to the American political parties, Khodorkovsky focused on the U.S. think-tanks and

---

[26] *The New York Times* November 5, 2003.

180 Firm Stakeholders vs. State Predators

organizations, "including a $1 million donation to the Library of Congress and a $500,000 pledge to the Carnegie Endowment for International Peace."[27] Yukos's westernized corporate governance also proved a magnet to foreign investors. Fiona Hill, a Russia analyst at the Brookings Institution, noted that "the [American] think tanks were all joking about who wanted to take money to fund the Mikhail Khodorkovsky chair of good corporate governance."

In line with my argument, Yukos's stakeholders have exerted broad efforts to support the firm and its main shareholder once under attack. Domestic NGOs sprang up to defend Khodorkovsky. One NGO, Sovest' [conscience], put public pressure on Duma deputies, organized televised demonstrations in front of the FSB (security service) headquarters, and drew Amnesty International to Khodorkovsky's cause. Foreign stakeholders also weighed in. Senator McCain told the U.S. Senate that the Yukos case was jeopardizing the United States-Russia relationship and called for an investment blockade of Russia. More credibly, an alliance of "prominent world leaders" led by the former prime minister of Canada, Jean Chrétien, "tried all kinds of tax settlement negotiations throughout 2004" on behalf of Yukos, according to Yukos's CFO, Bruce Misamore.[28] Yukos's dramatic improvement in its treatment of minority shareholders since the 1990s also paid off handsomely in the way the company's conflict with the Russian government was covered in the Western media. Tellingly, *The Economist* lashed out against Putin's overall record by stating that "the attack on Yukos, *the best-run and most western-looking of Russian companies*, was the worst of all."[29] The U.S. residency of Yukos's CFO as well as Yukos's U.S. assets also allowed the firm to seek Chapter 11 bankruptcy protection in a Houston court.

Despite Khodorkovsky's massive philanthropy and foreign support networks, the state imprisoned the tycoon and pushed through the auction of Yukos's main oil-producing asset, YugO-skneftegaz, now a subsidiary of the majority state-owned firm Rosneft. Alliances clearly did not save Yukos's main shareholder.[30]

It is, however, a mistake to treat Khodorkovsky and Yukos as synonymous. According to various estimates, Khodorkovsky controlled 30–60 percent of Yukos before the state's attack (on his arrest, Khodorkovsky transferred this stake to his partner Nevzlin, self-exiled in Israel). As a publicly traded corporation, Yukos had more than 50,000 owners.[31] Have the

---

[27] Ibid.

[28] *QFinance* 2009 (emphasis added).

[29] *The Economist* December 9, 2004.

[30] Still, Khodorkovsky's 2013 release would have been unlikely without the persistent lobbying on his behalf by Germany's former prime-minister Genscher and chancellor Merkel. Upon being released from prison, Khodorkovsky was flown to Germany in the private jet of Ulrich Bettermann, a German investor in Russia.

[31] By March 2003, around 60 percent of Yukos belonged to Group Menatep, of which Khodorkovsky controlled slightly more than half; 10 percent belonged to the fund Veteran

Yukos Redux

firm's stakeholders had any impact on its standoff with the state beyond Khodorkovsky? In fact, the firm's alliances have *protracted, delegitimized, and partly reversed* the expropriation of Yukos.

To begin, in December 2004, the Houston court granted Yukos a temporary injunction blocking any operations with Yukos's assets, including the planned auction of the Yugeskneftegaz subsidiary. This verdict prompted an international banking consortium to cancel its deal with the Russian state proxies aiming to finance the government's purchase of the subsidiary.[32] The Russian government proceeded with the auction but was forced to obfuscate the winning bidder and the source of finance, destroying the legitimacy of the auction.[33]

By using foreign courts, Yukos's stakeholders have achieved six other important victories against the Russian government. First, based on the claim by Veteran Petroleum Trust representing the former employees of Yukos (as well as the claims of two other Yukos-related entities), an arbitration tribunal convened in The Hague ruled in November 2009 that Yukos's former shareholders are entitled to seek compensation for the company's expropriation under the Energy Charter Treaty (a multilateral convention protecting investments and securing transits in the energy field, in force since 1998), and the ultimate ruling is binding on Russia under international law.[34] In July 2014, the tribunal ruled in favor of Yukos shareholders, dismissing Moscow's arguments about tax collection and eloquently concluding that the Kremlin had perpetrated "a devious and calculated expropriation."[35] The eye-popping $50 billion awarded to the collateral victims of Russia's sovereign is the largest arbitration award in history, twenty times larger than the previous record for damages against a government. While collecting a sum equivalent to 2.5 percent of Russia's 2013 GDP from the Russian sovereign will be challenging, analysts agreed that "the decision holds the potential to shift leverage … from Moscow toward companies in the tug of war over access to reserves and profits…. Russia would not be able to act by fiat or without fear of paying a cost."[36] According to Stratfor, a private intelligence agency, "the legacy provisions of the ECT ensure that the

---

Petroleum, a pension vehicle for Yukos's former employees; 23 percent was in free float; the remainder was owned by the Yukos corporation itself. *Profil'* August 30, 2010.

[32] This decision gave the judge the right to arrest the U.S. assets of Gazprom and six explicitly listed Western banks (J.P. Morgan, Deutsche Bank, Caylon, BNP Paribas, Dresdner, ABN AMRO), should they ignore the moratorium. *Kommersant* December 18, 2004.

[33] In early 2005, a scandal erupted when Russia's independent media presented leaked documents showing that the purchase of Yugeskneftegaz was financed from the state budget, an embarrassing circumstance belying the Kremlin's officially proclaimed distance from the auction. *Vedomosti* June 3, 2005.

[34] The tribunal overruled the Russian government's objections to the Treaty's applicability; these objections cited Russia's exit from the Treaty in 2009 and the technical lack of the Treaty's initial ratification by the Duma. For details, see Giorgetti 2010.

[35] *The Guardian* July 28, 2014.

[36] *The New York Times* December 1, 2009.

Yukos ruling will apply to a wide range of existing energy investments in Russia for the next 20 years," which, Stratfor notes, is crucial given that "Russia ... has increased its dependency for massive injections of foreign investment and know-how to rebuild its energy infrastructure."[37] More immediately, Yukos shareholders can be entitled to seize certain assets of the Russian government abroad in their effort to collect damages – the refineries and pipelines of Rosneft and Gazprom could become prime targets in this process.

Second, in October 2007, a court in Amsterdam ruled that the bankruptcy of Yukos, resulting from retroactive tax claims by the Russian state, contradicts Dutch legislation.[38] The Netherlands' refusal to accept the legitimacy of Yukos's bankruptcy in Russia triggered subsequent lawsuits, which have *reversed the expropriation of Yukos's non-Russian assets* (valued at several billion dollars and largely owned by the subsidiaries Yukos Finance BV and Yukos Capital S.a.r.l., registered in the Netherlands and Luxembourg). The rights to manage, transfer, and derive income from assets have all been profoundly affected to Yukos's advantage.

Third, the replacement of Yukos's original management team by the bankruptcy receiver Eduard Rebgun (appointed by the Russian bankruptcy order) was nullified and the original management reinstated. Fourth, in 2010, the Amsterdam Appeals court ruled that the Russian bankruptcy administrator had no authority to transfer the shares of Yukos Finance to the former subsidiary of Rosneft, Promneftstroy.

The fifth court-based victory concerns the Yukos case at the European Court of Human Rights. The very admission of the case to the ECHR constituted an early victory, an outcome for which the reorganization of Yukos assets abroad by foreign CEOs proved decisive.[39] While the original claim was submitted to ECHR in 2004 (application no. 14902/04), the wheels of justice grind slowly in Strasbourg; by the time the Court was deliberating on the admissibility of the case, Yukos had ceased to exist in Russia as a legal entity, which, the Russian Federation argued, put the ECHR outside of its jurisdiction. However, in 2009, the Court had admitted the case of an entity defunct since 2007, based on the latter's foreign subsidiaries. Since the problem of defining the claimant and "victim" in Yukos's case played a large part in Court's deliberation on its admissibility – the Court, perhaps understandably, does not see protecting billionaires' rights as its top priority – the presence of Veteran Petroleum pensioners in the background aided Yukos's prospects. A more spectacular victory came in July 2014 when the court awarded Yukos shareholders $2.6 billion, an amount unprecedented in the human rights field.[40]

---

[37] Stratfor 2013.

[38] *Kommersant* November 1, 2007.

[39] *Profil'* 2010.

[40] Interestingly, in 2011, the ECHR issued an inconclusive ruling on the alleged expropriation, allowing both Yukos representatives and the Russian government to declare victory while keeping mum on the compensation issue. According to ECHR in 2011, Yukos was denied a fair trial

Yukos Redux   183

Sixth and perhaps most importantly, Yukos shareholders have already collected some heavy monetary awards: $400 million against Rosneft and $1.2 billion against Promneftstroy (for Yukos Capital and Yukos Finance respectively).[41] In June 2010, Rosneft – the symbol of the Putin state's power – acknowledged defeat, stating tersely that "Rosneft will abide by the decision of the Supreme Court of the Netherlands"[42]; by August, the money was paid. A Yukos lawyer for this case interviewed by the author hints at the intensity of stakeholders' efforts preceding the victory:

> After the court of appeals in the Netherlands confirmed that the sum must be exacted, Rosneft naturally did not pay. After that and not without battle-like engagement [*ne bez boevogo uchastiia*], we have tracked their tankers and arrested a couple of [Rosneft] tankers with oil in Rotterdam. They unfroze the tankers, but in order to unfreeze them, they showed their secret contracts. Based on [these] contracts, we traced the subsidiaries of Rosneft and ... their accounts. Their accounts turned out to be in England: so in England, we obtained a court order [*sudebnyi prikaz*] and froze these accounts. When the sum in these accounts – and those were trading accounts which means there's constant turnover ... – kept climbing ... they said "ok," and brought [us] a bank guarantee. After that there was yet another small suit in a London court. Only then, they paid. To get money from the Russians voluntarily is impossible.... They never agree to a settlement. One must punish them very severely.

The quote underscores the importance of "battle-like engagement" even when the protection-oriented activity is conducted in the rule-of-law domain of Western courts. Crucially, this engagement is often conducted by a company's stakeholders, de facto on behalf of its majority owners. That is precisely what happened with Yukos. The animating force behind its legal battles abroad has consisted of the company's foreign management team and its pensioners (through Veteran Petroleum[43]), combining the expertise of the former with the clear motivation of the latter. Such motivation would not have existed had Yukos not provided its labor with generous pension benefits linked to company's shares, that is, to company's property rights. As Khodorkovsky presciently said at the launch of the "Veteran" program – which, in addition to the equity fund, involved substantial assistance with housing and post-retirement

---

in Russia and penalties imposed by the Russian state were disproportionate. At the same time, the Court ruled that the attack was not politically motivated. According to legal specialists interviewed by the author, the latter decision involved two considerations. As a matter of legal precedent, the 2004 case of *Gusinsky vs. Russia* at the ECHR (application no. 70276/01), in which the expropriation of Gusinsky's media assets *was* found politically motivated, established a high benchmark for proof of political motivation, which the Yukos case failed to reach; serendipitously for Mr. Gusinsky, the state offered him its extortion terms in writing. As a matter of political expediency, the ECHR currently receives the majority of its claims from Russian citizens, the enforcement of its rulings being critically dependent on the continued cooperation of the Russian state: the Court may have been loath to provoke Russia unnecessarily in this context.

[41] *Reuters* January 7, 2011; *The Economist* March 25, 2010.

[42] *Expatica* June 28, 2010.

[43] *FundsHub* January 10, 2008.

184   *Firm Stakeholders vs. State Predators*

relocation from the Northern regions – the mammoth initiative "will promote the harmonization of shareholders' interests with those of company's workers."[44] As to the expertise of Western stakeholders, the company's American CFO discloses some of the sophisticated legal strategizing:

> During 2004 and 2005 we scoured the world for legal structures to protect Yukos's international assets and we found a structure in the Netherlands called a Stichting, a Dutch "foundation" structure. We now have formed two Stichtings in which we have put all of Yukos's international assets. The Stichtings have served us extremely well ... [in] battling off attacks from Rosneft and other entities and fronts of the Russian government, which keep trying to seize those assets.[45]

But what about Mr. Nevzlin, the majority owner of Yukos shares after Khodorkovsky's imprisonment? After all, the accumulated penalties won against Russian entities in Western courts will be eventually paid out to Yukos's original shareholders. Says a New York-based Yukos lawyer (author's interview): "without a doubt, Menatep and Mr. Nevzlin ... will get a big chunk.... I cannot say that Mr. Nevzlin is undertaking any serious efforts to exact [the payments]. He's living his own life, he has his own business ... – thank god he's not interfering." With billions at stake, Mr. Nevzlin's indifference is remarkably stoic. Having the campaign to reclaim Yukos's property rights outsourced must provide some comfort.

Ten years after the Russian government had decided to dismantle Yukos, the ghosts of the oil giant continued to haunt the sovereign, even starting to bite. The bottom line of the Yukos saga? In modern weak states, a determined sovereign may expropriate his target, even if the latter is a well-connected multi-billion-dollar corporation. However, expropriating a company with stakeholder alliances is hard work. From the sovereign's perspective, a company's stakeholders open the expropriation to punishing reversals, increase its costs, and make its trajectory less predictable.

Beyond Yukos: Stakeholder Alliances versus Principal Expropriation

Of even broader import, Yukos's allies may have provided a positive externality to property rights' security in Russia beyond the firm's boundaries. The issue concerns the widespread popular support in Russia for the revision of privatization results[46] and the little-noticed 2005 campaign by the government's Audit Chamber[47] to implement such revision. The campaign was spearheaded

---

[44] *Skvazhina* May 4, 2001.

[45] *QFinance* 2009.

[46] In 2006, around 50 percent of Russians supported some form of renationalization, while an additional 30 percent demanded additional post-hoc payments from the owners for the privatized assets. Denisova et al. 2008, 287.

[47] The Audit Chamber is a watchdog monitoring the use of government funds and property; privatization-related issues fall clearly into its mandate.

Yukos Redux

by the chairman of the Chamber, Sergei Stepashin, a professional technocrat "long famous for trying to catch political wind in his sails."[48] Stepashin personally signed an exhaustive 185-page report on privatization results, officially issued by the Chamber, which in effect booby trapped the property rights of new owners. Meticulously reviewing the 1993–2003 rounds of privatization sector by sector, the report slams wide-ranging violations, ominously concluding that while the legislative basis for the privatization was underdeveloped,

> This does not mean "wholesale amnesty" [*zaochnaia amnistiia*] to persons who have committed violations.... On the basis of proven ... facts, the courts must restore the violated rights of the legal owner – the state ... which can be done either through the unconditional return to the state of illegally privatized property, or through various monetary compensations.[49]

Stepashin was scheduled to deliver the report to the Duma on December 8, 2004; the Communist Duma fraction, in particular, eagerly awaited the hearing.[50] However, Stepashin's presentation was abruptly rescheduled for spring and then suspended indefinitely. The report, which had been anticipated to become the "de facto directory for the General Procuracy"[51] – i.e., the yellow pages for expropriation targets – was buried on the webpage of the Audit Chamber and never saw the limelight. Who defused the bomb? A Russian economist opined that Stepashin "had his mouth shut" because "president [Putin] is apprehensive about the new counter-measures by the West, and not just the USA which have already stood up for Yukos through the Texas court. The president rebuffed this interference [by the Texas court] ... but what if such lawsuits start hitting [Russia] en masse?"[52] While today the issue of revising privatization in Russia is largely moot because many choice assets are privately owned by Kremlin-connected state officials,[53] in 2004 the danger of "re-privatization" à la Tymoshenko was clear and present. That the freshly reelected Russian president did not yield to the populist temptation based on Stepashin's "revolutionary document"[54] is at least partly the result of the furious campaign unleashed by Yukos stakeholders.

Finally, to provide a comparative perspective, let us note that in Ukraine, stakeholders *have* effectively protected a "political billionaire" against the sovereign. Victor Pinchuk is Ukraine's answer to Mikhail Khodorkovsky. As a

---

[48] *Kommersant* January 17, 2005.
[49] Stepashin 2004, 146.
[50] *NEWSru* December 8, 2004.
[51] *Kommersant* 2005.
[52] *Stoletie* February 11, 2005.
[53] This does not mean that the issue is not periodically weaponized during elections; during the 2012 presidential election, for example, Putin borrowed the idea of a windfall tax (whose sum was "to be determined") on companies privatized in the 1990s from his contenders Prokhorov and Mironov. Two other candidates, Zyuganov and Zhirinovsky, supported a more radical revision of privatization results.
[54] *Stoletie* 2005.

186   *Firm Stakeholders vs. State Predators*

son-in-law of ex-president Kuchma, discredited by the Orange Revolution, Pinchuk was intimately tied to (in addition to financing) the ancien régime, and a natural target for the post-revolutionary government of Tymoshenko. As thousands of Ukrainians demanded justice on Kyiv's Maidan square, an in-depth analysis of various tycoons' prospects by Ukraine's *Dzerkalo Tyzhnia* singled out Pinchuk as "a prime candidate for being un-dressed" during re-privatization (see Chapter 5).[55] Yet by 2009, five years after the Orange Revolution, Pinchuk continued to be the country's second-richest person *and* the second most politically influential businessman (eternally behind Akhmetov).[56] Pinchuk definitely kept his assets, partly because of his pragmatism[57] and certainly because of his vast international and local support networks. The previously mentioned NZF plant defended by workers was Pinchuk's; the 2,000 interior troops sent to seize the factory Tymoshenko's.[58] Top Ukrainian experts have attributed the oligarchs' ability to persevere relatively unscathed through Ukraine's re-privatization campaign to the support by labor. According to Oleksandr Paskhaver, an economist and former presidential adviser,

> Among the active opponents of reprivatization were the employees of large strategic enterprises. The majority of these were successful enterprises ... that traditionally implemented substantial [*vahomi*] social programs (salary increases, building of accommodations, general assistance of the social sphere, etc.). The protest potential of labor collectives at such enterprises was amplified by [their] fears ... of losing the customary social benefits [*zvychnykh sotsial'nykh pil'h*].[59]

At the height of the re-privatization fever, Andrii Yermolaiv, the president of the social research center "Sofiya," noted that "the declared [re-privatization] program would demand from the president a special approach to those enterprises that now successfully follow their investment obligations and where *mechanisms of solidarity exist between the owners and the labor collective*. Otherwise, the government will create new social conflicts aimed against itself."[60] The center of sociological research at the Kyiv National Shevchenko University surveyed 400 employees at Pinchuk's NZF plant in April 2005. According to the survey, 85 percent of employees thought that "in deciding upon the reprivatization of enterprises, the government must consider the opinion of their labor collectives." 38 percent of employees were ready to actively resist re-privatization. Among the latter, the following forms of resistance were most popular: public

---

[55] *Dzerkalo Tyzhnia* October 27, 2004.

[56] The ratings are conducted annually by Ukraine's *Fokus* magazine.

[57] After officially supporting Yanukovych in the 2004 elections, the magnate defected from the Kuchma regime at the height of the Revolution, and formally quit politics altogether in 2006 by leaving the parliament where he had served as a Labor Ukraine deputy since 1998.

[58] According to several interviewed experts, Tymoshenko followed the advice of Pinchuk's business rival, Kolomoisky.

[59] Paskhaver et al., 45.

[60] *Dzerkalo Tyzhnia* December 3, 2005 (emphasis added).

Yukos Redux

protests (56 percent), written petitions to the government (37 percent), and strikes (12 percent).

As for international allies, Pinchuk has firmly established himself as Ukraine's bridge to the West, which even his nemesis Tymoshenko had to acknowledge. In a 2004 interview, Tymoshenko grudgingly recognized Pinchuk's role in "conducting a series of negotiations with very influential and authoritative representatives of the USA," during which he promised to dissuade his father-in-law from seeking a third presidential term. (Pinchuk hosted Bush senior on the latter's private trip to Ukraine, before being invited to Bush's Texas ranch.) According to Tymoshenko, Pinchuk "took these obligations to these extremely influential ... [Americans] upon himself ... in order to preserve his business and his reputation in these [international] circles which he, spending lots of words and money, is trying to enter."[61] Enter he did. In his charity work, Pinchuk partnered with Bill Clinton and George Soros, while in the domain of foreign policy, Pinchuk began promoting Ukraine's EU integration through high-level events run by Pinchuk's Yalta European Strategy, an organization with a winning YES acronym and an influential board of European intellectuals and ex-politicians. This is not to say that Pinchuk does not genuinely enjoy the company of high-caliber foreigners,[62] only that it has paid off. Pinchuk's new friend Soros noted as much when asked in April 2004 why Pinchuk was giving Soros airtime on his ICTV channel and supporting the Hungarian billionaire's "legal clinics" program in Ukraine: "I think ... [Pinchuk] wants to keep his current position independently of how the new power [in Ukraine] will turn out." While Pinchuk has not missed a chance to highlight his 2006 departure from Rada, saying that power and business should be separated, his alliance-building is nothing but politics by other means. When interviewed by the author, the CEO of the Victor Pinchuk Foundation (an impressive well-funded organization whose eighteen projects target public health, education, and art while smartly promoting Ukraine's image abroad) shared that "Victor's philanthropic projects and international activities *have impact on business because things are so personal in this part of the world.* At the beginning Ukraine's political leaders were suspicious. But then they said 'wow!'" At the same time, an interviewed small entrepreneur shared a not atypical sentiment in the country: "look, I can't say that I like billionaires or Jews very much, but I would vote for Pinchuk. He is doing something for the people." To have "the people" as a stakeholder is a feat even Khodorkovsky would have been proud of.

---

[61] *Dzerkalo Tyzhnia* August 21, 2004.

[62] One cannot but admire the eclecticism of Pinchuk's taste in foreign friends who span geopolitics, academia, and Hollywood. Among the players Pinchuk has courted are the former NATO Commander-in-Chief Wellesley Clark and Zbigniew Brzezinski but also Steven Spielberg (who refers to Pinchuk as "my friend Victor"), Francis Fukuyama, and the Nobel-prize economist Robert Engle.

SURVEY EVIDENCE: STAKEHOLDER ALLIANCES VERSUS AGENT PREDATION

Overall, qualitative evidence implies that stakeholder alliances increase PR security. But how generalizable are these findings? This question is explored here with survey data.

Conventional emphasis on the role of the sovereign in securing PR neglects the firm-level sources of PR security; accordingly, analyses of PR security typically focus on cross-country variation. To be consistent with the bottom-up theoretical framework presented here, however, an empirical proxy for PR security, would have to vary across firms. The measures of ownership and income threats to PR, as evaluated by respondent firms in my survey, fit these requirements well.

The main measure of my dependent variable, *OwnershipThreat*, was introduced in Chapter 3; it is the average of six measures of ownership threats from state actors.[63] (Table 3.1 provides details on the individual threat measures; Table 2.1 provides summary statistics for all variables.) The basic equation to be estimated is:

$$OwnershipThreat = \beta_0 + \beta_1 Community + \beta_2 Foreigners + \beta_3 Country + \\ + \beta_4 MerchantGroup + + \beta_5 TaxShare + \beta_6 Loyalty \\ + \beta_7 NonPrivatized + \Sigma \beta_8 Size + + \Sigma \beta_9 Sector \\ + \Sigma \beta_{10} Ownership + \Sigma \beta_{11} Region + e. \quad (1)$$

Since threat averages refer to a continuous latent variable, an OLS model is used. Robust standard errors are used to account for heteroskedasticity. *Community* and *Foreigners* are proxies for alliances. *Community* equals 1 if a firm considers its "support of regional community and labor" to be "very significant" and 0 otherwise.[64] *Foreigners* equals 1 if the firm has a foreign creditor or a foreign investor and 0 otherwise. Theoretically, credit relations and ownership stake are good proxies for meaningful alliances, as threats to PR would likely affect the creditors or co-owners of the firm. The foreign identity of these allies is important as a result of selection effects because bigger and more powerful

---

[63] While common in social science research, note that the averaging of Likert-derived data relies on the assumption of interval status for ordinal measures. This assumption is reasonable here since our question phrasing suggests that the space between two successive ordinal categories, while not strictly constant, is of the same order of magnitude. Also, the threat-intensity scale possesses a natural zero point ("no threat"). See Wang et al. 1999.

[64] Firms were asked to evaluate their support on a 1–4 scale ("no support" to "very significant support"). My theoretical framework suggests that only a substantial volume of benefits transferred by the firm to its community stakeholders would incentivize the latter to protect the firm in case of expropriation. Dissembling by firms is also less likely to occur at extreme response values, which are easier to verify. Accordingly, the dummy equals 1 if the firms rated their support as very significant. Specific forms of support listed by firms in the follow-up questions include sponsorship of cultural events, support of facilities for children, church charity, subsidized housing or mortgages, payment for medical care, payment for holiday packages, and others.

Survey Evidence: Stakeholder Alliances versus Agent Predation 189

foreign firms are more likely to invest in the Russian market. The numbers on discrete alliances are in line with the available data on the region.[65]

A number of control variables that could influence both a firm's extent of stakeholder alliances and the security of its ownership are included. First, the macro-institutional environment could play a role. The *Country* variable is used to control for macro-institutional design; this is a dummy coded as 0 for Russia and 1 for Ukraine. As discussed in Chapter 5, both sovereigns committed to secure property by 2007 (when the survey was implemented), but they did so in different ways. While Russia institutionalized policy access for encompassing business associations, known in the literature as "merchant groups," Ukraine empowered its parliament vis-à-vis the presidency while also increasing media freedom and court independence. The significance of the *Country* variable would suggest that one of these commitment devices may be more effective for secure ownership than the other. The variable *MerchantGroup* further probes the importance of state commitment; this dummy equals 1 if the company participates in a *national* business association and 0 otherwise.[66]

According to the reputational restraint school, firms may be protected from state expropriation by virtue of paying taxes since the government would not want to jeopardize its revenue source. *TaxShare* provides a rough estimate of the firm's share of total tax revenue levied from enterprises in the region (*oblast*). This variable equals 1 if the share is below 5 percent, 2 if the share is in the 5–19 percent range, and 3 if the firm pays 20 percent or more of taxes collected in the region.

The firms' propensity for "loyalty" strategies vis-à-vis state officials (e.g., preemptive bribe payments or the establishment of government connections) could be a confounding factor. An attitudinal proxy is particularly appropriate here. On the one hand, a company's *endorsement* of loyalty strategies, either because of their perceived effectiveness or on normative grounds, can be expected to correlate with a firm's behavior (which is difficult to elicit with a direct question). On the other hand, even if the firm is not actually pursuing a loyalty strategy, its attitude toward such strategies *as such* may influence the firm's perception of PR threats as well as its readiness to pursue stakeholder alliances. Survey respondents were asked to estimate the effectiveness of voluntary "informal payments" (*neformal'nye otchisleniia*) to state officials in protecting the firms in respondent's region from state predation.[67] *Loyalty* equals 1 if a firm considers such payments ineffective; 2 – somewhat effective; 3 – very effective. As a robustness check for this control variable, I used

---

[65] Eighty-two percent of firms support communities and labor in some form, with 7 percent reporting "very significant support"; more than 3 percent have found foreign investors or creditors. For related studies, see Starodubskaya 2005; Dolgopyatova et al. 2007.

[66] *MerchantGroup* is distinct from the variable *BusinessAssociation* (used in Chapter 3), which measures participation in *any* association (including a local one).

[67] Such voluntary "incentive payments," *initiated by firms* to cope with legal uncertainty, should not be confused with the bribes extracted under pressure by officials.

several other questions, including (a) perceived "effectiveness of government connections in protecting firms in your region from state predation"; (b) membership of firm owners in a political party; and (c) perceived "importance of closer cooperation with the regional government for the enforcement of firm owners' legal rights."[68] These alternative questions serve as a validity check for *Loyalty* and decrease the probability of reverse causation for this variable.

The firm's privatization legacy could influence both its alliances and its ownership security. As a result of former state ownership, for example, a firm may have welfare-related obligations to its employees; the government may also threaten to revise the results of privatization, as was the case in Ukraine after the Orange Revolution. To control for privatization legacy, *NonPrivatized* equals 1 for firms that had been created de novo, and 0 for companies that had been partially or fully privatized.

I also control for the size, sector, and ownership of firms. *SizeMedium* and *SizeLarge* are dummies for firms that have more than 100 and more than 500 employees respectively. *Sector* and *Ownership* are dummies for industrial sectors and key ownership categories. Regional dummies control for potential cross-regional heterogeneity.

Table 6.1 presents the effects of alliance variables on the intensity of state threats to property rights.

Model 1 corresponds to Equation 1. Both alliance variables display the expected negative sign and are significant. While the level of statistical significance is the same for both alliances (0.05), the substantive impact of alliances with communities and labor is larger by thirty percent than that of alliances with foreigners. Among the proxies for rival hypotheses, only *Country* has a significant negative impact on PR threats.

The substantive impact of alliances is large. Taken together, alliances with foreigners and with community and labor reduce ownership threats by more than two thirds of a point on a 1–4 threat intensity scale. Given that the maximum hypothetical threat reduction is three points (from 4 to 1, i.e., from "very high threat" to "no threat"), this impact of alliances amounts to almost 25 percent of the maximum hypothetical threat reduction.

As a robustness check, Model 2 extends the dependent variable to include threats to income as well as to ownership. *PropertyThreat*, the dependent variable in Model 2, is the average of nine state threats to entrepreneurs' property rights (i.e., all threats listed in Table 3.1). Both alliance variables remain significant, although the significance level for *Foreigners* drops to 0.1. The substantive impact of alliances decreases by 12 percent for *Community* and by 35 percent for *Foreigners*, as compared to their impact on *OwnershipThreat*. The weaker impact of alliances in Model 2 suggests that alliances provide a better protection against threats to ownership than against threats to income. This is

---

[68] Note that (b) offers a *behavioral* proxy as compared with the original attitudinal proxy, while (c) also ensures that the endorsement of loyalty vis-à-vis *local* officials is tested.

TABLE 6.1. *Effect of Alliances on Security of Property Rights in Russia and Ukraine*

	(1)	(2)	(3)	(4)	(5)
	OwnershipThreat	PropertyThreat	IncomeThreat	OwnershipThreat	OwnershipThreat (Russia only)
Community	−0.41** (0.16)	−0.36** (0.15)	−0.26 (0.16)	−0.41** (0.16)	−0.34 (0.31)
Foreigners	−0.31** (0.12)	−0.20* (0.11)	−0.08 (0.14)	−0.32** (0.13)	−0.42** (0.17)
Country	−0.85*** (0.22)	−0.59*** (0.18)	−0.28 (0.16)	−0.86*** (0.22)	
MerchantGroup	0.09 (0.09)	0.07 (0.08)	0.04 (0.09)	0.09 (0.09)	0.18 (0.11)
TaxShare	0.08 (0.06)	0.08 (0.06)	0.06 (0.07)	0.08 (0.06)	0.07 (0.08)
Loyalty	0.05 (0.06)	0.05 (0.06)	0.08 (0.07)	0.05 (0.06)	−0.01 (0.09)
NonPrivatized	−0.02 (0.13)	−0.05 (0.12)	−0.14 (0.13)	−0.02 (0.13)	0.16 (0.17)
SizeMedium	0.08 (0.13)	0.08 (0.13)	0.08 (0.15)	0.08 (0.13)	0.09 (0.20)
SizeLarge	0.03 (0.13)	0.00 (0.12)	−0.05 (0.14)	0.03 (0.13)	0.06 (0.19)
ForcedFunding				0.02 (0.08)	0.03 (0.11)
Financial					−0.14 (0.09)
N	300	303	299	300	200
P > F	0.0000	0.0000	0.0000	0.0000	0.0000
R^2	0.28	0.24	0.18	0.28	0.14
Dummy Variables	Sector	Sector	Sector	Sector	Sector
	Ownership	Ownership	Ownership	Ownership	Ownership
	Region	Region	Region	Region	Region

* $p < 0.10$, ** $p < 0.05$, *** $p < 0.01$. OLS model with robust standard errors (in parentheses). Dependent variables are averages of respondents' estimates of threat intensity.

confirmed by Model 3 in which the dependent variable, *IncomeThreat*, is the average of income threats *only* (i.e., of three threats, as listed in Table 3.1). In Model 3, none of the alliance variables are significant. This finding makes sense within the theoretical framework advanced here. To be maintained, alliances demand the resources of business owners; to be effective, alliances require the considerable efforts of stakeholders. These resources and efforts are much more likely to be invested and exerted when property rights are threatened by agent predation than (merely) by siphoning.

What about the rival hypotheses? The significance as well as the large size of the *Country* coefficient both with respect to *OwnershipThreat* and *PropertyThreat* suggest that the macro-institutional design may also play an important role in establishing PR security. One way to interpret the *Country* coefficient would be this: Democratic checks on the upper executive (as they materialized in the wake of the Orange Revolution in Ukraine) improve PR security significantly better than the encompassing merchant groups enjoying institutionalized cooperation with the state sovereign (as they emerged after Putin's assumption of power in Russia). According to this interpretation, the concurrent significance of the bottom-up non-state alliances as well as certain top-down "commitment devices" of the sovereign implies equifinality; the reduction of state threats to PR security can be achieved via multiple paths.

While equifinality cannot be ruled out, two additional considerations suggest that given principal-agent problems in the bureaucracy, the democratic route to state commitment in fact does little to secure PR. First, once a measure of entrepreneurs' blame attribution for insecure PR to the local (as opposed to the central) state agencies, is inserted into Equation 1, the *Country* coefficient loses its significance altogether. *LocalBlame*, conversely, is significant and positively related to threat intensity.[69] This implies that *Country*'s impact in Table 6.1 may derive in part from the Russian *local* cadres' relatively greater rapaciousness compared to their Ukrainian counterparts and not necessarily from the manner in which the Ukrainian state principal was restrained at the time of the survey.[70] Second, Ukraine does not fare better than Russia in terms of the threats' *predictability*. When asked how predictable the state threats are "for the next year," Ukrainian entrepreneurs judged them to be significantly *less* predictable than their Russian counterparts.[71] This militates against the story of democratic checks on the executive as a superior commitment device for the sovereign. (In other words, if commitment via parliamentary empowerment is to have any meaning, then Ukraine's lower threat levels should be matched

---

[69] The variable *LocalBlame* was introduced in Chapter 4. Once *LocalBlame* is inserted, *Community* continues to reduce threats at a significant level, while *Foreigners* loses statistical significance.

[70] Of course, having only two countries in the sample hampers precise specification of the *Country*'s causal pathways.

[71] On a 1–4 scale, higher numbers indicating greater predictability, Ukrainian entrepreneurs judged the predictability of state threats to be 2.17 on average, compared with the Russian average of 2.44, a difference significant at the 0.01 level.

by their higher predictability relative to a country with a less democratically restrained sovereign.) Informal interviews further substantiate this point. As the director of InvestUA, Ukraine's state agency responsible for attracting foreign investment, shared with me in 2007:

> Yes, money is flowing to Russia, and you know what the difference is? Why is money also flowing to China? There are no fair courts there, no democracy, etc. There is one thing of which China has more than Russia and Russia more than Ukraine. Predictability of power [*predskazuemost' vlasti*]. And here it's "Two Ukrainians – three hetmans" [i.e., too many chiefs, not enough Indians].

The insignificance of *MerchantGroup*, foreshadowed by Chapter 5, also indicates the limits of the state commitment paradigm. The reason may be that while the literature expects high-level collaboration to insure business against threats by the state principal, my survey inquires into *local* predation. When principal-agent dilemmas are severe, one should not expect the sovereign to be able to commit on behalf of the agents. The Yukos case, moreover, strongly suggests that sovereign-supported merchant groups do not protect firms against today's state *principals* either. Yukos was an active participant in RUIE, Russia's federal big-business association. By October 2003, the association had written three official letters to Russia's president, nearly begging the sovereign in their last letter to stop the assault:

> We are asking Vladimir Vladimirovich Putin to intervene personally in order to calm down the parties in the conflict that will have no winners.... The new threats by Procuracy, [as well as] the unfolding revision of all laws and rules, according to which business has lived for a long period, create a dangerous situation to which we cannot fail to react.[72]

Putin rejected any negotiations with RUIE over Yukos: the principal-supported merchant group clearly failed to shield Yukos from the principal. By contrast, as the previous section showed, Yukos's foreign and labor stakeholders *have* achieved important victories against the Russian sovereign.

TaxShare does not improve PR security either, providing some evidence against the "reputational restraint" paradigm. Companies with larger tax contributions are not better protected against agent predation, possibly because principal-agent dilemmas within the state apparatus drive a wedge between sovereign rationality and the state actors' behavior on the ground. Says the owner of several retail stores in western Ukraine, whom I interviewed in 2011:

> They [the municipal authorities] did not want me to open a store here while my license was registered in another town, as they would lose taxes that way. But is there any actual gratitude for investment and such? Of course not.... The new county chief from the Party of Regions gathered the largest local entrepreneurs in the council here. But it was Soviet-style nonsense [*sovdepiia*]. They showed us some presentations, but they

---

[72] *Grani* October 22, 2003.

did not want any feedback from us.... I still went to the meeting with my accountant because we were afraid there might be sanctions if we didn't show up.

An expert on raiding in Russia points out that agent predation marginalizes taxation as a factor:

Why should the state protect a business owner? ... Raiders are often state officials; they strengthen the status quo. Because the status quo is based on the fact that the officials can rob [*grabit'*] whomever they want. And what does a business owner give to the state? Taxes? Who needs taxes in our country? ... The state [officials] need those who give them bribes.[73]

Interestingly, the ineffectiveness of tax contributions against PR threats in the 2000s in my data contrasts with Gehlbach's (2010) findings for Russia in the 1990s.[74] This discrepancy could be explained in two ways. First, the 1990s in Russia were a period of severe fiscal crises, which may have made tax revenue more politically important as compared to the fiscally stable 2000s. Second, Gehlbach's analysis proceeds from the viewpoint of *politicians* in charge of their staff, whereas I draw attention to the independently acting bureaucrats.

Loyalty is likewise insignificant in all models. Alternative codings yield the same result; no matter whether *Loyalty* refers to a firm's stance on bribe payments or government connections or the owners' actual membership in a political party, it does not mitigate PR threats. My interviews suggest that loyalty's insignificance stems from political instability. In Russia, Moscow's unprecedented criminal prosecution of the Nenets Autonomous Region's governor coincided with the Kremlin's consideration of an "anti-governor bill" (simplifying the firing of regional government heads[75]), which alarmed regional cadres at the time of the survey. In Ukraine, instability stemmed from the fallout from the Orange Revolution (see Chapter 5).

Endogeneity

What if the causal relationship between alliances and PR security flows in the opposite direction? More protected firms, one could argue, have more resources to invest in community projects and are more attractive to foreign investors. Firms that do better financially could also hire better lawyers, spend more on political connections, and so on – hence reducing PR threats – while at the same time spending more on alliance-building. My response is based on conceptual considerations, survey data, and qualitative interviews.

---

[73] CPT 2008, 34.

[74] The central argument of Gehlbach's book is that "anticipated tax compliance" drives "collective-goods provision" by the state to specific firms (p. 87).

[75] While the elections of regional governors had been replaced by presidential appointments in 2004, governors' *dismissals* by Moscow remained strikingly rare despite evidence of massive legal violations by some governors. The bill, proposed at the end of 2006, would have allowed the president to fire governors for criminal code violations regardless of their severity, potentially

Survey Evidence: Stakeholder Alliances versus Agent Predation

To begin, note that conceptually, there is less reason to expect endogeneity once the characteristics of the examined environment are accounted for. One should not expect firms in most developing countries to invest in corporate social responsibility just because they have more resources. While in Western markets such investments can boost a firm's profits through consumer preferences, consumers in countries like Russia or Ukraine do not take such considerations into account.[76] Furthermore, while foreign investors would naturally prefer well-protected companies, both foreign investors and predators are usually attracted to the same type of companies: those with high cash flows and significant upward potential. One Russian CEO expressed this paradoxical relationship between profitability and PR security in my interview as follows: "If you are not a target, something is wrong with your business."

Importantly, the causal mechanisms underlying the rival endogeneity hypothesis cannot account for the stark difference between the effectiveness of alliances against ownership threats and their ineffectiveness against income threats (Models 1 and 3 in Table 6.1). Indeed, if the *availability of resources* is the true causal mechanism connecting threats to alliances, then it is precisely the firms facing *lower income threats* (i.e., higher available cash flows) that should be strongly associated with *greater stakeholder alliances*.

While the risk of endogeneity is unlikely in these circumstances, an empirical proxy for the firms' financial condition would considerably strengthen my case. The inference would also benefit if the scenario in which companies are pressured by the state to invest in welfare-related projects could be controlled for. These proxies are inserted in Models 4 and 5 in Table 6.1. Model 4 runs the original equation with the addition of *ForcedFunding*, a dummy equaling 1 for companies that agreed with the statement: "Local authorities sometimes exert pressure on the enterprise to spend additional resources on public projects in the region, charity, or employee support." (Roughly one third of entrepreneurs in each country agreed with the statement.) The significance and size of alliance variables remain unchanged; in fact, the coefficient on *Foreigners* increases slightly in Model 4. The results do not seem to be driven by the local governments' pressure on firms to be "socially responsible." Model 5 inserts another proxy, *Financial*, which gauges the companies' financial condition; enterprises were asked to evaluate their "current financial and economic performance" on a 1–4 scale, increasing values meaning better performance. Since this question was not included in the Ukrainian part of the survey, Model 5 pertains only to the Russian subset. While the *Community* coefficient barely misses significance level, the coefficient on *Foreigners* retains its significance and grows in size by 30 percent. Meanwhile, all of the other controls remain insignificant. These results are robust to dichotomous recodings of *Financial* based on various

---

making *kompromat* (documented malfeasance) more effective as a means of informal pressure on the regional administrative networks.

[76] Starodubskaya.

thresholds. The Russian data alleviates concerns about the firms' financial condition as the most plausible source of bias.

Finally, the problem of endogeneity was a key focus of my informal interviews in the region. The interview data convey that to the extent PR security influences alliances, it should bias results *against* finding the effect in Table 6.1. Specifically, reverse causation evident in the interviews begins with *less* protected firms investing more in alliances so as to protect themselves against PR threats (more on this in the next section). This initially reverse relationship between alliances and PR threats conforms fully with my theory and results. At time t-1, a firm may experience a negative shock to its PR security; at time t, the owners build alliances; at time t+1, the threat to a firm's PR abates. Such a causal mechanism biases the results in the opposite direction of my findings, implying that Table 6.1 *underestimates* the long-term impact of alliances because the survey ignores the time gap required between the owners' investment in alliances and the capacity of alliances to deter or resolve PR conflicts. Once established, alliances seem to have a clear protective impact, as according to the head manager of the Emerging Markets Equity Funds at Fidelity Investments, interviewed by the author in 2005: "A lot of Russian companies like to have EBRD as a shareholder because it provides protection ... if you find that EBRD has a stake in a company, it's hard to shake down a company because you'll have all EU governments involved, and it's a pain ... so they [the Russian state officials] don't do it."

Individual Threats

For a more nuanced picture of alliances' impact on specific PR threats and another robustness check, I also use the nine measures of state threats *individually* as dependent variables. An ordered probit model with robust standard errors is used to reflect the ordinal status of individual threat measures. I estimate an equation identical to that of Model 4 in Table 6.1 except for the dependent variable, which is now $Threat_i$, the ith measure of threat intensity where i = 1, 2, ... 9. Stakeholder alliances have a statistically significant impact on seven out of nine PR threats, as summarized in Table 6.2. Simulation is used to translate ordered probit coefficients into substantive quantities of interest.[77] Along with the coefficients' significance levels, Table 6.2 reports the *change in the probability* of a firm reporting "no threat" (i.e., of obtaining 1 on a 1–4 threat intensity scale) as a result of a particular alliance. This marginal effect is the change in the likelihood of an alliance *eliminating* a perceived threat altogether.

As before, the size of alliances' impact is considerable. Depending on the threat, alliances with community and labor increase the probability of a "no

---

[77] Stata's *Clarify* package is used to simulate 1,000 coefficients for all model parameters and convert these into marginal effect estimates (first differences).

TABLE 6.2. *Substantive Impact of Alliances on Discrete Threats (Ordered Probit First Differences)*

Firms having alliances with …	are … % more likely to report	that they do not perceive any threat relating to …	Pseudo R²	P > χ²
community and labor	46*** (21)	illegal inspections by state organs	0.25	0.0009
	44*** (13)	raiding, illegal ownership capture	0.49	0.0000
	39*** (27)	extortion by taxation agencies	0.51	0.0001
	34*** (11)	state barriers to transfers of land, productive assets, etc.	0.10	0.0000
	34*** (21)	state pressure for financing various social funds	0.29	0.0000
	26** (12)	state interference with hiring or firing of labor	0.12	0.0000
	18* (13)	hostile use of state resources by competitors	0.18	0.0000
foreign creditors and investors	58** (37)	raiding, illegal ownership capture	0.49	0.0000
	34*** (10)	state interference with hiring or firing of labor	0.12	0.0000
	18** (12)	illegal inspections by state organs	0.25	0.0009
	6* (6)	extortion by taxation agencies	0.51	0.0001
merchant groups	14* (13)	raiding, illegal ownership capture	0.49	0.0000
	8* (5)	state pressure for financing various social funds	0.29	0.0000

* p < 0.10, ** p < 0.05, *** p < 0.01. Summary of ordered probit regression results with corresponding marginal effects. Second table column reports how the probability of a firm reporting "no threat" changes as a result of having an alliance (standard errors in parentheses). For example, companies that have alliances with community and labor are 46 percent more likely to report that illegal inspections by state organs are not a threat. Stata's Clarify package used for simulation of first differences.

threat" response by 18–46 percent; alliances with foreigners make a "no threat" response more likely by 6–58 percent. On average, firms with alliances are 32 percent more likely to report "no threat" for the seven threats on which alliances exert a significant impact; for six out of these seven threats, at least one alliance variable is significant at the .01 level. Alliances with community and labor contribute to eliminating seven threats, as compared to four threats eliminated by alliances with foreigners. For comparison, the table also includes "merchant groups," which eliminate two threats. Both the significance level (0.1) and the size of the impact (8–14 percent) are much lower for the top-down merchant groups as compared to the bottom-up stakeholder alliances. Neither the merchant groups nor the stakeholder alliances seem to protect against requests for bribes or the illegal administrative barriers to obtaining licenses and operation permits. On balance, the analysis of individual threats supports the claim that stakeholder alliances exert a powerful impact on the protection of entrepreneurs' property rights.

BEYOND SPECIFIC COUNTRIES, BEYOND INDIVIDUAL FIRMS

Would stakeholder alliances improve PR security beyond the countries examined here? That the results hold for both Russia and Ukraine is promising. These countries diverge widely on their democratic constraints on the executive branch (in the 2004–11 period) and on the availability of natural resources, two factors that could have an impact on the political economy of property rights. Hence, the theory should apply in different settings. Prima facie, there is no reason why the findings would be limited to postcommunist countries. If anything, the theory can be expected to apply even better to many economies in Africa and some in Latin America, where agent predation is rampant. As long as the firm does not face the Leviathan himself, allies matter. In other words, while potentially less effective against the threats to ownership that are directed by the state principal and implemented through a vertically accountable state machine, stakeholders do protect the firm against disorganized threats. Consider the case of China, where many private firms seek to list their equity abroad to prevent the local government from interfering with the management of the firm's assets; foreign regulators would publicize any state interference inflicting credible reputational damage on the relevant state actors.[78]

The key boundary condition for the theory of stakeholder alliances involves political stability and state capacity. Higher political stability and state capacity make the firms more likely to rely on state-oriented (rather than stakeholder-oriented) strategies because the state actors have longer time horizons as well as stronger incentives and a greater ability to shield the firm from PR threats. Longer time horizons of state actors create space for a strategic dialogue with firms and allow state employees to behave like "stationary bandits." Higher

---

[78] Author's interviews at Chinese and foreign investment banks, Beijing, October 2005.

Beyond Specific Countries, Beyond Individual Firms

state capacity, in turn, decreases agency costs within the state apparatus; if the state principal controls her agents, they have less leeway to engage in predation. However, the threshold at which political *in*stability or *low* state capacity renders state-oriented firm strategies futile is such that in many developing countries, stakeholder alliances should improve PR security.

Do the firm-based arrangements discussed here amount to more than spatially limited and temporary solutions to the problem of PR insecurity? Yes, based on two factors.

First, dynamic learning *across firms* occurs as enterprises that are more successful at defending their rights are emulated by others. In many instances, alliance-building is used by firms as a *conscious strategy* to secure PR, and there is no reason to assume that PR protection would be different from other business strategies that, as a rule, spread widely once shown effective. The intentionality of alliance building is particularly visible when firms invest in this strategy following a clear shock to PR security. Russia's corporations, for example, started investing more in alliances with foreigners after Putin's administration signaled a credible threat to their PR.[79] Immediately after the authorities began investigating Yukos, the firm implemented an "SOS management" scheme, according to which foreign citizens would take over the leadership of the firm, should anything happen to Khodorkovsky. Approved in the summer of 2003, Yukos's organizational chart "for the case of a protracted war" featured prominent U.S. and Norwegian citizens, "a whole chain of managers concluding with Lord Jacob Rotschild."[80] Similarly conscious hedging against expropriation via stakeholder alliances took place in Ukraine during the 2004 business panic following the announcements of re-privatization; for example, most of Pinchuk's initiatives discussed earlier were launched during this time. Presumably, their impact was not lost on Pinchuk's fellow oligarch Rinat Akhmetov; only months separated the launch of Akmetov's SCM Foundation (a philanthropy vehicle) from that of the Victor Pinchuk Foundation. Importantly, smaller firms appear to be learning too. In an explicit effort to "teach" such strategies, one of the most respected leaders of Russian business, Igor Yurgens, noted at a 2008 business forum that "small and medium-sized businesses, unlike large companies, are unable to negotiate on an equal footing with local and regional governments. The ... adoption of ... social responsibility will make it possible [for these businesses] to solve a large number of conflicts ... [with] the government."[81] A Rada deputy and a prominent small-business advocate, Kseniia Liapina, said in her 2006 address to the Ukrainian entrepreneurs, "with the wave of populism today, whatever is done against entrepreneurs [by the state], is allegedly done for 'the masses.' We need to react to this ... through the social aspect, to show

---

[79] Markus 2008.
[80] *Kommersant* July 14, 2003.
[81] Yurgens 2008.

that entrepreneurs actually understand the social concerns much better [than the government]."[82]

Second, learning is likely to occur among the *state actors* too, raising the question of what would be observed in the resulting equilibrium. There is some evidence that mutually beneficial state-business arrangements featuring higher provision of public goods are replacing the hostility and particularistic rent-seeking in Russia.[83] The larger theoretical point emerging from my inquiry is that the locus of contestation between owners and potential predators is shifting from "buying" select bureaucrats to "buying" *non-state groups*, which are relatively more encompassing (communities, labor, etc.). In addition to being more durable, as a result of the incorporation of previously sidelined stakeholders, such arrangements also approximate Olson's "by-product" theory of public goods' provision.

Overall, the islands of accountability established by firm-based alliances are not incommunicado; in striving to survive, they are learning and expanding. As the predatory state agents take note, the primary function of stakeholder alliances shifts from conflict resolution to deterrence, from treatment to prevention. While the impact of stakeholder alliances occurs at the level of individual firms, the ramifications of this phenomenon are systemic.

---

[82] Author's transcript of the National Congress of the Council of Entrepreneurship at the Cabinet of Ministers. Kyiv, October 23, 2006.

[83] Based on large-N surveys of Russian firms, Frye et al. (2009, 48) show that between 2000 and 2007 "a tangible change has taken place in business-state relations at the regional level" as firms planning to invest locally have increasingly experienced the "helping hand" of the state. The study points toward an emerging state-business consensus but is silent on the causal mechanism involved. The alliance-based argument advanced here may fill this gap.

7

Firm Stakeholders and Rule of Law

Thucydides, a forefather of social science, opened his *History of the Peloponnesian War* by specifying what distinguished the Hellenic civilization from the nomadic tribes: secure property. Two and a half millennia later, the immortal Greek's intuition is echoed by a voluminous body of research on property rights. To contribute to this remarkable scholarship, this volume has advanced three arguments.

First, the *conventional diagnosis* of what makes property rights insecure in modern developing states is incomplete. By substantiating empirically the ideal type of "agent predation," I showed that it is the low-level bureaucrats (rather than the state rulers) who jeopardize the ownership rights (and not just the income rights) of entrepreneurs. Second, the *conventional solution* to insecure ownership – institutional constraints on the state principal – fails in the context of agent predation because the ruler cannot commit to PR security on behalf of his staff. Agent predation severs the link between sovereign commitment and ownership security. Third, the *novel solution* to the scourge of insecure PR resides in the stakeholder alliances around specific firms. Firm-level strategies – and not only the macro-institutional design – define the security of property rights.

How does the framework of PR security presented in this volume relate to the rule of law proper, that is, to the universally applicable rules predictably enforced by the state? The concluding chapter begins to explore this connection.

RULE OF LAW: THE LIMITS OF POLITICAL WILL AND LEGAL REFORM

Two narratives currently dominate the question of how the rule of law emerges.[1] The first narrative, popular among legal sociologists and historical

---

[1] For excellent overviews, see Levi; Haggard et al; Przeworski and Maravall 2003.

institutionalists, focuses on the *content of law*. Accordingly, legal rules that are logically consistent and do not fundamentally contradict the prevalent social norms are more likely to be universally enforced and followed. The second narrative, to which many political economists and policy-makers subscribe, stresses the *political will* of the rulers to impose the rule of law on a society (including the ruler herself). Some accounts examine the threat of foreign invasions or domestic revolutions that may force the ruler to take such a step, while others analyze how the rule of law expands in a top-down fashion from interelite interactions to the interactions between the elites and the populace.

Since the protection of property rights is a critical piece in the rule-of-law puzzle, the analysis of PR security can be used to evaluate these two narratives. The trends in Russia and Ukraine, I argue, favor the "legal content" narrative over the "political will" narrative, although *both* perspectives are ultimately wanting.

The "political will" narrative is particularly questionable in the context of weak states, where the state principal's control over his subordinates is low. Consider the example of Ukraine from Chapter 5; although President Yushchenko, who rode the Orange Revolution to power, demonstrated ample political will to shift the country to a new rule-of-law equilibrium, severe principal-agent dilemmas in the executive scuttled the project.

Ukraine holds another sobering lesson for the "political will" paradigm: To the extent the infusion of political will stems from a democratic revolution, the subsequent *failure* of the sovereign to impose the rule of law may *discredit democracy per se* in the eyes of the population. The failure of the Orange Revolution to secure the property rights of Ukraine's middle class may answer the puzzle of the democratically sanctioned rollback of achieved freedoms – that is, the puzzle of revolution's ultimate implosion, contrary to the euphoric predictions of Western social scientists and policy-makers alike.[2] As a shop owner from Ternopil' put it in my interview, "in the end, people have elected the guy [Yanukovych] whom they themselves had booted out for fraud. People have made a farce out of democracy." Among the interviewed entrepreneurs of all political convictions, the revolution's negative impact on PR security seemed to have discredited democratic institutions as such. This dynamic had been unmistakable well before the 2010 election of Yanukovych, which served as a wake-up call to outside observers. In their 2012 *New York Times* op-ed, the foreign ministers of five EU countries belatedly lamented "Ukraine's slide," wistfully noting that in "March 2007, hopes were high for a sustainable ... development of Ukraine ... a beacon of democracy in the former Soviet Union."[3] Nothing could be further from the truth. Interviewed by the author in February 2007, a large retailer in L'viv (and an erstwhile supporter of Yushchenko who had donated money to the initial 2004 protests on Maidan)

---

[2] E.g., Åslund and McFaul 2006.
[3] *The New York Times* March 4, 2012.

Rule of Law: The Limits of Political Will and Legal Reform

colorfully observed, "elections showed that we are fools who believe in fairy tales ... [such that] if we replace one group [in power] by another, things would change. Now we know that when corpses swap their places, the odor remains the same."

Pervasive agent predation shut down Ukraine's beacon soon after the Orange Revolution. The repercussions for *public attitudes toward the rule of law* have been lasting. In December 2012, a judge and his family were brutally murdered and beheaded in their home in Kharkiv. The pertinent and shocking point here is that many of the users' comments on the news websites in Ukraine focused on the judge's property holdings and *supported* the lynching as a warning to the rapacious officials. "Dear bureaucrats, given that ... nobody believes in honest justice, the cases of mob rule [*samosud*] could increase.... People are on the verge of enlightenment [*prozreniia*]," and "many more heads will have to roll [pun intended] before the authorities begin to reflect" read some of the more tempered comments. In this context, it is also noteworthy that the 2011 politicized jailing of Tymoshenko, the erstwhile Orange prime minister, by her nemesis Yanukovych was applauded by many otherwise *liberal-minded* Ukrainians. Upon her release, Tymoshenko faced a muted reception on Maidan on February 22, 2014, as the crowd celebrated Dmytro Yarosh, the militant leader of the extreme right.

By early 2014, many Ukrainians overcame their post-Orange lethargy – though certainly not their cynicism toward the existing democratic institutions – and stunned the world by forcibly ousting Yanukovych. The lesson of the Orange Revolution in this context is clear. No matter how well-intentioned the new state principal may be, or how democracy-compatible the new Constitution, runaway agent predation will remain a formidable obstacle to the rule of law – one that should be addressed head-on, lest the events of 2004 and 2014 repeat themselves in 2024. Somewhat paradoxically, agent predation both facilitates the crumbling of the *old* regime under popular pressure (a point brilliantly captured by one of the strategists behind the 2014 anti-Yanukovych uprisings[4]) and undermines the institutionalization of the *new* order.

Overall, while the political will of the elites to institutionalize the rule of law is important, the exclusive reliance on such top-down mechanisms in weak

---

[4] One of the widely shared "manifestos" on social media in Ukraine in the run-up to Yanukovych's ouster directly linked agent predation to systemic fragility, calling on the readers to exploit the situation. The author, based on his work experience in a regional administration, describes with great humor a typical annexation of a private kiosk that pits multiple state agencies against each other. "The moral of the story is: there is no unity whatsoever in the System. Parts of the System are in a brutal combat for black cash, and they absolutely hate each other.... This pertains not only to the [administrative] horizontal [relations] – but above all to the vertical [ones].... The basis for our struggle ... must be the mutual framing [*vzaimnaia podstava*] of the bureaucrats along the horizontal and vertical [administrative dimensions] as they fight for uncontrolled resources.... This system ... [will] unravel like wet paper in your hands." *Ukrains'ka Pravda* December 6, 2013.

states can generate severe unintended consequences undermining public trust in the government and in democracy. Meanwhile, the *logistics* of imposing discipline on a bureaucratic caste that for centuries has evaded effective central control are yet to be worked out. It is not for the lack of trying, as the initiatives of state principals throughout the region's history suggest. Russia's consummate reformer Peter I, for example, publicly executed three ministers, six governors, the general prosecutor (plus all his deputies), and hundreds of other bureaucrats whose heads sometimes embellished the poles in Moscow's squares; one of Peter's decrees stipulated that a bureaucrat should be hanged if he stole a sum from the budget that exceeded the cost of a coil of rope.[5] Yet neither Peter I's ferocity nor the bloodbath unleashed by Stalin fundamentally transformed the state apparatus.

The analysis of PR security in this volume resonates with the "legal content" approach to the rule of law because legal statutes can narrow or expand the scope for agent predation. A Ukrainian expert on state-business relations describes the connection as follows:

Our laws that cannot be implemented – i.e. that are unreasonably harsh or restrictive, contradicting practice and each other, ambivalent etc. – destroy this idyll [of rule of law].... Because all violators of a non-implementable law cannot be punished, the law can only be applied selectively. In this situation, a modest bureaucrat or a law-enforcement employee assumes the status of a boss [*nachal'nyka*] ... endowed with discretionary power ... that could be used for extortion.... With its roots in the times of Ivan the Terrible and Peter the Great, the Bolshevist manner of using law to relentlessly destroy [*lamaty navidlih*] social practices has led to a situation in which ... the charge of failing to pay the taxes amounting to HR 1,700 [\$ 337] suffices to open a criminal case, to conduct the extraction of documents, to arrest bank accounts.... Which is why in business you can venture beyond the simplified tax system [i.e., beyond very small-scale entrepreneurship, as per Ukrainian law] only in a tank.[6]

However, relying exclusively on law content – that is, on legal reforms – to jumpstart the rule of law presents two serious problems.

First, there is no tabula rasa onto which coherent laws resonant with social norms can be grafted. Many developing countries are burdened with mammoth, intractable legislation; imposing "coherence" on the thousands of acts regulating the conduct of state enforcers, inspectors, administrators, and gatekeepers, while also reforming corporate and company law, contract and tort law, and so forth is, to put it mildly, a long-term project.

Furthermore, the underlying social practices and norms are sometimes themselves problematic from the rule-of-law perspective, suggesting that the correspondence between norms and laws is not always the appropriate maxim. Decades of planned economy under the aegis of the all-owning but mismanaged state, for example, generated a permissive popular attitude toward property

[5] *Dzerkalo Tyzhnia* 2012.
[6] *Dzerkalo Tyzhnia* 2007.

Rule of Law: The Limits of Political Will and Legal Reform 205

rights; the banality of theft from "the state" should be familiar to anyone who lived in the Soviet Union. Aleksandr Orfyonov, a prominent Russian anti-raiding specialist, comments on the relationship between norms and PR security in modern times:

> Raiding is here to stay for at least 40 years. The roots of raiding? Remember [the writer Mikhail] Bulgakov who said "the rack and ruin are not in the bathrooms, but in the heads" [*razrukha ne v klozetakh a v golovakh*].... The mentality is such that there is no respect for the institution of private property.... The state does not respect private property and is ready to raid ... so common citizens [*riadovye grazhdane*] likewise think "why not." I could cite many examples when entrepreneurs in Russia themselves do not respect private property, e.g. that of minority shareholders.... I was struck to find on the website of one law firm the methods for protecting your firm from raiding takeovers, among which was "pay dividends to your minority shareholders." ... Often a private owner disrespectfully treats his own assets. Moscow, for example, has been swept by raids on educational facilities. What is a typical institute? It is a huge [privatized] building in which during the Soviet times up to 15–20 thousand people were employed. Now 200–300 people work there, and the rest [of the facilities] is rented out. The rent, on paper, is ridiculously low, but the true rent is much, much higher. The margin goes into the pocket of the general director. Well, at least he could renovate the building once in a while – but he does not, and the facilities are crumbling apart.... I've met many such general directors. He does not respect his property; he is eating through his assets [*proedaet svoi aktiv*]....[7] When finally all of us – the state, the people – start to understand that private property means first of all responsibility and not a chance to fill one's own pocket, then raiding will definitely begin to decline, but until then – don't hope for it.[8]

In this situation, it is no wonder that state agents point to certain social mores as an alibi, while the reformers are pushed toward measures that run counter to the established social norms. The chief of Ukraine's new State Service on Deregulation and Development of Entrepreneurship, Mykhailo Brods'kyi, readily blamed "the weak side of our people, their propensity to steal [*vorovitost'*]" for the entrenched bureaucratic predation while suggesting that "what must be deregulated is the mentality of our whole people."[9] Such statements betray an insulting condescension of the government toward its citizens.

More generally, cultural explanations of underdevelopment are prone to analytical reductionism and to a policymaking impasse. The supposedly popular attitudes, such as legal nihilism, are often the result, and not the cause, of governmental malfeasance.[10] Still, to discount entirely the challenge of instituting the rule of law in non-Western cultural settings is to greatly overestimate the efficacy of legal reforms.

The second problem with the "legal content" narrative is more straightforward. While legal reforms may *complicate* agent predation, they are unlikely

---

[7] Such neglect simplifies raiding because it lowers the official price of the asset.
[8] Presentation at the business forum AntiReider 2007 in Kyiv, Ukraine (March 29, 2007).
[9] *Dzerkalo Tyzhnia* 2012.
[10] Popova 2004.

to *stop* it, because state predators are often ready to shift from the grey-zone practices afforded by incoherent legislation to outright illegal tactics (see Chapters 3 and 4 for details).

The issue of *deliberate, self-interested malfeasance* apart, there is also a real problem of *general bureaucratic outlook*. In 2011, the Ukrainian Tax Service commissioned a professionally made cartoon to popularize the importance of tax compliance.[11] The fifteen-minute, beautifully drawn feature named *The City of Dreams* speaks volumes about the mindset of state servants. In the Ukrainian version of the "city upon a hill," the benevolent, larger-than-life city patriarch is none other than the tax inspector, while private businesses appear as rodents (!) that quite literally undermine the city by digging tunnels to conceal their unpaid taxes. It does not take psychoanalysis to extract the meaning from these dreams. In an interview with the TV channel Inter on July 11, 2011, Deputy Chief of the Tax Service Alexander Klimenko laughably referenced a 1943 Disney cartoon (urging Americans to "pay taxes to fight the Axis") as an inspiration for the Ukrainian feature. The Ukrainian entrepreneurs were not amused, and their web networks exploded with caustic commentary. This *cultural hostility* of state agents toward private business owners extends to foreign investors. Ulrich Grunenberg, the adviser on economy and trade at the German Embassy in Ukraine notes that

Foreign entrepreneurs feel that the state tax administration perceives them negatively, that it harbors suspicions that all of them are criminal elements who try to evade taxes ... and create illegal schemes in the Ukrainian economy. I have personally witnessed such attitude from the representatives of the tax administration.... Of course it is extremely unfair towards the majority of entrepreneurs to accuse them of criminal intent. Granted, some big businesses, the oligarchs, used to enjoy certain privileges. But one should not pile the honest and the guilty together and accuse them of something.[12]

The routine disregard for the rule of law on the part of state agents, in part driven by their rational self-interest and in part by the prevalent administrative culture, suggests that legal content is only part of the solution. For example, one should *not* expect that any of the currently proposed law-based remedies to the legitimacy deficit of privatized property in Russia – including a "final" legislative act concluding privatization, a one-time tax on assets akin to the Western "windfall tax," or the signing of a symbolic "social contract" at the federal level – would ultimately secure the property rights of the new owners.[13] The limits of law to combat agent predation have been recognized both by lawmakers themselves and by entrepreneurs. In Russia, the head of the Duma committee on security, Vladimir Vasil'ev, remarked in 2010 with respect to raiding: "Of course we will perfect the law ... but the question is,

[11] Available at: http://www.youtube.com/watch?v=yBZbs5JIIFU
[12] *Dzerkalo Tyzhnia* June 4, 2005.
[13] For more details, see Tambovcev.

Rule of Law and Stakeholder Alliances

how soon will this mechanism kick in? ... [In the interim,] we must create conditions in which raiders cannot work. So we have launched the project 'Civic Control' ... that addresses cases in which you cannot rely on the law enforcement organs."[14] The Civic Control project, whose motto is "to resist evil with force," involves a direct channel to the Duma for the investigative media uncovering corruption in the regions, and has effectively addressed multiple cases of administrative abuse, including that of FSB agents.[15] In Ukraine, speaking at a national congress of business representatives, the president of Ukraine's Association of Management Consultants quipped that, in their advisory legislative capacity after the Orange Revolution (see Chapter 5 on state principal's commitment), "business was relegated to the state of permanent pregnancy"; while ideas conceived by entrepreneurs have been acknowledged and sometimes legislated at the top, the results have never been delivered on the ground.[16] Speaking at the same event, a nationally recognized small-business activist trenchantly warned the entrepreneurs against expecting too much from advising the government on legal reforms: "Our participation in law-making will not solve much because law can be obviated.... *Don't hope that influence can be secured via law.... Influence is secured via action [vply-vovist' zakhyshchaet'sia diieiu].*" Unlike the narratives of top-down political will and legal reforms, this volume argues for bottom-up social action as the most promising avenue toward the rule of law.

RULE OF LAW AND STAKEHOLDER ALLIANCES

Chapter 6 presented evidence that firm-level social empowerment can directly improve the security of PR. This section argues that stakeholder alliances pertain to the rule of law in three additional ways.

First, business stakeholders contribute to resolving the "robber baron problem" referring to the fact that big business is often well-positioned to exploit lawlessness to its advantage and hence less interested in the rule of law. The recognition of this problem in the literature has decimated the naiveté of early transition (when transferring property into private ownership was seen as synonymous with creating a powerful rule-of-law constituency) yet has not offered alternatives.[17] My research suggests that in settings where even the tycoons need stakeholders to protect themselves, these stakeholders exert a *disciplining*

---

[14] Transcript of the Meeting of the Social-Conservative Club "Civic Platform" of United Russia, May 13, 2010. On file with author.

[15] Although originally a brainchild of United Russia, the party of power, Civic Control has been surprisingly efficacious at uncovering local corruption. For details, see http://gkontrol.com

[16] Author's transcript of the National Congress of the Council of Entrepreneurship at the Cabinet of Ministers. Kyiv, October 23, 2006.

[17] Glaeser and Shleifer (2003) go as far as claiming that in Russia-like settings, any attempts by the state at rule of law will be subverted and should be given up as such to conserve state resources.

208   *Firm Stakeholders and Rule of Law*

reverse influence on the tycoons. Pace the orthodox treatments[18] of oligarchy, the sovereign is not the only actor capable of "taming" the oligarchs.

Consider the case of Vimpelcom, part two, as an example. (See Chapter 6 for part one.) After its Norwegian ally Telenor helped Alfa Group protect Vimpelcom against state attacks, Alfa Group attempted to marginalize Telenor in Vimpelcom's decision-making, potentially depriving Telenor of the right to manage its assets. A tycoon-victim turned into a tycoon-bully. Throughout 2005, Telenor legally resisted Vimpelcom's expansion into Ukraine as intended by Alfa Group; through its "super-majority" provisions, Vimpelcom's charter effectively guarantees Telenor veto powers on the board of directors. After bombarding Telenor with four lawsuits to render the charter provisions invalid, Alfa Group turned to less legitimate tactics. In February 2006, "a more than peculiar declaration" amorphously named "On Russian-Norwegian Economic Relations" was born in the Duma, effectively accusing Telenor of sabotaging the countries' bilateral relations.[19] The proposal's authorship left few doubts. Notably, a similarly murky tactic was used by Alfa Group in 2005 to prevent Telenor from increasing its equity stake in Vimpelcom. Then, the Russian security services "recommended" the Federal Antimonopoly Service block Telenor's entirely legitimate move in what constituted "the implementation of private, corporate interests through the hands of an authoritative state structure," in the words of a Duma deputy.[20]

In February 2009, with a tactic typical of corporate raiders, Alfa seemed to have delivered Telenor a crippling blow; through a putative minority shareholder in Vimpelcom, the company Farimex (owning 0.002 percent of Vimpelcom), Alfa won a lawsuit against Telenor in a remote Russian court in Siberia accusing Telenor of inflicting damages of $1.7 billion on Farimex through resisting Vimpelcom's expansion into Ukraine in 2004–5. Most of Telenor's stake in Vimpelcom was arrested through a court order following the verdict. Even by the nasty, brutish standards of corporate conflicts in under-institutionalized settings, Vimpelcom's drama was striking; an unscrupulous majority owner, it seemed, used a stakeholder when it suited his interests, only to expropriate him afterward.

Yet Telenor reined in Alfa Group after all. The dubious 2006 Alfa-lobbied declaration was recalled in the Duma by the chair of the international affairs committee preceding the visit of Norway's foreign minister.[21] Vimpelcom was forced to officially retract its Alfa-supported offer to purchase Ukraine's Kyivstar because of Telenor's resistance.[22] The Federal Antimonopoly Service director conceded Telenor the right to increase its stake in Vimpelcom after

---

[18] Winters.
[19] *Izvestiya* February 3, 2006; *Novye Izvestiya* February 20, 2006.
[20] *Novye Izvestiya* 2006.
[21] Ibid.
[22] Vimpelcom's press release, June 1, 2006.

Rule of Law and Stakeholder Alliances

much futile pressure from Alfa Group.[23] Finally, upon Telenor's victories in a New York court and not without another chat between Norway's prime minister and Putin, Alfa backed off from its attack on Telenor's stake in Vimpelcom; in 2009 Alfa and Telenor came to an agreement on a joint strategy in Ukraine, and Telenor's stock jumped 15 percent after the announcement.[24] When tycoons such as Fridman of Alfa Group create alliances with non-state actors, the latter can discipline the former – a critical side effect for the rule of law (in addition to the primary function of stakeholder alliances in protecting tycoons' assets).

In the case of corporations, this "discipline" is often institutionalized via firm-level charters assuring company transparency (through accounting standards and external audits) and the commitment of majority owners to respect the rights of other corporate stakeholders (through the latter's veto powers, independence of board directors, etc.). Such institutionalization is necessary to secure the cooperation of stakeholders in the first place (why help a corporation that may cheat the helper?).[25]

The process suggests a dilemma for the tycoons choosing whether to bind their hands with respect to stakeholders or face the storms of property fights alone. If they decide to do the former,[26] *multilateral binding* occurs; the tycoons are disciplined by the stakeholders, while together they discipline the state predators.

The second way stakeholder alliances pertain to the rule of law is through *institutionalized firm transparency*, which is *necessary to attract foreign stakeholders* and can per se incentivize the state actors to play by the rules. The latter effect occurs because firm transparency (a) makes illegal state activity visible to the public, (b) ties the majority owners' hands with respect to slush funds available for bribes, or, critically, (c) decreases the leverage state actors could use to blackmail the firm.

The level of companies' transparency, represented through their organizational form, has a significant impact on some state threats, according to my survey data. Organizational form was proxied with dummy variables for open joint-stock company (Russian "OAO"), closed joint-stock company ("ZAO"),

---

[23] *Prime-Tass* August 9, 2006.

[24] *Kommersant* October 6, 2009; *Delo* May 20, 2009.

[25] The anti-raiding specialists in Russia and Ukraine invariably emphasize the improvement of corporate governance as a mechanism to secure the loyalty of stakeholders in the case of raiding attacks. Says a partner at a law firm specializing in such takeovers, "Often the root of an attack is a conflict within the enterprise when the slighted side – often minority shareholders or workers –, once it understands that it cannot protect its rights legally, searches for raiders or third parties to sell them this situation and get out.... Not a single company we've worked with [i.e., that has been illegally raided] had a functioning corporate governance system." Presentation at the business forum AntiReider 2007 in Kyiv, Ukraine (March 29, 2007).

[26] Regarding the point at which corporate insiders will invest in alliance-building strategies, the Russian data suggests that this happens when the present value of the costs associated with a potential state expropriation begins to exceed the present value of the benefits the insiders derive from expropriating minority shareholders. Markus, 2008.

limited liability company ("OOO"), and other forms. Measures of individual PR threats were regressed on organizational form as well as controls for size, region, sector, ownership, and de novo status. Two results stand out. First, the dummy for open joint-stock firms, that is, those facing *the highest disclosure requirements*, was consistently negative across all threats and significantly (at 0.05 level) reduced the threats of "administrative pressure for informal payments" as well as "illegal inspections by regulatory agencies." Second, the dummy for closed joint-stock companies, which are the *least transparent* was consistently positive across all threats and significantly (at 0.01 level) increased the threats of "extortion by taxation agencies" as well as "illegal inspections by regulatory agencies." (The analysis was run for Russia only, as the data on organizational form was not available for Ukraine.)

As three leading Russian political experts noted in their open letter protesting the Yukos expropriation, "our bureaucracy cannot stand clean and legal business. They are interested in keeping businesses in the 'shadows' ... [and] in pushing them into an illegal, criminal space. Because ... [a firm that is] the subject of a thick dossier in the prosecutor's office is much easier to command and to use as a money bag."[27] A former adviser to the Ukrainian prime minister interviewed by the author agrees: "Companies that do IPOs, e.g. in London, are better protected because they are transparent.... After three years of audits you need to list abroad, you have less shady operations [*tenevye skhemy*], so they [state actors] can't grab you anywhere. Also, when you get loans from the World Bank or the EBRD, and the sums of these are huge now in Ukraine, you obviously must be transparent."

The third and most important way in which my framework relates to the rule of law is this: Stakeholder alliances multiply the number of actors involved in a potential PR conflict, decisively facilitating the eventual involvement of the media, or sanctions from executive superiors. Through iteration, this scenario can lead to a gradual internalization of new rules of the game by state actors, while also increasing the resolve of property owners to confront state predators.

The latter point is especially pertinent for smaller firms. The smaller entrepreneurs' apathy concerning the void of functioning legal protections is a self-fulfilling prophecy. The cognitive resignation of small-business owners to agent predation induces a behavioral passivity that further tempts bureaucrats to break the law – appetite comes with eating. Stakeholder alliances break this vicious cycle.

The "robber baron problem" is mirrored by the "small shopkeeper problem" in that both result in the lack of *active demand for the rule of law* among the respective business strata. While recognizing the issues of big business, the literature has neglected the "small shopkeeper problem" by formulaically referencing the middle class as the agent of change. Pervasive apathy on the

---

[27] *Moskovksie Novosti* August 5, 2003.

Rule of Law and Stakeholder Alliances

part of small business owners, however, raises the question of how *latent* demand for legality celebrated in the literature can be translated into battle-like engagement.

My survey and interview data show that companies with non-state alliances display *higher readiness to publicly expose state predation*. According to the survey, Russian companies with either local or foreign alliances receive significantly more frequent coverage in the local press and on television; moreover, companies with alliances are 43 percent more likely to agree with the statement that they "can count on the media in the case of a serious and groundless interference with the management of the enterprise by state agencies" compared to firms without alliances.

This trend extends to Ukraine, where the battle over the marketplace in Vinnytsia illustrates the point.[28] After 1,300 stands had been leased out to market sellers by the old municipal administration, the new mayor personally annulled the lease, pressuring the sellers to relocate to the "official market-place" run by a private company connected to the mayor. In the process, several containers with sellers' goods were confiscated. After the businesspeople refused to give in, one seller was beaten by thugs. As I was interviewing the leader of the Vinnytsia Union of Private Entrepreneurs, police were waiting for her outside ("for her protection," they said). The businesswoman stressed that while small entrepreneurs usually have zero chance in such conflicts, their cause was helped by "high cooperation and connections with business associations in other regions who face similar problems.... When people get together, confidence rises." Two days later, the entrepreneurs' union was able to gather an array of journalists, a parliament deputy from Kyiv (responsible for small business policy), the mayor's deputy, the chiefs of the local tax agency and police, as well as a dozen local business representatives. During three hours, the mayor's deputy, visibly unaccustomed to being disagreed with, endured a cross-examination by the parliament deputy and business representatives on the fees and ownership structure of the "official marketplace," as well as the details of the ongoing conflict. Tangible outcomes achieved at this roundtable included (a) the police representative launching a criminal investigation into the beating of the entrepreneur, (b) the oblast procuracy publicly ordering the mayor-connected companies to stop extortion, (c) the mayor's administration admitting on record that land designations to mayor-connected firms were done with major violations and would be reviewed while also (d) promising that these firms would lose their right to collect taxes and "service fees," and (e) the mayor's administration officially guaranteeing caps on future trade-related fees to the entrepreneurs.

---

[28] This case study is based on twenty-one in-depth interviews by the author with entrepreneurs and city administration representatives in Vinnytsia in February-March 2007. The author was also present at the roundtable event.

As a reminder, this volume argued that "merchant groups" – national business associations enjoying the support of the state principal – are not effective at restraining agent predation. Vinnytsia's case illustrates a different argument, namely that unlike "merchant groups," genuine *non-state, bottom-up business organizations* can improve local PR security even in the absence of sovereign support. Theoretically, such organizations can be properly conceptualized as another form of stakeholder alliance.[29]

Vinnytsia's case exemplifies how accountability structures are built, exposing the sanctified edifice of the rule of law while still under construction. The case study is particularly noteworthy because the entrepreneurs had tried various strategies to protect their property rights, offering some within-the-case variation. For example, a year prior to the roundtable, the entrepreneurs began paying trade-related municipal taxes (*rynkovyi zbir*) directly to the city[30] instead of paying through the mayor-connected private intermediaries, as officially mandated. The purpose of this maneuver was simple: to demonstrate how much revenue the city was losing in the pockets of intermediary companies.[31] The city's response? The mayor's administration sent a directive, cosigned by the tax agency chief, to the local banks *prohibiting them from wiring entrepreneurs' cash into the city treasury*. For the reputational restraint framework, this is the peak of absurdity. Alas, once the ownership structure of the "tax"-collecting intermediaries is taken into account, this is modern-day agent predation at its finest. During the roundtable, an acrimonious exchange ensued between the business association director and the Rada deputy from Kyiv on the one hand, and the tax agency representative on the other. While the tax agent cited formalistic reasons (absence of proper payment receipts) for declining entrepreneurs' money, the deputy from Kyiv cut to the point: "This is such a disgrace [*han'ba*] for the tax service. If the money is going straight into the budget, you have to welcome this with both hands." The director of the entrepreneurs' union diagnosed the issue: "They don't want to do anything because the catch is good and it's well-shared [*dobre lovyt'sia i dobre dilit'sia*]." Yet predatory sharing as the modus operandi of local state agents did not survive the roundtable. Intermediary companies ceased their operations immediately

---

[29] According to the director of the Institute for Competitive Society in Kyiv, the bottom-up business associations took off in Ukraine around 1996 in response to "a radical toughening of administrative pressure on small and medium-size enterprises, especially by taxation agencies, customs services, and certification departments. These [organs] have become states within a state, self-sufficient and dictatorial. Businessmen have realized that if they protest against the government [individually], they threaten their businesses. Hence the need for business associations" (author's interview, Kyiv, November 7, 2006). More broadly, see Duvanova's (2013) excellent study of bottom-up business associations across the postcommunist space.

[30] These taxes are distinct from the service fees, the latter collected by a market-administering entity for the cleaning and protection of the premises. In Vinnytsia's case, private firms were allegedly collecting taxes on the city's behalf (in addition to service fees).

[31] According to interviewed entrepreneurs, trade-related tax revenues quickly rose beyond those officially forecast as a result of this maneuver.

Rule of Law and Stakeholder Alliances

thereafter, and by 2008, Vinnytsia's official market tax revenue was in line with or ahead of similar Ukrainian cities.[32]

Victories like the ones achieved at the roundtable involve painstaking work; the network-building by Vinnytsia entrepreneurs involved years of attending business conventions in Kyiv, where a working relationship with the parliament deputy was established and supportive relations with other associations across the country were nurtured. By Ukraine's standards of administrative impunity, the standoff between the entrepreneurs' association and the city administration was epic. As a bottom-up, non-state network, the Vinnytsia Union of Private Entrepreneurs persevered.

The case study above is fundamentally distinct from the narratives of top-down political will or grand legal reforms; instead, the key mechanism showcases the private actors' rising confidence vis-à-vis the state, confidence that is often rooted in alliances and channeled through the local media.

Note that this mechanism is focused on *clusters* of actors around *clear material interests*, and is hence also distinct from the modernization theory's emphasis on a *diffuse* and *value-driven* "middle class" as a builder of a legal order. Apart from the obvious problem of collective action, the middle class *en masse* is an implausible disciplinarian of the state in postcommunist countries, where it depends on the government for its livelihood. (In Russia, more than half of the middle class is state-dependent.[33]) It does not help that the middle class is prone to a short attention span. The latter may suffice for spectacular bursts of protests (that sometimes even topple the state principal, as in Ukraine) but not for the painstaking process of monitoring and sanctioning state agents on an ongoing basis. The 2011 anti-Putin rallies in Moscow, for example, inspired many foreign commentators for a longer time period than the protesters. The owner of a marketing firm in Moscow commented that his employees participated in the protests "because it was fashionable, nothing more. They felt strongly about the ... rallies ... but they also feel strong emotions about their iPhones."[34] The "office plankton," as some Russians derisively refer to the middle class, needs anchors to sustain it in action against state abuse. The employers and business owners can provide such anchors, and they are more likely to do so when their material interests (read: property rights) are threatened by the law-flouting state. A middle class *without* collective action and long-term dedication is but a feeding ground for predatory bureaucrats.

Another weakness of a diffuse, ideationally driven middle class – as opposed to the clusters of materially driven stakeholder alliances – is the ease with which its initiatives can be subverted by the state. The problem in modern developing (quasi-) democracies is not so much violent suppression but rather *subversion through imitation*. Ukraine, for example, witnessed a proliferation

---

[32] For comparative statistics on all cities' market tax revenue, see *DonbassUA* November 13, 2009.

[33] Remington 2011.

[34] *The New York Times* January 5, 2013.

of anti-corruption NGOs in the second half of the 2000s. While these NGOs were often funded by foreign donors, the Ukrainian *state* paradoxically joined the initiatives, leading to an unhealthy equilibrium. According to a Rada deputy interviewed by the author in 2012:

The civil anti-corruption initiatives are just like the government initiatives; they are about imitation.... Remember that the leaders of such initiatives ... are now compensated from two main sources: state power and the donors. In this situation, imitation is in the interest of all parties. For the state, such NGOs confirm that "not all is bad news [*ne vse tak plokho*]," and ... for the organizations, the imitation of fighting corruption procures resources. It has nothing in common with fighting it in substance.

The director of Ukraine's state agency for foreign investment (interviewed by the author in 2007) put it in similar terms while relating it to the Orange Revolution:

Civil society is not an empty slogan. But it has been devalued here especially due to the grant-eaters [*grantoedy*] who just take money and create a semblance of activity.... Real civil society begins with a reform of local self-governance [*mestnoe samoupravlenie*], with communities.... It is very good that we had ... the Orange Revolution. But the lesson is that it is not about a one-time act. It is about the everyday, hard work of controlling power.... It was a great ... moment of unity ... but nobody wants to keep on working.

The problems of popular under-motivation and bureaucratic subversion are less severe in the case of *smaller* groups defending their *core interests*, such as the firm-level stakeholder alliances. The Ukrainian Center for Sociological and Political Research (Sotsiovymir) surveyed 600 respondents in the city of Khmelnytskyi in 2006. The instrument included the following question: "Who supports most actively [*naiaktyvnishe spryiaie*] the residents of Khmelnytskyi in defending their rights in relations [*stosunkakh*] with the municipal authorities?" Among the eight response options, "mass media" was ranked first, and "church" was ranked third. In between, proudly occupying the second rank, were "entrepreneurs," while "civil organizations" took a distant sixth place. ("Municipal deputies" concluded the ranking in eighth place, suggesting that local self-governance is, indeed, ripe for reform.)

Although the preliminary findings in this section are promising, one must beware teleological expectations. Alliance-based accountability may stabilize as a partial-reform equilibrium precluding further progress toward Weberian bureaucracies that enforce the law predictably and fairly. Still, auspiciously, stakeholder alliances do *not* seem to decrease the "demand for law" by firms. In fact, when asked about the importance for business activity of independent and uncorrupt courts, or democratic control over the government, both Russian and Ukrainian companies with alliances rate these aspects as *more* important than do firms without alliances.[35]

---

[35] Entrepreneurs were asked "On a scale of 1–4, how important are these factors for the protection of entrepreneurs' right to legally manage their property and derive legal income from it?"

The Argument from a Comparative Perspective

At present, stakeholder alliances do facilitate the rule of law by constraining robber barons, by institutionalizing firm transparency, and by forcing state actors to internalize the new rules of the game. Note that even if in the long run this relationship is no longer to hold and stakeholder alliances prove to be a substitute for (rather than a precursor to) the ideal-typical rule of law, such "second-best institutions" fitting the local context are celebrated in the development literature as often *preferable* to the "best-practice" templates.[36] In the developed world, the state and big business invariably feature as the two founding fathers of capitalism; while capitalists like John Rockefeller and the earlier financiers of the Industrial Revolution are often credited with the rise of the Anglo-Saxon economies, the state has played a major role in the "catch-up nations" of Continental Europe and Eastern countries. The role of the remaining multitude of firms appears secondary at best. Governmental benevolence and competence, however, are in short supply in modern developing countries, as are the pools of private capital to be invested. This volume, conversely, elaborated the constructive role of "small" capitalists. This role is political: By forging alliances with stakeholders around their firms, owners force the state to respect their rights.

THE ARGUMENT FROM A COMPARATIVE PERSPECTIVE

The connection between firm-level stakeholder alliances, property rights, and the rule of law fits empirically with a number of historical precedents for the bottom-up and initially informal trajectories toward the more accountable and formal legal orders.

In China, for example, the incremental constitutional adjustments stipulating the protection of private property occurred as a result of a grass-roots informal process: "In the course of their daily interactions ... with local staff of the party-state, business owners have had a structural impact on the direction of formal institutional reforms."[37] This process involved a mass of individual entrepreneurs gradually becoming an important constituency for the Communist Party through their ongoing exchange. Alliances, conflict, and creative business strategizing are lacking in China's story of consensual state-business interaction and mutual learning, providing an interesting contrast to Russia and Ukraine.

Companies with either community and labor alliances, or with foreign alliances consistently rated the importance of the "democratic control of national government" as well as the "independent and competent courts system" *higher* than firms without alliances. Across the four comparisons (two alliance types and two hypothetical rule-of-law outcomes), firms with alliances considered these rule-of-law factors more important by 0.13–0.34 points. The largest gap is in the perceived importance of democratic control between firms with community and labor alliances and firms without such alliances.

[36] E.g., Rodrik. See also Allina-Pisano (2008) for a critique of "best-practice" reforms in the agricultural PR regimes of Russia and Ukraine.

[37] Tsai 2007, 140.

In countries as diverse as Peru, Egypt, and post–World War II Japan, the legally effective allocation of property rights emerged only to the extent *local informal consensus* regarding property rights' protection preexisted (and was later acknowledged by) formal national institutions.[38] In this framework, the informal consensus among the population about who owns what endows the population with the implicit power to sabotage government reforms. The key mechanism here is *customary decentralized lawmaking*, in which state actors "apply community standards," and in doing so "they find law, rather than making it."[39] Unlike the mechanism of stakeholder alliances, however, this interpretation assumes political will and relies heavily on legal content.

Western countries, too, provide illuminating parallels. The history of corporate governance legislation in the United States suggests that "private action may provide the lead that spurs collective public action."[40] Before the existence of external audits or legal requirements, J.P. Morgan of Federal Steel pioneered corporate transparency vis-à-vis the public in 1898, providing the public with a standard on which to base their demands for more formal and universal arrangements. As Theodore Roosevelt later put it, the state would not "accept the publication of what some particular company chooses to publish as a favor, instead of demanding what we think ought to be published from all companies as a right."[41] In the modern OECD economies, the antidote to the "quiet politics" through which the upper corporate management may undermine the democratic process and the rule of law has been the bottom-up engagement of the public in politics.[42] These parallels offer two insights. First, the role of super-wealthy private actors in the popular movements for the rule of law is ambivalent; while at times tycoons may lead such movements, they may also find themselves to be their very targets. Second, the strength of democratic institutions may decrease the importance of stakeholder alliances because vibrant democracies allow the public to correct transgressions against the rule of law through elections.

Even the canonical case of credible commitment by the British Crown, stressing a one-time institutionalization of the king's promises to his creditors, is undergoing a revision, suggesting that the ongoing, bottom-up, resistance-based, and informal mechanisms played a much larger role in enhancing the Crown's accountability than the narrative of top-down commitment has acknowledged. First, the coalitional politics and the strengthening of the Whig party, which gradually unfolded decades *after* the constitutional changes that presumably committed the monarch, may have had a larger impact on holding the latter financially accountable.[43] Second, at least to some extent, British property was

[38] De Soto 2003.
[39] Cooter 1994, 216.
[40] Dixit, 82.
[41] Strouse 2000, 439.
[42] Culpepper 2011.
[43] Stasavage 2003.

The Argument from a Comparative Perspective

secured through the *informal power of the gentry*, manifested through its pacts with recruited militias and rooted in its ability to manage property efficiently rather than through deals between the king and the great lords.[44] Third, the *British public at large*, while entirely neglected in the orthodox commitment narrative, in fact "held the government to account through the published media and direct action."[45] By offering detailed criticism of the financial mismanagement by the Crown *and* the Parliament *after the repeated failures of sovereign commitment*, as well as by withdrawing their support from the Crown's fundraising initiatives aimed at the public, the latter directly influenced the course of Britain's financial revolution.

Property, predation, and protection – these phenomena were empirically engaged and theoretically integrated in this volume because they are fundamentally important to politico-economic development. The constructive strategies of economic actors to address poor property rights' enforcement are critically under-theorized. Yet firms' alliance-based resistance to property rights infringements – unlike the defenses based on concealment, corruption, or violence – may contribute to the rule of law taking hold in rent-seeking economies. Roman Emperor Tiberius, seeking to curb local governors' rampant predation, said he wanted his "sheep shorn, not flayed." The current literature on PR enforcement tends to treat businesses as sheep, too. Yet, under agent predation, the strategies of sheep may matter more than the words of the Emperor.

---

[44] Rajan and Zingales 2004, 146.
[45] Murphy 2013, 195.

Bibliography

Acemoglu, D., and S. Johnson. "Unbundling Institutions." *Journal of Political Economy* 113, no. 5 (2005): 949–95.

Acemoglu, D., S. Johnson, and J. A. Robinson. "The Colonial Origins of Comparative Development: An Empirical Investigation." *American Economic Review* 91, no. 5 (2001): 1369–401.

Acemoglu, D., and J. Robinson. *Why Nations Fail: The Origins of Power, Prosperity, and Poverty*. New York: Crown Publishing Group, 2012.

Acemoglu, Daron. "Introduction to Economic Growth." *Journal of Economic Theory* 147, no. 2 (2012): 545–50.

Advisers.ru "Obshchestvennaya Palata Obsudila Metody Bor'by S Reiderstvom." September 22, 2010.

AFN News Agency "Prezident Ukrainy Zaveril, Chto Vozvrata K Reprivatizatsii Ne Budet." October 6, 2005.

Aidt, Toke S. "Economic Analysis of Corruption: A Survey." *The Economic Journal* 113, no. 491 (2003): F632–52.

Albertus, Michael, and Victor Menaldo. "If You're against Them You're with Us the Effect of Expropriation on Autocratic Survival." *Comparative Political Studies* 45, no. 8 (2012): 973–1003.

Alekseev, Y. "O Rezul'tatah Raboty Organov Predvaritel'nogo Sledstviya Mvd Rossii Po Protivodeystviyu Reiderskim Zahvatam." *Nedvizhimost' i Investitsii* 38, no. 1 (2009): 76–8.

Allina-Pisano, J. *The Post-Soviet Potemkin Village: Politics and Property Rights in the Black Earth*. Cambridge: Cambridge University Press, 2008.

ArcticWay "Korrupciya Mozhet Pogubit' Shtokman." January 13, 2011.

Argumenty i Fakty "Iskuplenie Grefa." June 18, 2003.

"Rosstat: Chislo Chinovnikov V RF Uvelichivaetsya, Rastut Ih Zarplaty." May 26, 2011.

"Klyuev Reshil Perekryt' Vse Lazeiki Reideram." February 9, 2012.

Arikan, G. Gulsun. "Fiscal Decentralization: A Remedy for Corruption?" *International Tax and Public Finance* 11, no. 2 (2004): 175–95.

Aslund, A. *How Capitalism Was Built: The Transformation of Central and Eastern Europe, Russia, and Central Asia.* Cambridge: Cambridge University Press, 2007.

Åslund, A., and M. McFaul, eds. *Revolution in Orange: The Origins of Ukraine's Democratic Breakthrough*: Washington, DC: Carnegie Endowment for International Peace, 2006.

Åslund, Anders. *How Ukraine Became a Market Economy and Democracy.* Washington, DC: Peterson Institute, 2009.

Asoni, A. "Protection of Property Rights and Growth as Political Equilibria." *Journal of Economic Surveys* 22, no. 5 (2008): 953–87.

Augustine, Saint. *The City of God.* Vol. 2 London: T. & T. Clark, 1888.

Aylmer, Gerald Edward. *The Crown's Servants: Government and Civil Service under Charles II, 1660–1685.* Oxford: Oxford University Press, 2002.

Bardhan, Pranab, and Dilip Mookherjee. "Decentralization, Corruption and Government Accountability." In *International Handbook on the Economics of Corruption*, edited by Susan Rose-Ackerman, 161–88: London: Edward Elgar Publishing, 2006.

Barnes, A. S. *Owning Russia: The Struggle over Factories, Farms, and Power.* Ithaca, NY: Cornell University Press, 2006.

Barzel, Yoram. *Economic Analysis of Property Rights.* Cambridge: Cambridge University Press, 1997.

A Theory of the State: Economic Rights, Legal Rights, and the Scope of the State. Cambridge: Cambridge University Press, 2002.

Bates, R. H. *Prosperity and Violence: The Political Economy of Development.* New York: Norton, 2001.

"State Failure." *Annual Review of Political Science* 11 (2008): 1–12.

When Things Fell Apart: State Failure in Late-Century Africa. Cambridge: Cambridge University Press, 2008.

Baumol, W. J. "Entrepreneurship: Productive, Unproductive, and Destructive." *Journal of Political Economy* 98, no. 5 (1990): 893.

Becker, Gary S., and George J. Stigler. "Law Enforcement, Malfeasance, and Compensation of Enforcers." *Journal of Legal Studies* 3 (1974): 1.

Bertelli, Anthony M., and Andrew B. Whitford. "Perceiving Credible Commitments: How Independent Regulators Shape Elite Perceptions of Regulatory Quality." *British Journal of Political Science* 39, no. 3 (2009): 517–37.

Bfm.ru "Duma Vyvela Tovarnoe Reiderstvo Za Zakon." April 7, 2010.

Blockmans, W. P. "Der Kaiser Und Seine Niederlandische Untertanen." In *Karl V. 1500–1558. Neue Perspektiven Seiner Herrschaft in Europa Und Ubersee*, edited by A. Kohler, B. Haider, and C. Ottner, 437–49. Vienna: Verlag der osterreichischen Akademie der Wissenschaften, 2002.

Boix, Carles. *Democracy and Redistribution.* Cambridge: Cambridge University Press, 2003.

Boyarchuk, D., V. Dubrovs'ky, K. Rus'kyh, and V. Baloshenko. "Koryguvannia Kursu Reform: Vse Za Planom, Chy Vidstup Po Vsih Frontah?" In *Populiarna ekonomika: monitoryng reform.* Kyiv: Case Ukraine, 2012.

Boycko, M., A. Shleifer, and R. Vishny. *Privatizing Russia.* Cambridge, MA: MIT Press, 1997.

Brown, David, John Earle, and Almos Telegdy. "The Productivity Effects of Privatization: Longitudinal Estimates from Hungary, Romania, Russia, and Ukraine." *Journal of Political Economy* 114, no. 1 (2006): 61–99.

Bibliography

Brown, J. D., J. S. Earle, and S. Gehlbach. "Helping Hand or Grabbing Hand? State Bureaucracy and Privatization Effectiveness." *American Political Science Review* 103, no. 2 (2009): 264–83.

Bruszt, Laszlo, and David Stark. *Postsocialist Pathways: Transforming Politics and Property in East Central Europe.* Cambridge: Cambridge University Press, 1998.

Bykovec, Vyacheslav. "Rol' I Misce Biznes-Asociacij V Systemi Dialogu Biznesu Ta Vlady." Union of Private and Privatized Enterprises, 2007.

Chabal, Patrick, and Jean-Pascal Daloz. *Africa Works: Disorder as Political Instrument.* Indianapolis: Indiana University Press, 1999.

Chaudhry, K. A. "The Myths of the Market and the Common History of Late Developers." *Politics and Society* 21 (1993): 245–74.

Cheloukhine, Serguei, and M. R. Haberfeld. *Russian Organized Corruption Networks and Their International Trajectories.* New York: Springer, 2011.

Chubb, Judith. "The Mafia, the Market and the State in Italy and Russia." *Journal of Modern Italian Studies* 1, no. 2 (1996): 273–91.

Claessens, S., and L. Laeven. "Financial Development, Property Rights, and Growth." *The Journal of Finance* 58, no. 6 (2003): 2401–36.

Clark, G. *A Farewell to Alms: A Brief Economic History of the World.* Princeton, NJ: Princeton University Press, 2007.

Coen, D. "The Evolution of the Large Firm as a Political Actor in the European Union." *Journal of European Public Policy* 4, no. 1 (1997): 91–108.

Cooter, Robert D. "Structural Adjudication and the New Law Merchant: A Model of Decentralized Law." *International Review of Law and Economics* 14 (1994): 215–31.

Cox, G. W. "War, Moral Hazard, and Ministerial Responsibility: England after the Glorious Revolution." *The Journal of Economic History* 71, no. 1 (2011): 133–61.

CPT. "Reprivatizatsiya Otkladyvaetsia." Moscow: Centr Politicheskih Tehnologii, 2005.

  "Reiderstvo Kak Social'no-Ekonomichesky I Politichesky Fenomen Sovremennoj Rossii: Otchet O Kachestvennom Sociologicheskom Issledovanii." Moscow: Centr Politicheskih Tehnologii, 2008.

Culpepper, Pepper D. *Quiet Politics and Business Power: Corporate Control in Europe and Japan.* Cambridge: Cambridge University Press, 2011.

D'Anieri, Paul. *Understanding Ukrainian Politics: Power, Politics, and Institutional Design.* Armonk, NY: M.E. Sharpe, 2006.

Darden, K. A. "Blackmail as a Tool of State Domination: Ukraine under Kuchma." *East European Constitutional Review* 10 (2001): 67.

De Mesquita, B. "An "a" for Dictation [Pyaterka Za Diktat]." *Esquire* 83 (2012).

De Mesquita, B., Alastair Smith, Randolph Siverson, and James Morrow. *The Logic of Political Survival.* Cambridge, MA: MIT Press, 2003.

De Soto, H. *The Mystery of Capital: Why Capitalism Triumphs in the West and Fails Everywhere Else.* New York: Basic Civitas Books, 2003.

Delo "Prem'er Norvegii Zastupilsia Za Sobstvennika 'Kievstara.'" May 20, 2009.

Delovaya Nedelya "Fridman Pristroil Neftedollary [Fridman Took Care of Oil Revenues]." August 6, 2003.

Delovaya Pressa "Kazakhstan Stremitel'no Navodnyaetsia Reiderami." October 31, 2006.

Den' "Komu Ohranyat' Banki." February 1, 2012.

Denisova, I., M. Eller, T. Frye, and E. Zhuravskaya. "Who Wants to Revise Privatization? The Complementarity of Market Skills and Institutions." *American Political Science Review* 103, no. 2 (2008): 284–304.

Der Spiegel "Strategische Krise Bei Gazprom: Der Gas-Goliath Geht in Die Knie." February 1, 2013.

Diermeier, D., J. Ericson, T. Frye, and S. Lewis. "Credible Commitment and Property Rights: The Role of Strategic Interaction between Political and Economic Actors." In *The Political Economy of Property Rights*, edited by D. L. Weimer, 20–42: Cambridge: Cambridge University Press, 1997.

Dimitrov, Martin *Piracy and the State: The Politics of Intellectual Property in China.* Cambridge: Cambridge University Press, 2009.

Dixit, A. K. *Lawlessness and Economics: Alternative Modes of Governance.* Princeton, NJ: Princeton University Press, 2004.

Dobek, Mariusz. "Property Rights and Institutional Change in the Czech and Slovak Republics." In *The Political Economy of Property Rights*, edited by D. L. Weimer, 182–204: Cambridge: Cambridge University Press, 1997.

Dolgopyatova, T., I. Ivasaky, and A. Yakovlev, eds. *Rossiyskaya Korporaciya: Vnutrenniaya Organizaciya, Vneshnie Vzaimodeystviya, Perspektivy Razvitiya.* Moscow: VShE, 2007.

DonbassUA "Rynki 'Otstegivayut' V Gorodskoy Byudzhet Kruglen'kie Summy (Dannye Po Regionam)." November 13, 2009.

Doner, R. F., and B. R. Schneider. "Business Associations and Economic Development: Why Some Associations Contribute More Than Others." *Business and Politics* 2, no. 3 (2000): 261–88.

Doner, Richard, Bryan Ritchie, and D. Slater. "Systemic Vulnerability and the Origins of Developmental States: Northeast and Southeast Asia in Comparative Perspective." *International Organization* 59 (2005): 327–61.

Duindam, Jeroen. *Myths of Power.* Amsterdam: Amsterdam University Press, 1995.

  Vienna and Versailles: The Courts of Europe's Dynastic Rivals, 1550–1780. Cambridge: Cambridge University Press, 2003.

Duvanova, Dinissa. *Building Business in Post-Communist Russia, Eastern Europe, and Eurasia: Collective Goods, Selective Incentives, and Predatory States.* Cambridge: Cambridge University Press, 2013.

DV-News "Putin Obyavil Vojnu Offshoram." December 19, 2011.

Dzerkalo Tyzhnia "Yulia Tymoshenko: 'Praty Budut' Usi'." August 21, 2004.

  "Pryvatyzaciya: Pejzazh Pislya Zminy Portretiv." October 27, 2004.

  "Lyustraciya Ekonomiky?" February 19, 2005.

  "Bystree, Prozrachnee I V Ramkah Zakona." June 4, 2005.

  "Grabli Patriotov." December 3, 2005.

  "Samotniy Repryvatyzator?" December 17, 2005.

  "Demokratiya Peremogla! Hai Zhyve Korol'?" January 12, 2007.

  "Gosudarstvo, Kru-Gom! Povernutsia Li Licom K Armii Te Kto Za Nee Otvechaet?" May 15, 2009.

  "Za Gody Nezavisimosti Kolichestvo Chinovnikov V Otdel'nyh Vedomstvah Vyroslo V 3 Raza." February 27, 2010.

  "Ot Perestanovki Lic – Summa Otkatov Ne Menyaetsia?" August 20, 2010.

Bibliography

"Gorizontal' Yanukovicha. Vlast' Reshilas' Na Administrativnuyu Reformu?" October 23, 2010.

"Dlya Chego Minoborony Nuzhny Den'gi Detei-Invalidov?" November 12, 2010.

"Administrativnaya Reforma, Ili Obratno V Sssr." February 11, 2011.

"Mikhaylo Brods'ky "Dobre, Shcho Reyting PR Upav, – Otzhe, Reformy Bude Pryskoreno"." January 20, 2012.

"Perpetum-Peredelum." January 20, 2012.

"Reidery Protiv Invalidov." August 10, 2012.

"Mozhno Li Schitat' Spravedlivym Nalogovoe Reiderstvo?" October 19, 2012.

Easter, Gerald. *Capital, Coercion, and Post-Communist States*. Ithaca, NY: Cornell University Press, 2012.

East European Gas Analysis "Gazprom Continues Losing Its Market Share in Europe." September 14, 2010.

EBRD. "Transition Report: Business in Transition." 2005.

Egorov, Georgy, and Konstantin Sonin. "Dictators and Their Viziers: Endogenizing the Loyalty–Competence Trade-Off." *Journal of the European Economic Association* 9, no. 5 (2011): 903–30.

Ekonomichna Pravda "Vid Byudzhetu Nasolody Do Byudzhetu Palytsi." December 10, 2012.

Ekspert "Voprosy K S'ezdu." October 22, 2001.

"Zavety Prezidenta 1." February 25, 2009.

"O Sumerkakh Reiderov." July 12, 2010.

"Boris Titov: "Demokratiya Dlia Nas Ne Fetish"." March 12, 2012.

Ekspert Ukraina "Nuzhen Shelkovyi Shnurok." July 2, 2007.

"Reid Doshel Do Serediny." July 2, 2007.

Ekspert Volga "Novyi Peredel." May 14, 2007.

Ellickson, R. C. "A Hypothesis of Wealth-Maximizing Norms: Evidence from the Whaling Industry." *Journal of Law, Economics, & Organization* 5, no. 1 (1989): 83–97.

Ensminger, Jean. "Changing Property Rights: Reconciling Formal and Informal Rights to Land in Africa." In *The Frontiers of the New Institutional Economics*, edited by John Drobak and John Nye, 165–96. San Diego, CA: Academic Press, 1997.

Epstein, D., and S. O'Halloran. "Administrative Procedures, Information, and Agency Discretion." *American Journal of Political Science* (1994): 697–722.

European Business Association. "Overcoming Obstacles to Business Success." 2009.

Expatica "Rosneft to Abide by Dutch Court Yukos Decision: Company." June 28, 2010.

Fails, M. D., and J. Krieckhaus. "Colonialism, Property Rights and the Modern World Income Distribution." *British Journal of Political Science* 40, no. 3 (2010): 487–508.

Faktor Riska "Istoki Reida V Rossii." August 13, 2006.

Feld, L. P., and S. Voigt. "Economic Growth and Judicial Independence: Cross-Country Evidence Using a New Set of Indicators." *European Journal of Political Economy* 19, no. 3 (2003): 497–527.

Financial Times "The Magnitsky Law." July 27, 2012.

Firmin-Sellers, K. "The Politics of Property Rights." *The American Political Science Review* 89, no. 4 (1995): 867–81.

Bibliography

Fish, S. "The Roots and Remedies for Russia's Racket Economy." In *The Tunnel at the End of the Light: Privatization, Business Networks, and Economic Transformation in Russia*, edited by S. Cohen, A. Schwartz, and J. Zysman: Berkeley: University of California Press, 1998.

FLB.ru "Reideru Pripomnili 'Moloko'." April 1, 2012.

Forbes "Business Brains." January 7, 2002.

Friedman, M. *"Capitalism and Freedom."* Chicago: University of Chicago Press, 1962.

Frye, Timothy. "Russian Privatization and the Limits of Credible Commitment." In *The Political Economy of Property Rights: Institutional Change and Credibility in the Reform of Centrally Planned Economies*, edited by D. L. Weimer, 84–108. Cambridge: Cambridge University Press, 1997.

"Credible Commitment and Property Rights: Evidence from Russia." *American Political Science Review* 98, no. 3 (2004): 453–66.

Frye, T., A. Yakovlev, and Y. Yasin. "The 'Other' Russian Economy: How Everyday Firms View the Rules of the Game in Russia." *Social Research: An International Quarterly* 76, no. 1 (2009): 29–54.

FundsHub "Offshorny Pensionny Fond Obankrotivshegosya Yukosa Veteran Petroleum Trebuet Kompencacii." January 10, 2008.

Gambetta, Diego. *The Sicilian Mafia: The Business of Private Protection.* Cambridge, MA: Harvard University Press, 1996.

Gans-Morse, Jordan. "Threats to Property Rights in Russia: From Private Coercion to State Aggression." *Post-Soviet Affairs* 28, no. 3 (2012): 263–95.

Gazeta.ru "Tri Goda Bez Prava Proverki." September 17, 2003.

"S Ogliadkoj Na Biznes." April 9, 2012.

"Samoreguliruemaya Korrupciya." April 22, 2012.

Gazeta Po-Ukrains'ky "Viyna Mizh Dvoma Mil'yarderamy [War between Two Billionaires]." September 9, 2005.

Gehlbach, S., K. Sonin, and E. Zhuravskaya. "Businessman Candidates." *American Journal of Political Science* 54, no. 3 (2010): 718–36.

Gehlbach, S., and P. Keefer. "Investment without Democracy: Ruling-Party Institutionalization and Credible Commitment in Autocracies." *Journal of Comparative Economics* (2011).

Gehlbach, Scott. *Representation through Taxation: Revenue, Politics, and Development in Postcommunist States.* Cambridge: Cambridge University Press, 2010.

Gehlbach, Scott, and Philip Keefer. "Private Investment and the Institutionalization of Collective Action in Autocracies: Ruling Parties and Legislatures." *The Journal of Politics* 74, no. 2 (2012): 621–35.

Gelderblom, Oscar. *Cities of Commerce: The Institutional Foundations of International Trade in the Low Countries, 1250–1650.* Princeton, NJ: Princeton University Press, 2013.

Gelderblom, Oscar, and Regina Grafe. "The Rise and Fall of the Merchant Guilds: Re-Thinking the Comparative Study of Commercial Institutions in Premodern Europe." *Journal of Interdisciplinary History* 40, no. 4 (2010): 477–511.

Gilinsky, Yakov. "Organizatsionnaya Prestupnost' V Rossii: Teoriya I Real'nost'." St.Petersburg: Institut Sotsiologii RAN, 1996.

Gilson, R. J., and C. J. Milhaupt. "Economically Benevolent Dictators: Lessons for Developing Democracies." *American Journal of Comparative Law* 59, no. 1 (2011): 227–88.

Bibliography

Gingerich, Daniel W. "Governance Indicators and the Level of Analysis Problem: Empirical Findings from South America." *British Journal of Political Science* 43, no. 3 (2013): 505–40.

Giorgetti, Chiara. "The Yukos Interim Awards on Jurisdiction and Admissibility Confirms Provisional Application of Energy Charter Treaty." *ASIL Insight* 14, no. 23 (2010).

Glaeser, E.L., and A. Shleifer. "The Rise of the Regulatory State." *Journal of Economic Literature* XLI, no. June (2003): 401–25.

Goldman, M. I. *The Piratization of Russia: Russian Reform Goes Awry.* London: Routledge, 2003.

Goreslavsky, A. "Kto V Dome Hoziain?" *Sovershenno Sekretno* 9, no. 148 (2001): 1–5.

Grafton, R. Quentin, and Dane Rowlands. "Development Impeding Institutions: The Political Economy of Haiti." *Canadian Journal of Development Studies/Revue canadienne d'études du développement* 17, no. 2 (1996): 261–77.

Grani "Tret'e Pis'mo Putinu O Dele Yukosa." October 22, 2003.

"Proekt Amnistii Predprinimatelei Dorabotayut V Techenii 3–4 Nedel'." May 25, 2013.

Gravois, John. "The De Soto Delusion." *Slate Magazine* (2005).

Greif, Avner. *Institutions and the Path to the Modern Economy: Lessons from Medieval Trade.* Cambridge: Cambridge University Press, 2006.

Greif, Avner, P. Milgrom, and B. R. Weingast. "Coordination, Commitment, and Enforcement: The Case of the Merchant Guild." *Journal of Political Economy* 102, no. 4 (1994): 745–76.

Gromadzki, Grzegorz, Veronika Movchan, Mykola Riabchuk, Iryna Solonenko, Susan Stewart, Oleksandr Sushko, and Kataryna Wolczuk. "Beyond Colours: Assets and Liabilities of 'Post-Orange' Ukraine." Kyiv, Warsaw: International Renaissance Foundation, 2010.

Grossman, Sanford, and Oliver Hart. "An Analysis of the Principal-Agent Problem." *Econometrica* 51 (1983): 7–45.

Grzymala-Busse, A., and P. J. Luong. "Reconceptualizing the State: Lessons from Post-Communism." *Politics & Society* 30, no. 4 (2002): 529–54.

Grzymala-Busse, Anna. "Beyond Clientelism Incumbent State Capture and State Formation." *Comparative Political Studies* 41, no. 4–5 (2008): 638–73.

Gudkov, L., and B. Dubin. "Privatizatsiya Politsii." *Vestnik obshchestvennogo mneniya* 1, no. 81 (2006): 58–71.

Guriev, Sergei. "*A Theory of Informative Red Tape with an Application to Top-Level Corruption.*" Moscow: New Economic School, 1999.

Guriev, S., A. Kolotilin, and K. Sonin. "Determinants of Nationalization in the Oil Sector: A Theory and Evidence from Panel Data." *Journal of Law, Economics, and Organization* 27, no. 2 (2011): 301–23.

Guriev, Sergei, and Andrei Rachinsky. "The Role of Oligarchs in Russian Capitalism." *The Journal of Economic Perspectives* 19, no. 1 (2005): 131–50.

Guriev, S., and K. Sonin. "Dictators and Oligarchs: A Dynamic Theory of Contested Property Rights." *Journal of Public Economics* 93, no. 1–2 (2009): 1–13.

Haber, S. H., A. Razo, and N. Maurer. *The Politics of Property Rights: Political Instability, Credible Commitments, and Economic Growth in Mexico, 1876–1929.* 2003.

Haggard, S., A. MacIntyre, and L. Tiede. "The Rule of Law and Economic Development." *Annual Review of Political Science* 11 (2008): 205–34.

Haggard, S., S. Maxfield, and B. R. Schneider. "Theories of Business and Business-State Relations." In *Business and the State in Developing Countries*, edited by S. Maxfield and B. R. Schneider, 36–62: Ithaca, NY: Cornell University Press, 1997.

Hall, R. E., and C. I. Jones. "Why Do Some Countries Produce So Much More Output Per Worker Than Others?" *Quarterly Journal of Economics* 114, no. 1 (1999): 83–116.

Hellman, J. S., G. Jones, and D. Kaufmann. "Seize the State, Seize the Day: State Capture and Influence in Transition Economies." *Journal of Comparative Economics* 31, no. 4 (2003): 751–73.

Hendley, Kathryn. "Assessing the Rule of Law in Russia." *Cardozo Journal of International and Comparative Law* 14 (2006): 347.

Hirschman, A. O. *Exit, Voice, and Loyalty: Responses to Decline in Firms, Organizations, and States*. Cambridge, MA: Harvard University Press, 1970.

Hobbes, T. *Leviathan*. New York: Liberal Arts, 1958.

Hough, J. F. *The Logic of Economic Reform in Russia*. Washington, DC: Brookings Institution Press, 2001.

Hume, David. *A Treatise of Human Nature*. Oxford: Oxford University Press, 1978.

Humphreys, Macartan, and Robert H Bates. "Political Institutions and Economic Policies: Lessons from Africa." *British Journal of Political Science* 35, no. 3 (2005): 403–28.

Hutchison, K. B. "Democracy and the Rule of Law." *International Law* 39 (2005): 663.

Interfax "Zakon Bessilen Pered Reiderami." October 13, 2009.

Izvestiya "Byurokratichesky Front. Deputaty Horoniat Zakonoproekt O Licenzirovanii." June 30, 2001.

"Po Zakonu Al'fy [According to Alfa's Law]." February 3, 2006.

"Dmitrii' Medvedev Razgranichil Torgovliu I Rei'derstvo." November 6, 2009.

"Korrupciya V Rosreestre: Kuda Uhodiat Narodnye Den'gi?" April 27, 2010.

"Reiderskikh Zakhvatov Stanovitsia Vse Bol'she." April 12, 2012.

Jensen, Nathan. "Political Risk, Democratic Institutions, and Foreign Direct Investment." *Journal of Politics* 70, no. 4 (2008): 1040–52.

Johnson, S., J. McMillan, and C. Woodruff. "Property Rights and Finance." *The American Economic Review* 92, no. 5 (2002): 1335–56.

Kaiser, Kai, and Stephanie Wolters. "Fragile States, Elites, and Rents in the Democratic Republic of Congo." In *In the Shadow of Violence: The Problem of Development in Limited Access Societies*, edited by Douglass Cecil North, John Joseph Wallis, Steven Benjamin Webb, and Barry R Weingast, 70–111. Cambridge: Cambridge University Press, 2013.

Kapeliushnikov, Rostislav, Andrei Kuznetsov, Natalia Demina, and Olga Kuznetsova. "Threats to Security of Property Rights in a Transition Economy: An Empirical Perspective." *Journal of Comparative Economics* (2012).

Kapital Strany "Boris Titov: Pravozashchitnik Mezhdu Biznesom I Vlast'yu." August 1, 2012.

Keefer, P., and S. Knack. "Polarization, Politics and Property Rights: Links between Inequality and Growth." *Public Choice* 111, no. 1 (2002): 127–54.

Bibliography

Khan, Mushtaq. "Determinants of Corruption in Developing Countries." In *International Handbook on the Economics of Corruption*, edited by Susan Rose-Ackerman, 216–46: London: Edward Elgar Publishing, 2006.

"Bangladesh: Economic Growth in a Vulnerable Lao." In *In the Shadow of Violence: The Problem of Development in Limited Access Societies*, edited by Douglass Cecil North, John Joseph Wallis, Steven Benjamin Webb, and Barry R Weingast, 24–69. Cambridge: Cambridge University Press, 2013.

Kiser, E. "Markets and Hierarchies in Early Modern Tax Systems: A Principal-Agent Analysis." *Politics & Society* 22, no. 3 (1994): 284–315.

Kleiner, Vadim. "How Should Gazprom Be Managed in Russia's National Interests and the Interests of Its Shareholders?" 2005.

Klitgaard, Robert. *Controlling Corruption*. Berkeley: University of California Press, 1991.

"Cleaning up and Invigorating the Civil Service." *Public Administration and Development* 17, no. 5 (1997): 487–509.

Kobrin, Stephen J. "Expropriation as an Attempt to Control Foreign Firms in LDCs: Trends from 1960 to 1979." *International Studies Quarterly* (1984): 329–48.

Kolennikova, O., L. Kosals, and R. Rybkina. "Kommercializatsia Sluzhebnoy Deyatel'nosti Rabotnikov Militsii." *Sotsiologiya prava* (2004): 73–83.

Kommersant "Demokraty Voznamerilis' Ob'edinit' Predprinimatelej." October 30, 1993.

"Zhivye I Mertvye." September 2, 1995.

"Sos-Menedzhment." July 14, 2003.

"Dlya Al'fa-Grupp 4,4 Milliarda Ne Den'gi [for Alfa Group 4.4 Billion Is No Big Deal.]." December 9, 2004.

"Odin I Bez Pokrytiya: Gazprom Idet Na Aukcion Bez Deneg." December 18, 2004.

"Plyus 'Yukosizaciya' Vsey Strany: Sergei Stepashin Obosnoval Peresmotr Itogov Privatizacii." January 17, 2005.

"Viktor Yushchenko Ravnopriblizil Oligarhov." October 17, 2005.

"Reidery Uhodiat Iz Saratova." May 23, 2006.

"Mert Otkryvaet Antireiderskuyu Kampaniyu." October 26, 2006.

"Velikaya Zakhvatnicheskaya Voina." April 16, 2007.

"Gollandiya Ne Priznala Yukos Bankrotom." November 1, 2007.

"Provoevavshiesia: Piatiletny Konflikt Al'fa-Grupp I Telenor Zavershen." October 6, 2009.

"Aleksandr Bastrykin Meniaet Pogony." September 24, 2010.

"Sergei Borisov, Prezident 'Opory Rossii.'" November 15, 2010.

"Do Primorskogo Gubernatora Delo Ne Doshlo." February 4, 2011.

"Vladimir Putin Prishel Za Energetikami." December 19, 2011.

"Upolnomochenny Budet Ne Tol'ko Zashchishchat' No I Napadat'." July 10, 2012.

Kommersant-Daily "German Gref Nashel Oporu V Dume." March 21, 2001.

"Duma Vygryzla Byurokratizm." June 8, 2001.

Kommersant Den'gi "Otpetye Zakhvatchiki." October 10, 2011.

Kommersant Ukraina "Yuri Yekhanurov Reshil Vernut' Eshe Odin Zavod." November 30, 2005.

"Mirovoe Razglashenie." December 8, 2005.

Bibliography

Kommersant (Volgograd) "Saratovcev Vyveli Pomolchat' Protiv Samarskih Reiderov [Saratov Residents Led to Protest against Samara Raiders]." April 7, 2006.
Korrespondent "Intsident S Lozinskim." June 23, 2009.
Kosals, L., and A. Dubova. "Vlkyuchennost' Rossiiskih Politseiskih V Tenevuyu Ekonomiku." *Otechestvennye Zapiski* 2, no. 47 (2012): 1–12.
Krasnov, M., K. Kabanov, S. Vasina, E. Panfilova, E. Golenkova, and G. Shantin. "Predlozheniya Po Povysheniyu Effektivnosti Bor'by S Reiderstvom (Nezakonnym Zahvatom Sobstvennosti)." *Nevizhimost' i investitsii. Pravovoe regulirovanie* 1, no. 38 (2009): 58–72.
Krymskaya Pravda "Zaslon on Byurokratii." December 29, 2012.
Kudelia, Serhiy. "The Sources of Continuity and Change of Ukraine's Incomplete State." *Communist and Post-Communist Studies* 45, no. 3 (2012): 417–28.
Kuzio, Taras. "Twenty Years as an Independent State: Ukraine's Ten Logical Inconsistencies." *Communist and Post-Communist Studies* 45, no. 3 (2012): 429–38.
Lebedev, Aleksandr. "Oppozitsiya Dolzhna Zabyt' Ob Otdyhe." *Snob.ru* (2012).
Leblang, D. A. "Property Rights, Democracy and Economic Growth." *Political Research Quarterly* 49, no. 1 (1996): 5.
Ledeneva, Alena V. *Can Russia Modernise? Sistema, Power Networks and Informal Governance*. Cambridge: Cambridge University Press, 2013.
Levi, Margaret. "The Predatory Theory of Rule." *Politics and Society* 10, no. 4 (1981): 431–65.
  Of Rule and Revenue. Vol. 13. Berkeley: University of California Press, 1989.
  "Why We Need a New Theory of Government." *Perspectives on Politics* 4, no. 1 (2006): 5–19.
Li, Quan. "Democracy, Autocracy, and Expropriation of Foreign Direct Investment." *Comparative Political Studies* 42, no. 8 (2009): 1098–1127.
Literaturnaia gazeta "Rei'derov Zakazyvali?" January 28, 2009.
Luong, P. J., and E. Weinthal. "Contra Coercion: Russian Tax Reform, Exogenous Shocks, and Negotiated Institutional Change." *American Political Science Review* 98, no. 1 (2004): 139–52.
Machiavelli, N. *Discourses on Livy*. Translated by H. C. Mansfield and N. Tarcov. Chicago: University of Chicago Press, 1998.
Mahoney, J. "After Kkv: The New Methodology of Qualitative Research." *World Politics* 62, no. 1 (2010): 120.
Malesky, E., and M. Taussig. "Out of the Gray: The Impact of Provincial Institutions on Business Formalization in Vietnam." *Journal of East Asian Studies* 9, no. 2 (2008): 249–90.
Mann, M. "Infrastructural Power Revisited." *Studies in Comparative International Development (SCID)* 43, no. 3 (2008): 355–65.
  The Autonomous Power of the State. Oxford: Blackwell, 1984.
Markus, Stanislav. "Capitalists of All Russia, Unite! Business Mobilization under Debilitated Dirigisme." *Polity* 39, no. 3 (2007): 277–304.
  "Corporate Governance as Political Insurance: Firm-Level Institutional Creation in Emerging Markets and Beyond." *Socio-Economic Review* 6, no. 1 (2008): 69–98.
Maxfield, S., and B. R. Schneider, eds. *Business and the State in Developing Countries*: Ithaca, NY: Cornell University Press, 1997.

Bibliography

McDermott, G. A. *Embedded Politics: Industrial Networks and Institutional Change in Postcommunism*. Ann Arbor: University of Michigan Press, 2002.

"Institutional Change and Firm Creation in East-Central Europe." *Comparative Political Studies* 37, no. 2 (2004): 188–217.

Medard, Jean-Francois. "Corruption in the Neo-Patrimonial States of Sub-Saharan Africa." In *Political Corruption: Concepts and Contexts*, edited by Arnold J Heidenheimer and Michael Johnston, 379–402. New Brunswick, NJ: Transaction Publishers, 2002.

MEDT. "Doklad "O Sostoianii Sistemy Gosudarstvennogo Kontrolia (Nadzora) I Municipal'nogo Kontrolia V Rossiiskoi Federacii". [Report "on the Condition of the System of State Control (Monitoring) and Municipal Control in the Russian Federation"]. Moscow, Russia, 2010.

Mishra, Ajit. "Corruption, Hierarchies and Bureaucratic Structure." In *International Handbook on the Economics of Corruption*, edited by Susan Rose-Ackerman, 189–215: London: Edward Elgar Publishing, 2006.

Moe, T. M. "The Politics of Structural Choice: Toward a Theory of Public Bureaucracy." In *Organization Theory: From Chester Barnard to the Present and Beyond*, edited by O. E. Williamson, 116–53: New York: Oxford University Press, 1995.

Montinola, Gabriella. "Change and Continuity in a Limited Access Order: The Philippines." In *In the Shadow of Violence: The Problem of Development in Limited Access Societies*, edited by Douglass Cecil North, John Joseph Wallis, Steven Benjamin Webb, and Barry R Weingast, 149–97. Cambridge: Cambridge University Press, 2013.

Morozov, Valerii. "Putin Naznachit 'Den' Dlinnykh Nozhey' Do Novogo Goda." *Snob. ru* (2011).

"Printsip Pervy: Antikorruptsionnost'." *Snob.ru* (2012).

Moskovksie Novosti "My Ne Sdaem Imena V Arendu [We Do Not Rent out Our Names]." August 5, 2003.

"Bazal't Pod Pressom." March 30, 2007.

"Zhertvy Vto." March 1, 2012.

Moskovskaya Pravda "Novyi Peredel Sobstvennosti." February 27, 2009.

Moskovskii Komsomolets "Reidery Prorvali Oboronku." April 11, 2008.

"Neprikasaemyi Bastrykin." November 19, 2009.

"Novyi Peredel Sobstvennosti." February 9, 2009.

Most Kharkov "Aleksandr Duker: Ya Prodolzhu Stroitel'stvo Esli Budut Garantii Prezidenta." September 26, 2011.

Murphy, Anne L. "Demanding 'Credible Commitment': Public Reactions to the Failures of the Early Financial Revolution." *The Economic History Review* 66, no. 1 (2013): 178–97.

Mushkat, Miron, and Roda Mushkat. "The Political Economy of Corruption in China: The Principal–Agent Dimension." *International Journal of Public Law and Policy* 2, no. 3 (2012): 263–86.

Nemtsov, Boris, and Vladimir Milov. "Putin. Itogi. 10 Let." In *Nezavisimy Ekspertny Doklad*. Moscow: Solidarnost', 2010.

NEWSru "Gosduma Otlozhila Slushanie Doklada Schetnoy Palaty Ob Itogah Privatizacii." December 8, 2004.

"Timoshenko Gotova Posadit' Za Reshetku Kirovogradskogo 'Strelka-Byutovca' Lozinskogo." June 26, 2009.

Bibliography

Nezavisimaia gazeta "Rei'derstvo Po–Tuvinski." May 24, 2012.

Nickson, Andrew. "Democratisation and Institutional Corruption in Paraguay." In *Political Corruption in Europe and Latin America*, edited by Eduardo Posada Carbó and Little Walter, 237–66. New York: St. Martin's Press, 1996.

North, D. C. *Institutions, Institutional Change, and Economic Performance.* Cambridge: Cambridge University Press, 1990.

North, D. C., and B. R. Weingast. "Constitutions and Commitment: The Evolution of Institutions Governing Public Choice in Seventeenth-Century England." *The Journal of Economic History* 49, no. 4 (1989): 803–32.

North, D. C., J. J. Wallis, and B. R. Weingast. *Violence and Social Orders: A Conceptual Framework for Interpreting Recorded Human History.* Cambridge: Cambridge University Press, 2009.

North, Douglass Cecil, and Robert Paul Thomas. *The Rise of the Western World: A New Economic History.* Cambridge: Cambridge University Press, 1973.

North, Douglass Cecil, John Joseph Wallis, Steven Benjamin Webb, and Barry R Weingast. *In the Shadow of Violence: The Problem of Development in Limited Access Societies.* Cambridge: Cambridge University Press, 2013.

Novaya Gazeta "Ekonomika Dolzhna Byt'. Gosudarstvo Usilivaetsia, a Ekonomika Osvobozhdaetsia?" July 5, 2001.

"Nepravitel'stvenny Doklad: Koleya Rossii." February 7, 2005.

"Aleksandr Bastrykin: 10 Tysiach Ugolovnyh Del Po Faktam Korruptsii Vozbuzhdeno Tol'ko V Proshlom Godu." May 18, 2009.

"Daniil Dondurej: 'Vse Soglasny Na Moral'nuyu Katastrofu'." November 9, 2011.

"Kartel' I Zakon." February 1, 2012.

"Chtoby Vyzhit' Putin Dolzhen Stat' Stalinym." December 3, 2012.

Novoe Vremia "Raby Omona." February 1, 2010.

Novy Region "V Sochi Sanatorii "Matsestinskaya Dolina" Zakhvatili Vooruzhennye Lyudi." July 7, 2008.

Novye Izvestiya "Delovaya Rossiya Pod Vpechatleniem." October 18, 2001.

"Ataka Na Telenor Sorvalas' [The Attack on Telenor Failed.]." February 20, 2006.

Offe, Claus. "The Attribution of Public Status to Interest Groups." In *Organizing Interests in Western Europe*, edited by Suzanne Berger. Cambridge: Cambridge University Press, 1981.

Ogoniok "Reideromafiya." May 16, 2007.

Oi, J. C., and A. Walder, eds. *Property Rights and Economic Reform in China*: Stanford, CA: Stanford University Press, 1999.

Olson, M. "Dictatorship, Democracy, and Development." *The American Political Science Review* 87, no. 3 (1993): 567–76.

Olson, Mancur. *"Power and Prosperity: Outgrowing Capitalist and Communist Dictatorships."* New York: Basic Books, 2000.

ORD "General Moskal' O Novoy 'Milicii S Narodom'." September 7, 2012.

OSCE. "Russian Federation, State Duma Elections – Statement of Preliminary Findings and Conclusions." Moscow: OSCE/ODIHR Election Observation Mission, 2011.

Ostrom, E. *Governing the Commons: The Evolution of Institutions for Collective Action.* Cambridge: Cambridge University Press, 1990.

Paskhaver, O., L. Verkhovodova, and K. Ageeva. *Pryvatyzacija ta Repryvatyzacija v Ukraini Pislya Pomaranchevoi Revolyucii.* Kiev: Milenium, 2006.

Bibliography

Pastukhov, V. "Law under Administrative Pressure in Post-Soviet Russia." *East European Constitutional Review* 11 (2002): 66.

Peregudov, Sergey. *Korporatsii, Obshchestvo, Gosudarstvo: Evolyutsiya Otnosheniy.* Moscow: Nauka, 2003.

Pistor, Katharina, Martin Raiser, and Stanislaw Gelfer. "Law and Finance in Transition Economies." *Economics of Transition* 8, no. 2 (2000): 325–68.

Podrobnosti "Kompaniya 'Khar'kov-Moskva' Obvinyaet Kernesa V Reiderstve." October 5, 2011.

Polsky, A. "When Business Speaks: Political Entrepreneurship, Discourse and Mobilization in American Partisan Regimes." *Journal of Theoretical Politics* 12, no. 4 (2000): 455–76.

Popova, Maria. "Implicit Objections to the Rule of Law Doctrine in Russian Legal Thought." *Journal of East European Law* 11, no. 2–3 (2004): 205–29.

Politicized Justice in Emerging Democracies: A Study of Courts in Russia and Ukraine. Cambridge: Cambridge University Press, 2012.

Post, Alison. *Foreign and Domestic Investment in Argentina: The Politics of Privatized Infrastructure.* New York: Cambridge University Press, 2014.

Pravda "Ostanovit' Nashestvie Reiderov." October 22, 2009.

Pravo "Medvedev: 'Vorovstvo Pri Goszakupkah Mozhno Snizit' Na 1 Trln'." October 29, 2010.

PricewaterhouseCoopers. "Ukraina: Ekonomichni Zlochyny U Period Kryzy." 2009.

"Rossiya – Obzor Ekonomicheskih Prestupleniy – 2011." 2012.

Prime-Tass "Vimpelcom Holders Can up Stakes without Permission Soon." August 9, 2006.

PriMetrica "Putin Removes Reiman and Scraps Ministry Following Spat with Vimpelcom." March 10, 2004.

PRiZ "'Pravovoe Reiderstvo' Ili Kak Zashchitit' Svoy Biznes?" November 23, 2011.

Profil' "Strashny Sud." August 30, 2010.

Pryadil'nikov, M. "The State and Markets in Russia – Understanding the Development of Bureaucratic Implementation Capacities through the Study of Regulatory Reform, 2001–2008." Dissertation defended at Harvard University, 2009.

Przeworski, A. *Democracy and the Market.* New York: Cambridge University Press, 1991.

Przeworski, Adam, and José María Maravall. *Democracy and the Rule of Law.* Vol. 5 Cambridge: Cambridge University Press, 2003.

QFinance "Lessons from Russia." 2009.

Qian, Y., and B. R. Weingast. "Federalism as a Commitment to Preserving Market Incentives." *The Journal of Economic Perspectives* 11, no. 4 (1997): 83–92.

Radnitz, Scott. "The Color of Money: Privatization, Economic Dispersion, and the Post-Soviet Revolutions." *Comparative Politics* 42, no. 2 (2010): 127–46.

Weapons of the Wealthy: Predatory Regimes and Elite-Led Protests in Central Asia. Ithaca, NY: Cornell University Press, 2010.

Rajan, R., and L. Zingales. *Saving Capitalism from the Capitalists: Unleashing the Power of Financial Markets to Create Wealth and Spread Opportunity.* Princeton, NJ: Princeton University Press, 2004.

Rajan, Raghuram, and Luigi Zingales. "The Emergence of Strong Property Rights: Speculation from History." National Bureau of Economic Research, 2003.

Razo, Armando. *Social Foundations of Limited Dictatorship*. Palo Alto, CA: Stanford University Press, 2008.

RBK Daily "Andrei Loginov O Ministerstvah." December 25, 2012.

Remington, Thomas F. "The Russian Middle Class as Policy Objective." *Post-Soviet Affairs* 27, no. 2 (2011): 97–120.

Reno, W. *Warlord Politics and African States*. Boulder, CO: Lynne Rienner, 1998.

Reuter, O. J., and T. F. Remington. "Dominant Party Regimes and the Commitment Problem." *Comparative Political Studies* 42, no. 4 (2009): 501–26.

Reuters "Prezident Ukrainy Zaveril, Chto Vozvrata K Reprivatizacii Ne Budet." October 6, 2005.

"Statoil Sees 'Serious' Shtokman Risks – Wikileaks." January 7, 2011.

"Yukos Unit Wins $1.2 Bln Refinery Proceeds Case." January 7, 2011.

RF. "Koncepciya Administrativnoj Reformy V Rossijskoj Federacii V 2006–2008 Godah [Conception of the Administrative Reform in the Russian Federation in the Years 2006–08], Approved by Government Order No 1789-R on October 25." 2005.

Robinson, J. A. "Economic Development and Democracy." *Annual Review of Political Science* 9 (2006): 503–27.

Rodrik, D. *One Economics, Many Recipes: Globalization, Institutions, and Economic Growth*. Princeton, NJ: Princeton University Press, 2007.

Rodrik, Dani. "Second-Best Institutions." *American Economic Review* 98, no. 2 (2008): 100–4.

Roland, Gerard. "Corporate Governance and Transition Economies." In *Annual World Bank Conference on Development Economics 2000*, edited by Boris Pleskovič and Nicholas Herbert Stern, 331–52. Washington, DC: World Bank Publications, 2001.

Root, H. L. "Tying the King's Hands." *Rationality and Society* 1, no. 2 (1989): 240.

Rose-Ackerman, Susan. *Corruption: A Study in Political Economy*. New York: Academic Press, 1978.

Corruption and Government: Causes, Consequences, and Reform. Cambridge: Cambridge University Press, 1999.

ed. *International Handbook on the Economics of Corruption*: London: Edward Elgar Publishing, 2006.

Rosenthal, Jean-Laurent. *The Fruits of Revolution: Property Rights, Litigation, and French Agriculture, 1700–1860*. The Political Economy of Institutions and Decisions. Cambridge, New York: Cambridge University Press, 1992.

Rosrazvitie. "Vrazhdebnye Pogloshcheniya V Ukraine." Kyiv, Ukraine, 2007.

Rossiiskaya Biznes Gazeta "Korporativnyi Shantazh." October 13, 2009.

Rossiiskaya Gazeta "Dmitri Medvedev Poruchil Silovikam Sledit' Za "Reiderami V Pogonakh"." July 2, 2010.

"Ob'edinit' Usiliya." July 19, 2010.

Rossii'skie vesti "'Oranzhevaia Revoliutsiia' I Rei'derstvo." May 14, 2012.

"Rei'derstvo – Osnova Kriminal'nogo Kapitalizma." October 22, 2012.

Russky Kur'er "Kto Spaset 'Bazal't'?" December 3, 2007.

Schlesinger Jr, A. "Has Democracy a Future?" *Foreign Affairs* (1997): 2–12.

Schneider, B. R. "Why Is Mexican Business So Organized?" *Latin American Research Review* (2002): 77–118.

Schoenman, Roger. *Networks and Institutions in Europe's Emerging Markets*. New York: Cambridge University Press, 2014.

Bibliography

Segodnya "Otbit'sia Ot Grefa. Chinovnikam Udalos' Otlozhit' Vopros O Sokrashchenii Kolichestva Vidov Litsenzirovaniya." May 15, 2001.

"Kriminal'naya Hronika 20 Let: Kak Ukraincy Narushali Zakon." June 11, 2012.

Semidid'ko, Andrei. "Korporativnye Konflikty: Nacional'nye Osobennosti Ukrainy." *Vrazhdebnye Pogloshcheniya v Ukraine* (2007): 26–8.

Sened, Itai. *The Political Institution of Private Property.* Cambridge: Cambridge University Press, 1997.

Shah, A. "Tailoring the Fight against Corruption to Country Circumstances." In *Performance Accountability and Combating Corruption,* edited by Anwar Shah. Washington, DC: The World Bank, 2007.

Shevtsova, Lilia. "Russia under Putin: Titanic Looking for Its Iceberg?" *Communist and Post-Communist Studies* (2012).

Shipan, C. R. "Regulatory Regimes, Agency Actions, and the Conditional Nature of Congressional Influence." *American Political Science Review* 98 (2004): 467–80.

Shlapentokh, Vladimir. *Contemporary Russia as a Feudal Society: A New Perspective on the Post-Soviet Era.* Palgrave Macmillan, 2007.

Shleifer, A., and D. Treisman. *Without a Map: Political Tactics and Economic Reform in Russia.* Cambridge, MA: MIT Press, 2001.

Shleifer, A., and R. W. Vishny. "Corruption." *The Quarterly Journal of Economics* 108, no. 3 (1993): 599–617.

Shleifer, Andrei, and Robert W. Vishny. *The Grabbing Hand: Government Pathologies and Their Cures.* Cambridge, MA: Harvard University Press, 1998.

Silva, E. *The State and Capital in Chile: Business Elites, Technocrats, and Market Economics.* Westview Press, 1996.

Skvazhina "10% Akciy Nk Yukos Peredano Fondu Veteran Petroleum." May 4, 2001.

Sliyaniya i Pogloshcheniya "Titov Vzyalsia Za Pervoe 'Reiderskoe' Delo." October 9, 2012.

Smirnov, G. "Organizovannaya Prestupnost' I Mery Po Ee Presecheniyu." Ekaterinburg: MVD RF, 1995.

Solnick, S. L. *Stealing the State: Control and Collapse in Soviet Institutions.* Cambridge, MA: Harvard University Press, 1999.

Sonin, K. "Why the Rich May Favor Poor Protection of Property Rights." *Journal of Comparative Economics* 31, no. 4 (2003): 715–31.

Sovetskaya Belorussiya "Zakony Protiv Reiderov." November 21, 2012.

Starodubskaya, Marina. "*Corporate Social Responsibility View of Ukrainian Business.*" Dissertation, defended at Kiev, Ukraine: International Institute of Business Centre, 2005.

Stasavage, D. *Public Debt and the Birth of the Democratic State: France and Great Britain, 1688–1789.* Cambridge: Cambridge University Press, 2003.

Stepashin, Sergei. "Analiz Prozessov Privatizacii Gosudarstvennoy Sobstvennosti V Rossiyskoy Federacii Za Period 1993–2003 Gody." Edited by the Audit Chamber of the Russian Federation: Olita, 2004.

Stereophile "Tube Supplies under Siege." May 20, 2006.

Stoletie "Pochemu Zatknuli Rot Stepashinu." February 11, 2005.

Stoner-Weiss, K. *Resisting the State: Reform and Retrenchment in Post-Soviet Russia.* Cambridge: Cambridge University Press, 2006.

Stratfor. "The Impact of Yukos on the EU-Russia Energy Relationship." Stratfor Global Intelligence, 2013.

Strebkov, D. "Neformal'naya Ekonomicheskaya Deyatel'nost' Politsii: Sravnitel'ny Analiz Transformiruyushchihsia Stran." Higher School of Economics, 2012.

Strouse, Jean. *Morgan: American Financier.* HarperCollins, 2000.

Stulz, R. M. "The Limits of Financial Globalization." *Journal of Finance* 60, no. 4 (2005): 1595–638.

Svensson, J. "Investment, Property Rights and Political Instability: Theory and Evidence." *European Economic Review* 42, no. 7 (1998): 1317–41.

Tambovcev, V., ed. *Prava Sobstvennosti, Privatizaciya I Nacionalizaciya V Rossii.* Moscow: Fond Liberal'naya Missiya, 2009.

Tansey, O. "Process Tracing and Elite Interviewing: A Case for Non-Probability Sampling." *PS: Political Science and Politics* 40, October (2007): 765–72.

Tema "Viktor Lozinsky: Stolichny 'Pochtal'on' I Provintsial'ny Barin." June 26, 2009.

The Economist "Vladimir Putin Takes on Democracy, the West and All-Comers." December 9, 2004.

"A Spectre of Litigation: Adverse Court Rulings Are Exhuming Russia's Most Infamous Expropriation." March 25, 2010.

"Gunvor: Riddles, Mysteries and Enigmas." May 5, 2012.

"Old-Fashioned Theft Is Still the Biggest Problem for Foreign Companies in China." February 23, 2013.

The Guardian "Russia Ordered to Pay $50bn in Damages to Yukos Shareholders." July 28, 2014.

The Moscow Times "Big Setbacks Give Gazprom Impetus for Change." September 27, 2012.

The New York Times "How Russian Oil Tycoon Courted Friends in U.S." November 5, 2003.

"Investors of the World, Here's the Word on Putin Inc." March 2, 2005.

"From Russia, with Dread." May 16, 2006.

"A Victory for Holders of Yukos." December 1, 2009.

"Leaked Cables Offer Raw Look at U.S. Diplomacy." November 29, 2010.

"Ukraine's Slide." March 4, 2012.

"As Putin's Grip Gets Tighter, a Time of Protest Fades in Russia." January 5, 2013.

The New Yorker "Net Impact: One Man's Cyber-Crusade against Russian Corruption." April 4, 2011.

Timmons, J. F. "The Fiscal Contract: States, Taxes, and Public Services." *World Politics* 57, no. 4 (2006): 530–67.

Tompson, W. "Putin's Challenge: The Politics of Structural Reform in Russia." *Europe-Asia Studies* 54, no. 6 (2002): 933–57.

"From "Clientelism" to a "Client-Centred Orientation"? The Challenge of Public Administration Reform in Russia." In *Economics Department Working Paper No. 536*: OECD, 2007.

Transparency International. "National Integrity System Assessment: Ukraine 2011." Kirovohrad, Ukraine, 2011.

Tribuna "Protivoyadie Ot Reidera." April 11, 2008.

Tsai, K. S. "Adaptive Informal Institutions and Endogenous Institutional Change in China." *World Politics* 59, no. 1 (2007): 116–41.

Tsai, L. L. "Solidary Groups, Informal Accountability, and Local Public Goods Provision in Rural China." *American Political Science Review* 101, no. 2 (2007): 355–72.

Bibliography

Ukraina-Centr "Bez Svideteley Ili Ubit Pri Zaderzhanii." June 24, 2009.

Ukrains'ka Pravda "K Yushchenko Prishli 20 Oligarhov I Posol Rossii." March 14, 2005.

"Kinakh Nastaivaet Chto U Kabmina Est' Spisok V 29 Predpriyatii." May 17, 2005.

"U Semenyuk V Chernom Spiske 199 Predpriyatii." May 30, 2005.

Ukrainskaya Pravda "Timoshenko I Litvin Pri Yushchenko Dogovorilis' O Garantiyah Sobstvennosti." June 16, 2005.

Ukrains'ka Pravda "Yushchenko Zadabrivaet 20 Oligarhov." October 14, 2005.

"Gpu Ustanovila Chto Lozinskii Umyshlenno Ubil Cheloveka." July 3, 2009.

"Vot Iz-Za Takikh Syuzhetov Kernes Zakryl Veshchanie Nezavisimogo Tv V Har'kove." September 28, 2011.

"V Odesi Vlashtuvaly "Maski-Shou" V Sotcial'nykh Idal'niakh." November 8, 2011.

"Zakhopyty Biznes V Ukraini Deshevshe, Nizh Kupyty." February 9, 2012.

"Strategiya Teplogo Okeanu." December 6, 2013.

"U Firtasha Rozpovily Pro Masshtaby Koruptsii Pry Yanukovychi." February 26, 2014.

Ukrainskie Novosti "Yushchenko, Timoshenko I Litvin Dogovorilis' O Garantiyah Prav Sobstvennosti." June 16, 2005.

Vedomosti "Minyust Naznachat Registratorom." December 5, 2000.

"Usilit'sia Li Vliyanie Rspp Na Priniatie Reshenii Pravitel'stvom?" June 27, 2001.

"Liberal'nee Grefa?" June 29, 2001.

"Kto Oplatil Yugansk." June 3, 2005.

"Samarskii Fuz." May 12, 2006.

"Dobrosovestnye Rei'dery." April 25, 2007.

"Bastrykin Meniaet Komandu." March 20, 2009.

"Bastrykin Uzhe Ne Protiv." February 12, 2010.

"Leonid Reiman Ushel V Otstavku." September 10, 2010.

"Mif o Biurokratii. Nevernaia Problema, Oshibochnoe Reshenie." February 17, 2011.

"Rei'derstvo Ili Tiur'ma." July 20, 2011.

"Chinovniki Meshayut Razvivat'sia Ekonomike Rossii." December 21, 2011.

"Bol'shinstvo Rossiyan Schitaet Chto 'Edinaya Rossiya' – Partiya Zhulikov I Vorov." April 29, 2013.

"Levada-Centr: Lozung "Rossiya Bez Putina" Podderzhivayut Uzhe 24% Rossiyan." May 7, 2013.

Versiya "Tiazhelaya Utrata: Chinovnikov Budut Uvol'niat' Sotniami, Esli Oni Vyjdut Iz Doveriya Rukovodstva." July 11, 2011.

Voslensky, M. *Nomenklatura: The Soviet Ruling Class–An Insider's Report.* New York, Doubleday and Co., 1984.

Volkov, V., E. Paneyakh, and K. Titaev. "Proizvol'naya Aktivnost' Pravoohranitel'nyh Organov V Sfere Bor'by S Ekonomicheskoy Prestupnost'yu." St. Petersburg, Russia: The Institute for the Rule of Law, 2010.

Volkov, Vadim. "Violent Entrepreneurship in Post-Communist Russia." *Europe-Asia Studies* 51, no. 5 (1999): 741–54.

"Standard Oil and Yukos in the Context of Early Capitalism in the United States and Russia." *Demokratizatsyia* 16, no. 3 (2008): 240–64.

Vremya Novostey "Rastushchiy Organizm: Za Desyat' Let Nepreryvnogo Sokrashcheniya Chinovnikov V Rossii Ih Chislo Postoyanno Uvelichivaestsya." July 30, 2010.

Vslukh "Soyuz Soglasiya I Primireniya." December 10, 2003.

Vzglyad "Skhvatka Za Chetvert' Megafona [The Battle for a Quarter of Megafon.]." July 26, 2005.

"Zoloto Za Schet Byudzheta." March 7, 2011.

Waller, Christopher J, Thierry Verdier, and Roy Gardner. "Corruption: Top Down or Bottom Up?" *Economic Inquiry* 40, no. 4 (2002): 688–703.

Wang, S. T., M. L. Yu, C. J. Wang, and C. C. Huang. "Bridging the Gap between the Pros and Cons in Treating Ordinal Scales as Interval Scales from an Analysis Point of View." *Nursing Research* 48, no. 4 (1999): 226.

Way, Lucan. "Kuchma's Failed Authoritarianism." *Journal of Democracy* 16, no. 2 (2005): 131–45.

Wedeman, Andrew. "Looters, Rent-Scrapers, and Dividend-Collectors: Corruption and Growth in Zaire, South Korea, and the Philippines." *The Journal of Developing Areas* 31, no. 4 (1997): 457–78.

Wegren, Stephen K. *Land Reform in the Former Soviet Union and Eastern Europe.* London: Routledge, 2003.

Weimer, D. L. "The Political Economy of Property Rights." In *The Political Economy of Property Rights: Institutional Change and Credibility in the Reform of Centrally Planned Economies,* edited by D. L. Weimer, 1–19. New York: Cambridge University Press, 1997.

——— ed. *The Political Economy of Property Rights: Institutional Change and Credibility in the Reform of Centrally Planned Economies.* New York: Cambridge University Press, 1997.

Weingast, B. R., and M. J. Moran. "Bureaucratic Discretion or Congressional Control? Regulatory Policymaking by the Federal Trade Commission." *The Journal of Political Economy* (1983): 765–800.

Weingast, Barry R. "The Role of Credible Commitments in State Finance." *Public Choice* 66, no. 1 (1990): 89–97.

——— "Constitutions as Governance Structures: The Political Foundations of Secure Markets." *Journal of Institutional and Theoretical Economics* 149, no. 1 (1993): 286–311.

Weymouth, S. "Political Institutions and Property Rights: Veto Players and Foreign Exchange Commitments in 127 Countries." *Comparative Political Studies* 44, no. 2 (2011): 211–40.

Williamson, O. E. *Markets and Hierarchies.* New York: Free Press, 1983.

Winters, J. A. *Oligarchy.* Cambridge: Cambridge University Press, 2011.

Woodruff, David. "Property Rights in Context: Privatization's Legacy for Corporate Legality in Poland and Russia." *Studies in Comparative International Development* 38, no. 4 (2004): 82–108.

——— "Law's Authorizations and Rule of Law Ideals: Lessons from Russia." *Georgia Journal of International and Comparative Law* 41 (2012): 157.

World Bank. "Where Is the Wealth of Nations." 2006.

Wright, Joseph. "Do Authoritarian Institutions Constrain? How Legislatures Affect Economic Growth and Investment." *American Journal of Political Science* 52, no. 2 (2008): 322–43.

Bibliography

Wyckoff, P. G. "The Simple Analytics of Slack-Maximizing Bureaucracy." *Public Choice* 67, no. 1 (1990): 35–47.

Yakovlev, A. "Evolyuciya Vzaimootnosheniy Mezhdu Gosudarstvom I Biznesom: Ot 'Privatizatsii Gosudarstva' K Zahvatu Biznesa?" In *Institutsional'nye problemy rossiyskoy ekonomiki*. Moscow: Higher School of Economics, 2005.

Yurgens, Igor. "Corporate Social Responsibility of Russian Companies (Speech at Economic Forum)." 2008.

Zerkalov, D. *Reiderstvo*. Kiev: Osnova, 2011.

Zmora, Hillay. *Monarchy, Aristocracy and State in Europe 1300–1800*. East Sussex, UK: Psychology Press, 2001.

Zudin, Aleksei. "Sistema Predstavitel'stva Rossiyskogo Biznesa: Formy Kollektivnogo Deystviya." Moscow: Tsentr Politicheskikh Tekhnologii, 1997.

"Associacii I Koordinaciya Vzaimodejstviya Rossijskogo Biznesa I Gosudarstva." Higher School of Ecnomics, 2010.

Index

Abramovich, Roman, 1
Africa, 4, 6, 9, 198, 216
agent predation, 2, 3, 6, 11, 12, 13, 15, 16, 212
   coexistence with principal expropriation,
      35, 87, 118
   concept, 27, 31
   consequences of, 22, 35, 36, 38, 79–82,
      109–12, 121–67, 168, 192, 194, 198,
      203, 210, 217
   dynamic trends, 82–5
   history of, 118–19, 204
   in broader post-communist region, 82–5
   in Russia and Ukraine compared, 71–3
   and intra-state conflict, 68–71, 87, 89–97,
      107, 203n4
   key arguments, 35
   and rule of law, 202–7
   subnational variation, 113–17
   and types of state actors, 33–5
   varieties of, 32–3
   versus income threats, 53–68, 75–82
   versus organized expropriation, 86–119
Akhmetov, Rinat, 117, 147, 149, 163,
     186, 199
Alekperov, Vagit, 149
American Chamber of Commerce, 175
annexation, 33, 37, 55, 56, 60, 63, 64, 75, 79,
     154, 167, 168, 169, 171, 175, 203n4
   definition, 32
Arab Spring, 22
Audit Chamber, 127, 184, 184n47, 185, 233

Bakai, Ihor, 147
Belarus, 50, 64, 96, 108

Bendukidze, Kakha, 122n5
Berezovsky, Boris, 1
bespredel, 117
Brods'kyi, Mykhailo, 68, 69, 100, 102, 205
Browder, Bill, 52, 53
bureaucracy, 11, 12, 34, 36, 38, 39, 68, 70, 75,
     87, 90, 92, 97, 106, 118, 119, 134, 142,
     192, 210
   and administrative reform, 97–102, 135–6
   size, 97
   types engaged in agent predation, 33
business aggressiveness, 110–12
business associations, 10, 14, 22, 26, 36, 43,
     63, 80, 81, 103, 111, 121–43, 189, 192,
     193, 198, 211, 212
   bottom-up vs. sovereign-supported, 213
   politicization, 140
   subversion by state agents, 138
business institutionalization, 14, 36, 128, 129,
     130, 131, 132, 133, 134, 136, 137,
     150n94
   and state commitment, 142
Business Russia, 103, 105n52, 121, 126,
     126n14, 127, 128, 128n19, 131, 134,
     136, 138, 141, 141n68
business stakeholders. *See* stakeholder
   alliances
business start-ups, 50

Catherine the Great, 163
CCI, 121, 124, 125, 126, 127, 128n20, 134,
     136, 137, 137n52, 138, 138n57,
     139n60, 140, 141n68
Chamber of Commerce and Industry. *See* CCI

239

240   *Index*

China, 4, 9, 23, 26, 34, 38, 42, 64, 160, 193, 198, 215
Chubais, Anatoly, 49, 149
Civic Control, 207
Civic Rada, 150
constitution, 51, 51n10, 52, 52n11, 52n12, 124, 143, 143n73, 203
Coordination Council of Entrepreneurs' Unions, 131
corporate social responsibility, 37, 178, 195
corruption. *See* income threats; siphoning
corruption data, 53, 82
corruption literature, 20–1
courts, 22, 33, 38, 52, 54, 56, 58, 59, 62, 68, 101, 103, 123, 125, 126, 128, 138, 144, 145, 164, 170, 171, 173, 175, 189, 193, 208, 214
   foreign, 180, 181, 182, 183, 185
credible commitment. *See* state commitment

decree, presidential, 49, 98, 145, 148, 150, 151, 155
Delovaia Rossiia. *See* Business Russia
developmental state, 23
Duma, 44n97, 57, 91, 94, 103, 104, 105, 105n52, 123, 125, 126, 130, 133, 134, 135, 136, 137n52, 138, 139, 180, 181n34, 185, 206, 208, 220, 227, 230

Eastern Europe, 4, 9, 10, 50
elections, 41, 51, 89, 91, 92, 96, 100, 107, 108, 115, 123, 129, 130, 141n68, 144, 145, 146, 147n83, 148, 151, 159, 185n53, 186n57, 194n75, 202, 203, 216
embeddedness, 4n14
endogeneity, 194–6
Entrepreneurs' Council at the Cabinet of Ministers, 155
EU Business Association, 175
Europe, medieval, 6, 8, 10, 25, 216
European Court of Human Rights, 182
Evtushenkov, Vladimir, 149
expropriation. *See* principal expropriation; agent predation
extortion, 22, 32, 33, 37, 64, 65, 66, 67, 68, 71, 76, 76t3.1, 83n83, 86, 103, 116t4.2, 117n78, 144, 146, 154, 167, 173, 183n40, 197t6.2, 204, 210, 211
   definition, 32
   legitimation of, 160

Fridman, Mikhail, 122n5, 133, 173, 209, 221
FSB. *See* security services

Gazprom, 96, 149, 181n32, 222, 223, 227, 234
Georgia, 51, 153, 162
Gorbachev, Mikhail, 52, 119, 122
Gref, German, 134, 134n36, 135, 135n40, 136, 136n44, 137n52, 139, 227
Gunvor, 95, 96, 234

Illarionov, Andrei, 53
income rights, 2, 8, 13, 16, 18, 20, 21, 29, 30, 40, 53, 57, 62, 67, 72, 75, 76, 77, 80, 82, 201
   definition, 18, 28
   and stakeholder alliances in survey, 192
Interpipe, 163
intervention, 37, 64, 71, 167, 173
   definition, 33

judiciary. *See* courts

Katyrin, Sergei, 125, 140
Kazakhstan, 64
Khodorkovsky, Mikhail, 53, 88, 122n5, 133, 142, 179, 180, 180n31, 181, 183, 184, 185, 187, 199
Khrushchev, Nikita, 118
Kinakh, Anatoly, 235
Kivelidi, Ivan, 130, 131n28
Krivorozhstal', 163, 165
Kuchma, Leonid, 41, 49, 50, 52, 143, 144, 146, 147, 147n83, 149, 154, 155, 156, 157, 163, 186, 186n57, 221, 236
Kuzhel', Oleksandra, 155
Kyrgyzstan, 51

Latin America, 6, 10, 26, 129, 198, 216
law
   anti-raiding reforms, 102–6
   contract security in survey, 80, 81, 111, 112
   customary, 216
   deregulation, 69, 72, 100, 101, 107, 134–7, 150, 158
   in raiding, 55, 56, 58, 60, 112, 169, 171
   lobbying by business associations, 121–7, 134–7
   on privatization, 48
   on property protection, 51, 107, 148, 150, 206
   and state extortion. 16, 17, 18, 43
law enforcement. *See* police; security services
Lazarenko, Pavlo, 144
Lebedev, Alexander, 88, 88n6, 97n29, 228
legislature. *See* parliaments

Index

legitimacy of private ownership, 38, 74,
 162n117, 184, 186
Liapina, Kseniia, 155, 199
limited access order, 7

mafia, 2, 19, 27, 31, 42, 73
 private vs. state, 74
Magnitsky, Sergei, 88, 223
Marx, Karl, 52, 57
Medvedev, Dmitry, 61, 89, 91, 98, 99, 101,
 104, 113, 128, 142n69, 174, 226,
 231, 232
merchant groups. *See* business associations
methodology, 13
 case selection, 13, 35, 43
 interviews, 43–4
 survey, 14–15, 44–6, 75
middle class, 17, 117, 146, 165, 202, 210, 213
Miller, Alexei, 149

nationalization, 6, 32, 57, 184n46
Navalny, Alexei, 34n67, 88, 106
new institutional economics, 25, 223

open access order, 13
OPORA, 56, 105, 121, 125, 126, 127, 128,
 128n19, 130, 131, 132, 133, 134,
 136, 137, 137n50, 138, 139, 141n67,
 141n68, 142n69
Orange Revolution, 14, 22, 36, 41, 50, 90,
 113, 163n120, 165n128, 186, 192,
 194, 207, 214
 and property rights, 143–67
 and rule of law, 202–3
Our Ukraine, 148, 164
ownership rights, 8, 11, 13, 16, 21, 22, 25,
 27, 28, 29, 30, 31, 33, 35, 36, 37, 39,
 40, 42, 43, 53, 54, 56, 59, 62, 63, 64,
 65, 66, 67, 72, 75, 76, 76n69, 77, 80,
 82n80, 83, 114, 120, 157, 167, 201
 definition, 18, 28, 29
 and stakeholder alliances in survey, 190

parliament, 10, 14, 25, 49, 91, 103, 115, 120,
 125, 130, 143, 144, 148, 167, 189,
 211, 217
 and constraints on sovereign in
 Ukraine, 145
Party of Regions, 107, 115, 148n86, 164, 193
peace agreements on privatized assets,
 151, 165
People's Party, Ukraine, 165
Peter I, 87, 204

Pinchuk, Victor, 149, 163, 185, 186, 186n58,
 187, 187n62, 199
piranha capitalism, 11–12, 87, 90, 121
 See also state concept
 definition, 32 *See also* agent predation;
 principal expropriation
police, 6, 8, 11, 22, 33, 38, 58, 60, 61, 63, 65,
 69, 73, 74, 75, 88, 105, 109, 154, 155,
 161, 177, 211
 size, 99
policy implications, 39, 201, 204, 215
Poroshenko, Petro, 148
Potanin, Vladimir, 122n5, 149
predation. *See* principal expropriation; agent
 predation
predatory state, 13
Primakov, Yevgeny, 124, 125
principal expropriation, 6–8, 11, 34, 113, 117
 See also agent predation versus
 organized expropriation
 coexistence with agent predation, 118
 coexistence with agent
 predation, 35, 87
 concept, 21, 28–31, 32, 97
 and effectiveness of stakeholder alliances,
 36, 179–87
 impact on firm incentives, 112
 in Russia, 8, 40, 179, 193
 in Ukraine, 41, 167, 185
 and reputational restraint, 8
 and state commitment, 9
principal-agent dilemma, 2, 5, 12, 20, 21, 27,
 30, 34, 40, 68, 70, 92, 192, 193, 202
 and theory of property rights' security,
 12, 21
privatization, 4, 4n14, 6, 9, 14, 19, 24, 39, 40,
 42, 43, 47, 47n1, 48, 49, 49n3, 49n4,
 50, 50n7, 51n8, 52, 57n23, 59n27,
 71, 79n74, 81, 128, 148, 149, 161,
 162, 162n116, 162n117, 163n120,
 163n122, 164, 164n126, 165, 170,
 184, 184n47, 185, 185n53, 186, 190,
 199, 206
 results, 50
Prokhorov, Mikhail, 185n53
property rights
 allocation of, 4, 5, 19, 39, 207, 216
 See also privatization
 history, 47–51
 definition, 18
 importance of security, 3–4, 5
 private threats to, 5, 9, 73
 in survey, 77

242   *Index*

property rights (*cont.*)
  security of, 8–11, 12, 22–7, 36–9
    empirical proxies, 14
    security versus allocation, 4, 19
    state threats to, 2, 6–8, 11–12, 15–17,
        40–2, 53–73, 75–85, 86–102, 109–19,
        153–67
    ideal types, 27–32
    predictability, 80, 83
public goods, 29, 200
Putin, Vladimir, 1, 2, 8, 8n34, 14, 31, 34,
    34n67, 35n68, 36, 40, 41, 42, 49, 52,
    53, 62, 64, 69, 87, 88, 91, 92, 94, 95,
    96, 97, 98, 99, 101, 104, 106, 113, 114,
    121, 123, 126, 126n14, 128, 128n19,
    128n20, 129, 130, 131, 132, 133, 134,
    134n36, 135, 135n40, 136, 137, 140,
    141, 141n68, 141n69, 142, 142n69,
    143, 149, 171, 172, 174, 180, 183, 185,
    185n53, 192, 193, 199, 209, 213, 222,
    227, 229, 230, 231, 233, 234

Rada, 44n97, 90, 92, 143, 144, 145, 145n78,
    145n79, 146, 146n80, 148, 148n86,
    150, 151, 164, 187, 199, 212, 214
raiding, 15, 29, 54–64, 87, 142, 169, 171, 172,
    175, 176, 205 *See also* annexation
  extent, 56, 76
  legal reforms, 102–6
  propensity for, in survey, 110–12
  stages, 58
  types, 56, 62
reprivatization, Ukraine, 162–6
reputational restraint, 8, 9, 9n37, 23n27, 24,
    26, 36, 40, 42, 189, 193, 212
robber baron problem, 207
Rosneft, 180, 182, 183, 184, 223
Roundtable of Russia's Business, 130, 131
RUIE, 99n37, 121–4, 124n11, 126, 128,
    128n19, 129n22, 131, 133, 138,
    142n69, 178, 193
Rukh, 158
rule of law, 3, 17, 25, 38, 50n8, 106, 201,
    207n17
  demand for, 210
  and legal reform, 68, 69, 102–6,
    157, 204–7
  and political will, 202–4
  and stakeholder alliances, 207–17
Russia's Federation of Independent Trade
    Unions, 176
Russian Union of Industrialists and
    Entrepreneurs. *See* RUIE

Saakashvili, Mikheil, 162
samodeiatel'nost', 117
SBU. *See* security services
SCM, 163, 199
second-best institutions, 38, 215
security services, 33, 72, 75, 88, 90, 92, 93,
    105, 107, 109, 142, 160, 164, 171, 180,
    207, 208
Shokhin, Aleksandr, 124n11, 131n31, 178,
    178n25
siphoning, 30, 31, 32, 33, 35, 75, 86, 157, 192
    See also agent predation versus income
    threats
  concept, 28–31
skimming, 30, 31, 35, 40
  concept, 28–31
Skolkovo, 92
small shopkeeper problem, 210
Socialist Party of Ukraine, 148n86, 164
Soros, George, 187
sovereign, 6, 86n1 *See also* state concept
sovereign initiatives against agent
    predation, 89, 97–109, 156, 162, 172,
    174, 203
sovereign priorities, undermined by agent
    predation, 89–97
Soviet legacies, 4, 6, 47, 49, 51, 73, 95, 100,
    101, 118, 124, 143, 156, 158, 159,
    170, 205
stakeholder alliances
  cases, 168–87
  and rule of law, 207–17
  survey, 188–98
  theory, 12, 17, 36–8, 39, 42, 177, 178, 179,
    184, 192, 198–200
Stalin, 41, 118, 204
state apparatus. *See* bureaucracy; police;
    security services; tax agencies
state capacity, 21, 21n21, 22, 35, 40,
    114, 198
state capture, 19, 27n49, 39, 112
state commitment, 2, 9–11, 13, 14, 22–7, 35,
    39, 42, 120–54, 166, 189, 192
  critique of, 20, 22–4, 25, 120
  and federal ombudsman, 141
  in medieval Britain, 216
state concept, 5, 7–8, 11–12, 19, 22, 27, 30,
    86n1
state corporations, 50
state failure, 3, 6, 19, 20, 27
state principal. *See* sovereign;
    state concept
state unitary enterprises, 50n5

Index

243

state weakness, 2, 5, 15, 22, 102, 184, 202
See also principal-agent dilemma
Surkov, Vladislav, 92

tax agencies, 11, 55, 58, 65, 66, 69, 76, 84, 93,
108, 124, 153, 160, 206, 210, 211, 212
extortion in survey, 77
size, 100
tax payments, as protection, 8, 178, 193, 212
taxation, 8, 9, 21, 23, 26n42, 30, 31, 32, 40,
42, 123, 151n99, 194
teleology, 214
threats to property rights, definition, 28
Titov, Boris, 126, 141, 141n69, 142, 142n69,
223, 226, 233
Turkmenistan, 85
Tymoshenko, Yulia, 50, 91, 95, 96, 96n25,
100, 108, 148, 150, 156, 157, 162, 163,
163n120, 164n126, 185, 186, 186n58,
187, 203, 222

Ukraine's Association of Business
Incubators, 154
Union of Right Forces, 130
United Russia, 34, 34n67, 91, 92, 94n18, 104,
104n48, 126, 141, 141n67, 141n68,
207n14, 207n15
US-Russia Business Council, 172
USSR. *See* Soviet legacies
Uzbekistan, 50

Vekselberg, Viktor, 149
Victor Pinchuk Foundation, 187
Vinnytsia Union of Private Entrepreneurs,
211, 213

WTO, 9, 123, 124, 128, 137, 137n52

Yabloko, 133, 141n67
Yalta European Strategy, 187
Yanukovych, Viktor, 35n68, 41, 90, 92, 96,
96n25, 100, 101, 102, 107, 108, 109,
144, 145, 161, 186n57, 202, 203,
203n4
Yekhanurov, Yurii, 49, 150, 151,
151n99, 227
Yeltsin, Boris, 41, 49, 87, 113, 129, 130
Yukos, 14, 35n68, 43, 53, 132, 168, 175,
179, 180, 180n31, 181, 182,
182n40, 183, 184, 185, 193,
199, 210, 223, 225, 227, 232,
233, 234, 235
Yushchenko, Viktor, 36, 41, 96, 102, 113,
144, 145, 146, 146n80, 150, 154, 155,
156, 157, 161, 162, 163, 163n122,
164n126, 202, 227, 235
and state commitment, 147–51

Zhirinovsky, Vladimir, 185n53
Zinchenko, Oleksandr, 148
Zyuganov, Gennady, 129, 185n53

For EU product safety concerns, contact us at Calle de José Abascal, 56–1°,
28003 Madrid, Spain or eugpsr@cambridge.org.

www.ingramcontent.com/pod-product-compliance
Ingram Content Group UK Ltd.
Pitfield, Milton Keynes, MK11 3LW, UK
UKHW011318060825
461487UK00005B/154